ELEMENTS OF ACCOUNTS

BALANCE-SHEET APPROACH

for Elementary and Intermediate Stage Students
Ninth edition completely revised

by ANDREW BASTON
B.Com. (Dunelm.)
Formerly Head of Management, Business and Liberal
Studies Department, Watford Technical College

CASSELL · LONDON

CASSELL & COMPANY LTD

35 Red Lion Square • London WC1R 4SJ

and at

SYDNEY, AUCKLAND
TORONTO, JOHANNESBURG

First edition 1952
Second (revised) edition 1954
Fourth (revised) edition 1960
Sixth (revised) edition January 1964
Ninth (revised) edition January 1968
Ninth edition, second impression March 1970
Ninth edition, third impression July 1971
Ninth edition, fourth impression September 1972

I.S.B.N. 0 304 93247 7

Printed in Hong Kong by
The Continental Printing Co. Ltd.
972

PREFACE TO THE FIRST EDITION

It has often been alleged, and with considerable truth in many cases, that students who have completed a course in book-keeping are able to do exercises of a set type, but that when they meet a problem which must be solved by the application of first principles they are without resource to deal with it.

The present book is an attempt to remedy this state of affairs. The method employed is to take the balance sheet as the starting-point and to develop the system of accounts from it. Students are thus presented at the beginning with the end-objectives of book-keeping and work back to the detailed routines, which are then seen in their true perspective.

This shift of emphasis results in a much clearer appreciation of the principles and in a considerable saving of time. Time is saved because it is found that the processes of book-keeping are much more quickly learnt when the student knows the purposes that they serve.

The book covers the syllabuses of most examining bodies up to the intermediate standard, and puts the student in a position to study profitably an advanced text-book on accountancy. It should be useful to students taking the new National Certificate course and other courses of a similar type; as an introduction for students taking professional examinations; and in the intensive end-on secretarial courses run in most technical colleges and some grammar schools. The author has also used it successfully with pupils in a technical secondary school.

The author is greatly indebted to L. Gartside, Esq., B. Com., Head of the Commerce Department of the South-West Essex Technical College, who read the MS. and made many valuable suggestions.

Grateful acknowledgement is made to the various examining bodies for permission to reproduce their examination papers.

PREFACE TO THE SECOND EDITION

In preparing the Second Edition, the author is greatly indebted to Mr. F. Troughton, of Lanchester College of Technology, Coventry, for his many valuable suggestions and his assistance in calling attention to the errors that appeared in the original edition.

PREFACE TO THE SIXTH EDITION

In the Sixth Edition a section on Merchandise Accounts has been inserted and the section on Accounting Machines rewritten. In addition, a number of illustrative examples have been added, and in several chapters the number of exercises has been increased and emendations made to the text.

Mr. V. Marland, A.A.C.C.A., A.C.C.S., has read the text and suggested a number of improvements, for which the author tenders his thanks.

It has not been found practicable to provide a key to the exercises, but those who would find answers an advantage or who would like a greater number of exercises are referred to the author's *Book-Keeping Exercises* (Cassell) which can profitably be used in conjunction with this book.

PREFACE TO THE NINTH EDITION

In preparing this reprint, all sums of money have been converted to the new decimal currency to be introduced in 1971. Exact conversion is not possible for any sum less than one shilling or 5p, so teachers who have worked solutions to examples will find that in many cases their results will not correspond exactly with those obtained with the new figures.

The opportunity has been taken to make some small but important improvements to the text.

Contents

1

THE BALANCE SHEET

Suppose three brothers, X, Y and Z, owned equal shares in a bicycle, worth £10; a boat, worth £20; and a radio set, worth £18. These things would be known as their assets.

The total value of these three assets is £48. The share of each brother would thus be £16. All this information could be set out in a statement in the following form:

				£						£
X's share	...	...	...	16	Bicycle ..	...	...	...	10
Y's share	...	..	...	16	Boat	..	..	..	..	20
Z's share	...	..	..	16	Radio	..	...	...	..	18
				£48						£48

Such a statement is known as a Balance Sheet. A Balance Sheet could be drawn up for any individual, or for any group of individuals (such as a business), owning things in common. It shows on the right-hand side a list of the things owned, and their value. This is the assets side. On the left-hand side is shown the list of those who own the assets and the share each would receive if the assets were turned into money at the value shown. The left-hand side is called the liabilities side.

Obviously both sides must be equal in amount, because all the property shown on the assets side must be owned by someone. This brings us to our first equation:

$$L \text{ (for liabilities)} = A \text{ (for assets)}$$

Now let us see the effect of some transactions on this Balance Sheet.

I. Let us suppose that brothers Y and Z relinquish their claim to the assets by giving their shares to X. There would then be only one claimant to the assets, and the Balance Sheet would read as follows:

BALANCE SHEET

				£						£
X's share	...	...	...	48	Bicycle ..	...	...	...	10
					Boat	..	...	..	..	20
					Radio	..	...	...	...	18
				£48						£48

II. X now buys an engine for the boat from D for £25; but, having no money, he purchases it on credit; i.e., he receives the engine at once and agrees to pay for it later.

1

After this transaction, he is clearly no richer than he was before. True, his assets have been increased by the addition of the motor; but he is in debt for it. In other words, his net worth is the same. His Balance Sheet would now be as follows:

BALANCE SHEET

			£					£
Due to D	...	...	25	Bicycle ..	...	...	...	10
X's share	...	...	48	Boat ..	...	..	..	20
				Radio ..	...	...	..	18
				Engine ..	...	...	...	25
			£73					£73

The liabilities side of the Balance Sheet now shows two items. They both represent claims to the assets. The first is a claim by a person outside the business. He (D) cannot point to any particular item and say it is his—even the engine does not belong to him once he has sold it. The debt must, nevertheless, be regarded as a claim to the assets, since, if X had no undisclosed property, it could be met only out of the assets. These outside claims are known as liabilities, and give the name to the side of the Balance Sheet on which they are placed.

The second claim is that of the owner of the assets, the person whose Balance Sheet is being shown. This second claim is known as X's *net worth*, or, more usually, as his *capital*.

The Balance Sheet has not changed its form. It still shows the assets on the right-hand side, and the claims to those assets on the left. But the claims have been divided into two parts, distinguishing between outside claims (debts) and the claim of the proprietor (proprietorship or capital). The first part might contain a number of separate items. It could be shown in theoretical form as follows:

BALANCE SHEET

Liabilities Capital	Assets

From this we get a new equation known as the book-keeping equation:

$$L+C=A$$

Clearly, if any two of these items are known, the other can be found by simple arithmetic.

Thus

    (a) If the liabilities are £1,000 and the capital £2,000, the assets must be £3,000.

    (b) If the liabilities are £1,000 and the assets £2,500, the capital must be £1,500.

(c) If the capital is £4,000 and the assets £4,500, the liabilities must be £500.

III.   Let us look a little closer at capital. We shall suppose that X sells all his assets and pays his debts out of the proceeds, and that they realize not £73 as shown, but £80. When D is paid for the engine, X will have £55 left, and his Balance Sheet will now read:

BALANCE SHEET

	£					£
Capital X	55	Cash				55

This brings out the point that the liabilities are claims to a fixed amount, but that the capital is a claim to whatever is left of the assets after the liabilities have been paid. The assets may change in value, or they may be worth more or less than the value shown on the Balance Sheet. If so, this will correspondingly change the amount of capital, but it will not affect the amount of the claim represented by the liabilities. Capital is therefore defined as the amount by which the assets exceed the liabilities.

The Business Cycle

It is upon this fact that business really depends, because a man enters business for the purpose of increasing his capital. It is more usually expressed as 'making a profit'. The business cycle might be described as follows:

A trader begins a trading period with certain assets and liabilities, the excess of the assets over the liabilities being his capital.

Some of these assets he exchanges for others of a greater value; for example, he sells them for more than he paid for them, and thus makes a profit. This increases his capital.

Other assets he buys to keep and to use. As time goes on, the value of these assets falls because:

(a) They wear out or are used up.
(b) They get out of date.
(c) Things, like leases, expire.

This loss reduces his capital. If the increase is greater than the loss, then he has made a profit. Obviously, the only way to find out whether or not a profit has been made is to keep track of the values of the assets and liabilities, and that is why he keeps books. Book-keeping could be defined as a record of the changing nature and value of assets and liabilities.

This is illustrated in the series of diagrams at the end of this chapter.

One other small point should be noticed. An unsuccessful business man might find that his liabilities exceeded his assets. In that case he would have no capital, and the difference between the assets and liabilities would then be called a 'deficiency'. The book-keeping equation would need to be rewritten as

$$L=A+D$$

A person or business whose liabilities exceed the assets is said to be insolvent.

THE BOOK-KEEPING PROCESS

STAGE I

A business man commences with certain assets and liabilities. The difference is his capital.

$$\begin{array}{ccc} L & + & C & = & A \\ (\text{£300}) & & (\text{£400}) & & (\text{£700}) \end{array}$$

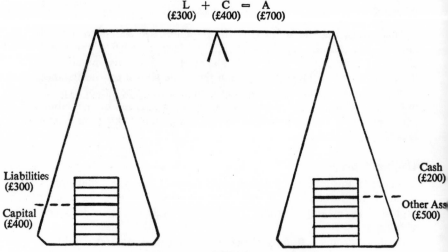

Liabilities
(£300)

Capital
(£400)

Cash
(£200)

Other Assets
(£500)

STAGE II

Additional assets costing £200 are acquired, but liabilities are increased by the same amount (*i.e.*, goods are bought but not paid for immediately).

$$\begin{array}{ccc} L & + & C & = & A \\ (\text{£500}) & & (\text{£400}) & & (\text{£900}) \end{array}$$

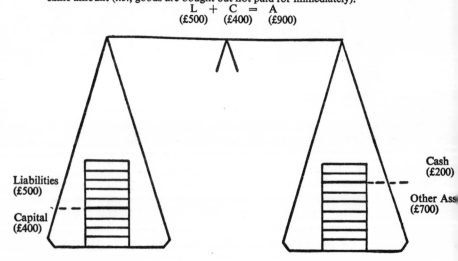

Liabilities
(£500)

Capital
(£400)

Cash
(£200)

Other Assets
(£700)

STAGE III

Some liabilities are extinguished by the sacrifice of assets of equal value (*e.g.*, debts of £100 are paid in cash).

$$\underset{(£400)}{L} + \underset{(£400)}{C} = \underset{(£800)}{A}$$

STAGE IV

Some assets are exchanged for others of a greater value (*i.e.*, goods costing £300 are sold for £500). This increases capital by the amount of the profit, £200.

$$\underset{(£400)}{L} + \underset{(£600)}{C} = \underset{(£1,000)}{A}$$

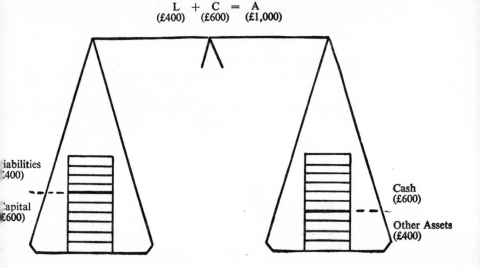

STAGE V

Assets diminish in value through being used up to the extent of £100 (*e.g.*, a car is worth less after a year's use). This reduces capital.

$$L + C = A$$
$$(£400) \quad (£500) \quad (£900)$$

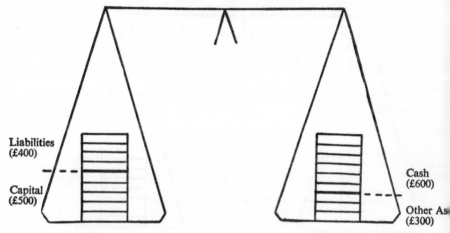

The difference between the capital at the end (£500) and the capital at the beginning (£400) is the final profit (£100).

The process is then repeated from Stage II.

WRITTEN EXERCISES

Instructions to Students
  (i) Use single sheets of foolscap paper until you are told to use ruled book-keeping paper.
 (ii) Put your name at the top of each page.
(iii) Head each exercise with the number of the exercise and the date on which it was begun.
 (iv) Use a ruler for every line you draw.
  (v) Keep separate sheets in a folder in date order with the latest one on top.

1.   Complete the following tables. When marking, allow one mark for an entry in the correct column, and one mark for the correct figure. No marks should be given for any figure in the wrong column.

Liabilities	Capital	Assets	Deficiency
£	£	£	£
117		295	
	3,215	11,961	
1,911	2,816		
9,203		5,844	
	62,372	106,412	
9,383			1,417

Liabilities	Capital	Assets	Deficiency
£ 12,713	£	£ 19,495	£
		60,422	9,210
14,566	10,862		
8,448			1,617
	11,573	15,918	
16,301		20,606	
2,534	7,781		
	826	4,962	
		9,184	305
7,439		3,281	

2. Draw up a Balance Sheet showing your own assets and liabilities. You may invent suitable items.

CLASS QUESTIONS

1. What is an asset?
2. What is a liability?
3. How may the amount of capital owned by the proprietors of a business be calculated?
4. What is the book-keeping equation?
5. Why must the book-keeping equation always be true?
6. If the liabilities are greater than the assets, what name is given to the difference?
7. Give six examples of assets.
8. What is meant by the word 'insolvent'?
9. Give six examples of liabilities.
10. Which are usually bigger, assets or liabilities?
11. Why is capital classed with the liabilities?
12. If you were given the liabilities and the capital of a business, how would you find the assets?
13. If you were given the assets and the capital of a business, how would you find the liabilities?
14. In what way does the capital differ from other liabilities?
15. How does a business man make a profit?
16. Give three ways in which the value of assets may decrease.
17. How does book-keeping assist a business man to measure his success or failure?
18. Define book-keeping.

2

THE BALANCE SHEET

(continued)

IT is necessary to look a little more closely at the nature of assets and liabilities.

Assets

These consist not only of property or things possessed, but of any advantages to which a money value can be attached. The term therefore includes:

(a) Property of all kinds (such as money, goods, buildings).
(b) Debts due from other people.
(c) Goods and services paid for in advance.

Debts Due from Other People

A debt usually arises as a result of a transaction. For example, A may sell goods to B on the understanding that B will pay at a later date. A has not yet got the money, but he has a legal claim to it. Because he has this legal claim, he will (almost certainly) get the money; if he had no such claim, he certainly would not. The claim, therefore, is worth money to him, and for this reason it would be included in his assets.

Goods Paid for in Advance

If money due to a person or business can be treated as an asset, then clearly any goods due to him would equally be an asset. They would be due to him if they had been paid for in advance.

Services

Services, like goods, are worth money. That is why people, including business men, are prepared to pay for them. Though in this sense they are assets, they would appear in a Balance Sheet only if a money value could be attached to them.

For example, the performers at a concert give a service to the audience. Now if you possessed a ticket, costing £0·50 for a concert you would include it as an asset in your personal Balance Sheet, because until the concert took place, you would probably be able to sell it. After the concert had taken place, however, the ticket would be worth nothing and could no longer be classed as an asset. That is the nature of services—they perish in the act of being given.

For this reason, only services that are due to you because they have been paid for in advance can be regarded as assets for Balance Sheet purposes. This subject will be dealt with in more detail later.

(If the services result in a saleable asset—as when a cabinet-maker makes a desk out of a piece of timber—the saleable asset would be put in the Balance Sheet, but not the labour as such.)

Fixed and Current Assets

Assets are divided into two groups—fixed and current (see the Balance Sheet on p. 10).

Fixed assets consist of property of a durable nature, likely to be retained for a considerable period, at least a year. When, for instance, A. Brown draws up his Balance Sheet on 1st September of the following year, it is probable that his present house will still be found amongst his assets. It may have deteriorated a little but it will be there at substantially the same figure.

A business, like a private person, also possesses fixed assets, such as buildings and equipment of all kinds, the amount varying with the type of business. They are bought to be used and not to be sold at a profit.

Current assets consist of items, each of which is held for a short time—less than a year.

The chief current assets held by a business are stock, debtors (*i.e.,* debts owing to the business) and cash. These are the resources used in the trading activities of the business—the buying and selling to make a profit. Without them there could be no trade and therefore no profit, only a factory or a warehouse standing idle.

In the process of trade there is a cycle of events causing continual change in the constitution of the current assets. Stock is sold on credit (*i.e.,* to be paid for later) and is thus replaced by debtors; the debtors pay and are replaced by cash; fresh stock is bought and so on. Thus the amount of each current asset held can vary up or down at short notice. The more rapidly the current assets can be circulated or worked, the more profit, generally speaking, can be made.

Liabilities

These consist of the claims of outside persons and would include amongst other things:

Bank overdraft.
Debts for goods and services.
Loans.
Income tax due.
Rent due.
Services for which other people have paid you in advance.

It should be observed that if you buy something without paying for it at the time, you have acquired both an asset and a liability. For example, if you buy a desk for £50 on credit, you have the desk, which is an asset; but also you owe the £50, which is a liability. Similarly, if somebody lends you £100, the money received is an asset, and would appear as part of your cash; but, as you must pay it back, there is also a liability for this amount. When the term 'loan' is used, it is the liability to repay that is referred to. The actual money lent would be referred to as cash, not as a loan.

It should also be noticed that the liabilities of one person are the assets of somebody else. In your own Balance Sheet you are concerned only with your own assets and liabilities.

Like assets, liabilities are divided into long-term and current liabilities, the latter being those debts which must be paid quickly and certainly within about a year. Current liabilities arise largely through purchases of goods for resale and are thus linked to current assets.

What a Balance Sheet is

A Balance Sheet is a statement of the assets and liabilities of a person or a business, on a given date, arranged in the form of the book-keeping equation $L+C=A$.

A hypothetical personal Balance Sheet of A. Brown on 1st September, 19—, is shown below:

BALANCE SHEET OF A. BROWN
AS AT 1ST SEPTEMBER, 19—

Liabilities	£	Assets	£	£
		Fixed Assets		
Capital	22,500	House and Furniture	5,000	
		Car	500	
		Shares	1,000	
				6,500
Current Liabilities		*Current Assets*		
Debts due for sundry purchases	500	Debt due from		
		C. Drew ..	1,500	
		Cash at Bank ...	15,000	
				16,500
	£23,000			£23,000

In this Balance Sheet, A. Brown holds assets valued at £23,000. Of this, the various people from whom he has bought goods on credit (*i.e.*, without paying immediately) can claim £500. He himself has a legal claim to the remainder.

The Heading of the Balance Sheet

Notice that the heading contains three things:

(*a*) The name of the document—Balance Sheet.
(*b*) The name of the person (or business) whose Balance Sheet is being drawn up.
(*c*) The date.

The Importance of the Date

It is important to show the date on which the Balance Sheet is drawn up, because the assets and liabilities do not remain unchanged indefinitely; they constantly fluctuate. Suppose, for instance, on 2nd September, A. Brown paid the tradesmen the amounts due to them. His liabilities would then be £500 less, and so would his assets, because he would have £500 less in the bank. Since every transaction will affect the Balance Sheet, it follows that a Balance Sheet is a true statement of assets and liabilities only so long as no fresh transaction takes place. Therefore a Balance Sheet can be known to be correct only at the time it is drawn up. Hence it is very important that the date should be shown. As the date refers to all items, it is included in the heading and not written against each item. The date should be stated in full, including the year.

Order of Assets

The assets are shown on the right-hand side of the Balance Sheet in this country, fixed assets first, followed by current assets.

There are no rules defining the order in which fixed assets are entered but current assets are arranged in the order in which they could be turned into cash, with cash appearing as the last item. The normal arrangement is therefore:

Stock.
Debtors.
Cash.

Prepayments (*i.e.,* goods or services paid for in advance) are rarely turned into cash and for that reason would appear first.

An asset that can be turned easily into cash is described as a 'liquid' asset, and assets arranged in the above order are said to be in order of liquidity.

Order of Liabilities

Capital and long-term loans are shown first, in that order, followed by current liabilities which thus appear opposite current assets.

Current liabilities should be shown in the order in which they must be paid, the most urgent appearing last.

The Cash Position

The current assets include the cash with which the liabilities are paid. It is a matter of great importance in business, that debts should be paid when they fall due, and therefore the business man should so organize his activities that he always has sufficient cash to meet his commitments. He would take into account that against the outflow of money to his creditors (for purchases) there is an inflow from his debtors (through sales). The inflow must at least be equal to the outflow.

Capital Employed and Working Capital

A business man has certain assets, fixed and current, at his command, and in general it is his function to employ them to obtain the greatest return, measured by profit.

The scale of activity on which he can embark in any given business is determined by the amount of his assets. The total of the assets is known as the

Capital Employed

His fixed assets make possible a certain level of output. Equally he needs a sufficient amount of working capital to enable him to employ the fixed assets and dispose of the output through trading.

The working capital is provided by the current assets, but as he must meet current liabilities from the current assets, the working capital consists of the excess of the current assets over the current liabilities.

Thus in the balance sheet below, the capital employed is £18,000 and the working capital £2,000.

BALANCE SHEET

	£			£
Capital	17,000	Fixed assets		15,000
Current liabilities	1,000	Current assets		3,000
	£18,000			£18,000

Working Capital

Let us suppose that, on 2nd September, 19—, A. Brown decides to commence a business to be known as Eureka Motors, and that he thinks he can afford to invest £10,000 in this business. He would see his bank manager, open an account for Eureka Motors, and transfer £10,000 from his own account to that of the business. His personal Balance Sheet after this transaction would read as follows:

BALANCE SHEET OF A. BROWN AS AT 2ND SEPTEMBER, 19—

	£		£	£
Capital ... — —	22,500	*Fixed Assets*		
		House and Furniture	5,000	
		Car	500	
		Shares	1,000	
		Investment in Eureka		
		Motors ..	10,000	
				16,500
Current Liabilities		*Current Assets*		
Debts for sundry purchases	500	Debt due from		
		C. Drew ..	1,500	
		Cash at Bank ..	5,000	
				6,500
	£23,000			£23,000

On the same date the position of Eureka Motors would be shown in the following Balance Sheet:

BALANCE SHEET OF EUREKA MOTORS
AS AT 2ND SEPTEMBER, 19—

Liabilities		£	Assets			£
Capital (A. Brown)	...	10,000	Cash at Bank ..	...	..	10,000

A. Brown and Eureka Motors are Two Separate 'Persons'

It is important to notice that A. Brown's Balance Sheet is not at all the same thing as the Balance Sheet of Eureka Motors. The Balance Sheet of Eureka Motors shows how the business stands; the Balance Sheet of A. Brown is a statement of the financial position of A. Brown. The business could be in difficulties while A. Brown was prosperous (and vice versa), because A. Brown possesses assets that do not belong to the business. It is true that he might have to use some of these assets to meet the liabilities of the business if it became insolvent; but, until he does so, they are his and his alone. In a similar way, the business might be sold and he might devote the proceeds to the purchase of things for himself, but, until he does so, the assets are the property of the business.

WRITTEN EXERCISES

Instructions to Students
(i) Read once more the instructions to students given in the first chapter.
(ii) If you make an error, draw a single line with a ruler through what is wrong, and write the correct words or figures above.
(iii) Never scratch out a figure that is wrong.
(iv) Write neatly—avoid blots.
(v) Do not allow the edges of your papers to get torn or dirty.
(vi) Keep your ruler clean.

1. Write definitions of the following terms:

(a) Assets.
(b) Fixed assets.
(c) Current assets.
(d) Liabilities.
(e) Current liabilities.
(f) Capital.
(g) Working capital.
(h) Insolvency.
(i) Deficiency.
(j) Book-keeping.

2. Arrange the following into two columns, one containing assets, the other liabilities. Underline the fixed assets.
Typewriter.
Insurance premium due.
A drilling machine.
The bill for the drilling machine.
A pair of scales.
A bill owing to your doctor.
Money in your safe.
A load of coal.
The bill for the coal.

Money in the bank.
A loan from a friend.
Unexpired rates.
War Savings Certificates.
Rent paid in advance.
Sum of money overpaid on a bill.
Overdue rent on house you live in.
Bank overdraft.
Stock of goods on hand.

3. A shopkeeper has a capital of £6,235. Make a list of the assets and liabilities he might possess.

4. Make a list of the kinds of assets and liabilities that might be possessed by

(a) A farmer.
(b) A railway.
(c) A shipping company.
(d) A hotel.

(e) A laundry.
(f) A shop.
(g) A builder.
(h) A garage.

In each of the exercises below separate the current assets from the fixed assets and the current liabilities from the fixed liabilities.

5. Arrange the following assets in the correct order for a Balance Sheet:

(a) Debts due to you.
(b) Buildings.
(c) Land.
(d) Cash in hand.

(e) Tools.
(f) Motor vans.
(g) Stock of goods.
(h) Cash at bank.

6. Prepare the Balance Sheet of E. Fox on 30th September, 19—, from the following list of assets and liabilities. Ascertain and insert his capital.

	£
Bank overdraft	3,000
Cash in hand	50
Debts due to E. Fox	2,000
Debts due by E. Fox.	1,200
Stock of goods	2,500
Income Tax due	300
Plant and machinery	5,000
Buildings	7,000

7. Show the Balance Sheet of G. Hogg, a doctor, who has the following assets and liabilities on 30th September, 19—, and insert the capital: Cash in hand £40. Cash at bank £760. Subscription due to B.M.A. £10. Due to D. Bile (chemist) £5. Due to International Drugs Ltd. £120. Bills outstanding from patients £350. Surgery fittings £1,000. Stock of bottles £50. Stock of drugs £180. Car £500. House £4,000.

8. Find the capital and prepare the Balance Sheet of Isaac Jay, grocer, on 30th September, 19—, from the following list of assets and liabilities: Premises £3,000. Stock of goods £900. Shop fittings £250. Office furniture and fittings £200. Wages of assistants outstanding £20. Loan from Building Society £2,000. Interest due on loan from Building Society £100. Loan from K. Lett £400. Vans £750. Cash £18. Cash at bank £82. Debts owing £125.

9. Make a list of (a) ten fixed assets and (b) ten current assets, likely to be owned by a school.

10. Insert suitable liabilities into the following Balance Sheet of M. Nunn, a builder, on 30th September, 19—.

BALANCE SHEET OF M. NUNN
AS AT 30TH SEPTEMBER, 19—

	£	*Fixed Assets*	£	£
Capital ... — —	3,600	Yard	2,000	
		Equipment ..	1,500	
				3,500
		Current Assets		
		Stock of Materials	500	
		Work in Progress	400	
		Debtors ..	700	
		Cash	20	
				1,620
	£5,120			£5,120

CLASS QUESTIONS

1. What is a Balance Sheet?
2. What is included under the heading of 'Assets'?
3. If a man had assets valued at £50,000 and liabilities of £40,000, how much capital would he possess?
4. What three things are included in the heading of a Balance Sheet?
5. Why is it important to show the date on which a Balance Sheet was drawn up?
6. Is the date shown opposite each item on a Balance Sheet?
7. On which side of a Balance Sheet are the assets written?
8. In what order are the current assets shown?
9. In what order are the liabilities shown?
10. Which usually appear first on a Balance Sheet, fixed or current assets?
11. If a man bought £1,000 of shares by cheque, what effect would this have on his Balance Sheet?
12. What is meant by a 'liquid asset'?
13. Define Working Capital.
14. Why are fixed assets bought?
15. For what are current assets used?

3

EFFECT OF TRANSACTIONS
ON THE BALANCE SHEET

A BALANCE SHEET is an equation. If it is correctly drawn up, the liabilities plus the capital must always be equal to the assets, because both sides of a Balance Sheet refer to the same group of assets, the liabilities side showing the division of the property listed on the assets side if it were turned into money. This is true before a transaction takes place. It is also true after a transaction takes place.

It follows from this that a transaction must have two effects, because if it had only one effect then only one side of the equation (*i.e.*, of the Balance Sheet) would be changed. The side that had been changed would no longer be equal to the other side, which had not been changed.

For example, suppose that as a result of a transaction a new asset has been acquired. This will increase the assets side of the Balance Sheet. Now, if the liabilities side is not increased by the same amount, or, alternatively, the assets side reduced in some other way by that amount, the Balance Sheet will be out of balance. Therefore one of these two things must happen.

Let us therefore trace the effect of:

    I. a purchase;
    II. the payment of a debt

upon a Balance Sheet, using as our basis the Balance Sheet of Eureka Motors as it stood on 2nd September, 19—. It then appeared as follows:

BALANCE SHEET OF EUREKA MOTORS
AS AT 2ND SEPTEMBER, 19—

Liabilities	£	Assets	£
Capital (A. Brown)	10,000	Cash at Bank	10,000

I. The Effect of a Purchase

A purchase will always have the effect of increasing the assets, either by an addition to an existing asset or by the acquisition of a new one. Simultaneously, however, there is a second effect, because the business must either pay for the new asset at once, or accept the liability to pay at a future date.

(*a*) In the former case, the effect is to *decrease another asset*; *e.g.*, Eureka Motors buys six cars at £500 each, paying for them by cheque.

16

(i) The assets will be increased by the addition of stock £3,000.

(ii) The assets will be decreased by the reduction of cash at bank £3,000.

The Balance Sheet will now appear:

BALANCE SHEET OF EUREKA MOTORS
AS AT 3RD SEPTEMBER, 19—

Liabilities		£	Assets			£
Capital (A. Brown) ...	..	10,000	Stock	.. ..		3,000
			Cash at Bank	— ...		7,000
		£10,000				£10,000

(b) If the business agrees to pay on a later date, the effect is to *incur a liability*; e.g., on 4th September, 19—, Eureka Motors buys land value £400 on credit.

(i) The assets will be increased by the addition of land £400.

(ii) The liabilities will be increased by the amount owing for the land £400.

The Balance Sheet will now appear:

BALANCE SHEET OF EUREKA MOTORS
AS AT 4TH SEPTEMBER, 19—

		£			£	£
			Fixed Assets			
Capital	...	10,000	Land	... ...		400
Current Liabilities			*Current Assets*			
Creditor ..	— ...	400	Stock ..	...	3,000	
			Cash ... —	..	7,000	
						10,000
		£10,400				£10,400

(c) A third possibility is that payment may be made in part, the rest to remain as a liability. The effect would be a *decrease in another asset plus the incurring of a new liability*.

This is a combination of (a) and (b); e.g., on 5th September, 19—, Eureka Motors purchases premises for £10,000, paying £2,000 by cheque and borrowing £8,000 from the Church Building Society.

(i) The assets will be increased by the addition of premises £10,000.

(ii) The assets will be decreased by the reduction of cash at bank £2,000.

(iii) The liabilities will be increased by the amount owing to the Building Society £8,000.

The Balance Sheet will now appear:

BALANCE SHEET OF EUREKA MOTORS
AS AT 5TH SEPTEMBER, 19—

	£			£	£
Capital	10,000	*Fixed Assets*			
Long-term Loan from Building		Premises ..	.. 10,000		
Society	8,000	Land	.. 400		
Current Liabilities					10,400
Creditor ... — ...	400	*Current Assets*			
		Stock ..	... 3,000		
		Cash	.. 5,000		
					8,000
	£18,400				**£18,400**

II. The Effect of Paying a Debt

For the person who owes it, a debt is a liability. One effect of the payment of a debt, therefore, must always be to reduce the liabilities by the amount of debt extinguished. As in the case of making a purchase, there is simultaneously a second effect. Two of the possibilities are shown in the following examples.

(*a*) *The decrease of an asset.* This will occur if, for example, the debt is paid by cheque. Suppose that on 6th September, 19—, Eureka Motors pays half the debt of £400 for land. The effects would be:

 (i) The liabilities will be decreased by the reduction of this debt from £400 to £200.

 (ii) The assets will be decreased through reduction of cash at bank by £200.

The Balance Sheet will now appear:

BALANCE SHEET OF EUREKA MOTORS
AS AT 6TH SEPTEMBER, 19—

	£			£	£
Capital	10,000	*Fixed Assets*			
Long-term Loan from Building		Premises ..	.. 10,000		
Society	8,000	Land	.. 400		
Current Liabilities					10,400
Creditor	200	*Current Assets*			
		Stock ..	.. 3,000		
		Cash	.. 4,800		
					7,800
	£18,200				**£18,200**

(b) *The incurring of a new liability.* Let us now assume that on 7th September Eureka Motors decides to pay off the £200 still due for the land, and borrows this £200 from the Building Society. The effects would be:

    (i) The liabilities will be decreased by the extinction of the debt for £200.

    (ii) The liability 'Loan from Building Society' will be increased from £8,000 to £8,200.

The Balance Sheet would then read:

BALANCE SHEET OF EUREKA MOTORS
AS AT 7TH SEPTEMBER, 19—

	£			£	£
		Fixed Assets			
Capital	10,000	Premises ..	.. 10,000		
Long-term Loan from Building		Land	.. 400		
Society	8,200				10,400
		Current Assets			
		Stock ..	.. 3,000		
		Cash	... 4,800		
					7,800
	£18,200				£18,200

Summary of Effect of Transactions

BALANCE SHEET

	Liabilities	Assets
1		±
2	+	+
3	−	−
4	±	

These are the four basic possibilities, but it may happen that a complicated transaction may have the combined effects of more than one case. (See (c) on page 17.)

The Meaning of Double Entry

The first effect of any transaction is to put the Balance Sheet out of balance; but simultaneously there is always a second effect which compensates for the first and restores the balance. For instance, the first effect of purchasing an asset is to make the assets side larger than the liabilities side; the second effect is to decrease another asset by the same amount or to increase a liability. In both cases the result is to put the Balance Sheet in balance again. Every transaction has thus a double effect, one counterbalancing the other. Double entry book-keeping consists in recording both effects.

WRITTEN EXERCISES

Instructions to Students
(i) Write legibly.
(ii) In writing figures, keep units exactly under units, tens under tens, etc.
(iii) Do not fold your papers.
(iv) Keep a sheet of paper in your folder for scrap working, etc.
(v) Keep no papers in your folder except those needed for book-keeping.

1. State the effect on a Balance Sheet of the following transactions, showing in each case which assets and/or liabilities are affected—
    (a) Payment by cheque of a debt of £50 due by the business.
    (b) Purchase on credit of a piece of machinery for £700.
    (c) Receipt of £15 cash in payment of a debt due to the business.
    (d) Payment of £10 into the bank from the office cash.
    (e) Sale of a typewriter for £40, the money being received by cheque.
    (f) Sale of a piece of land for £5,000 of which £1,000 was received by cheque on account.

2. State the effect on a Balance Sheet of selling office furniture for £500—
    (a) If it were paid by cheque.
    (b) If it were sold on credit.
    (c) If £250 were paid by cheque on account.

3. The purchase of a machine for £1,000 would increase the asset Machinery by that amount. State what other effect it would have if—
    (a) It were bought on credit.
    (b) It were paid for by cheque.
    (c) £300 were paid by cheque on account.
    (d) It were paid by cheque, but there were a bank overdraft of £200.
    (e) It were paid by cheque, but there were £600 only in the bank.

4. Suggest two possible further effects that each of the following transactions could have. In every case give the name of the other asset or liability affected—
    (a) Assets increased by the purchase of a van.
    (b) Liabilities decreased by the payment of a debt by cheque.
    (c) Assets decreased by the sale of buildings.

5. E. Harvey commences business on 1st January, 19—, as a dental surgeon, with £6,000 in the bank.
    Jan. 2. Purchases premises by cheque £4,000.
       ,, 3. Purchases equipment on credit from T. Smith £500.
       ,, 4. Sells part of equipment at cost for £100, received by cheque.
       ,, 5. Withdraws £10 from bank. This money is kept in the surgery for use in making cash payments when necessary.
       ,, 6. Purchases stationery for cash £3.
       ,, 7. Buys postage stamps £2.
Show his Balance Sheet on 1st January, 19—, and again after each transaction.

6. F. Walter commences business on 1st February, 19—. His initial capital is £12,500 in the bank.
    Feb. 2. Purchases the following assets from R. Tubb on credit—
           Van £300.
           Premises £5,000.
           Stock £4,000.

Feb. 3. Pays R. Tubb in full.
  ,, 4. Purchases furniture by cheque £350.
  ,, 5. Sells van to East Motors Ltd. on credit £300.
  ,, 6. Purchases new van by cheque £450.
Show his Balance Sheet on 1st February and again after each transaction.

7. The following were the assets and liabilities of S. Bates on 1st April, 19—:
    Cash at bank £100.
    Cash in hand £40.
    Stock £1,500.
    Premises £10,000.
    R. James, creditor £640.
Find his capital and show his Balance Sheet on that date.
April 2. Made loan in cash to T. Glass £10.
  ,, 3. Paid R. James by cheque £500.
  ,, 4. Purchased office equipment on credit from D. Beck £400.
  ,, 5. T. Glass repaid his loan by cheque £10.
  ,, 6. Paid into bank from office cash £20.
Show his Balance Sheet after each transaction.

8. C. Dent possessed the following assets and liabilities on 1st March, 19—:
    Cash at bank £1,000.
    L. Pitts, debtor £400.
    W. Smith, creditor £200.
    Office furniture and equipment £600.
    Stock £3,000.
Find his capital and show his Balance Sheet on that date.
March 2. Purchased stock on credit from T. Gill £500.
  ,, 3. Paid W. Smith by cheque £200.
  ,, 3. L. Pitts paid by cheque £250.
  ,, 4. Withdrew from bank for office cash £20.
  ,, 5. Purchased stationery by cash £10.
  ,, 6. Purchased new typewriter £50, paying £30 by cheque and giving
      old one in part exchange £20.
Show C. Dent's Balance Sheet after each transaction.

CLASS QUESTIONS

1. What is the first effect of any transaction on a Balance Sheet?
2. What are the possible effects of a purchase of goods upon a Balance Sheet?
3. If a liability is increased, what further effects could this have on a Balance Sheet?
4. Give an example of a transaction that increases one asset, decreases another and increases a liability.
5. Give two possible effects of decreasing a liability.
6. Explain what is meant by double entry book-keeping.

4

ASSETS AND LIABILITIES RECORDED INDIVIDUALLY

EVERY transaction affects the Balance Sheet. It would be possible to draw up a new Balance Sheet after each transaction, but it is not a practical method of book-keeping. The amount of work would be enormous, and the possibility of error very great; moreover, a Balance Sheet is only required at certain intervals—say, six months, or a year—when definite trends in the business have had time to establish themselves, and day to day variations have cancelled out. These intervals are known as 'accounting periods' or 'financial periods'. They are usually of six months' or one year's duration, but may be shorter.

Now, a Balance Sheet can be taken out at any time provided the values of the assets and liabilities at that time are known. They will be known if every change that has taken place in those values since the previous Balance Sheet is recorded when it takes place (*i.e.*, when transactions take place).

For example, let us suppose that a business commences on 1st January with £100 in the bank, receives during the month four cheques to a total value of £150 and pays out three cheques to a total value of £120. The amount of money in the bank at the end of the month would be £100+£150—£120, a net sum of £130. This fact can be arrived at by simple arithmetic without taking out a Balance Sheet each time a cheque is received or paid out.

Similarly, the value of every other asset and liability as it stands at the end of the month can be calculated. A Balance Sheet could then be taken out, and it would balance provided no mistake had been made in the calculations.

Let us take as an illustration the affairs of Eureka Motors. The Balance Sheet on 7th September was as follows:

BALANCE SHEET OF EUREKA MOTORS
AS AT 7TH SEPTEMBER, 19—

	£			£	£
		Fixed Assets			
Capital	10,000	Premises ..	..	10,000	
Long-term Loan from Building		Land	..	400	
Society	8,200				10,400
		Current Assets			
		Stock ..	..	3,000	
		Cash	..	4,800	
					7,800
	£18,200				£18,200

22

Let us further suppose that the transactions during the following week were as follows:

Sept. 8. Paid by cheque £2,000 of loan from Building Society.
(Asset, cash at bank, reduced by £2,000.
Liability, Building Society loan, reduced by £2,000.)

„ 9. Breakdown ambulance purchased on credit from S. Black £750.
(New asset, breakdown ambulance, acquired £750.
New liability, to S. Black, acquired £750.)

„ 10. Withdrew from bank for office cash £50.
(Asset, cash at bank, reduced by £50.
New asset, cash in hand, acquired £50.)

„ 11. Paid S. Black by cheque £750.
(Asset, cash at bank, reduced by £750.
Liability, to S. Black, extinguished £750.)

„ 12. Sold half of land for cheque £200.
(Asset, cash at bank, increased by £200.
Asset, land, reduced by £200.)

The table below shows how the value of the assets and liabilities changes as a result of these transactions, and in the last column their value on 12th September, after the changes have taken place. The starting point must obviously be their value on 7th September, and this is shown in the first column.

	Value on 7th Sept.	8th Sept.	9th Sept.	10th Sept.	11th Sept.	12th Sept.	Final Value
Assets.	£	£	£	£	£	£	£
Cash at bank	4,800	−2,000		−50	−750	+200	2,200
Stock	3,000						3,000
Land	400					−200	200
Premises	10,000						10,000
Breakdown ambulance			+750				750
Office cash				+50			50
Liabilities.							
Building Soc. loan	8,200	−2,000					6,200
Capital	10,000						10,000
S. Black			+750		−750		

The values of the assets and liabilities as they stood on 12th September are shown in the final column. These can now be arranged in the form of a Balance Sheet.

BALANCE SHEET OF EUREKA MOTORS
AS AT 12TH SEPTEMBER, 19—

	£			£	£
			Fixed Assets		
Capital	... 10,000		Premises ..	.. 10,000	
Building Society Loan	... 6,200		Land	.. 200	
			Breakdown Ambulance	750	
					10,950
			Current Assets		
			Stock ..	.. 3,000	
			Cash at Bank	.. 2,200	
			Cash in Hand	.. 50	
					5,250
	£16,200				£16,200

WRITTEN EXERCISES

1. Repeat question No. 8 at the end of Chapter Three, showing the Balance Sheets of C. Dent on 1st March, 19—, and 6th March, 19—, only.

2. The following were the assets and liabilities of F. Long, a furniture dealer, on 1st May, 19—:

> Cash at bank £7,500.
> Warehouse £11,000.
> D. North (creditor) £800.
> Stock of furniture £1,300.

Draw up his Balance Sheet on that date.

> May 2. Rented office premises and paid by cheque one year's rent in advance £500.
> „ 3. Purchased stock on credit from L. Miller £3,700.
> „ 4. Purchased office equipment by cheque £600.
> „ 5. Paid D. North by cheque.
> „ 6. Purchased vans by cheque £1,400.
> „ 6. Withdrew from bank for office cash £50.

Show the Balance Sheet of F. Long on 6th May, 19—.

3. The following were the assets and liabilities of L. Rich, a cycle dealer, on 1st July, 19—:

> Cash in till £80.
> Cash at bank £720.
> Stock £1,600.
> T. Short (debtor) £100.
> W. Wise (creditor) £500.

Draw up his Balance Sheet on 1st July, 19—.

> July 1. Paid into bank £60.
> „ 2. Purchased stationery for cash £8.
> „ 3. T. Short paid by cheque £50.
> „ 4. Paid W. Wise by cheque £500.
> „ 6. Paid rates in advance £20.

Show the Balance Sheet of L. Rich on 6th July, 19—.

5

ACCOUNTS

It was shown in the previous chapter that changes in the value of assets and liabilities could be calculated arithmetically, but the method shown would not be suitable if the number of transactions were very large. Moreover, the calculation itself did not show whether the item was an asset or a liability, and gave no indication of the nature of the transaction.

To overcome such difficulties, these calculations are embodied in 'accounts' ('account' is usually abbreviated to 'a/c').

A separate account (sometimes more than one) is opened for each asset and each liability. It takes, roughly, the form of the letter 'T'.

The name of the asset or liability to which the account refers is written on the horizontal line. The vertical line divides the account into two 'sides', one to show additions and the other to show deductions. Thus the 'pluses' are kept together on one side and the 'minuses' on the other, and the difference between the two sides will show the value of the asset or liability.

Debit and Credit

The left-hand side of an account is known as the 'debit side'. It is usually abbreviated to 'Dr.' An entry on the debit side is called a 'debit entry'.

The right-hand side is known as the 'credit side', abbreviated to 'Cr.' An entry on the credit side is called a 'credit entry'.

It is customary for the sides of the account to be indicated in the heading. An account headed 'Cash at Bank' would appear as follows:

CASH AT BANK ACCOUNT

Dr.   **Cr.**

The Balance

The difference between the two sides of an account (which, as stated above, represents the value of the asset or liability) is known as the 'balance'.

If the debit side is larger than the credit side, the balance is a 'debit balance'.

If the credit side is larger than the debit side, the balance is a 'credit balance'.

If there is only one item in an account, the balance is equal to that item. If the item is on the debit side, the balance will be a debit balance. If the item is on the credit side, the balance will be a credit balance.

The balance is so called because if a sum equal to the difference between the sides is placed on the smaller side, both sides would then be equal, or 'in balance'.

Entering Accounts

At the beginning of the accounting period, a Balance Sheet will be drawn up, showing the amounts of the assets and liabilities on that date. The first step in opening a set of books will be to open an account for each of these assets and liabilities, including capital.

(*a*) ASSETS. The value of an asset, as shown in the Balance Sheet, is entered on the debit side of its account. It is called a 'balance' partly because on that date, the first of the accounting period, there are no other entries in the account.

Any additions to that asset will, in consequence, be entered on the debit side also.

Deductions from the value of the asset will be shown on the credit side.

(*b*) LIABILITIES. For practical reasons the amount of a liability, as shown in the Balance Sheet, will be entered on the credit side of its account. It will also be called a balance.

Additions to a liability will also be entered on the credit side. Deductions from a liability will be entered on the debit side.

(c) CAPITAL. The rules for entering the Capital Account are the same as those for liabilities, because capital is shown on the liabilities side of the Balance Sheet.

The Final Balance Sheet

At the end of the accounting period a new Balance Sheet is drawn up from the information provided in the accounts. The debit balances are the assets and the credit balances are the liabilities.

Relation of the Debit to the Credit Side of an Account

It is clear from the rules given above that an entry on the debit side of an account may mean one of two things:

either (a) An increase of an asset.

or (b) A subtraction from the credit side (i.e., a decrease of a liability).

Similarly, an entry on the credit side of an account may mean:

either (a) An increase of a liability.

or (b) A subtraction from the debit side (i.e., a decrease of an asset).

It should be observed that normally the only way to make a subtraction from either side is to make an entry on the opposite side.

SUMMARY OF RULES FOR ENTERING ACCOUNTS

Debit (a) Assets	*Credit* (a) Liabilities
(b) Additions to assets	(b) Additions to liabilities
(c) Deductions from liabilities	(c) Deductions from assets

How to Make an Entry

The date of each transaction is entered in the accounts, and a brief description of its nature.

It was customary to preface the description with the word 'To' on the debit side, and the word 'By' on the credit side. The practice has little, if any, significance, and has largely been dropped. It will not be followed in this book.

Illustration: As an illustration, the example used in Chapter Four will be reworked, this time using accounts. It should be compared step by step with that example. We begin with the Balance Sheet of Eureka Motors on 7th September, 19—:

B

BALANCE SHEET OF EUREKA MOTORS
AS AT 7TH SEPTEMBER, 19—

	£			£	£
			Fixed Assets		
Capital	.. 10,000		Premises ..	.. 10,000	
Building Society Loan	.. 8,200		Land	.. 400	
					10,400
			Current Assets		
			Stock ..	.. 3,000	
			Cash at Bank	.. 4,800	
					7,800
	£18,200				£18,200

The company's transactions were as follows:

Sept. 8. Paid by cheque £2,000 of loan from Building Society.
„ 9. Breakdown ambulance purchased on credit from S. Black £750.
„ 10. Withdrew from bank for office cash £50.
„ 11. Paid S. Black by cheque £750.
„ 12. Sold half of land for cheque £200.

The first step is to open an account for each asset and liability and record therein its value as shown in the Balance Sheet. In accordance with the principles laid down in this chapter, the amount of each asset will be shown on the debit side, and the amount of each liability on the credit side. As the assets are equal to the liabilities (including the capital) the total of the debit entries will be equal to the total of the credit entries. These initial amounts will be called balances.

BUILDING SOCIETY ACCOUNT

Dr.				Cr.
				£
	Sept. 7 Balance			8,200

CAPITAL ACCOUNT

Dr.				Cr.
				£
	Sept. 7 Balance			10.000

BANK ACCOUNT

Dr.				Cr.
		£		
Sept. 7 Balance ..	.. 4,800			

STOCK ACCOUNT

Dr.				Cr.
		£		
Sept. 7 Balance ..	.. 3,000			

PREMISES ACCOUNT

Dr.				Cr.
		£		
Sept. 7 Balance ..	... 10,000			

LAND ACCOUNT

Dr.		Cr.
	£	
Sept. 7 Balance	400	

Now let us see the effect of the transactions on these values:

Sept. 8.   Paid by cheque £2,000 of loan from Building Society.

(a) When this money is paid there will be £2,000 less in the bank. The decrease in the value of this asset is shown by a credit entry in the Bank Account. The balance of the Bank Account at this stage would then be £2,800.

(b) With this payment, the liability to the Building Society will be reduced by £2,000. The liability appears on the credit side of the Building Society Account. To show a reduction, an entry will be made on the debit side of that account.

These two accounts, as they stand after this transaction, are shown below:

BANK ACCOUNT

Dr.			Cr.
	£		£
Sept. 7 Balance	4,800	Sept. 8 Building Society ..	2,000

BUILDING SOCIETY ACCOUNT

Dr.			Cr.
	£		£
Sept. 8 Bank	2,000	Sept. 7 Balance	8,200

To record the double effect of this transaction two entries are required, one on the debit side and one on the credit side. Before this transaction took place the total entries on the debit side were equal to the total entries on the credit side, because the debit entries represented the assets side of the Balance Sheet, and the credit entries represented the liabilities side. After this transaction, the total debits will still equal the total credits, because the same amount has been added to each side.

It should be noticed that the explanation in words against an entry consists of the name of the other account which is affected by the transaction. Thus, in the Cash at Bank Account, the description is 'Building Society', and in the Building Society Account the description is 'Bank'. This is the general rule to be followed in writing descriptions.

The name of the account in which the entry is made should never be used as a description. For example, in the Capital Account, no item should be described as 'Capital', because, if it were not an addition to or subtraction from capital, it would not be there. In other words, such a description would give no information.

Sept. 9.   Breakdown ambulance purchased on credit from S. Black £750.

(a) A new asset has been acquired, which must be shown as a separate item in the next Balance Sheet. Therefore, a new account must be opened for it; and, because it is an asset, it will be entered on the debit side.

(b) At the same time, a liability, which did not exist before the purchase, has come into existence. A new account, in the name of S. Black, must be opened in which to record it. As a liability, it will be entered on the credit side.

BREAKDOWN AMBULANCE ACCOUNT

Dr.					Cr.
				£	
Sept. 9	S. Black	..	..	750	

S. BLACK ACCOUNT

Dr.				Cr.
				£
	Sept. 9	Breakdown Ambulance		750

As before, to record the effect of this transaction on the assets and liabilities, both a debit and a credit entry are necessary. The total on the debit side will therefore still be equal to the total on the credit side.

Sept. 10.   Withdrew from bank for office cash £50.

(a) When this money is withdrawn, there will be £50 less in the bank. As the Bank Account must show how much money there is in the bank, this withdrawal must be recorded. The money in the bank is an asset, and is therefore shown on the debit side. Any reduction in the amount must consequently be shown on the credit side.

(b) This £50, however, has not been spent. It is held in the office in the form of cash. To show that the business now possesses £50 in cash which it did not have before, a new account, the 'Cash Account', must be opened, and the amount entered on the debit side.

BANK ACCOUNT

Dr.								Cr.
				£				£
Sept. 7	Balance	...	..	4,800	Sept. 8	Building Society	..	2,000
					„ 10	Cash	..	50

CASH ACCOUNT

Dr.					Cr.
				£	
Sept. 10	Bank	..	...	50	

Sept. 11.   Paid S. Black by cheque £750.

(a) This will further reduce the amount of money in the bank, so another credit entry will be required in the Bank Account.

(b) At the same time the liability to S. Black is extinguished. This liability was shown as a credit entry in the S. Black Account. The extinction of the debt will be shown by a debit entry in the S. Black Account.

BANK ACCOUNT

Dr.								Cr.
				£				£
Sept. 7	Balance	...	..	4,800	Sept. 8	Building Society	..	2,000
					„ 10	Cash	..	50
					„ 11	S. Black	..	750

S. BLACK ACCOUNT

Dr.   Cr.

		£			£
Sept. 11	Bank	750	Sept. 9	Breakdown Ambulance	750

Sept. 12. Sold half of the land for cheque £200.

(a) The cheque will be paid into the bank and will increase the amount of money held there. This increase will be shown by a debit entry in the Bank Account.

(b) The money was received for the part of the land which was sold. Having sold half the land, the business has only half left. The reduction is shown by a credit entry in the Land Account.

BANK ACCOUNT

Dr. Cr.

		£				£
Sept. 7	Balance	4,800	Sept. 8	Building Society		2,000
" 12	Land	200	" 10	Cash		50
			" 11	S. Black		750

LAND ACCOUNT

Dr. Cr.

		£			£
Sept. 7	Balance	400	Sept. 12	Bank	200

For the sake of clarity, the accounts are now repeated, as they should stand after these transactions have been entered. The balances of the accounts show the present value of the assets and liabilities, so the balance of each account is also shown.

BUILDING SOCIETY ACCOUNT

Dr. Cr.

		£			£
Sept. 8	Bank	2,000	Sept. 7	Balance	8,200
		(Cr. Balance £6,200)			

CAPITAL ACCOUNT

Dr. Cr.

			£
	Sept. 7	Balance	10,000
	(Cr. Balance £10,000)		

BANK ACCOUNT

Dr. Cr.

		£				£
Sept. 7	Balance	4,800	Sept. 8	Building Society		2,000
" 12	Land	200	" 10	Cash		50
			" 11	S. Black ...		750
	(Dr. Balance £2,200)					

STOCK ACCOUNT

Dr. Cr.

		£
Sept. 7	Balance	3,000
	(Dr. Balance £3,000)	

PREMISES ACCOUNT

Dr.				Cr.
		£		
Sept. 7	Balance	 10,000		
		(Dr. Balance £10,000)		

LAND ACCOUNT

Dr.						Cr.
		£				£
Sept. 7	Balance	 400	Sept. 12	Bank	.. ..	200
		(Dr. Balance £200)				

BREAKDOWN AMBULANCE ACCOUNT

Dr.				Cr.
		£		
Sept. 9	S. Black	 750		
		(Dr. Balance £750)		

S. BLACK ACCOUNT

Dr.						Cr.
		£				£
Sept. 11	Bank	 750	Sept. 9	Breakdown Am-		
				bulance		750
		(A/c Balanced)				

CASH ACCOUNT

Dr.				Cr.
		£		
Sept. 10	Bank	 50		
		(Dr. Balance £50)		

A Balance Sheet can be taken out at any time, because the balances of the accounts at any time show the values of the assets and liabilities. The accounts shown above have been balanced on 12th September. A Balance Sheet as at that date can therefore be taken out.

The debit balances represent assets and the credit balances liabilities. The Balance Sheet is shown below. It should be noted that the order in which the balances should appear in the Balance Sheet is not necessarily the same as the order in which the accounts happened to be opened.

BALANCE SHEET OF EUREKA MOTORS
AS AT 12TH SEPTEMBER, 19—

	£			£	£
		Fixed Assets			
Capital	.. 10,000	Premises ..	.. 10,000		
Building Society Loan	.. 6,200	Land	200		
		Breakdown Ambulance	750		
					10,950
		Current Assets			
		Stock ..	.. 3,000		
		Cash at Bank	.. 2,200		
		Cash in Hand	.. 50		
					5,250
	£16,200				£16,200

Difference between a Balance Sheet and an Account

A Balance Sheet is a statement, *at a given moment of time,* of all the assets and all the liabilities of a business.

An Account refers to one asset or one liability, and shows all the changes that have taken place, throughout the accounting period, in that asset or liability.

Debtors and Creditors

If a man owes you some money, the amount of the debt will be an asset; he is called a debtor, because the amount owing will be shown on the debit side of an account in your books.

Similarly, a debt owed by you will be a liability; it will be shown on the credit side of an account, and the person to whom you owe the money will therefore be called a creditor.

As each debt owed either to you or by you is a separate claim, it is necessary in practice to open a separate account for each debtor and each creditor. For the sake of conciseness they are lumped together in the Balance Sheet as debtors or creditors, and a list is attached showing the individual amounts.

Note. If a man owes you some money, he is your debtor and the amount will be entered on the debit side of his account in your books because it is an asset. But if he is your debtor, then you are his creditor, and the same debt is a liability to him. He also keeps books, in which he will keep an account of his transaction with you, and in that account the debt will appear on the credit side. The account he keeps of the transactions between you and him should be identical with the one you keep, except *that the sides would be reversed.*

The Meaning of Double Entry in Accounts

It was shown in Chapter Three that every transaction has a double effect on the Balance Sheet. Either effect, taken alone, would put the Balance Sheet out of balance, but the two effects, taken together, necessarily restore the balance.

This principle may now be restated. Every book-keeping transaction has two effects. One of these effects must be an addition to an asset or a reduction of a liability, because a business man could have no other reason for entering into a transaction. Either of these would be shown by a debit entry. But every advantage gained must be paid for, either at once or later, which means that an asset, such as cash, is reduced, or a liability increased. Either of these would be shown by a credit entry. Thus every transaction involves both a debit entry and a credit entry.

If more than two accounts are affected by any transaction, the total of the debit entries will be equal to the total of the credit entries.

DOUBLE EFFECT OF A TRANSACTION

FIRST EFFECT		SECOND EFFECT	
Effect on Account	Effect on asset or liability	Effect on asset or liability	Effect on Account
Debit Entries	Increase of asset	(1) Decrease of another asset or (2) Increase of a liability	Credit Entries
	Decrease of liability	(1) Decrease of an asset or (2) Increase of another liability	

Why Assets are Debited and Liabilities Credited

There are two main reasons why assets are shown on the debit side of accounts and liabilities on the credit side.

(a) If this is done, the assets will be clearly distinguished from the liabilities, because a debit balance will represent an asset and a credit balance a liability.

It is obviously very important in the ordinary conduct of business that there should be no confusion between assets and liabilities, and to enter these on different sides of accounts does simplify the drawing up of the Balance Sheet, in which they must be shown on different sides.

This purpose would equally be served if the sides were reversed (i.e., assets on the credit side and liabilities on the debit), but long custom has decided that the sides of an account should be used as explained above.

(b) As was pointed out in the previous section, when this practice is followed, each transaction results in one debit entry and one credit entry. The total debits should therefore be equal to the total credits. If they are equal, there is presumptive evidence that the accounts are correct. There is thus a check upon the accuracy of the working. (See next chapter on the 'Trial Balance'.)

WRITTEN EXERCISES

1 and 2. Repeat exercises No. 7 and No. 8 at the end of Chapter Three, using accounts in the form of a letter 'T'. Before entering the accounts, observe the effect of the transaction on the Balance Sheet.

3 and 4. Repeat exercises No. 2 and No. 3 at the end of Chapter Four, using accounts.

5. The following is the Balance Sheet of S. Clark on 31st December, 19—:

BALANCE SHEET OF S. CLARK
AS AT 31ST DECEMBER, 19—

	£		£	£
		Fixed Assets		
Capital	.. 44,662	Plant and		
		Machinery	.. 17,600	
		Vans	.. 4,203	
		Office Furniture	.. 710	
				22,513
Current Liabilities		*Current Assets*		
Creditors	.. 6,291	Stock ..	.. 18,233	
		Debtors ..	.. 8,165	
		Cash at Bank	.. 2,042	
				28,440
	£50,953			£50,953

Open an account in the form of a letter 'T' for each asset and liability, and enter the balances under the date 1st January, 19—.

During January, the following transactions took place:
Jan. 1. Drew £20 from the bank to be held in the office in the form of cash. (Open a Cash Account.)
 „ 5. Received by cheque from debtors £3,500.
 „ 8. Paid creditors £4,000 by cheque.
 „ 12. Bought new van valued £600 by cheque.
 „ 12. Sold old van, value £400, on credit.
 „ 20. Bought office furniture on credit for £250.
Enter these transactions in the accounts and show the Balance Sheet of S. Clark on 31st January, 19—.

6. The following is the Balance Sheet of R. Tile on the 31st December, 19—

BALANCE SHEET OF R. TILE
AS AT 31ST DECEMBER, 19—

	£		£	£
		Fixed Assets		
Capital	.. 24,930	Freehold Property ..	8,350	
Bank Overdraft ..	... 1,054	Fixtures and Fittings	960	
				9,310
Current Liabilities		*Current Assets*		
Creditors .. —	... 4,067	Stock ..	.. 12,285	
		Debtors ..	.. 8,406	
		Cash in Hand	.. 50	
				20,741
	£30,051			£30,051

Open an account for each asset and liability and enter the balances under the date of 1st January, 19—.

Transactions during January:
Jan. 10. Received by cheque from debtors £5,000.
 „ 12. Paid £30 into the bank from cash in hand.
 „ 15. Paid creditors £3,000 by cheque.
 „ 20. Purchased vans £1,000 on credit.
 „ 25. Sold office desk for cheque £20.

Pass these transactions through the accounts and draw up the Balance Sheet of R. Tile on 31st January, 19—.

7. Show by means of accounts the effects of the following transactions. Give also a written explanation of each entry, showing whether it is an increase or a decrease of an asset or liability.

(*Example:* The purchase by cheque of office furniture costing £100.

OFFICE FURNITURE ACCOUNT			BANK ACCOUNT		
Dr.		Cr.	Dr.		Cr.
	£				£
Bank	100			Furniture	100

The asset 'Office Furniture' was increased by £100. The asset 'Bank' was reduced by £100.)

(a) The payment by cheque of a debt to T. Smith for £50.
(b) The purchase, on credit, of machinery for £750 from Messrs. Latex.
(c) The receipt of £20 in cash in payment of a debt owed to you by R. Jones.
(d) The payment of £45 office cash into the bank.
(e) The purchase, by cheque, of a motor van for £250.
(f) The investment by the proprietor of a further £1,000 in the business by means of a cheque.
(g) The withdrawal of £100 by cheque for office purposes.
(h) The destruction, through an accident, of a motor van valued at £250.
(i) The receipt of a cheque for £25 as commission.

8. Explain the transactions which gave rise to each of the following pairs of entries:

(a)

CREDITORS ACCOUNT			BANK ACCOUNT		
Dr.		Cr.	Dr.		Cr.
	£				£
Bank	60			Creditors	60

(b)

CASH ACCOUNT			BANK ACCOUNT		
Dr.		Cr.	Dr.		Cr.
		£		£	
	Bank	100	Cash	100	

(c)

CASH ACCOUNT			BANK ACCOUNT		
Dr.		Cr.	Dr.		Cr.
	£				£
Bank	50			Cash	50

(d)

CAPITAL ACCOUNT			BANK ACCOUNT		
Dr.		Cr.	Dr.		Cr.
	£				£
Bank	100			Capital	100

(e)

DEBTORS ACCOUNT			BANK ACCOUNT		
Dr.		Cr.	Dr.		Cr.
		£		£	
	Bank	80	Debtors	80	

(f)

DEBTORS ACCOUNT			FURNITURE ACCOUNT		
Dr.		Cr.	Dr.		Cr.
		£		£	
	Furniture	45	Debtors	45	

(g)	CREDITORS ACCOUNT			FURNITURE ACCOUNT		
Dr.			Cr.	Dr.		Cr.
			£		£	
	Furniture		70	Creditors	70	

(h)	CAPITAL ACCOUNT			FIXTURES AND FITTINGS ACCOUNT		
Dr.			Cr.	Dr.		Cr.
	£					£
Loss by Fire	15			Loss by Fire		15

(i)	RENT ACCOUNT			BANK ACCOUNT		
Dr.			Cr.	Dr.		Cr.
			£		£	
	Bank		30	Rent	30	

(j)	CAPITAL ACCOUNT			BANK ACCOUNT		
Dr.			Cr.	Dr.		Cr.
			£		£	
	Bank		750	Capital	750	

9. Amongst your assets on 1st January, 19—, is a debt of £400 owed to you by W. Pepper. Open an account for W. Pepper and enter the debt as a balance. The following transactions then took place between you:

Jan. 3. He purchased goods on credit £75.
 ,, 6. He returned goods to you, damaged, £15.
 ,, 8. He paid the amount due from him on 1st January by cheque.
 ,, 10. You bought office furniture from him on credit £100.
 ,, 12. You paid him by cheque the amount due to him.

(a) Complete the W. Pepper Account as it appeared in your books. (Do not complete the double entries.)

(b) Show your account as it appeared in his books. In each case state the balance.

10. On 1st February, 19—, you owed P. Corn £48.

Feb. 9. You paid P. Corn £30 by cheque on account.
 ,, 12. Purchased goods from P. Corn on credit for £25.
 ,, 20. Sent cheque £50 to P. Corn, the excess above the amount due to him to be held by him against further purchases.

Without completing the double entries, show—

(a) The P. Corn Account in your books.
(b) Your account in P. Corn's books.

In each case state the balance.

11. The following were the assets and liabilities of R. Welsh, draper, on 1st June, 19—:

Cash in hand £300.
Bank overdraft £1,000.
Stock £2,500.
Premises £12,000.
Due to Building Society £8,000.

Draw up his Balance Sheet on 1st June, 19—, and enter the balances in accounts.

June 2. Purchased van on credit from S. Scott £600.
 ,, 3. Paid cash into bank £250.
 ,, 4. R. Welsh increased his capital by paying into bank £4,000.
 ,, 5. Paid S. Scott £600.
 ,, 6. Purchased stock by cheque £1,500.

Pass these transactions through the accounts and show the Balance Sheet of R. Welsh on 6th June, 19—.

CLASS QUESTIONS

1. How often are Balance Sheets ordinarily drawn up?
2. What is the name of the interval of time between Balance Sheets?
3. What is the purpose of accounts?
4. Why are there two sides to an account?
5. What names are given to these two sides?
6. What is a 'balance'?
7. When is a balance said to be (a) a debit balance or (b) a credit balance?
8. What does a balance represent?
9. On which side of an account is an asset shown?
10. On which side of an account is a liability shown?
11. How are additions to the value of (a) an asset and (b) a liability shown in the accounts?
12. How is capital treated in the Capital Account—as an asset or a liability?
13. When a Balance Sheet is drawn up at the end of an accounting period where are the values of (a) the assets and (b) the liabilities to be found?
14. What two reasons can be given for (a) a debit entry and (b) a credit entry?
15. What is the difference between a Balance Sheet and an account?
16. Summarize the rules for (a) debit entries and (b) credit entries.
17. In writing a description of an entry in an account, what general rule is followed?
18. Why is the name of an account not used as a description of an entry in that account?
19. What is the minimum number of entries required for each transaction?
20. Why is it that, before the entry of any transactions, the total of all the debit items equals the total of all the credit entries?
21. Why is it that after the entry of transactions the total of all the debit items still equals the total of all the credit items?
22. How are deductions from the value of (a) an asset and (b) a liability shown in the accounts?

6

THE LEDGER AND TRIAL BALANCE

ACCOUNTS are kept in a book called the ledger. It would be a waste of time to rule accounts by hand every time an account had to be opened; so, as all accounts are ruled in the same way, ruled ledgers are used. The ruling is shown below, the columns being numbered for reference:

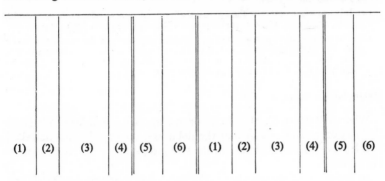

| (1) | (2) | (3) | (4) | (5) | (6) | (1) | (2) | (3) | (4) | (5) | (6) |

Explanation of Ruling

The heading of the account is written on the top line. On the same line, at the left and right ends respectively, the abbreviations 'Dr.' and 'Cr.' are written.

The columns on the left of the double vertical line down the centre are the debit columns. They are repeated on the right of the line for the credit side. The use of these columns is shown below:

(1) The month.

(2) Day of the month—shown simply in figures (*e.g.*, 1, 19, 27).

(3) Particulars.

(4) Folio. A folio is a page in a book-keeping book. Each page in the ledger is numbered and each account would appear on a different page. In the folio column, the number of the page on which the corresponding double entry is found would be entered. This greatly facilitates checking, especially when there are a great number of entries.

(5) (6) These are the money columns.

Illustration: The Bank Account from the worked example at the end of the previous chapter (page 31) is as follows:

39

BANK ACCOUNT

Dr. | | | | | | | | Cr.

19—			£	19—			£
Sept. 7	Balance b/d	..	4,800	Sept. 8	Building Society		2,000
" 12	Land	.. ..	200	" 10	Cash		50
				" 11	S. Black ..	...	750
				" 11	Balance c/d	..	2,200
			£5,000				£5,000
Sept. 12	Balance b/d	..	2,200				

Note. Entering the Account

(a) It is important to write the figures in alignment, units under units, tens under tens, and so on. If there are no pence it is clearer to put a dash.

(b) The year is an important part of the date, especially if the transactions are few in number and spread over a number of years. If the year changes before the page is complete, the new year is indicated in the date column, immediately above the first entry in the new year.

Balancing an Account

When a Balance Sheet is to be drawn up, it is usual first to balance the accounts. This means that the debit and credit sides are cancelled out, leaving only the balance, as the starting-point for the next accounting period.

In the account shown above, the debit side amounts to £5,000 and the credit side to £2,800. There is therefore a debit balance of £2,200. The method of balancing is shown below:

First Step. The amount of the balance is inserted on the smaller side. This is a check upon arithmetical accuracy, because if no mistake has been made, both sides should now total up to the same amount.

Second Step. The credit side now consists of four entries, but there are only two on the debit side. Obviously if one of the sides continues to grow much faster than the other the longer side may be several pages ahead of the shorter side, making it difficult to compare them. To prevent this, they are brought together at the end of each page or when the account is balanced. The totals of the two sides are entered on the same line (the line after the last entry on the longer side), and the unused lines on the short side are cancelled in the manner shown in the above Bank Account. The cancellation prevents the later insertion of entries in the blank lines.

Third Step. As stated at the beginning of this section, there is a debit balance in this account. It is now entered on the debit side immediately below the total, thus completing the double entry. The date is the first day of the new accounting period, which is the day following the last day of the previous period.

Note. The entry in the folio column, 'c/d', is an abbreviation for 'carried down', and 'b/d' for 'brought down'.

Balancing Accounts Containing One Line Only

(*a*) If an account contains one entry only, it is unnecessary to enter the total. The following is an example:

CASH ACCOUNT (9)

Dr.								Cr.
19—				£	19—			£
Sept. 11	Bank ...	...	3	50	Sept. 11 Balance ...		c/d	50
Sept. 12	Balance	...	b/d	£50				

Notice that, after ruling, 'ditto' signs must not be used for the month.

(*b*) If an account contains one entry on each side and is in balance, it is ruled off only, *e.g.*:

S. BLACK ACCOUNT (8)

Dr.				£	19—			Cr.
19—				£				£
Sept. 11	Bank	...	3	750	Sept. 9 Breakdown Ambulance ...		7	750

The Trial Balance

In the previous chapter it was stated:

(*a*) That the balances with which the accounts were opened consisted of the assets and liabilities (including capital) on that date. As the assets were entered on the debit side, and the liabilities on the credit side, the total of the debits would equal the total of the credits. This is true because the total assets are equal to the total liabilities plus the capital.

$$(L+C=A)$$

(*b*) That each subsequent transaction involved one entry on the debit side, and an equal entry on the credit side.

It follows that the total debit entries are still equal to the total credit entries *provided no mistake has been made*.

Now it is impossible to guarantee that no mistake will ever be made. Therefore, as soon as the transactions are double-entered in the accounts, it is usual to make a preliminary check upon the accuracy of the entries by taking out a 'Trial Balance', to see if the total of all the debit entries is equal to that of all the credit entries. This could take the form of a list of the accounts showing the total of the debit entries, and the total of the credit entries in each. A Trial Balance in this form, based on the worked example at the end of the previous chapter, is as follows:

TRIAL BALANCE

	Dr. £	Cr. £
Building Society A/c.	2,000	8,200
Capital A/c.		10,000
Bank A/c.	5,000	2,800
Stock A/c.	3,000	
Land A/c.	400	200
Premises A/c.	10,000	
Breakdown Ambulance A/c.	750	
S. Black A/c.	750	750
Cash A/c.	50	
	£21,950	£21,950

The balance in the Building Society Account is a credit one of £6,200. Now if this had been shown in the Trial Balance instead of the totals, each side of the Trial Balance would have been reduced by £2,000. But it would still have balanced. It follows that a Trial Balance can be constructed by making a list of the balances instead of totals. It would be a more useful statement because the figures used would be those required for a Balance Sheet. Moreover, it obviates the possibility of making a calculating mistake in the amount of the balance, since this also is tested by a Trial Balance in this form. The previous Trial Balance is now rewritten to include only the balances.

TRIAL BALANCE

	Dr. £	Cr. £
Building Society A/c.		6,200
Capital A/c.		10,000
Bank A/c.	2,200	
Stock A/c.	3,000	
Land A/c.	200	
Premises A/c.	10,000	
Breakdown Ambulance A/c.	750	
S. Black A/c.	—	—
Cash A/c.	50	
	£16,200	£16,200

The debit balances, being debit balances of accounts, will represent assets, and the credit balances will represent liabilities.

Errors Disclosed by a Trial Balance

If the two sides of a Trial Balance are not equal, this is proof of the existence of error. There may, of course, be more than one error. Such errors may be traced to the following causes:

(*a*) Misreading of figures through bad writing or bad alignment.
(*b*) Mistakes in the addition of the Trial Balance.

(c) Entry of a balance on the wrong side of the Trial Balance.

(d) Omission of a balance.

(e) A mistake in the calculation of the balance.

(f) Omission of either a debit or a credit entry in the accounts.

(g) Entry of one figure on one side of the accounts and a different figure on the other side.

Tracing Errors Disclosed by a Trial Balance

The following steps should be taken to trace the error:

(a) If the Trial Balance is badly written, rewrite it.

(b) Add each side of the Trial Balance again. If you added *upwards* the first time, start at the top and add *downwards* the second time, and vice versa.

(c) Find the amount of the discrepancy, so that you will know when the error or errors have been found.

(d) Check the balance in each account, and write the balance in pencil in the account on the *larger* side.

(e) Tick the balance in the account and in the Trial Balance if it is entered correctly.

If this does not disclose the error, it must be sought in the accounts themselves. A short cut may be taken in exercises, where the number of entries is small, by searching first for any item of either the same size, or half the size, of the discrepancy, and checking these first. (If the item is the same size as the error it may have been omitted from one side; if it is half the size of the error, it may have been entered twice on the same side.)

(f) Go through the books from the beginning, ticking each correct entry in pencil in the folio column. Insert and tick any entries omitted on either side, or correct those in which wrong figures have been entered. The error, if it is still untraced, will be accounted for by the unticked entries.

Errors the Trial Balance will not Disclose

The existence of error is proved if a Trial Balance is not in balance· But the fact that it is in balance does not prove that the books are correct, because mistakes may be made that will not upset the equilibrium of the two sides. A Trial Balance can prove only that the total of the debit entries in the accounts is equal to the total of the credit entries. The following are examples of errors that would not be disclosed:

(a) The complete omission of a transaction (*i.e.*, no entry on either side of the books).

(b) An entry in a wrong account, if the amount is correct and the side correct (both entries for a transaction might be entered in the wrong accounts).

(c) Compensating errors. The effect of one mistake may be cancelled by another mistake, of the same size, acting in the reverse direction.

WRITTEN EXERCISES

Instructions to Students

(i) Rule lightly.

(ii) Before ruling a line, decide how long it should be and make it that length. Ragged lengths are untidy.

(iii) If you are ruling double lines, they should both be the same length and the same distance apart throughout their length.

(iv) Ruled lines that are supposed to join should join exactly.

(v) All ruled lines should be the same thickness.

In all future exercises in which accounts are written up, the accounts should be numbered and the folio columns used.

1.   Re-write exercises 9 and 10 from the previous Chapter, using ledger paper.

2.   E. Toms commenced business on 1st January, 19—, with £5,000 in the bank·
Show his Balance Sheet on that date.

Open the necessary accounts and enter the balances shown in the above Balance Sheet. Pass the following transactions through the ledger, opening new accounts when necessary.

Jan. 2.   Purchased premises for £8,000, paying £2,000 by cheque and borrowing the balance from the 'Brick Building Society'.

  „   3.   Purchased machinery £3,000 on credit from F. Johns.

  „ 10.   Purchased fixtures and fittings for £500 from O. Luke on credit.

  „ 13.   Purchased van £500 by cheque.

  „ 20.   Paid O. Luke £350.

  „ 25.   Drew £20 from the bank for office purposes (not private purposes).

  „ 28.   Sold part of fixtures on credit to I. Mark for £60.

(a) Take out a Trial Balance.

(b) When it is correct, balance off accounts. Draw up a Balance Sheet as on 31st January, 19—.

3.   V. Dry had the following assets and liabilities at 1st January, 19—ı

				£
Cash in hand ..	...	...	...	20
Cash at bank ..	...	.-.	...	450
Debtors ..	...	...	...	1,100
Creditors ...	...	..-	...	900
Stock	...	..	..	2,000
Loan to T. Salt	..	..	..	3,000

Find his capital and draw up his Balance Sheet on that date. Open accounts and enter the balances from the Balance Sheet. Pass the following transactions through the books:

Jan. 6.   Received £750 by cheque from debtors.

  „ 10.   Paid creditors by cheque £800.

  „ 12.   Purchased office furniture on credit for £500.

  „ 15.   Bought office supplies by cheque £50.

  „ 28.   Withdrew £15 for office cash.

Take out a Trial Balance, balance the accounts, and draw up a Balance Sheet showing V. Dry's position on 31st January, 19—.

4. On 1st March, 19—, L. Cade had the following assets and liabilities:

					£
Cash in hand	...	—	—	—	22
Cash at bank	...	—	—	—	350
Stock	..	...	...	...	600
Debtors	...	...	...	—	500
Creditors	..	...	...	...	400
Office Furniture		...	...	...	200

Ascertain his capital and draw up his Balance Sheet on that date. Open accounts for all assets and liabilities, then pass the following transactions through the accounts:

Mar. 2. Purchased van on credit £300.
  ,, 9. Received £20 in cash from debtors.
  ,, 14. Paid debts by cheque £250.
  ,, 18. Received cheques in payment of debts £350.
  ,, 20. Paid £30 into the bank, from cash in hand.
  ,, 26. Bought office furniture by cheque £100.
  ,, 30. L. Cade drew cheque £25 for office cash.

5. Correct and complete the following Trial Balance, taken from the books of N. Fay on 31st January, 19—:

			Dr. £	Cr. £
Cash in hand	..	...	20	
Cash at bank	...	..	1,000	
Stock	..	...	2,000	
Debtors	..	...		800
Creditors	..	...	700	
Loan from A.B.		...	1,250	
Machinery	...	...	5,000	
Premises	...	...	6,000	
Capital ...	...	...		

When the Trial Balance is complete, draw up the Balance Sheet of N. Fay on 31st January, 19—.

6. The following is the account of G. Carr in the books of R. Smith:

G. CARR ACCOUNT

Dr.				£	Cr.				£
19—					19—				
Jan. 1	Balance b/d.			100	Jan. 16	Cheque	..	..	120
,, 14	Sales	..	..	50	,, 31	Balance c/d.		..	30
				£150					£150
Feb. 1	Balance b/d.		..	30					

(a) Explain each of the entries in the above account in your own words and state:

    (i) Whether G. Carr was a debtor or a creditor on 15th January.
    (ii) The amount of the debt on that date.

(b) Show the account of R. Smith in G. Carr's books during the same period.

7.   The following is the Cash at Bank Account in the books of R. Smith:

CASH AT BANK ACCOUNT

Dr.						Cr.
19—			£	19—		£
Jan. 1	Balance b/d.	...	350	Jan. 3 Goods		50
„ 4	Cash ...	...	25	„ 10 V. Dry		80
„ 6	L. Toms ...	...	70	„ 20 Office Furniture ..		500
„ 16	G. Carr ...	...	120	„ 26 Stationery ...		25
„ 31	Balance c/d.	...	90			
			£655			£655
				Feb. 1 Balance b/d. ...		90

(a) Explain each of the entries in the above account in your own words.
(b) What was the state of R. Smith's banking account on

(i) 12th January?

(ii) 18th January?

8.   Draw up the Balance Sheet of N. Green on 31st December, 19—, from the following Trial Balance:

	Dr. £	Cr. £
Cash in hand	·80	
Stock	320	
Machinery	1,250	
Fixtures	100	
Buildings	2,500	
Bank overdraft ..		500
Loan from Building Society		1,000
Debtors: L. White ..	20	
S. Black ..	30	
Creditors: N. Brown ..		40
T. Pink ..		50
Wages due		75
Interest due to Building		
Society		25
Rates due		20
Capital		2,590
	£4,300	£4,300

9.   Show by means of accounts the effects of the following transactions:

(a) The receipt of machinery, valued at £120, in settlement of a debt to you of £120.
(b) The Purchase on credit of a showcase costing £28.
(c) The payment in cash by you of a debt of £15.
(d) The balance of the Office Furniture Account includes an amount of £40 for a chair which was, in fact, delivered to the proprietor's own home for his private use. Make the necessary correction in the business accounts.
(e) The sale of a portion of the premises for £500 for which a cheque was received.
(f) A cheque received from a debtor was entered in the books in error at £10 above its actual value. Make the necessary correction.
(g) The purchase for cash of stationery and stamps for £5.
(h) The proprietor withdrew £20 from the bank for office cash.
(i) The sale on credit of part of the office furniture for £55.
(j) The receipt of a cheque for £75 in payment of a debt due to you.

10. Explain the transactions which gave rise to each of the following pairs of entries:

(a)

DEBTORS ACCOUNT			
Dr.			Cr.
			£
	Cash		28

CASH ACCOUNT			
Dr.			Cr.
	£		
Debtors	28		

(b)

PREMISES ACCOUNT			
Dr.			Cr.
			£
	Bank		2,000

BANK ACCOUNT			
Dr.			Cr.
	£		
Premises	2,000		

(c)

DEBTORS ACCOUNT			
Dr.			Cr.
	£		
Bank (Error)	9		

BANK ACCOUNT			
Dr.			Cr.
			£
	Debtors (Error)		9

(d)

STATIONERY & STAMPS ACCOUNT			
Dr.			Cr.
	£		
Cash	10		

CASH ACCOUNT			
Dr.			Cr.
			£
	Stamps		10

(e)

CAPITAL ACCOUNT			
Dr.			Cr.
	£		
Stamps (Theft)	3		

STATIONERY & STAMPS ACCOUNT			
Dr.			Cr.
			£
	Capital (Theft)		3

(f)

MACHINERY ACCOUNT			
Dr.			Cr.
	£		
Motor Vans (Error)	450		

MOTOR VAN ACCOUNT			
Dr.			Cr.
			£
	Machinery (Error)		450

(g)

CASH ACCOUNT			
Dr.			Cr.
	£		
Bank	30		

BANK ACCOUNT			
Dr.			Cr.
			£
	Cash		30

(h)

CAPITAL ACCOUNT			
Dr.			Cr.
	£		
Bank	36		

BANK ACCOUNT			
Dr.			Cr.
			£
	Capital		36

(i)

CREDITORS ACCOUNT			
Dr.			Cr.
	£		
Furniture	48		

FURNITURE ACCOUNT			
Dr.			Cr.
			£
	Creditors		48

CLASS QUESTIONS

1. What is the name of the book in which accounts are kept?
2. Name the columns on each side of the book.
3. Explain how 'ditto' signs can be used to save time.
4. What does the word 'folio' mean?
5. Explain how the folio column is used.
6. How are the two sides of an account kept the same length?
7. Why are unused lines in an account cancelled?
8. Under what date is the balance entered—
    (a) When the account is closed?
    (b) When the balance is carried down?
9. What is a Trial Balance?
10. Why are both sides of a Trial Balance equal?
11. Mention six mistakes that would prevent a Trial Balance from balancing.
12. Mention three errors that a Trial Balance would not disclose.
13. If a Trial Balance were out of balance, what steps would you take to discover the error?
14. At what point in the keeping of books is a Trial Balance extracted?

7

THE EFFECT OF TRANSACTIONS ON CAPITAL

IF a transaction consists of an exchange of assets of equal value, or the cancellation of a liability through giving an asset of the same value, the difference between the assets and the liabilities will remain unaltered, and no profit will have been made.

If, on the other hand, one asset is exchanged for another of greater value, the difference in value between these assets will be a profit. Because the assets have been increased without a corresponding increase in liabilities, the capital will be increased by the same amount as the assets. In other words, a profit is an increase of capital. This is so because a profit belongs to the proprietor, and the amount he owns is shown by the amount of his capital.

The usual way in which a trader makes a profit is to sell goods at a price higher than that which he paid for them.

Let us assume that the following is a Balance Sheet of Eureka Motors:

BALANCE SHEET OF EUREKA MOTORS
AS AT 6TH SEPTEMBER, 19

	£		£	£
		Fixed Assets		
Capital	10,000	Premises	10,000	
Building Society Loan	8,000	Office Furniture	400	
				10,400
Current Liabilities		*Current Assets*		
Creditors	400	Stock	3,000	
		Cash at Bank	5,000	
				8,000
	£18,400			£18,400

The stock £3,000 consists of six cars purchased for £500 each. They are shown in the Balance Sheet at cost price. Suppose one of these cars is sold for £800 cash. The stock will now consist of five cars bought for £500 each and will therefore stand at £2,500; that is, £500 less. The car was sold for £800, therefore the cash will be increased by £800. The net effect is an addition to the assets side of £300, and that difference is profit. As the profit belongs to the proprietor it will be added to the capital on the liabilities side and the new Balance Sheet will appear as follows:

BALANCE SHEET OF EUREKA MOTORS
AS AT 7TH SEPTEMBER, 19—

	£	£			£	£
			Fixed Assets			
Capital ...	... 10,000		Premises ..	.. 10,000		
Add Profit	.. 300		Office Furniture	.. 400		
		10,300				10,400
Building Society						
Loan ..	..	... 8,000				
Current Liabilities			*Current Assets*			
Creditors ...	...	... 400	Stock ..	.. 2,500		
			Cash at Bank	.. 5,800		
						8,300
		£18,700				£18,700

When a sale is made, money is obtained. Students therefore often jump to the conclusion that profit must always consist of money. This, however, is not necessarily, or even usually, true; because the money acquired as a result of a sale would probably be used in the purchase of other assets (*e.g.,* more stock). Profit is part of capital and as such is part of the excess of assets over liabilities, in whatever form the assets are held.

Other Transactions that Affect Capital

Capital can be affected only by a change in the relative value of assets and liabilities. Profit causes such a change. Other possible causes are:

(a) *A Loss.* The process would be similar to that shown for the making of a profit, the difference being that there would be a reduction of the margin between assets and liabilities and the loss would be deducted from capital.

(b) *An Addition to Capital.* If the proprietor decided to increase his investment, he would bring fresh assets into the business. These would be shown on the assets side of the Balance Sheet, and the amount by which they were increased added to the capital.

(c) *A Withdrawal of Capital.* The owner of capital in a business might find it necessary to withdraw some part of it. The effect on the Balance Sheet would be the reverse of the effect of an addition; *i.e.,* the assets and the capital would both be reduced. Apart from such reductions, however, it is customary for a proprietor who depends upon a business for his living to withdraw sums of money at intervals for personal and domestic expenses, or he may withdraw goods if they happen to be useful to him. Such withdrawals are withdrawals of capital; they are known as 'drawings'.

Drawings are not a Reduction of Profit

It is important to understand that drawings are a reduction of capital, but not a reduction of profit. If a business man makes a profit of £100 and goes for a holiday with this money, it would be wrong to say he had not made any profit. He has made the profit and then spent it. On the other hand, he might withdraw money for his own use even if he had made no profit.

This point is made clear by a consideration of the following example.

Suppose a trader commenced business with a capital of £1,000, made no profit, but withdrew £100 for his own use. His capital at the end of the year could be arrived at in the following way:

Initial capital	...	..	£1,000
Drawings ..	...	...	100
Final capital	...	..	£900

If now we assume that the same trader had made a profit of £200 during the year, his final capital would be as follows:

Initial capital	...	...	£1,000
Add profit	...	..	200
			1,200
Less drawings	...	...	100
Final capital	...	..	£1,100

It will be observed that, in the second case, his final capital was greater than in the first case by £200—the full amount of the profit. Clearly the profit had not been reduced by the drawings. Both drawings and profit have an independent effect upon capital.

Finding Profit by a Comparison of Initial and Final Capital

If a profit is made:

$$\text{Initial Capital} + \text{Profit} = \text{Final Capital}$$
$$\text{or Final Capital} - \text{Initial Capital} = \text{Profit}$$

It is assumed in this equation, however, that the final capital is intact—that none of it has been drawn out. If money has been withdrawn by the proprietor, those drawings must be added back to the final capital before subtracting the initial capital (to find profit). The equation would then be:

$$\text{Initial Capital} + \text{Profit} = \text{Final Capital} + \text{Drawings.}$$

Any one of these terms can be found if the other three are known, simply by finding the difference between the two sides.

For example, suppose a trader had an initial capital of £1,000 and a final capital of £1,500, and had withdrawn £200, his profit would be calculated as follows:

	£
Final Capital + Drawings	1,700
Initial Capital	1,000
Profit	£700

Again, if his initial capital were £800, his profit £400, and his final capital £900, his drawings would be:

	£
Initial Capital + Profit ..	1,200
Final Capital	900
Drawings	£300

WRITTEN EXERCISES

1. A. Seath has a capital on 1st January, 19—, of £4,000. On 30th June his capital is £4,600.

(a) How much profit has he made?

It was then disclosed that before ascertaining his capital on 30th June, he had withdrawn £100 for his own use.

(b) What would his capital have been on that date if he had not withdrawn the £100?

(c) What would his profit have been for the half-year?

2. Complete the following table:

Capital (July)	Profit	Capital (Dec.)	Drawings
£	£	£	£
4,180		4,520	200
6,600		6,700	250
1,800		1,500	350
10,500	150		300
7,400	400	7,200	
	100	9,000	275
25,000	1,500		500
	1,000	1,200	450
15,000	1,200	15,200	

3. The following is the Balance Sheet of Mr. O. Winter on 1st January, 19—:

BALANCE SHEET OF O. WINTER
AS AT 1ST JANUARY, 19—

Liabilities		£	Assets		£
Debts owed by him ..	..	820	Cash in Hand ...	...	15
Capital .. .	...	11,291	Cash at Bank ...	...	792
			Debts owed to him	...	1,044
			Stock	...	1,800
			Vans	...	960
			Land and Buildings	...	7,500
		£12,111			£12,111

It was then found that
    (*a*) The stock had been overvalued by £150.
    (*b*) A van, valued at £300, had been destroyed by fire the previous night.
    (*c*) The amount owed by him should have been £800—not £820.
Draw up a corrected Balance Sheet.

    4. On 1st January, 19—, George Chappel commenced business with £2,000 in the bank. His position on the following 31st December was as follows:

Machinery £1,200	Fixtures and fittings £120
Sundry creditors £240	Cash at bank £195
Sundry debtors £310	Stock 31/12/19— £645
Cash in hand £45	

During the year he had withdrawn £20 every month including December. Find his net profit for the year and prepare his Balance Sheet on 31st December.

CLASS QUESTIONS

1. What is profit?
2. What is the usual way of making a profit?
3. For what reasons, other than the making of a profit, can the value of capital change?
4. Are drawings a reduction of profit?
5. What is the equation by which profit can be ascertained?

8

THE TRADING ACCOUNT

THE nature of profit was discussed in the previous chapter. It is now necessary to show how profit is passed through the accounts.

The amount of profit resulting from a sale is calculated arithmetically by subtracting the cost of goods from the amount for which they were sold. If, for example, something is bought for £500 and sold for £750, the amount of profit, obvious though it is, would in fact be found by doing the following sum:

	£
Proceeds of sales..	750
Cost of goods sold	500
Profit (by subtraction)	250

The selling price, £750, contained the cost of the goods, £500, plus the profit £250. When the cost is subtracted the profit is left.

It is this calculation which must be incorporated in the books. The method is best shown by taking an example.

Let us therefore take the position of Eureka Motors on 1st September, 19—. On that date the capital was £10,000 consisting entirely of cash at bank, and the Balance Sheet was as follows:

BALANCE SHEET OF EUREKA MOTORS
AS AT 1ST SEPTEMBER, 19—

	£		£
Capital (A. Brown)	10,000	Cash at Bank	10,000

Let us now assume that the business acquires six cars for nothing on 2nd September, and sells them all at £750 each, a total of £4,500, on the same day. As nothing was paid for the cars, the whole of the selling price would be profit and would have to be added to capital by means of a credit entry in the Capital Account (since profit increases capital).

The Capital Account would then appear:

CAPITAL ACCOUNT (A. BROWN)

Dr.   Cr.

			£
19—			
Sept. 1	Balance	... ..	10,000
„ 2	Sales ..	... ..	4,500

54

If now it is assumed that in fact £500 each was paid for the cars (a total of £3,000), the profit made would be only the difference between £3,000 and £4,500, that is, £1,500. Clearly the £3,000 would have to be deducted from the capital. The deduction would be made by a debit entry in the Capital Account, the net effect being that the capital would be increased only by the difference, or profit. The Capital Account after the deduction of purchases (representing costs) would appear:

CAPITAL ACCOUNT (A. BROWN)

Dr.						Cr.
19—		£	19—			£
Sept. 2	Purchases ..	.. 3,000	Sept. 1	Balance	...	.. 10,000
„ 2	Balance c/d.	.. 11,500	„ 2	Sales ..	...	.. 4,500
		£14,500				£14,500
			Sept. 3	Balance b/d.		£11,500

The arithmetical calculation with which we started has now reappeared in the Capital Account with cost and sales side by side. The sales are on the credit side because they contain the profit; and the purchases, or cost, are on the debit side as a deduction from sales.

The debit entry for the sales would be in the Cash Account or Bank Account (if the money were received) or in the personal account of the buyer (if the goods were sold on credit). Similarly, for the purchases the double entry would be on the credit side of the Cash Account, the Bank Account, or the personal account of the vendor (*i.e.*, the seller).

It should be noted that, for the time being, we have dispensed with the Stock Account. Eureka Motors had no stock at the beginning (because it was bought later); there was none at the end (because it was all sold). Thus, when the Balance Sheets were taken out there was no stock to record.

The Trading Account

There are various criticisms of the method so far adopted for dealing with profit. For example:

(*a*) There is no clear statement of what the profit is. It is still a difference—the difference between £3,000 and £4,500 (or between £10,000 and £11,500).

(*b*) If there were many purchases and sales (and these could run into thousands), the Capital Account would be overburdened with detail.

To meet these objections, the Capital Account is divided into two parts by opening a new account, called the Trading Account, and it is in this account that the profit is calculated. The Trading Account is a sub-division of the Capital Account, so the same principles apply—sales are entered on the credit side and purchases on the debit side. If the sales are greater than the purchases there will be a profit and it will appear as a credit balance in the Trading Account. It will be transferred to the Capital Account by a debit entry in the Trading Account and a credit entry in the Capital Account.

The Capital Account and the Trading Account, after these purchases and sales had been recorded, would appear as follows:

TRADING ACCOUNT

Dr.							Cr.
19—			£	19—			£
Sept. 2	Purchases ..	..	3,000	Sept. 2	Sales ..	.. ..	4,500
„ 2	Profit (to Capital A/c.) ..	..	1,500				
			£4,500				£4,500

CAPITAL ACCOUNT (A. BROWN)

Dr.							Cr.
19—			£	19—			£
Sept. 2	Balance c/d.	..	11,500	Sept. 1	Balance	..	.. 10,000
				„ 2	Profit	..	.. 1,500
			£11,500				£11,500
				Sept. 3	Balance b/d.		£11,500

A loss, of course, would be shown as a debit balance in the Trading Account, and would be transferred *to the debit side of the Capital Account.*

It will be observed that as the profit was transferred from the Trading Account to the Capital Account, it was not brought down in the Trading Account. A balance is either brought down or transferred—never both.

Purchases and Sales Accounts

One more modification to the system must be introduced at this stage.

It is usual to take out a Trading Account at balancing time (the end of the accounting period) only. To enter the day-to-day purchases and sales, two new accounts are therefore opened—a Purchases Account and a Sales Account. The purchases and sales are entered here, and the totals are transferred to the Trading Account when the profit for a period is being ascertained.

These two accounts are sub-divisions of the Trading Account, and the same rules apply as for entering the Trading Account; namely, purchases on the debit side of the Purchases Account, and sales on the credit side of the Sales Account. No entry is made on the credit side of the Purchases Account except the one necessary to transfer the total to the Trading Account. Similarly, the only entry on the debit side of the Sales Account is the entry to transfer the total of the sales to the Trading Account, at the end of the financial period.

The burden of details is thus transferred to these accounts, only the totals appearing in the Trading Account. This is an advantage; but, as will be seen later, it is not in itself a sufficient answer to the problem of dealing with the vast number of transactions involved.

A second advantage is that in this way the total value of the purchases and of the sales is disclosed. This is important information that would have to be extracted in any case because the business man wants to know whether they are expanding or contracting in relation to previous years.

Use of the Purchases and Sales Accounts

The full accounts relating to these transactions are now shown below. It is assumed that the goods were bought and sold for cash and the double entry is therefore shown in the Bank Account: *e.g.,*

    (*a*) Purchased six cars at £500 each

           (i) Debit Purchases Account.
           (ii) Credit Bank Account.

    (*b*) Sold six cars at £750 each

           (i) Debit Bank Account.
           (ii) Credit Sales Account.

If they had been bought and sold on credit, the double entries would have been in personal accounts.

The foregoing transactions would appear in the books as follows:

BALANCE SHEET OF EUREKA MOTORS
AS AT 1ST SEPTEMBER, 19—

	£			£
Capital	.. 10,000	Cash at Bank		.. 10,000

BANK ACCOUNT (1)

Dr.   Cr.

19—			£	19—			£
Sept. 1	Balance	..	10,000	Sept. 2	Purchases	2	3,000
„ 2	Sales	.. 3	4,500	„ 2	Balance c/d.		11,500
			£14,500				£14,500
Sept. 3	Balance b/d.		£11,500				

PURCHASES ACCOUNT (2)

Dr.						Cr.
19—			£	19—		£
Sept. 2	Bank	...	1	3,000	Sept. 2 Trading A/c.	3,000

SALES ACCOUNT (3)

Dr.					Cr.
19—			£	19—	£
Sept. 2	Trading A/c.		4,500	Sept. 2 Bank ...	4,500

TRADING ACCOUNT OF EUREKA MOTORS
FOR PERIOD ENDED 3RD SEPTEMBER, 19—

Dr.						Cr.
			£			£
Purchases	..	..	3,000	Sales		4,500
Profit	...	... ...	1,500			
			£4,500			£4,500

CAPITAL ACCOUNT (4)

Dr.						Cr.
19—			£	19—		£
Sept. 2	Balance c/d.	..	11,500	Sept. 1 Balance	..	.. 10,000
				„ 2 Profit	...	.. 1,500
			£11,500			£11,500
				Sept. 3 Balance b/d.		£11,500

BALANCE SHEET OF EUREKA MOTORS
AS AT 3RD SEPTEMBER, 19—

			£				£
Capital	...	...	.. 11,500	Cash at Bank	...	...	.. 11,500

Notice that the Trading Account, being an account, covers the whole of the accounting period. Hence the heading 'for period ended . . .' When the period covered is stated in the heading, the date need not be repeated with each item.

The Purpose of the Trading Account

The purpose of the Trading Account is to ascertain whether, as a result of trading, a profit or a loss has been made, and how much. It follows from this that the purchases entered in the Purchases Account are the purchases only of goods bought for resale, and the sales included in the Sales Account refer only to the same goods. Other assets, such as a typewriter for use in the office, may be bought or sold, at a profit or a loss; but, if you are not trading in them, their purchase and sale will not be entered in these accounts, and will not appear in the Trading Account. Special accounts will be opened for them.

A certain amount of confusion sometimes arises because it is felt that, since the purchases represent additions to stock and sales represent the disposal of stock, the difference should be the amount of stock held, just as the balance of the Cash Account shows the amount of cash in hand. But this is not so, because the goods shown on the debit side are entered at cost price, and the same goods, when sold, appear on the credit side at selling price. The same goods, that is to say, appear at different prices on different sides of the account; so that, if no goods remained in the possession of the trader at all, all having been sold, there would still be a balance in the account, equal to the profit made.

In the Trading Account, therefore, we are not concerned with the size of the asset, stock, but with the size of a liability, capital. The entry of sales on the credit side means that capital has been increased, not that stock has been reduced. Capital has been increased because the sales include profit. Similarly, purchases are entered on the debit side as a reduction of capital, not as an addition to stock. When sales were added to capital, too much was added—the cost of the goods as well as the profit. The cost of the goods must therefore be deducted.

This point must be clearly understood. The Trading Account could serve either of two purposes, but not both. If the purchases and sales were entered at the same prices, it would show the amount of stock in hand, but the trader would have to find some other way of discovering his profit. If the purchases and sales are entered at cost price and selling price respectively, the Trading Account will show his profit but he will have to find some other way of ascertaining his stock. It is the latter alternative which has been chosen, so the problem of ascertaining stock will have to be faced. It will be dealt with in the next chapter.

WRITTEN EXERCISES

1. On 1st January, 19—, E. Wilkes had capital consisting of £500 in the bank. Draw up his Balance Sheet on that date. On the 15th January, he bought fifteen wireless sets by cheque for £20 each and sold them all on 20th January at £30 each, receiving the amount by cheque. Show his profit arithmetically, then pass these transactions through the books and show the Balance Sheet of E. Wilkes on 31st January, 19—.

2. E. Tye had the following assets on 1st January, 19—:
   Cash at bank £400.
   Premises £6,600.
   Vans £1,000.
Prepare his Balance Sheet on that date. On 10th January, he bought goods on credit from T. Smith for £1,200, and sold them all on credit to W. Green for £1,500 on 25th January. Open all the necessary accounts, pass these transactions through the books, and show his Balance Sheet on 31st January, 19—.

c

3. On 1st January, 19—, S. Little had the following assets and liabilities:

Cash in office £25   Creditors £300
Bank overdraft £200   Premises £6,000
Debtors £800   Furniture and fittings £500

Ascertain his capital and show his Balance Sheet on that date.

Jan. 12. He bought goods on credit £600.
  „ 15. He bought on credit a typewriter for use in his own business £48.
  „ 25. He sold all goods on credit £800.
  „ 27. He purchased furniture by cheque for £100.
  „ 28. His debtors paid him £250 by cheque.
  „ 30. Withdrew for his own use £40 by cheque.

Open accounts and enter his assets and liabilities as on 1st January, 19—.
Pass the above transactions during January through the books. Take out a Trial Balance.
Show his Balance Sheet on 31st January, 19—.
What was his bank overdraft on 28th January?

4. Mr. G. Turner commenced business on 1st January, 19—, with £1,000 in the bank. On 4th January, he purchased goods by cheque for £450, all of which were sold on 20th January for a total of £400.

(a) Show his Balance Sheet on 1st January, 19—.
(b) Open all necessary accounts to record his position and pass his transactions through the books.
(c) Show his Balance Sheet on 31st January, 19—.

CLASS QUESTIONS

1. Why must profit be shown in the Capital Account?
2. On which side of the Capital Account would profit be entered?
3. On which side of the Capital Account would a loss be entered?
4. Why is a Trading Account opened in addition to the Capital Account?
5. How is the amount of profit on a sale calculated arithmetically?
6. What form does the Trading Account take?
7. Why are sales entered on the credit side of the Trading Account?
8. Why are purchases entered on the debit side of the Trading Account?
9. What is the double entry for a purchase of goods for cash?
10. What kind of goods are included under the term 'purchases' in the Trading Account?
11. What is the double entry for a sale of goods on credit?
12. How is profit transferred from the Trading Account to the Capital Account?

THE TRADING ACCOUNT

(continued)

IT was stated at the end of the previous chapter that, as the Trading Account was used to arrive at the profit, some other method must be adopted to ascertain stock.

The method adopted is to 'take stock'. An inventory (*i.e.,* a list) is made of the goods on hand, each item is priced, and the total value is found by adding together the prices of the separate items.

Now let us suppose that, as before, Eureka Motors purchased six cars at £500 each on the 2nd September, but that on 30th September only five had been sold, at £750 each. The stock on hand on that date would therefore be one car, bought for £500.

The Trading Account of Eureka Motors, on 30th September, showing these purchases and sales, would be as follows:

TRADING ACCOUNT OF EUREKA MOTORS
FOR MONTH ENDED 30TH SEPTEMBER, 19—

Dr.		Cr.
	£	£
Purchases 3,000	Sales ... — 3,750	

From this account it would appear that only £750 profit had been made. In fact, the profit on five cars, each bought for £500 and sold for £750, would be £1,250.

The reason for the discrepancy is plain. Only five cars were sold, but the cost of six cars has been deducted from the proceeds of the sales. Clearly only the cost of five cars should have been deducted. The cost of five cars was £2,500. If this sum is deducted from the £3,750 realized on the sales, the correct profit, £1,250, will be shown. The purchases must therefore be reduced from £3,000 to £2,500 by subtracting from them the value of the unsold car.

The method of deducting the value of the unsold car from the purchases is to enter it on the opposite side, *i.e.,* the credit side, of the Trading Account. It will be credited at the value at which it was included in the purchases—the cost price.

The Trading Account for September showing the purchases, sales, and stock would then appear as follows:

TRADING ACCOUNT OF EUREKA MOTORS
FOR MONTH ENDED 30TH SEPTEMBER, 19—

	£		£
Purchases	3,000	Sales	3,750
Profit	1,250	Stock 30/9/19—	500
	£4,250		£4,250

The question then arises, what is to be done with the unsold car?
Obviously it will be offered for sale during the next accounting period,
ending, let us say, on 31st October. If it were sold during October, and
there were no other purchases or sales, the profit would be shown in
the following calculation:

	£
Selling price	750
Cost price	500
Profit	£250

If this calculation is put in the form of a Trading Account, the sales,
as before, will be shown on the credit side. The stock, which must be
deducted from the sales, would therefore appear on the debit side;
and the Trading Account for October would be as follows:

TRADING ACCOUNT OF EUREKA MOTORS
FOR MONTH ENDED 31ST OCTOBER, 19—

Dr.   Cr.

	£		£
Stock 1/10/19—	500	Sales	750
Profit	250		
	£750		£750

The Stock Account

From the above statements, it is apparent that the double entry for
the stock which is credited in the Trading Account at the end of one
accounting period, is on the debit side of the Trading Account for the
next accounting period. But a difficulty arises here. The Trading Account
for the next accounting period will not be opened until the end of that
period, which may be six months or a year later. It is impossible to
double enter an item in a non-existent account.

The solution is to open a Stock Account and to debit the stock
there. There it will lie until the next Trading Account is opened, when
it will be transferred to that Trading Account by:

(*a*) A credit entry in the Stock Account (closing the Account).

(*b*) A debit entry in the Trading Account.

The Stock Account is thus purely a matter of convenience, to retain the figure for stock until it is wanted. It is shown below, together with the Trading Accounts for September and October:

TRADING ACCOUNT OF EUREKA MOTORS
FOR MONTH ENDED 30TH SEPTEMBER, 19—

Dr.							Cr.
			£				£
Purchases	...	...	.. 3,000	Sales ..	..	..	.. 3,750
Profit ..	...	...	.. 1,250	Stock 30/9/19—		...	.. 500
			£4,250				£4,250

STOCK ACCOUNT

Dr.						Cr.
			£			£
Oct. 1 Balance	..	..	500	Oct. 31 Trading A/c.	..	500

TRADING ACCOUNT OF EUREKA MOTORS
FOR MONTH ENDED 31ST OCTOBER, 19—

Dr.							Cr.
			£				£
Stock 1/10/19—			500	Sales	...	...	... 750
Profit ..	..	...	... 250				
			£750				£750

The £500 stock held on 1st October is known as the 'Final' or 'Closing' Stock of the accounting period ending on 30th September, and as the 'Opening', 'Commencing' or 'Initial' Stock for the accounting period commencing on 1st October.

The closing stock is entered on the credit side of the appropriate Trading Account. The opening stock is entered on the debit side of the Trading Account.

Illustration Involving Opening and Closing Stock

To show how stock is dealt with when, as is usual, the trader owns some stock at the beginning of an accounting period and still has some left at the end, let us suppose that on 30 September, 19—, Eureka Motors had cash at bank £10,000 and three cars bought for £500 each, and that the following transactions took place during October:

(a) Seven cars were bought by cheque at £500 each.
(entries—debit Purchases Account £3,500;
credit Bank Account £3,500).

(b) Eight cars were sold for cheques at £750 each.
(entries—debit Bank Account £6,000;
credit Sales Account £6,000).

The opening stock was three cars costing £500 each, *i.e.*, £1,500. The closing stock on 31st October is arrived at by adding the opening stock, three cars, to the seven cars bought (making ten cars) and subtracting the eight cars sold. This leaves two cars as the closing stock.

Starting from the assets and liabilities as they stood on 30th September, the initial Balance Sheet, the accounts and the final Balance Sheet would be as under:

BALANCE SHEET OF EUREKA MOTORS
AS AT 30TH SEPTEMBER, 19—

	£		£
Capital .. — — ..	11,500	Stock	1,500
		Cash at Bank	10,000
	£11,500		£11,500

CAPITAL ACCOUNT

Dr.				Cr.
		£		£
Oct. 31 Balance c/d. ..	13,500	Oct. 1 Balance	11,500
		„ 31 Profit	2,000
	£13,500		£13,500
		Nov. 1 Balance b/d.	£13,500.

TRADING ACCOUNT OF EUREKA MOTORS
FOR MONTH ENDED 31ST OCTOBER, 19—

Dr.				Cr
		£		£
Stock 1/10/19—	1,500	Sales	6,000
Purchases .. — ..	3,500	Stock 31/10/19—	1,000
Profit .. ... — ..	2,000		
	£7,000		£7,000

STOCK ACCOUNT

Dr.				Cr.
		£		£
Oct. 1 Balance	1,500	Oct. 31 Trading A/c. ..	1,500
Nov. 1 — — ..	£1,000		

PURCHASES ACCOUNT

Dr.				Cr.
		£		£
Oct. - Bank ... — ..	3,500	Oct. 31 Trading A/c. ...	3,500

SALES ACCOUNT

Dr.								Cr.
			£					£
Oct. 31	Trading A/c.	..	6,000	Oct. -	Bank	...	...	.. 6,000

BANK ACCOUNT

Dr.								Cr.
			£					£
Oct. 1	Balance	...	.. 10,000	Oct. –	Purchases	..	..	3,500
„ –	Sales ..	...	.. 6,000	„ 31	Balance c/d.	..	..	12,500
			£16,000					£16,000
Nov. 1	Balance b/d.		£12,500					

BALANCE SHEET OF EUREKA MOTORS
AS AT 31ST OCTOBER, 19—

		£	£					£
Capital	..	.. 11,500		Stock	..	...	...	.. 1,000
Add Profit	...	... 2,000		Cash at Bank	...	...	.. 12,500
			13,500					
			£13,500					£13,500

The stock on hand on 1st November, £1,000, would be the initial stock for November and would be transferred to the debit side of the Trading Account on 30th November. On 31st October it existed as an asset, and was included in the Balance Sheet.

Illustration of Stock Account: To show the Stock Account over a number of trading periods, let us suppose that a business prepares its accounts annually and takes stock on 31st December each year. The following were the stocks of goods on hand on the dates shown:

			£
December 31,	19–1	..	3,640
do.	19–2	..	4,194
do.	19–3	..	4,436
do.	19–4	..	4,750

The Stock Account would be as follows:

STOCK ACCOUNT

Dr.							Cr.
19–2			£	19–2			£
Jan. 1	Balance	... ...	3,640	Dec. 31	Trading A/c.	...	3,640
19–3				19–3			
Jan. 1	Balance	... ...	4,194	Dec. 31	Trading A/c.	...	4,194
19–4				19–4			
Jan. 1	Balance	... ...	4,436	Dec. 31	Trading A/c.	...	4,436
19–5							
Jan. 1	Balance	... ...	4,750				

The stock, £3,640, on 31st December, 19–1, was the final, or closing, stock for the year 19–1. It was also the initial, or opening, stock for 19–2, and it is as the opening stock that it first appears in the Stock Account. This applies also to successive years.

The Final Form of the Trading Account

The final form of the Trading Account in which account is taken of both opening and closing stock, would be as follows:

TRADING ACCOUNT OF . . .
FOR PERIOD ENDED . . .

Dr.		Cr.
(a) Opening stock	(c) Sales	
(b) Purchases	(d) Closing stock	

The opening stock plus the purchases together give the total cost of the goods offered for sale during the period. When the closing stock is deducted from this, what is left is the cost of the goods actually sold and the difference between this figure and the amount received for the goods (*i.e.*, the sales) is the profit. It is in fact a presentation in book-keeping form of the following arithmetical calculation, the figures used being those employed in the Trading Account in the previous section.

Sales		£6,000
Opening stock ..	£1,500	
Add purchases ..	3,500	
Cost of goods offered		
for sale ..	5,000	
Less closing stock..	1,000	
Cost of goods sold ...		£4,000
Profit		£2,000

The Trading Account is, in fact, sometimes presented in this way. Using the figures employed in the above example, it would appear as follows:

TRADING ACCOUNT

Dr.	£	£		Cr.	£
Opening Stock ...	1,500			Sales	6,000
Add Purchases ..	3,500				
Cost of goods offered					
for sale	5,000				
Less Closing Stock	1,000				
Cost of goods sold ..		4,000			
Profit		2,000			
		£6,000			£6,000

Merchandise Accounts

The figures necessary for the calculation of the cost of goods sold (shown in the previous section) are normally incorporated in the Trading Account. Sometimes, for the sake of clarity, they are entered instead in an account called a Merchandise Account, and only the resulting figure, the cost of goods sold, transferred to the Trading Account. The Trading Account then contains only the sales on the credit side and the cost of sales on the debit, the difference being profit. This is shown in the illustration below, using the same figures as in the previous section. When this is done, the opening and closing stocks are entered directly in the Merchandise Account, and no Stock Account need be kept.

On the debit side in the example below, the balance (opening stock) is the balance brought down from the previous period, and the figure for purchases is transferred from the Purchases Account.

On the credit side, the balance (closing stock) is obtained by stock taking and is carried down as the opening stock for the next trading period. The cost of goods sold, transferred to the Trading Account, is found as the difference between the two sides when the other figures have been entered.

MERCHANDISE

	£		£
Balance (opening stock) b/d.	1,500	Trading Account (Cost of Goods Sold)	4,000
Purchases	3,500	Balance (closing stock) c/d.	1,000
	£5,000		£5,000
Balance b/d.	1,000		

PURCHASES

	£		£
Creditors (or Cash) ...	3,500	Merchandise	3,500

SALES

	£		£
Trading Account	6,000	Debtors (or Cash) ...	6,000

TRADING ACCOUNT

	£		£
Merchandise (Cost of Goods Sold)	4,000	Sales	6,000
Gross Profit	2,000		
	£6,000		£6,000

Relation of Trading Profit to Sales

It should be noted that the profit will vary in direct proportion to the sales so long as prices remain constant. If the sales are doubled, the cost of the goods sold will be doubled and so will the amount of profit. If a business sells more than one type of article, and makes a different rate of profit on each type, this statement would require modification. Clearly, if the increase in sales consisted chiefly of goods on which the highest rate of profit was earned, the average rate of profit would be increased.

The Drawings Account

The device of using accounts to obtain totals in those cases in which totals are required, can be applied to a wide variety of cases besides those of purchases and sales. It enables information to be presented in a concise and understandable form. A further case in which this device is an advantage is that of drawings. If the proprietor drew a monthly cheque for his private expenses, for example, there would be twelve entries for drawings alone on the debit side of the Capital Account in the course of a year. This is more detail than is required. A Drawings Account is therefore opened. Each withdrawal is debited in the Drawings Account as it is made, instead of in the Capital Account. At the end of the accounting period, the total is transferred to the debit side of the Capital Account.

WRITTEN EXERCISES

1.   N. Love started business on 1st February, 19—, with £8,000 in the bank, and stock £2,000. Show his Balance Sheet on that date, open accounts, and enter balances.

> Feb. 5. Purchased goods by cheque £1,000.
> „   10. Sold goods on credit to J. Croft £1,200.
> „   14. Sold goods for cheque £1,500.
> „   20. Purchased goods on credit from E. Pearson £400.
> „   25. Withdrew for own use £100.

Enter these transactions in the accounts, take out a Trial Balance, prepare a Trading Account for February, and show N. Love's Balance Sheet on 28th February. His stock on that date was £1,600.

2.   V. Robins commences business on 1st January, 19—, with cash at bank £5,000 and stock £1,000. Show his Balance Sheet on that date, open accounts and insert balances.

> Jan. 5. Purchased goods by cheque £2,000.
> „   10. Sold goods for cheque £2,600.
> „   15. Bought goods by cheque £800.
> „   20. Sold goods for cheque £1,500.
> „   25. Withdrew by cheque for his own use £100.

Pass these transactions through accounts. Take out a Trial Balance, prepare a Trading Account, balance off the accounts, and show his Balance Sheet on 31st January, 19—. Stock on that date was £950.

3. A cycle dealer had the following assets and liabilities on 1st March, 19—:

		£
Cash in hand	... ..	100
Cash at bank	.. ...	250
Premises ..	.. ..	3,000
Stock	.. ..	1,000
Creditor: The Red Cycle Co.		150
Rates due	.. ..	10

Find his capital and draw up his Balance Sheet on that date. Open accounts and enter balances.

Mar. 1. Sold for cash two bicycles at £15 each.
 ,, 3. Paid rates due in cash.
 ,, 4. Paid £90 of cash in hand into the bank.
 ,, 10. Purchased on credit from Accessories Ltd., tools and accessories £75.
 ,, 15. Sold to the New Cycle Club, bicycles in return for cheque £300.
 ,, 20. Paid Red Cycle Co. cheque £150.
 ,, 25. Withdrew by cheque for private expenses £25.

Pass these transactions through the books, take out a Trial Balance, balance accounts, and draw up a Balance Sheet on 31st March, 19—. Closing stock £850.

4. The assets and liabilities of C. Lewis, furniture dealer, on 1st February, 19— were as follows:

		£
Cash at bank	... ...	800
Premises ..	... ...	9,500
Stock	... ..	8,000
Fittings ..	.. ..	750
Debtor: A. Bell ..	..	150
Creditor: Collins & Co.		600
Vans	.. ..	2,000

Find his capital, draw up his Balance Sheet, open accounts, and enter balances.

Feb. 1. Paid Collins & Co. by cheque, £600.
 ,, 5. A. Bell purchased furniture on credit £250.
 ,, 8. Extended premises at cost of £1,500, the amount being a debt to Cross & Co.
 ,, 10. Withdrew from bank for business purposes £20.
 ,, 15. Purchased bankrupt stock by cheque £500.
 ,, 20. A. Bell paid £300 by cheque on account (i.e., the debt was not paid in full).
 ,, 25. Withdrew by cheque for private purposes £40.
 ,, 28. Cash sales during month £1,100 (banked).

Pass these transactions through the accounts, take out a Trial Balance, balance the accounts, and draw up a Balance Sheet on 28th February, 19—. The stock on that date was £7,600.

5. On 1st March, 19—, H. Winter bought fifty wireless sets for £15 each. They all required new cabinets, which he bought and fitted at a cost of £1·50 each. During March he sold fifteen sets for £20 each. During April he sold thirty-two sets, also for £20 each, but three sets were returned, in perfect condition, after sale.

Show, by means of separate trading accounts for the months of March and April, what his profits were in each of those months. Show also the Stock Account for March and April. (*Adapted from R.S.A.*)

6. On 1st January, 19—, E. Lyons had the following assets and liabilities:
Cash in hand £40. Cash at bank £360. Stock £1,000. Debtors: N. Smith £25; R. Mayer £45. Creditor: J. Peel £110.

Find his capital, draw up his Balance Sheet as on 1st January, 19—, and enter the balances in accounts.

Jan.	3.	Purchased goods from J. Peel on credit £200.
„	5.	Purchased goods by cheque £100.
„	7.	Paid J. Peel £110 by cheque.
„	8.	Sold goods to N. Smith on credit £50.
„	12.	Sold goods to R. Mayer on credit £40.
„	14.	Cash sales to date £240.
„	14.	Paid into bank from office cash £250.
„	18.	Purchased goods by cheque £75.
„	20.	R. Mayer paid by cheque £45.
„	24.	Sold goods on credit to N. Smith £30.
„	31.	Cash sales (banked) £280.

Pass these transactions through the accounts, and take out a Trial Balance. Prepare a Trading Account, assuming closing stock to be £975. Show the Balance Sheet of E. Lyons as at 31st January, 19—.

7. C. Brett had stock on hand £3,500 on 1st January, 19—. The following were his purchases and sales for January:

Purchases			£	*Sales*				£
Jan. 3.	Cash		115	Jan. 2.	L. Perring ..		...	77
„ 5.	J. Smith	..	84	„ 6.	Cash	..	...	322
„ 8.	L. Oliver ..		31	„ 9.	S. Wright ..		...	93
„ 15.	T. Ellam ..		163	„ 13.	Cash	...	...	286
„ 20.	E. Alland ..		410	„ 20.	Cash	...	...	432
„ 26.	V. Cummings	..	226	„ 27.	Cash	...	...	601

His stock on 31st January, 19—, was £3,115.

Show (a) his Stock Account, (b) Purchases Account. (c) Sales Account, (d) Trading Account, all balanced as on 31st January, 19—.

8. The following were the balances in the books of S. Stanley on 30th November, 19—, after trading for eleven months from 1st January, 19—:

	Dr. £	Cr. £
Capital A/c.		5,000
Stock A/c. (1st Jan., 19—)	2,000	
Bank A/c.	400	
Purchases A/c.	6,000	
Sales A/c.		8,000
Various fixed assets ...	4,600	
	£13,000	£13,000

Open accounts and enter these balances.

Dec.	5.	Sold goods on credit to G. Marsh £80.
„	12.	Purchased goods on credit from E. Allen £50.
„	14.	Cash sales to date (banked) £200.
„	15.	Purchases by cheque £30.
„	31.	Cash sales to date (banked) £350.

Enter these transactions, take out a Trial Balance, prepare a Trading Account for the year and a Balance Sheet as at 31st December, 19—. Balance accounts. Stock on 31st December was valued at £2,170.

9. The balances in the accounts of C. Dobbs on 31st May, 19—, after trading for five months, are as follows:

	Dr. £	Cr. £
C. Dobbs: Capital Account ..		7,500
Drawings Account ..	400	
Sundry fixed assets	6,000	
Purchases (Merchandise) ..	5,500	
Sales		7,200
Stock Account (1st Jan., 19—)..	3,000	
Bank overdraft		200
	£14,900	£14,900

Open accounts and enter these balances.

June 2. Purchased goods on credit from F. Wilson £300.
„ 5. Sold goods on credit to E. Gibson £400.
„ 10. Purchased goods on credit from C. Hill £800.
„ 15. Drawings: C. Dobbs £30.
„ 30. Cash sales for month (paid into bank) £1,200.
„ 30. Drawings: C. Dobbs £50.

Enter these transactions, take out a Trial Balance, prepare Trading Account for the half-year, and a Balance Sheet as at 30th June, 19—. Balance accounts. Stock on 30th June, 19—, was £2,400.

10. From the following information show the Capital Account, Drawings Account, Trading Account, and Stock Account of A. Soft.

		£
A. Soft: Capital Account		9,500
A. Soft: Drawings Account	March 31	320
	June 30	350
	Sept. 30	300
	Dec. 20	320
Stock 1st Jan., 19—		2,500
31st Dec., 19—		2,800
Purchases 1st Jan. to 31st Dec.		5,600
Sales 1st Jan. to 31st Dec.		7,500

11. At 1st January, 19—, a trader's stock is valued at £4,000 and he wishes to end the year with a stock valued at £3,000. His manufacturing wages and inwards carriage are expected to amount to £1,200 and £300 respectively. He estimates that his sales for 19— will amount to £12,000 and that his gross profit will be 25 per cent of this sum. Calculate the value of the purchases you would advise him to make.
Your answer should take the form of an estimated trading account. (R.S.A.)

12. Find the value of the closing stock at 30th June, 19–2, from the following information:

	£
Sales	4,400
Purchases	2,300
Stock 1st July, 19–1	400

Sales were marked up 100 per cent on cost price.

13. A. Brown is a merchant who marks his selling price of goods at 25 per cent above cost. His books reveal the following information at 30th June, 19–2:

	£
Stock at 1st July, 19–1	2,468
Stock on hand at 30th June, 19–2 ...	3,155
Stock purchased during year	12,687

You are required to find:
(a) What was the cost of the goods he sold?
(b) What was the value of his sales?
(c) How much profit did he make?

(Univ. of Melb. Inter Cert.)

14.   T. Thomas is a merchant who marks his selling price of goods at 25 per cent above cost. His accounts at 30th June, 19–2, include:

		£
Purchases for the year	.. ..	15,687
Stock on hand at 30th June, 19–2	..	4,426
Stock on hand at 1st July, 19–1	..	4,739

You are required to prepare a statement of his trading for the year and so determine—

(a) the cost of the goods he sold;
(b) the amount of profit he made;
(c) the amount of his sales.
(d) Using Merchandise and Trading Accounts record the above information.

(*Univ. of Melb. Inter. Cert., modified.*)

CLASS QUESTIONS

1. Why are sales entered on the credit side of the Trading Account?
2. What is meant by closing stock?
3. Why is closing stock entered on the credit side of the Trading Account?
4. In which other account and on which side is closing stock entered?
5. What is opening stock?
6. On which side of the Trading Account is opening stock entered?
7. Where is the double entry for opening stock?
8. What is the relation between closing stock at the end of one period and opening stock at the beginning of the next?
9. Why is a Stock Account opened?
10. In the final form of the Trading Account, what entries would you expect to find on the debit side?
11. What entries would you expect to see on the credit side of the Trading Account?
12. What two items added together give the cost of all goods offered for sale?
13. If the closing stock is deducted from the cost of all goods offered for sale, what does the remaining figure represent?
14. What must be deducted from sales to give profit?

10

THE TREATMENT OF STOCK

Taking Stock

THE Trading Account can show only one balance, or difference, as has been pointed out; therefore it cannot tell the trader both the amount of his profit and the value of his stock, each of which would be a separate balance. In practice, he uses the Trading Account to ascertain his profit. He is compelled, therefore, to find the value of his stock independently of the Trading Account.

The simplest and most accurate method is to make an inventory of his stock at the end of each accounting period, and to compute its value by pricing each article. In addition, some firms find it possible to keep stock records outside the ordinary system of book-keeping. These would take the form of separate cards for each item of stock, additions being shown on one side and issues on the other, the difference being the present stock, which could be priced when the need arose. Even so, it would be necessary at intervals to check the information given in the stock records, by taking stock.

The Valuation of Stock

When, as a result of stock-taking, the amount of stock is known the question arises as to what value should be put upon it. It is obvious that the higher the figure at which it is valued, the greater will be the profit shown for the accounting period in which it was bought, and the less will be the profit during the ensuing period.

To illustrate this, let us take the first example employed in the previous chapter. In this example, six cars were purchased at £500 each, and five cars were sold at £750 each. When profit was ascertained, the remaining car was valued at cost price—£500—and the profit is shown in the following calculation:

	£	£
Selling price		3,750
Cost price	3,000	
Less stock at cost price	500	
Net cost of goods sold ...		2,500
Profit — — —		£1,250

The profit of £1,250 thus consisted of £250 on each of the five cars sold.

Now suppose the unsold car had been valued at selling price; that is, at £750. The profit would then have been arrived at by the following calculation:

	£	£
Selling price		3,750
Cost price	3,000	
Less cost of one car at selling price	750	
Net cost of goods sold ...		2,250
Profit		£1,500

The profit, that is to say, would be equal to £250 on each of the six cars, when in fact only five cars were sold. It is quite clear that if a profit is made on the sixth car, it cannot be made before the car is sold. This becomes even clearer when the next accounting period is examined. There is an asset, consisting of one car valued at £750. It is sold for £750. The profit shown when the car was sold would therefore appear to be nothing at all.

It is clear from this that any stock unsold when profit is being calculated should be valued at cost price. Any higher valuation would mean that profit was assumed on a sale that had not taken place. The matter might have been stated more simply, of course, by saying that, since the closing stock is a deduction from the purchases, it should be deducted at the price at which it was included in the purchases—that is, at purchase (or cost) price. But it is important to understand the principles involved, because difficult cases arise, particularly with manufacturing concerns, whose stock consists of partly manufactured goods. Such cases can only be decided by reference to first principles.

Effect of Changes in Price

An interval usually elapses between the purchase of goods and their sale. During that interval the market price of the goods a trader has bought may either rise or fall. Let us assume first that they rise, and that, confining ourselves to the same example, the purchase price of the cars he bought at £500 rose to £600. In valuing his stock at the end of the accounting period, he would be entitled to price them at either £500 or £600, and either could be described as the cost price, with equal truth. Which should be chosen?

Now, if the cost price has risen, the selling price will in all probability be higher also. This means that when he does sell the car, he will make more profit than he expected. But the important point to remember is that he will have made no profit whatever until the car is sold; and to value the stock at £600 now, before it is sold, would be to assume that £100 of the profit had already been made. It has not, and therefore he should value the stock at the original, lower price.

The price, however, may not rise. It may fall to say £400 instead of rising to £600. In this case, which price does he use? If he may not anticipate profits, it might be argued that he ought not to anticipate losses. But in fact he does, and in this case his stock of cars would be priced at £400 each. It is a matter of ordinary business prudence that, if a trader knows that a loss is probable, he allows for it as soon as he becomes aware of it. If the loss does not in fact occur, he is no worse off, in the end, for having prepared for it. But he might be very much worse off in the end if he had shut his eyes to a probable loss, which did, in fact, fall upon him.

One further possibility must be considered. Goods may deteriorate, become shop-soiled, or go out of fashion whilst in stock. If this should happen, all such goods must be revalued at prices that would be lower than either market price or cost price.

To sum up, a trader will value his stock at the end of an accounting period, at either the cost price or the market price, whichever is lower, and will deduct from this price any allowance for deterioration.

Function of the Stock Account

The value of the stock entered in the Stock Account is found by taking stock. It is not the function of the Stock Account to give this information. The whole purpose of the Stock Account is to retain the figure at which the stock stood at the beginning of the accounting period so that it can be transferred to the Trading Account when it is opened at the end of the period. Nothing that happens to the stock during the accounting period can alter the figure at which it stood originally, which must be known in order to ascertain profit. If this figure were altered in any way, the Trading Account would not show the total cost of the goods offered for sale. It would therefore not show the cost of the goods actually sold, nor, consequently, the correct amount of profit made. From this it follows that no receipts, issues, or losses of stock, for any reason whatever, should be entered in the Stock Account.

Loss of Stock

Normally, changes in the amount of stock take place through purchases and sales. It is quite possible, however, that some stock may be lost through an accident such as fire. If this occurs it can have no effect upon the amount of stock which was on hand at the beginning of the period, before the loss occurred. As this is the figure the Stock Account is intended to show, the loss should clearly not be credited in the Stock Account.

Obviously, however, a loss has been suffered and the profit shown for the period should be less by the amount of the loss. What entries are necessary to record this loss? The answer is that profit is automatically reduced without a specific entry. When stock is taken at the end of the period, the goods that have been destroyed will not be included in the closing stock; and, as the closing stock is thereby reduced, the profit will be reduced by the same amount.

To make this clear, let us take the illustration used in the previous chapter. In that illustration Eureka Motors had on 1st October an opening stock consisting of three cars bought at £500 each. During October seven more cars were bought at £500 and eight were sold at £750 each, leaving two cars unsold on 31st October. If the two unsold cars are valued at £500 each, the Trading Account would be as follows:

TRADING ACCOUNT OF EUREKA MOTORS
FOR MONTH ENDED 31ST OCTOBER, 19—

Dr.							Cr.
			£				£
Stock 1/10/19—	..	..	1,500	Sales ..	..	..	6,000
Purchases	..	..	3,500	Stock 31/10/19—	..	..	1,000
Profit ..	..	..	2,000				
			£7,000				£7,000

Let us now assume that one car was completely destroyed by fire in the garage during October. This would not alter the fact that Eureka Motors owned three cars on 1st October, so the opening stock would not be affected. Nor would there be any difference in the number bought or the number sold, but they would possess only one car on 31st October instead of two; so the closing stock would be only £500. In those circumstances, the Trading Account would appear:

TRADING ACCOUNT OF EUREKA MOTORS
FOR MONTH ENDED 31ST OCTOBER, 19—

Dr.							Cr.
			£				£
Stock 1/10/19—	..	..	1,500	Sales ..	..	..	6,000
Purchases	..	..	3,500	Stock 31/10/19—	..	..	500
Profit ..	..	..	1,500				
			£6,500				£6,500

It will be seen that the profit is automatically reduced, and that therefore a smaller sum is added to capital in consequence of the fire.

If, however, a successful claim is made on an insurance company, the effect is the same as if the goods had been sold to the insurance company. When the cash is received—

(a) debit the Cash Account;
(b) credit the Insurance Indemnity Account.

At the end of the accounting period, the balance of the Insurance Indemnity Account would be transferred to the Trading Account, on the credit side—like sales.

Stock Withdrawn by the Proprietor

If the proprietor takes any property belonging to the firm for his own use, the property so withdrawn is drawings in exactly the same sense as money taken by the proprietor is drawings.

If that property takes the form of stock (*i.e.*, goods bought for resale) the effect upon the books would be the same as that of goods lost through accident. Any goods he had taken would not be included in the closing stock. This would reduce the figure arrived at for profit, and a smaller sum would therefore be added to capital. It would be smaller by the amount of stock withdrawn (see illustration in previous section).

A business man, however, must know how much profit he has made; and, therefore, drawings, which are quite independent of profit, should not be deducted from profit. If no entries are made, the goods withdrawn will be deducted automatically from profit. To correct this, they must be added back to profit and then deducted from the capital. The entries would be:

(*a*) credit Purchases Account (or a special Sales to Staff Account which would be deducted from Purchases before their transfer to the Trading Account);

(*b*) debit Drawings Account.

This entry reduces purchases on the debit side by the amount that the proprietor's withdrawals had reduced closing stock on the credit side. The profit shown will therefore be increased by the amount by which it had previously been reduced, and will thus be unaffected by the withdrawals.

Date of Stock-taking

The date on which stock should be taken is the last day of the accounting period, after all transactions on that day have been completed. It may, however, be a big task, taking several days to complete, in which case it must be begun early or finished late.

(*a*) *Stock taken before the end of the accounting period.* If the stock of any article is taken a few days before the end of the accounting period, and transactions take place in the intervening time, it is clear that the figure arrived at will be wrong. In the first place, some goods may have been bought. These will have to be added. Sales, on the other hand, would have to be deducted, at cost price. The resulting figure will be the closing stock, provided no other changes have taken place. Other possible changes which should be deducted would include the destruction of goods by fire, drawings by the proprietor in the form of goods, and goods returned to the supplier if they were unsatisfactory. Other additions to the stock would include goods accepted in payment of a debt, and goods returned by customers. All such changes must be calculated at cost price.

(*b*) *Stock taken after the expiration of the accounting period.* The adjustment of the figure for stock, if it has been taken some time after the end of the accounting period, is similar in principle, but each transaction would have the opposite effect. For example, if 31st December were the end of the accounting period and stock were taken on 4th January, the stock might include some goods bought between these dates. These goods were obviously not on hand on 31st December, so they must clearly be deducted from the stock shown on the 4th January. In a similar way, sales would have to be added back (at cost price). Each of the alterations referred to in the previous section (*a*) would also have to be allowed for, remembering that, if they were additions when stock was taken early, they are subtractions when stock is taken late, and vice versa.

WRITTEN EXERCISES

1. On 1st January, 19—, S. Farder had in stock 100 bags of potatoes which had cost him an average of £0·375 per bag. During January he purchased 80 bags at a cost of £0·40 each and he sold 50 bags at £0·60 a bag, 20 bags at £0·625 a bag, and 70 bags at £0·55 a bag. The potatoes he had left were some of those which cost him £0·40 a bag. Draw up a Trading Account for the month of January, 19—, showing the amount of profit or loss which arose from the transactions, and show the Stock Account.   (*U.E.I., modified.*)

2. On 1st January, 19—, E. Barker had a capital of £5,000 which included a stock of 1,200 articles which cost him £0·50 each. During January he purchased a further 1,000 similar articles at £0·45 and sold 1,500 at £0·75 each. He also took 100 for his own use, charged against him at £0·50 each. Of his remaining stock, 20 had been damaged by water and were considered to be worth only £0·25 each. Show (*a*) his Trading Account, (*b*) his Capital Account for the month of January, (*c*) his Stock Account.

3. H. Walls had a stock consisting of 100 articles bought at £1 each, on the 1st January, 19—. His purchases during the month consisted of 200 at £1·05 each bought on 8th January and 500 at £0·95 bought on 20th January. On 25th January he sold 600 at £1·25 each, 10 of which were returned to him in perfect condition.

(*a*) How many articles had he in stock on 31st January?
(*b*) At what price should his stock be valued on that date?
(*c*) Show his Trading Account and Stock Account as they would appear on 31st January, 19—.

4. A business makes up its accounts annually on 31st December. Stock-taking took place in a certain year on 27th December. From the following particulars ascertain the value of stock on 31st December. All figures given are at cost price.

	£
Stock, December 27 19—	8,456
Purchases, December 27–31	48
Sales, December 27–31	200
Goods returned by customers, December 27–31	5

5. A business makes up its accounts annually on 31st December. Stock-taking took place in a certain year on 3rd January following. From the following particlars ascertain the value of the stock on 31st December. All figures are given at cost price.

				£
Stock, January 3	..	...	...	4,200
Purchases, January 1–3		..	..	150
Sales, January 1–3	..	..	..	120
Goods returned to suppliers, January 1–3	..	..	..	..	10

6. On 1st January, 19—, a trader had in stock 4,000 articles which he valued at £0·10 each. During the month he bought 2,400 more, costing £0·125 each, and sold 6,000 at £0·15 each. Prepare a Trading Account for the month showing his gross profit.   (*R.S.A., modified.*)

7. A firm commenced on 1st June, 19—, with a stock of 1,000 articles costing £0·30 each. During the month it purchased 3,000 similar articles at £0·25 each and sold 2,200 at £0·40 each. During the month 100 of the articles were returned to the firm in good saleable condition, by purchasers. At 30th June, 50 of the articles in stock had become damaged and were worthless. The saleable stock on hand was valued at £0·25 each.

Show, in the form of a Trading Account, the gross profit or loss made on these articles during the month.   (*R.S.A., modified.*)

8. Copy out the following ledger account. Complete and close it off for the year ended 31st December, 19—, and state what amount would appear in the Balance Sheet on that date.

STOCK ACCOUNT

Dr.		Cr.
19—	£	
Jan. 1 Balance	890·00	

(The stock on following 31st December was £920.)   (*R.S.A., modified.*)

9. F. Wilson had the following assets and liabilities on 1st January, 19—:

			£
Cash at bank	..	..	500
Debtor: D. Wills		...	100
Stock	..	..	850
Premises ..	..	..	4,000
Creditor: N. Craven	..		150

Show his Balance Sheet on that date and enter the balances in accounts.

Jan.	4.	Bought goods by cheque £180.
„	10.	Paid N. Craven in full by cheque.
„	15.	Sold goods on credit to T. Farr £60.
„	20.	D. Wills paid £50 by cheque on account.
„	31.	Cash sales for month £500 (banked).

Pass these transactions through the books, and take out a Trial Balance. Prepare a Balance Sheet as on 31st January, 19—, assuming stock on that date to be £680. What was the cost of the goods sold?

10. The Z. Co. closes its books annually on 31st March, and stock-taking usually takes place a few days later.

In 19— the annual stock-taking took place on the evening of 3rd April, when the total value of stock then actually on hand, taken at selling price, was found to amount to £1,951·50.

Purchases during the period 1st-3rd April amounted to £35·675 and sales during the same three days to £65·60, and the ratio of gross profit to sales is fixed at 25 per cent.

You are required to ascertain the value of stock on hand at the close of business on 31st March, 19—, for the purposes of the annual accounts.   (*R.S.A., modified.*)

11.   Ernest Eagles conducts a business which regularly makes a gross profit of 20 per cent on sales. His accounts are balanced at 31st December. On 31st March, 19–3, his stock was destroyed by a fire except for some slightly burned goods that were sold as salvage for £300. His books were intact, and disclosed:

		£
Stock at 31st Dec., 19–2 ..	...	6,000
Purchases to 31st Mar., 19–3	...	8,300
Sales	...	10,500

Prepare an account showing the manner of arriving at the claim presented to the Insurance Company.   (*Institute of Book-keepers.*)

12.   You have prepared the accounts of a retailer of china and glassware for the year ending 31st March, 19–2. On examining them the proprietor points out to you that there appears to be no charge against the profits in respect of breakages in his shop which amounted to about £100 during the year.

Give your explanation of the position.   (*R.S.A.*)

CLASS QUESTIONS

1. What is the simplest method of ascertaining the value of stock?
2. What other method is available?
3. What is the effect on profit of
    (a) too high a valuation of closing stock?
    (b) too low a valuation?
4. At what price is closing stock valued?
5. Why does a trader allow for possible losses?
6. What effect has the deterioration of stock on the price at which it is valued?
7. What entry would be needed to record the fact that some of the stock had perished completely?
8. If a claim is made on an insurance company for loss of stock, how is that claim treated in the books?
9. What entries are made when the proprietor withdraws some stock for his own use?
10. If a firm takes stock one week *before* the end of the accounting period, are additions to stock during that week added to the stock or subtracted from it?
11. If a firm takes stock one week *after* the end of the accounting period, are additions to stock made during that week added to the stock or subtracted from it?

11

THE PROFIT AND LOSS ACCOUNT

IT has already been shown that:
- (a) Profit is an increase of capital and is obtained by enlarging the gap between the value of assets and the value of liabilities.
- (b) The method employed by a trader to increase this gap is to exchange assets for others of a greater value (*e.g.*, by selling goods for more than they cost).

It now remains to show that there is a continual tendency for the gap between assets and liabilities to close because:
- (a) Liabilities, being legal claims to certain fixed sums of money, remain unaltered until they are paid; and
- (b) Assets tend to fall in value.

Reasons for the Falling Value of Assets

There are four main reasons for the fall in the value of assets:
- (a) They may wear out, like furniture, machinery, or motor vans.
- (b) They may get out of date when a better article comes on the market. The value of an out-of-date asset may fall to a very low figure long before it is actually used up.
- (c) They may lose value through the passage of time. A lease on premises for ten years, for instance, would lose one-tenth of its value each year.
- (d) They may be consumed, like petrol in a car, or stationery, or postage stamps.

Effect on the Balance Sheet

Let us take as an illustration the following Balance Sheet of Mr. X on 1st January, 19—:

BALANCE SHEET OF X
AS AT 1ST JANUARY, 19—

	£		£	£
		Fixed Assets		
Capital	9,500	Machinery	3,260	
		Motor Vans ...	1,000	
		Lease of Premises (5 years)	500	
				4,760
Current Liabilities		*Current Assets*		
Creditors	600	Stationery and Stamps	40	
		Stock	4,500	
		Cash	800	
				5,340
	£10,100			£10,100

If the creditors were paid in full, both cash and creditors would be reduced by £600, leaving a cash balance of £200. The difference between assets and liabilities would not be changed.

If, at the end of the year, all the stock had been sold for £6,000, received in cash, a profit of £1,500 would have been made and the capital would be increased from £9,500 to £11,000. The Balance Sheet after these two transactions is shown below:

BALANCE SHEET OF X
AS AT 31ST DECEMBER, 19—

	£		£	£
Capital ... — — ...	11,000	*Fixed Assets*		
		Machinery	3,260	
		Motor Vans ..	1,000	
		Lease of Premises (5		
		years)	500	
				4,760
		Current Assets		
		Stationery and Stamps	40	
		Cash	6,200	
				6,240
	£11,000			£11,000

At this stage, X reviews the value of his assets, and comes to the following conclusions:

  (1) All the stationery and stamps, except £10, had been used up.
  (2) The motor vans were a year older and were considered to be worth only £800.
  (3) There were only four years left of the lease instead of five years, reducing its value from £500 to £400.
  (4) The machinery, after being used the whole year, was worth only £3,000.

The new Balance Sheet, showing the assets at their value at the end of the year, would appear as follows:

BALANCE SHEET OF X
AS AT 31ST DECEMBER, 19—

	£		£	£
Capital — — ...	10,410	*Fixed Assets*		
		Machinery	3,000	
		Motor Vans	800	
		Lease of Premises (4		
		years)	400	
				4,200
		Current Assets		
		Stationery and Stamps	10	
		Cash ... — ..	6,200	
				6,210
	£10,410			£10,410

The reductions in the value of the assets were not accompanied by an increase in the value of any other assets or the acquisition of any new ones. They represent simply a reduction of capital, a loss. Such losses are inevitable in business.

Method of Showing these Losses in Accounts

I. The asset that has diminished in value is credited with the amount it has lost. It will be remembered that a credit entry may be regarded as a subtraction from the debit side. The asset that has to be reduced will have been entered on the debit side when it was acquired.

II. The amount lost must then be deducted from capital. As the capital is entered on the credit side, this will mean a debit entry.

The Capital Account, however, has already been divided into two parts—the Capital Account proper and the Trading Account. To show the loss through the diminished value of assets, a further sub-division of the Capital Account is required. It is called the Profit and Loss Account.

The profit shown in the Trading Account, instead of being credited directly to the Capital Account, is credited instead to the Profit and Loss Account. The losses suffered through diminishing assets are debited to the Profit and Loss Account, which has the same effect as debiting them to the Capital Account, because the Profit and Loss Account is part of the Capital Account. The remaining profit is then transferred to the Capital Account.

The process is shown in the diagram given below:

TRADING ACCOUNT

Dr.	Cr.
Gross Profit (Excess of credit side over debit side)	

PROFIT AND LOSS ACCOUNT

Dr.	Cr.
Losses (Through diminishing value of assets) Net Profit (Transferred to Capital Account)	Gross Profit (Transferred from Trading Account)

CAPITAL ACCOUNT

Dr.	Cr.
	Net Profit (Transferred from Profit and Loss Account)

Applying these principles to the affairs of X, we now show his Trading Account, Profit and Loss Account, and Capital Account, putting into effect his adjustment of the value of his assets.

TRADING ACCOUNT OF X
FOR YEAR ENDED 31ST DECEMBER 19—

	£		£
Stock (1st Jan.)	4,500	Sales	6,000
Gross Profit (to Profit and Loss			
A/c.)	1,500		
	£6,000		£6,000

PROFIT AND LOSS ACCOUNT OF X
FOR YEAR ENDED 31ST DECEMBER, 19—

	£		£
Stationery	30	Gross Profit	1,500
Motor Vans	200		
Lease	100		
Machinery	260		
Net Profit	910		
	£1,500		£1,500

CAPITAL ACCOUNT

	£			£
Dec. 31 Balance c/d. ..	10,410	Jan. 1 Balance		9,500
		Dec. 31 Net Profit ...	..	910
	£10,410			£10,410
		Jan. 1 Balance b/d.		£10,410

The accounts for the assets that have diminished in value would appear as under:

STATIONERY ACCOUNT
Dr.   Cr.

19—		£	19—		£
Jan. 1 Balance		40	Dec. 31 Profit and Loss A/c...		30
			„ 31 Balance c/d.		10
		£40			£40
19—					
Jan. 1 Balance b/d. ...	...	£10			

MOTOR VANS ACCOUNT
Dr.   Cr.

19—		£	19—		£
Jan. 1 Balance		1,000	Dec. 31 Profit and Loss A/c.		200
			„ 31 Balance c/d. ..		800
		£1,000			£1,000
19—					
Jan. 1 Balance b/d. ...	...	£800			

LEASE OF PREMISES ACCOUNT

Dr.						Cr.
19—			£	19—		£
Jan. 1	Balance	... ...	500	Dec. 31	Profit and Loss A/c.	100
				„ 31	Balance c/d ..	400
			£500			£500
19—						
Jan. 1	Balance b/d. ..	..	£400			

MACHINERY ACCOUNT

Dr.						Cr.
19–1			£	19—		£
Jan. 1	Balance	... ..	3,260	Dec. 31	Profit and Loss A/c.	260
				„ 31	Balance c/d. ..	3,000
			£3,260			£3,260
19—						
Jan. 1	Balance b/d. ..	..	£3,000			

Accounts of Partners

Illustration: C. Stone and R. Cant are in partnership, sharing profits and losses equally. The following is a list of the balances in their books on 31st December, 19—:

	Dr.	Cr.
	£	£
Cash at bank	200	
Stock (1st Jan., 19—) ..	2,200	
Purchases and sales ..	6,500	8,000
Debtor: D. Mack	300	
Creditor: P. Kay		350
Shop fittings	450	
Premises	6,000	
Motor vans	600	
Wrapping materials	50	
Capital: C. Stone		4,500
R. Cant		4,400
Drawings: C. Stone ..	500	
Drawings: R. Cant ..	450	
	£17,250	£17,250

Open accounts and enter the above balances. Prepare a Trading Account, Profit and Loss Account, and Balance Sheet as on 31st December, 19—, making allowance for the following valuations:

(1) Stock 31st December, 19—, £2,000.

(2) Of the wrapping material, £30 worth has been used.

(3) Deduct 5 per cent from the value of premises and 25 per cent from motor vans.

(4) Shop fittings have been valued at £400.

Show also the Capital·Accounts and Drawings Accounts of partners.

TRADING ACCOUNT OF C. STONE AND R. CANT
FOR YEAR ENDED 31ST DECEMBER, 19—

Dr.   Cr.

19—		£	19—		£
Jan. 1	Stock	2,200	Dec. 31	Sales..	8,000
Dec. 31	Purchases	6,500	,, 31	Stock	2,000
,, 31	Gross Profit ..	1,300			
		£10,000			£10,000

PROFIT AND LOSS ACCOUNT OF C. STONE AND R. CANT
FOR YEAR ENDED 31ST DECEMBER, 19—

Dr.   Cr.

19—		£	19—		£
Dec. 31	Shop Fittings ...	50	Dec. 31	Gross Profit ..	1,300
,, 31	Premises	300			
,, 31	Motor Vans ..	150			
,, 31	Wrapping Matls. ..	30			
,, 31	Net Profit				
	C. Stone	385			
	R. Cant	385			
		£1,300			£1,300

CAPITAL ACCOUNT: C. STONE

Dr.   Cr.

19—		£	19—		£
Dec. 31	Drawings	500	Dec. 31	Balance	4,500
,, 31	Balance c/d. ..	4,385	,, 31	Net Profit	385
		£4,885			£4,885
			19—		
			Jan. 1	Balance b/d	.. £4,385

DRAWINGS ACCOUNT: C. STONE

Dr.   Cr.

19—		£	19—		£
Dec. 31	Bank	500	Dec. 31	Capital A/c. ..	500

CAPITAL ACCOUNT: R. CANT

Dr.   Cr.

19—		£	19—		£
Dec. 31	Drawings	450	Dec. 31	Balance	4,400
,, 31	Balance c/d.. ..	4,335	,, 31	Net Profit	385
		£4,785			£4,785
			19—		
			Jan. 1	Balance b/d ...	... £4,335

DRAWINGS ACCOUNT: R. CANT

Dr.   Cr.

	£			£
19—		19—		
Dec. 31 Bank	450	Dec. 31 Capital		450

BALANCE SHEET OF C. STONE AND R. CANT
AS AT 31ST DECEMBER, 19—

	£	£		£	£
C. Stone Capital A/c.			*Fixed assets*		
1/1/19— ..	4,500		Motor Vans ...	450	
Add Profit ..	385		Shop Fittings ...	400	
	———		Premises	5,700	
	4,885			———	6,550
Less Drawings..	500		*Current assets*		
	———	4,385	Wrapping Materials	20	
R. Cant Capital A/c.			Stock	2,000	
1/1/19— ..	4,400		Debtor	300	
Add Profit ...	385		Bank	200	
	———			———	2,520
	4,785				
Less Drawings..	450				
	———	4,335			
Current Liabilities					
Creditor ...		350			
		———			———
		£9,070			£9,070

Gross Profit and Net Profit

There are now two stages in the ascertainment of profit:

    Stage I. In the Trading Account the difference between the cost and the selling value of goods is found. This is known as the 'Gross Profit'.

    Stage II. The gross profit is adjusted to make allowance for any other losses. What remains is then known as the 'Net Profit'.

This description of net profit is not quite complete because the losses referred to may be offset, or partly offset, by profits not shown in the Trading Account. For example, rent may be received for part of the premises sublet, or a commission received for arranging a sale on behalf of another business. Such profits would be added to the gross profit in the Profit and Loss Account. Again, some assets may actually increase in value—for example, buildings at the end of a war—though any such gains would be treated with great circumspection by a business man in case the enhanced values were not maintained.

The net profit cannot be known with complete certainty. Its magnitude depends partly upon the figure at which assets are valued. As a rule, this valuation will be an estimate. The actual value will not be known until they are sold.

It is quite possible to have a gross profit and a net loss (which would, of course, be carried to the debit side of the Capital Account, since its effect is to reduce the amount of capital). If there is a gross loss, the net loss will usually be greater than the gross loss.

WRITTEN EXERCISES

1. The following is the Trial Balance of A. Trader on 31st December, 19—:

	Dr. £	Cr. £
Cash at bank	350	
Stock (1st Jan., 19—)	1,500	
Office supplies	40	
Petrol, oil, etc.	120	
Motor vans (1st Jan., 19—)	960	
Premises (1st Jan., 19—)	4,000	
Machinery (1st Jan., 19—)	3,000	
Debtors	130	
Creditors		450
Purchases	6,000	
Sales ..		7,500
Capital		8,150
	£16,100	£16,100

Open accounts and enter balances. Prepare a Trading Account, stock on 31st December, 19—, having been valued at £1,400.

Transfer gross profit to the Profit and Loss Account and find net profit with the aid of the following information:

(a) £25 of office supplies have been consumed.
(b) Petrol and oil in stock is valued at £20.
(c) The value of motor vans is to be reduced by 25 per cent, premises by 5 per cent, and machinery by 20 per cent.

Balance off all accounts and show A. Trader's Balance Sheet as at 31st December, 19—.

2. The following is a list of the balances of N. Wood in his books on 31st December, 19—:

	Dr. £	Cr. £
Cash at bank	500	
Purchases and sales	4,000	6,000
Stock (1st Jan., 19—)	2,000	
Debtors and creditors	100	200
Shop fittings (1st Jan., 19—)	500	
Lease of premises (1st Jan., 19—)	1,000	
Motor vans (1st Jan., 19—)	400	
Spare parts, etc., for van	100	
Drawings: N. Wood	1,100	
Capital: N. Wood		3,500
	£9,700	£9,700

Open accounts and enter balances. Take out Trading Account and Profit and Loss Account and Balance Sheet as at 31st December, 19—. Assets on that date were revalued as follows:

(a) Stock £1,800; (b) Shop fitting £400; (c) Lease of premises £950; (d) Motor van £250; (e) Spare parts, etc., for van £60.

CLASS QUESTIONS

1. What is profit?
2. How is it obtained?
3. Why is there a tendency for the gap between assets and liabilities to close?
4. Give four reasons to explain why assets tend to fall in value.
5. Do assets ever appreciate in value? If so, give examples.
6. What entry is made in the account of an asset the value of which has fallen?
7. What effect has such a fall in value on capital?
8. What main sub-divisions are there of the Capital Account?
9. What is gross profit?
10. In which account is it calculated?
11. What is net profit?
12. In which account is net profit calculated?
13. Give two examples of profits that must be added to gross profit.
14. Why is it that net profit cannot be known with complete certainty?
15. If there is a gross loss, would you expect the net loss to be smaller?

THE PROFIT AND LOSS ACCOUNT
(continued)

Rate of Loss on Assets

ALL assets must be examined and valued at the end of each accounting period to discover how much loss has been sustained on them. From this point of view, assets fall into three main classes, according to the rate at which they are used up.

(*a*) Fixed assets, which wear out very slowly.
(*b*) Goods or services with a short life.
(*c*) Goods or services which are used up before they are paid for.

(*a*) **Fixed Assets.** Assets such as machinery, buildings, office furniture, and motor vans, last a long time and appear in successive Balance Sheets. As already explained, they are known for this reason as fixed assets.

The fall in value of such assets is known as depreciation.

The method of recording depreciation in the books has already been described, but an illustration is given below.

A business buys a machine for £500, paying for it by cheque. At the end of the first year, its value is estimated to be £400.

1. The purchase of the machine would mean the creation of an asset (machinery £500) and the reduction of another asset by the same amount (cash at bank £500). It is a substitution of one asset for another and obviously involves no reduction in capital.

MACHINERY ACCOUNT

Dr.						Cr.
				£		£
Cash	..	—	—	...	500	

CASH AT BANK ACCOUNT

Dr.					Cr.
					£
	Machinery	..	...	..	500

2. The machine was worth £400 at the end of the year. The depreciation was therefore £100. This would be shown as follows:

MACHINERY ACCOUNT

Dr.						Cr.
				£		£
Cash	...	—	—	...	500	Depreciation ... — — 100

PROFIT AND LOSS ACCOUNT

	£
Depreciation of Machinery ..	100

In the Balance Sheet, the amount of depreciation is shown as a deduction from the asset. This disposes of any doubt that depreciation has in fact been allowed for, in arriving at the value of the asset. The method is shown below:

BALANCE SHEET OF . . .

AS AT . . . .

	£	£
Machinery	500	
Less Depreciation ..	100	
	——	400

The difficulty with depreciation is not in understanding the entries, which are simple, but the practical one that faces the business man in determining how much depreciation to allow. The only certain method of finding the value of an asset, and therefore the amount of depreciation, is to sell the asset. This method is not open to the business man, who wants to keep the asset. The alternative is for him to estimate the value. His estimate may be wrong. If he overrates the asset, he will write off too little depreciation, and the profit shown will be too large. If he underrates the asset, he will write off too much depreciation, and the profit shown will be too small.

His method is:

1. To estimate (i) the useful life of the asset, (ii) the price it will fetch at the end of its life. This gives him the total loss from depreciation.
2. To spread the loss over its life in a reasonable way.

If the price it fetches is less than he expected, the difference will have to be carried to the Profit and Loss Account as a loss. If the price is greater, there will be a profit to be added to the gross profit in the Profit and Loss Account.

Three methods of spreading the loss from depreciation over the life of an asset may be mentioned:

1. The Straight Line (or Fixed Instalment) method, whereby the total loss is divided by the number of years, and the same amount deducted from the asset at the end of each year.
2. The Reducing Instalment method, whereby the same percentage of its value is deducted each year, calculated upon its value at the beginning of the year.

D

3. Revaluation of the asset at the end of each year, the difference between its value at the beginning of the year and at the end being carried to the Profit and Loss Account.

The subject is further discussed in Chapter 33. But it should be pointed out that the writing off of depreciation does not necessarily mean that the money is available to replace the asset—the money may be tied up in other things.

(b) **Goods or services that have a short life.** An asset may be said to have a short life if it is likely to be used up within about a year. The term of its usefulness, of course, may extend over more than one accounting period, or may be partly in one period and partly in another.

Examples of such assets are:

> Rent
> Rates and taxes
> Telephone
> Insurance
> Feeding stuff for animals
> Stores of petrol and oil, etc., for motor vans
> Wrapping materials, etc.
> Stationery

It may appear at first sight that, if a man pays rates or taxes, he has submitted to a levy but has not purchased an asset. In fact he does receive a very real return for them in the form of made-up roads, street lighting, traffic regulation, police protection, etc. The special feature of rates and taxes is that they are payments for services he is compelled to buy. They are none the less services.

The treatment of these assets is precisely the same as the treatment of fixed assets. Whatever part of them is used up—it may be the whole of them—by the end of the accounting period is a reduction of capital and is therefore credited in the accounts that record them and debited to Profit and Loss Account.

As an example, let us take the case of insurance. In return for an annual premium, a man is secured against certain losses for a period of one year. It is an asset that cannot, therefore, last for more than one year, for if he pays another premium to extend the insurance, he has, in effect, bought another asset. If he took out a Balance Sheet at the end of the year for which the premium was paid, that asset would be worth nothing, and the whole sum paid for it would have to be deducted from his capital. If, on the other hand, he took out a Balance Sheet before that date he would still be insured for some time to come, and only the proportion that had expired would be transferred to the Profit and Loss Account. For example:

A man took out a fire insurance policy and paid an annual premium of £12 on 1st May, 19–1. He drew up his Balance Sheet on 31st December, 19–1. His accounts and his position on 1st May, 19–1, are shown below.

1.   *The payment of the premium.*

FIRE INSURANCE ACCOUNT

Dr.					Cr.
19–1				£	
May 1	Cash ..	...	..	12	

CASH ACCOUNT

Dr.			Cr.
	19–1		£
	May 1 Fire Insurance	..	12

2.   *The state of the asset on 31st December when eight months of the insured premiums have expired.*

If the cost of twelve months is £12, the proportionate cost for one month is £1. After eight months £8 will have expired and will be transferred to the Profit and Loss Account as a loss. The value of the insurance for the remaining four months will be £4.

FIRE INSURANCE ACCOUNT

Dr.				£					Cr. £
19–1				£	19–1				£
May 1	Cash	...	...	12	Dec. 31	Profit & Loss	..		8
					„ 31	Bal. c/d.	..	..	4
19–2				£12					£12
Jan. 1	Bal. b/d.	..	...	£4					

PROFIT AND LOSS ACCOUNT

Dr.			Cr.
19–1		£	
Dec. 31	Fire Insurance	8	

BALANCE SHEET OF . . .
AS AT 31ST DECEMBER, 19–1

Liabilities	£	Assets		£
(The capital would be reduced by the amount of the expired insurance, £8, deducted from the profit in the Profit and Loss Account)		Fire Insurance unexpired	...	4

Thus both the asset Fire Insurance and the liability Capital have been reduced by £8 from their original value.

This example shows a debit balance of £4 in the Fire Insurance Account on 1st January, 19–2. On 1st May, 19–2, a further premium of £12 would become due, and would be paid, increasing the amount on the debit side to £16. The total annual cost of this insurance, however, is the annual premium of £12; therefore only £12 would be transferred to the Profit and Loss Account on 31st December, 19–2, leaving once again a debit balance of £4 in the account on 1st January, 19–3. The Fire Insurance Account from 1st May, 19–1, to 1st January, 19–3, is as follows:

FIRE INSURANCE ACCOUNT

Dr.				Cr
19–1		£	19–1	£
May 1	Bank	12	Dec. 31 Profit and Loss A/c.	8
			„ 31 Balance c/d. ..	4
		£12		£12
19–2			19–2	
Jan. 1	Balance b/d. ..	4	Dec. 31 Profit and Loss ..	12
May 1	Bank	12	„ 31 Balance c/d. ..	4
		£16		£16
19–3				
Jan. 1	Balance b/d. ..	£4		

Unexpired payments, such as the £4 remaining in the Insurance Account above, are sometimes referred to as 'payments in advance'.

In practice, as has been said, it is necessary for a business man to examine all assets at the end of the accounting period to discover their value at that time (and, therefore, the amount of any loss on them). For *examination* purposes, however, it is assumed, unless you are informed to the contrary, that such assets as those described in the present section are completely used up, and are therefore to be transferred to the Profit and Loss Account in full.

An asset wholly transferred to the Profit and Loss Account is said to be 'written off'. Where part only is transferred, it is 'written down'.

(c) **Goods or services that are used up before they are paid for.** These consist largely of services, such as carriage of goods and labour (wages), which are not usually paid for until after they have been given. Thus at the time of payment, the benefit is already completely used up, because, as far as that particular payment is concerned, the business man has no further claim upon the giver nor can the service be stored and used at a later date. In the act of receiving the service, it is destroyed. There is therefore no doubt that the whole amount must be written off.

Examples of services of this character are:

Wages	Cleaning
Salaries	Repairs
Carriage of goods	Postage
Commissions paid	General expenses
Heating and lighting	Office expenses, etc.

Because at the time of entry in the books such services have been completely used up, it is not usual to describe them as assets, since an essential part of the definition of an asset is that it should have a money value. Instead they are described as expenses. An expense is anything for which money has been paid but which has no present value. Nevertheless they are treated in accountancy in precisely the same way as assets for the following reasons:

(a) Value is received in return for the money paid, *e.g.,* labour is received in return for wages and salaries, light and heat in return for the payment for electricity. Therefore there is a debit entry to record their receipt as there would be for something of a more lasting nature.

(b) They are consumed instantly as they are given. There is therefore a credit entry in the account for the service to record the fact of consumption, as there would be with any asset, with a corresponding debit entry in the Profit and Loss Account, to show the reduction in capital consequent upon the consumption.

It is, of course, possible that a service which normally falls in this class is paid in advance. If so, the effect is simply to transfer it to the previous class—those with a short life. Whatever proportion was paid in advance would remain in the account as an asset, and only that part which had been received and used up would be transferred to the Profit and Loss Account.

A much more likely occurrence is that such a service would be received and not entered in the books because no payment was made for it. This difficulty will be dealt with in a later chapter.

Summary

The book-keeping procedure is summarized in the following diagram.

ASSET

Dr.				Cr.
AMOUNT PURCHASED	A	AMOUNT USED (To P. & L. A/c.)		B
		BALANCE IN HAND (C/d. as asset)		C
BALANCE IN HAND (B/d. as asset)	C			

A is the total amount purchased during the financial period, *plus* any balance in hand at the beginning of the period.

B is the total amount consumed during the financial period. If the financial period were one year, then, in the case of rent, B would be the annual rental; in the case of salaries, B would be the annual salary bill.

C is the present value of the asset and is equal to the amount not yet consumed or expired. In the case of rent or salaries C would be the amount that had been paid in advance (or was unexpired) at the end of the financial period.

Clearly A=B+C

If A is known and B is known, C can be found by subtracting B from A; *e.g.*, if rent paid is £100, and the annual rental is £80, the amount paid in advance (representing the right to use premises or land for a further period) would be £20 (£100 – £80).

Again, if A is known and C is known, B can be found by subtracting C from A; *e.g.*, if total rent paid were £100 and £20 were unexpired, £80 (*i.e.*, £100—£20) equals the amount consumed.

The amount to be carried to the Profit and Loss Account is always the amount consumed during the financial period.

Capital Expenditure and Revenue Expenditure

Assets are divided into fixed assets and current assets. The fixed assets are retained in the business for use. The current assets are the resources used in the trading activities of the business.

Capital Expenditure is all expenditure incurred in the acquisition of new fixed assets or which results in an increase in the value of the fixed assets already possessed.

All other expenditure is Revenue Expenditure, because it is incurred not in the acquisition of fixed assets but in the pursuance of trading activities. Some examples:

(1) The purchase of a machine for use is capital expenditure. It is entered amongst the fixed assets at cost. But a machine cannot be used until it is transported to the factory and installed where it is to be used. Therefore the cost of transport and installation is an unavoidable part of the cost of the machine and both are part of the capital expenditure incurred in purchasing the machine.

(2) A payment may be partly capital and partly revenue expenditure, as when a fixed asset is repaired and the money spent on it not only restores but actually enhances its value above the figure appearing in the books. The amount by which the value is enhanced would be capital expenditure. The rest is revenue expenditure.

The importance of the distinction is that in the main, revenue expenditure is deducted from capital in the Trading or Profit and Loss Account, but capital expenditure is not so deducted because it provides assets equal to the expenditure.

These two terms are frequently used and must be understood, but the division of expenditure into capital and revenue does not modify the principles laid down in this chapter. In the main, revenue expenditure is transferred to the Trading or Profit and Loss Account but only to the extent to which the goods or services bought have been consumed. For example, the payment of an insurance premium would be revenue expenditure, but only that part of it that had expired would be transferred to the Profit and Loss Account. Again, the purchase of goods for resale is revenue expenditure, but only the cost of the goods actually sold is deducted in the Trading Account.

Capital expenditure is not transferred as such to the Profit and Loss Account. But the fixed assets bought are used up over a period of time and the amount consumed is transferred to the Profit and Loss Account as depreciation.

To sum up, a business requires both fixed and current assets to sustain its activities, and the use of both is directed to the same end—the making of a profit. In pursuing this aim, both the fixed and current assets are consumed, and the part consumed is a deduction from capital. The difference between them is the rate at which they are consumed.

WRITTEN EXERCISES

1. In the following table, the letters A, B and C refer to the diagram on page 95. Complete the table.

Account	A £	B £	C £
(1) Rent ..	500	400	
(2) Salaries	3,000		100
(3) General Expenses ..	150		
(4) Insurance	75	50	
(5) Telephone	25		10
(6) Furniture	1,000		950
(7) Wrapping Materials	50		Nil
(8) Wages	2,000		
(9) Rates and Taxes	350		60
(10) Lighting	15		
(11) Stationery and Postage	45		
(12) Carriage	30		

What name would be given to the sum of money shown at C in the above accounts numbers 1, 2, 4, 5, 9?

2. Show each of the accounts in the above table.

3. In a merchant's books, the Rent Account shows a debit balance of £50 on 1st January, 19—. Explain this entry. On 1st May of the same year a year's rent (£150) is paid in advance. Show the Rent Account balanced on 31st December of that year.

4. The Insurance Account of a business shows a debit balance of £4 on 1st January, 19—. If the annual premium is paid on 1st March, how much would you expect it to be? When the account was balanced on 31st December, what sum would be carried down as insurance paid in advance?
Show the Insurance Account, balanced on 31st December, 19—.

5. On 1st January, 19—, H. Bassett had the following assets and liabilities: Cash at bank £400. L. Allsort owed him £500. Stock £1,000. Machinery £5,000. Premises £8,000. Rates (prepaid) £20. He owed C. Drop £300.

Show his Balance Sheet as it appeared on 1st January, 19—. Open accounts and enter balances.

His transactions for the year are summarized below. All receipts and payments were by cheque.

	£
Purchases	2,000
Sales	2,700
Received from L. Allsort	500
Paid C. Drop	300
Paid rates on 1st April for one year commencing on that date	80
Wages	500
Heating, lighting	25
General expenses	10
Stationery	20

Pass these transactions through the accounts, take out a Trial Balance, prepare a Trading Account and Profit and Loss Account, balance accounts, and take out a Balance Sheet as on 31st December, 19—. His stock on that date was £1,200. £20 of the sum paid for heating and lighting had been consumed, a ton of coal, valued at £5, being still unused. £10 of stationery is still on hand. Depreciate machinery by 10 per cent and premises by 5 per cent.

6. On 1st December, 19—, after eleven months' trading, V. Robins had the following balances in his books:

	£
Cash at bank	1,100
Creditors: G. Murdock	100
M. Marsh	140
Fixtures and fittings (1st Jan., 19—) ..	900
Stock (1st Jan., 19—)	2,000
Machinery (1st Jan., 19—)	8,000
Lease of premises (4 years to run) (1st Jan., 19—)	1,200
Wages	6,000
General expenses	200
Rates (paid to 31st Mar. following year) (Balance at 1st April, 19—)	240
Purchases	4,000
Sales	12,000
Capital (1st Jan., 19—)	11,400

Arrange these in the form of a Trial Balance and enter balances in accounts.

His transactions during December were:

			£
Dec.	4.	Purchased goods on credit from M. Marsh ..	260
„	10.	Purchased goods for cash	50
„	20.	Purchased chairs for office by cheque	20
„	21.	Drew cheque for private expenses	250
„	31.	Wages for month (by cheque)	600
„	31.	Sales for month (by cheque)	1,000

Enter these transactions, prepare a Trading Account and Profit and Loss Account and a Balance Sheet as at 31st December, 19—, assuming stock on that date to be worth £2,400.

Write £300 off the lease.

Depreciate machinery by 15 per cent; fixtures and fittings by 10 per cent.

The annual payment for rates is £192; £48 is therefore unexpired.

7. From the following information prepare a Profit and Loss Account and Balance Sheet on 31st December, 19—, for H. Wright.

	Dr. £	Cr. £
Gross profit		2,800
Rent	400	
Rates and taxes	600	
Salaries	1,500	
Stock (1st Jan., 19—) ..	2,500	
Stationery	50	
Insurance	20	
Petrol and oil	30	
Heating and lighting ..	24	
Commission received ..		204
Office expenses	10	
Carriage	70	
Motor vans (1st Jan., 19—)	1,000	
Furniture (1st Jan., 19—) ..	300	
Capital (1st Jan., 19—) ..		3,500
	£6,504	£6,504

(a) £100 of rent, and £200 of rates and taxes, were unexpired on 31st December, 19—.

(b) Stocks on 31st December were: stationery £40; petrol and oil £20.

(c) Depreciate vans 20 per cent and furniture 5 per cent.

8. On 31st December, 19–1, the Balance Sheet of a trader showed an item 'Insurance paid in advance £21·30.' During the ensuing year the following annual payments for various insurances became due on the dates shown and were paid:

Mar. 31.   Fire Premium on buildings   £3,000 at £0·10 per £100.
June 30.   Fire Premium on stock   £5,000 at £0·25 per £100.
Dec. 1.   Staff Fidelity Premium   £12·50.

Write up the Insurance Account as it would appear after the accounts for the business had been closed for the year ended 31st December, 19–2. Calculations may be made in months. (*R.S.A., modified.*)

9. John Smith, a retail trader, lives in a flat above his shop. The rent of the whole building is £200 per annum and may be regarded as divisible equally between business and private occupation. The rent was paid up to 31st December, 19—. During the following year, Smith made no payment to the landlord, but the landlord accepted goods from Smith's stock valued at £200 (at selling price) in full settlement.

Open the necessary accounts and enter these transactions.
(*Institute of Bankers, modified.*)

(*Note.* If £100 of the rent is for private occupation of premises, this £100 must be regarded as drawings.)

10. X Ltd. purchased a seven-year lease of certain shop premises for £8,000. A further sum of £2,000 was expended in various alterations, and it was estimated that at the end of the lease the cost of restoring the premises to their original condition (for which the company were liable) would be about £500.

Show the ledger account for the first two years, providing for depreciation.
(*R.S.A.*)

(*Note.* The £2,000 spent on alterations is to be treated as an addition to the lease. Depreciation must cover the £500 that would have to be spent at the termination of the lease.)

11.   From the following Balance Sheet of C. English as at 31st March, 19— calculate the answers to the questions given below:

BALANCE SHEET OF C. ENGLISH
AS AT 31ST MARCH, 19—

		£					£
Creditors	... ..	1,450	Cash at Bank ...	...	...		150
Capital ..	.. £4,800		Debtors..	..	...	..	2,350
Add Net Profit	.. 250		Stock ..	..	..	..	1,000
	———		Furniture and Fittings		..		260
	5,050		Machinery	..	..	£550	
Less Drawings	... 240		*Less* Depreciation ..		50		
	———	4,810				———	500
			Land and Buildings	..		..	2,000
		———					———
		£6,260					£6,260

(*a*) What is the total of English's circulating assets?
(*b*) What is the total of his fixed assets?
(*c*) What is his working capital?
(*d*) If English had not depreciated his machinery, what would his capital be?
(*e*) If furniture and fittings are only worth £200, what should the net profit be?
(*f*) If on 1st April a machine was bought on credit for £150, what would the
       creditors then be?   (*R.S.A.*)

12.   Do you know the difference between Capital and Revenue items? Identify each of the following items, and give your reasons:

The cost of building a new extension to the existing factory, £5,000.
The cost of removing several power machines from one part of the factory to
   another, and resetting them in concrete, £300.
Building another six feet on the height of the factory's chimney stack, £500.
Painting the whole of the outside woodwork and metalwork of the factory
   building, £600.
On the new extension for the factory being completed, providing central heat-
   ing, £1,000.
Removing and cleaning the existing boiler used for central heating, £150.
                                                   (*Institute of Book-keepers.*)

CLASS QUESTIONS

1. Into what three classes may assets be divided, according to the rate at which they
   are used up? Give two examples of each.
2. What is the loss on fixed assets called?
3. What portion of any asset is transferred to Profit and Loss Account at the end of
   the accounting period?
4. What is meant by (*a*) 'Writing down' an asset?
                     (*b*) 'Writing off' an asset?
5. Which class or classes of assets are normally written off?

13

SERVICES RECEIVED BUT UNPAID

IT was stated in the previous chapter that a service may have been received, and used up, but no entry made in the books because no payment had been made for it. To understand this it is necessary to understand the difference between cash and credit transactions.

Cash and Credit Transaction

The word credit, as used here, is only remotely and by inference connected with the debit and credit side of the Ledger. It means simply that a person or a business has been trusted to pay at a later date for some benefit received in the present.

If you buy something on credit, the asset you have bought will be debited in the appropriate asset account, and there will be a credit entry in the account of the person to whom you owe the money, to record the fact that you are in debt for this sum. When you pay, the Cash Account (or the Bank Account) will be credited, and there will be a debit entry in the creditor's account, cancelling the debt. Because of the time given to pay the debt (*i.e.,* because of the credit allowed) the transaction is broken into two parts, each requiring a double entry. For example:

(*a*) The acquisition of the asset and the creation of the debt:

On 1st January, a van is purchased on credit from W. Case for £1,000.

VAN ACCOUNT

Dr.				Cr.
19—			£	
Jan. 1	W. Case	...	...	1,000	

W. CASE ACCOUNT

Dr.				Cr.
		19—		£
		Jan. 1	Van ..	..	.. 1,000

(*b*) The extinction of the debt through payment:

If, in the above example, the van were paid for on 30th January, the entries would be:

W. CASE ACCOUNT

Dr.					Cr.
19—			£	19—	£
Jan. 30	Bank		1,000	Jan. 1 Van	1,000

101

BANK ACCOUNT

Dr.   Cr.

	19—				£
	Jan. 30 W. Case	..	..	1,000

On the other hand, if the van had been bought for cash, the whole transaction would be entered as follows:

VAN ACCOUNT

Dr.   Cr.

19—				£	
Jan. 1 Bank..	..	..	1,000	

BANK ACCOUNT

Dr.   Cr.

	19—				£
	Jan. 1 Van ..	..	..	1,000

Entries Relating to Services

When services as distinct from goods are bought, the purchase is usually treated as a cash transaction. Suppose, for example, you engage an assistant of 1st January, 19–1, at a salary of £80 a month, payable on the first day of the following month. You will not, each day or each week, make a record of the amount you owe him to date, though in fact your debt to him begins to grow (the book-keeping term is 'accrue') from the moment you hand him one month's salary until you pay him the next. Instead, you will wait until the agreed date, pay what is due and enter it

   (*a*) On the credit side of the Cash Account.

   (*b*) On the debit side of the Salaries Account.

Your assistant will not appear in the books as a creditor.

Now, in the example given, at the end of the accounting period (say the year ended 31st December) a month's salary has been earned by your assistant during December, but it will not be paid until 1st January in the following period. There will be no record in the books to show that you owe him this money. It is, however, an expense incurred during the financial period which ended on 31st December, and if the profit made during that period is to be correctly assessed, that expense must be deducted from the gross profit in the profit and loss account.

If, as in this case, the amount due but unpaid is known, or easily calculated, it is brought into account in the following way:

(1) Debit the appropriate account (in this case salaries account) with the amount outstanding. It is described as a balance.

(2) The whole cost of the service consumed has now been entered on the debit side of the account. This amount is transferred to the profit and loss account by a credit entry in the account for the service and a debit entry in the Profit and Loss Account.

(3) Bring down the amount outstanding as a credit balance. It will then appear as a liability in the Balance Sheet.

The Salaries Account as it would appear after these entries had been made on 31st December is shown below. It should be remembered that the assistant was appointed on 1st January and that eleven months' salary, £880 (*i.e.,* £80 on the first day of each month from February to December inclusive) will have been entered.

SALARIES ACCOUNT

Dr.				Cr.
19–1		£	19–1	£
Dec. 1	(Amount paid to date)	880	Dec. 31 Profit and Loss A/c.	960
„ 31	Balance c/d.. ..	80		
		£960		£960
			19–2	
			Jan. 1 Balance b/d. ..	80

Now let us see what happens if the same arrangement continues for another year. On the first day of each month from January to December inclusive, £80 salary will be paid, making a total of £960. The Salaries Account will then appear:

Dr.	SALARIES ACCOUNT			Cr.
19–2		£	19–2	£
Dec. 1	(Amount paid to date)	960	Jan. 1 Balance b/d.	80

This leaves a balance once more of £880. But once more, on 31st December, £80 has been earned but not paid. This should be debited in the account and £960, the cost of a whole year's service, should be transferred to the Profit and Loss Account. As in the previous year, the £80 due but unpaid would be carried down as a credit balance on 31st December, 19–2.

The Salaries Account continued to the 1st January, 19–3, is shown below:

SALARIES ACCOUNT

Dr.						Cr.
19–2			£	19–2		£
Dec. 1	(Amount paid to date)		960	Jan. 1	Balance b/d. ..	80
„ 31	Balance c/d. ..		80	Dec. 31	Profit and Loss A/c.	960
			£1040			£1040
19–3				19–3		
Jan. 1	Cash		£80	Jan. 1	Balance b/d. ..	£80

The same principle will apply to wages. For example, wages may be paid on Friday of each week, but made up only to the previous Wednesday. When he receives his wages on Friday, each workman will have two days' pay 'lying on'. Now, if the 31st December falls on a Friday, the wages bill for two days will be outstanding. It would be treated in exactly the same way as the salary illustrated above. That is, it would be debited in the Wages Account and carried down as a credit balance and the whole amount of the wages, including the amount due but unpaid, would be transferred to the Profit and Loss Account.

In these examples (salaries and wages) the amount due but unpaid was known and usually this will be the case. It could happen, however, that the determination of the amount due at the end of a financial year involved a difficult calculation. For example, suppose premises were rented at an annual figure of £624 and that up to 15th October £489 had been paid, the next instalment being due on 15th January of the following year. As there are 77 days to 31st December (assuming this to be the end of the financial year) the amount due up to 31st December could be calculated as $77/365 \times £624$. However, the amount to be set against the profit is one year's rent, £624. It would be simpler, in examination work, to transfer this amount to the profit and loss account and find the amount due but unpaid as the balance of the account, than to work out this difficult calculation.

RENT ACCOUNT

19–1		£	19–1		£
Oct. 15	Bank	489	Dec. 31	Profit and Loss A/c	624
Dec. 31	Balance c/d	135			
		£624			£624
			19–2		
			Jan. 1	Balance b/d	135

The principle established is that each year (if the Balance Sheet is a yearly one) the total value of the services consumed will be transferred to the Profit and Loss Account. If less than this has actually been paid, there will be a credit balance, which will appear in the Balance Sheet as a liability. If more has been paid, there will be a debit balance, which, of course, will be an asset (*see* previous chapter).

The principles discussed in this chapter are shown diagrammatically below. This diagram should be compared with that shown on page 95.

Dr.				Cr.
Services received and paid for	A	Services consumed (to P. and L. A/c.)	B	
Service received but not paid for (c/d. as liability)	C			
		Amount due (b/d. as liability)	C	

SERVICES RECEIVED BUT UNPAID   105

A is the total value of services received and paid for during the financial period.

B is the total amount consumed during the financial period. In the case of salaries, B would be the annual salary bill.

C is the value of the services received but not paid for at the end of the financial period

Clearly $A+C=B$

If A is known and C is known, then B can be found by adding A to C. For example:

> If salaries received and paid for are £950, and the sum due for services received is £50, then the amount to be transferred to the Profit and Loss Account would be £1,000.

Again, if A is known, and B is known, C can be found by subtracting A from B. For example:

> If the rent paid during the year is £300 and the annual rent is £400, then the rent due at the end of the year would be £100.

Summary of Rules for Dealing with Services

I. Debit the account with the amount of money paid (credit entry in Cash or Bank Account).

II. If the service has been paid for in advance, credit the account with the unexpired amount and bring it down to the debit side as an asset.

III. If an amount is accrued (*i.e.,* due but not paid), debit the account with this amount and bring it down to the credit side as a liability.

IV. Transfer the balance then remaining in the account to the Profit and Loss Account. This represents the amount consumed.

Income other than through Sales

In addition to the profit derived from the sales of its products, a business may have other income from such sources as commission, rent for premises sub-let, etc. To ascertain the net profit for a given financial period, such income should be added to profit in the Profit and Loss Account. The amount to be added is the amount actually earned within the period, whether it has been received or not.

The method of dealing with such income is similar to that used to record expenses except that, being income, the sides are reversed.

(I) The account is credited with all money received (the debit entry will be in the Bank Account).

(II) If (a) Income has been earned during this financial period but not received, the amount outstanding will be entered on the credit side of the account and brought down to the debit side as a balance. It will be an asset and will appear on the Balance Sheet, added to debtors.

If (b) Payment has been received in advance, and some of it refers to the following financial period, the amount relating to the following period will be entered on the debit side of the account and brought down to the credit side as a balance. It will appear on the liabilities side of the Balance Sheet, but should not be added to creditors because, unlike the creditors, it has not to be paid by the business in cash. It will disappear with the lapse of time. The creditors on the Balance Sheet should show the amount of money to be found.

(III) The difference between the two sides which represents the amount earned during the period is transferred to the Profit and Loss Account by a debit entry in the income account and a credit entry in the Profit and Loss Account.

Note that Step II is required only if an amount is outstanding or prepaid.

Illustration: Commission received during the year to 31st December 19–1 is £265. This includes £15 which was due but unpaid on 1st January 19–1. An assignment which will not be completed until February 19–2 has been undertaken and should, when finished, yield a further £120. It is estimated that on 31st December 19–1 £95 of this £120 has been earned. Show the Commission Account balance on 31st December 19–1.

COMMISSION ACCOUNT

19–1		£	19–1		£
Jan. 1	Balance	15	Dec. 31	Bank	265
Dec. 31	Profit and Loss	345	„ 31	Accrued c/d	95
		£360			£360
19–2					
Jan. 1	Balance	95			

WRITTEN EXERCISES

1. The following table gives some information concerning the accounts named on 31st December, 19—. The letters A, B and C refer to the diagram on page 104. Complete the table.

Account	A (Amount paid to date) £	B (Amount to be transferred to P. and L.) £	C (Amount due but unpaid) £
Rent	250	300	
Wages	5,000		100
Interest		480	40
Salaries	1,200		50
Lighting	25		5
Fees	15	21	

2. Show each of the accounts in the above table.

3. The financial year of a certain firm runs from 1st April in one year to 30th March in the next. On 1st April, 19–1, the Rent Account shows a credit balance of £60. Explain this entry. On 2nd April, 19–1, one year's rent, £240, is paid. How much rent will be due on 31st March, 19–2? Show the Rent Account balanced on that date.

4. In a merchant's books, the Rates Account shows a debit balance of £18 on 1st January, 19–1. On 1st April of the same year, six months' rates, £36, for the period 1st April to 30th September, are paid, but no further payments are made that year. Show the Rates Account balanced on 31st December, 19–1.

5. R. Tyne is a paper merchant and has the following assets and liabilities on 1st January, 19—: Cash in hand £10; Cash at bank £100; Debtors £600; Creditors £400; Stock £1,200; Furniture and fixtures £300; Rent due £80; Van £500.

Find his capital and draw up his Balance Sheet on that date. Open accounts and enter balances.

Jan. 1. Paid motor insurance £30 by cheque.
„   2. Purchased goods on credit £450.
„   4. Received by cheque from debtors £350.
„   6. Paid rent due by cheque £80.
„   8. Paid creditors by cheque £300.
„   12. Sold goods on credit £650.
„   15. Sold van valued at £200 and received cheque for that amount.
„   20. Paid office cleaning £5 by cash.
„   24. Paid van licence £10 by cheque.
„   31. Cash sales for month £150, of which £130 had been paid into the bank.
„   31. Paid month's wages by cheque £40.
„   31. General expenses for month paid in cash £8.
„   31. Drawings (by cheque) £20.

Pass the above transactions through the accounts, take out a Trial Balance, Trading Account, and Profit and Loss Account, and show his Balance Sheet on 31st January, 19—. Stock on 31st January was valued at £1,150; motor insurance at £27; and licences at £9. The van was assumed to have depreciated by £5. Rent accrued during January £10.

6. What information is conveyed to you by the following balances standing in the ledger at 30th June, 19–1 after balancing the accounts and preparing the final accounts for the half year ended 30th June, 19–1?

(a) A debit balance on Rent Account
(b) A credit balance on Wages Account
(c) A debit balance on Packing Materials Account
(d) A credit balance on Bank Account as shown in the Cash Book.
(*College of Preceptors*)

7. From the following particulars show R. Oldfield's Rates Account, correctly closed and balanced on 31st December, 19—.

			£
Jan. 1.	Rates prepaid, brought forward from previous year		37·25
Apr. 17.	Paid by cheque, rates for half year (1st April to 30th September, 19—)		76·40
Nov. 20.	Paid by cheque, rates for half year (1st October, 19— to 31st March following year)		76·40

(*L. Ch. C., modified.*)

8.   W. Cash commenced business at 1st February, 19—, as a horse dealer, with a capital of £5,000 in the bank. Show his Balance Sheet on that date. Open accounts and enter balances.

Feb. 1.   Rented stables and land at £20 per month and paid first month's rent by cheque.
„   1.   Engaged assistant at £10 per week.
„   2.   Withdrew from bank for office cash £50.
„   3.   Purchased by cheque feeding stuffs and straw £50.
„   6.   Purchased by cheque stable equipment £40.
„   7.   Purchased horses by cheque £2,000.
„   10. Purchased trap and harness by cheque £100.
„   18. Purchased horses by cheque £1,000.
„   21. Sold horses and received cheque £2,100.
„   28. Wages £30 paid in cash.
„   28. Withdrew by cheque for own use £30.
„   28. Received invoice from veterinary surgeon £10. This was not paid.

Pass the above transactions through accounts, take out a Trial Balance, ascertain net profit, and draw up W. Cash's Balance Sheet as at 28th February, 19—.

Assume that the value of horses held on that date was £1,500; that £40 of the feeding stuff and straw has been consumed; and that the rates due on the premises but not paid were £5. Allow no depreciation of fixed assets.

9.   In the books of X & Co. the wages due but unpaid on 1st January, 19—, were shown as £650. On 31st December of the same year, the Wages Account shows that the total sum paid out during the year was £26,745 (which included the £650 owing). The wages, however, are made up to the Tuesday of each week. In the last week of that year Tuesday fell on 28th December. Three days' wages, amounting to £595, had therefore accrued on 31st December, but would not be paid until the following week. Show the Wages Account as it would appear on 31st December of that year.

10.   Show how the Insurance Account, the Packing Materials Account, the Light and Heat Account and the Carriage Inwards Account would appear after the following items had been entered, the final accounts prepared and the ledger accounts completely balanced for the half year to 30th June, 19—.

			£
Jan.	1.	Stock of packing materials	54
„	1.	Insurance prepaid to 31 March, 19—	18
Feb.	10.	Paid carriage on purchases by cheque	6
Apr.	1.	Paid *annual* insurance premium by cheque	78
„	14.	Paid by cheque electricity a/c	12
„	14.	Paid by cheque gas account	7
May	26.	Purchased packing materials from Packings Ltd.	89
June	4.	Paid carriage on purchases by cheque	14
„	30.	Amount due for gas and electricity	16
		Stock of packing materials	63

(College of Preceptors)

11.   On 1st April, 19—, S. Exton, an undertaker, bought a motor hearse for £300. Show the entry for this in the appropriate account in his ledger, write off depreciation at 20 per cent per annum, and bring down the balance on 31st March of the following year.   *(R.S.A., modified.)*

12.   William Robinson sub-lets the flat over his shop at an annual rent of £48, payable quarterly. During 19— the tenant at the flat pays the rent due from him on 25th March, 24th June, and 29th September, but at 31st December has not paid the quarter's rent due.

Show the Rent Account in William Robinson's books after the preparation of his Profit and Loss Account for the year ending 31st December, 19—.   *(R.S.A.)*

13.   The payments made by J. Wilton to his travellers on account of commission and salaries for 19–2 amounted to £2,500 and for 19–3 £3,000. The amounts due and unpaid were as follows:

		£
31st December, 19–1	....	50
31st December, 19–2	..	45
31st December, 19–3	..	48

Show the Salaries and Commission Account for 19–2 and 19–3 (closed at 31st December in each year).

(*R.S.A.*)

14.   Robinson's financial year ends on 31st October.

From the following information you are required to write up his Rent and Rates Account for the financial years ended 31st October, 19–2 and 19–3 respectively, balancing at 31st October and bringing out clearly the transfer to Robinson's Revenue Account at those dates.

19–1		£
Oct. 15.	Paid rates for the year ended 31st March, 19–2 ..	60
Dec. 31.	Paid rent for half year to date	96
19–2		
June 30.	Paid rent for half year to date	96
Nov. 10.	Paid rates for the year ended 31st March, 19–3	72
Dec. 31.	Paid rent for half year to date	96
19–3		
June 30.	Paid rent for half year to date	96
Oct. 10.	Paid rates for the year ended 31st March, 19–4	84

(*L. Ch. C.*)

14

RETURNS, CASH AND TRADE DISCOUNT, BAD DEBTS

Adjustments to Purchases and Sales

IF goods are sold, an asset is acquired in their place, sometimes in the form of cash, but more often in the form of debts; these are owed by the purchasers, who thus become debtors. Similarly, if goods are bought, a liability is acquired, usually in the form of obligations to pay the sellers, who thus become creditors. Now, if these assets and liabilities do not realize the sum of money at which they are entered, the difference will be an addition to, or a subtraction from, capital; that is, a profit or a loss. An adjustment to the capital will therefore have to be made in the Trading Account or the Profit and Loss Account. There are three main factors which affect the book values of debtors and creditors. These are:

(a) goods sold may be returned, thus reducing the item 'Debtors'. Similarly, goods bought may be returned, thus reducing the item 'Creditors';

(b) there may be allowances for cash discounts—
(i) by the proprietor to his debtors;
or (ii) by creditors to the proprietor;

(c) debtors may fail to pay their debts in full or even at all.

Sales and Purchases Returns

Cases will frequently arise in which a purchaser returns to the seller goods he has bought.

To the seller, this would be a cancellation of a sale and would be described from his viewpoint as a 'Sales Return', or, on the grounds that the goods are received into his stock, as 'Returns Inwards'.

To the buyer, on the other hand, a return of goods to the seller would be a cancellation of a purchase, and he would describe the return as a 'Purchases Return' or as 'Returns Outwards'.

Sales Returns or Returns Inwards

When the goods were sold, the record made by the seller would have been:

(a) a debit entry in the account of the buyer;
(b) a credit entry in the sales account.

If the goods are returned, these entries must be cancelled:

110

(a) *In the buyer's account.* The debit entry would be cancelled by a credit entry equal to the value of the goods returned.

(b) *Cancellation of the sale.* Theoretically this could be accomplished by a debit entry in the Sales Account. It is important, however, for a business man to know what proportion of his goods is being returned. He therefore opens a 'Sales Returns Account' or a 'Returns Inwards Account' and debits each return to this account. At the end of the accounting period the total (*i.e.,* the balance) is transferred to the Trading Account. In theory this total should be transferred to the debit side of the Trading Account, but it is more usual to show it as a deduction from sales on the credit side, as illustrated in the following example. In this way, the net figure for sales is obtained.

Example: On 3rd January, goods value £500 are sold to A. Letts. On 9th January, A. Letts returns goods, damaged, £30.

A. LETTS ACCOUNT (1)

Dr.						Cr.
19—			£	19—		£
Jan. 3	Sales (2)		500	Jan. 9 Sales Returns (3) ..		30
				„ 31 Balance c/d. ..		470
			£500			£500
Feb. 1	Balance b/d. ...		£470			

SALES ACCOUNT (2)

Dr.					Cr.
		£	19—		£
Trading A/c. (4)		500	Jan. 3 A. Letts (1)		500

SALES RETURNS ACCOUNT (3)

Dr.				Cr.
19—		£		£
Jan. 9 A. Letts (1)		30	Trading A/c. (4)	30

TRADING ACCOUNT OF . . . (4)
FOR . . . ENDED . . .

Dr.			Cr.
		£	£
	Sales (2)	500	
	Less Returns (3)	30	
			470

The credit entry in the account of the buyer reduces the item debtors, and the capital is reduced when the return is deducted from the sales in the Trading Account. It should be noted, however, that there is an offset, because the closing stock will be increased by the value of the returned goods. But, whereas the sales are reduced by the selling price of the returned goods, the stock is increased by the cost price only, the net effect being a loss of the profit which would have been made on the returned goods if the sale had been completed. No entry is made in the Stock Account (which shows only the opening stock for the financial period) for the returned goods. They would be included in the stock when it is taken at the end of the period (see Chapter Ten).

Two other possibilities may be considered:

(a) The buyer may not return the goods but may claim instead a reduction in price.

(b) The price charged to the buyer may be too high because of a mistake on the part of the seller.

A reduction in the price for either of these reasons would not be the same thing as a return of the goods, but it would have precisely the same effect—the sales, and the buyer's debt to the seller, would both be reduced. Because the effect is the same, the treatment is the same. In both cases the Sales Returns Account would be debited and the customer's account credited with the reduction.

Purchases Returns or Returns Outwards

The principles governing the Purchases Returns Account are exactly the same as those governing the Sales Returns Account, except, of course, that the entries are on opposite sides. An allowance in price is treated as a return, and no entries are made in the Stock Account. An example is given below:

January 4. Goods, charged at £200, are bought on credit from S. Trip.

January 10. It was agreed that the correct price of the goods should have been £190.

S. TRIP ACCOUNT (1)

Dr.				Cr.
19—		£	19—	£
Jan. 10	Returns Outwards (3)	10	Jan. 4 Purchases (2) ...	200
„ 31	Balance c/d. ..	190		
		£200		£200
			Feb. 1 Balance b/d. ...	£190

PURCHASES ACCOUNT (2)

Dr.				Cr.
19—		£		£
Jan. 4	S. Trip (1)	200	Trading A/c. (4)	200

PURCHASES RETURNS ACCOUNT (3)

Dr.   Cr.

			£	19—			£
Trading A/c. (4)	...	...	10	Jan. 10 S. Trip (1) ...		...	10

TRADING ACCOUNT OF . . .
. . . ENDED . . .

Dr.   Cr.

		£	£	
Purchases (2) ..	..	200		
Less Returns (3)..		10		
		——	190	

Cash Discount

It is the practice in certain trades to encourage customers to pay promptly by allowing a certain amount of discount if they pay within a stipulated time. The discount is usually calculated as a percentage of the amount of the debt. If a trader allows discount of this kind to a debtor, it will be equivalent to a reduction in price—it will reduce both the amount of the debt owed to him and the amount of his profit. The reduction of the debt will be shown by a credit entry in the customer's (_i.e.,_ the debtor's) account, and the reduction of profit will be shown by a debit entry in the Profit and Loss Account. As there may be many such items, and only the total is required in the Profit and Loss Account, a summarizing account called the 'Discounts Allowed Account' is opened, and is debited with each item of discount allowed to customers. The total amount is transferred to the debit of the Profit and Loss Account at the end of the accounting period.

It is probable, of course, that the trader who allows discount to his debtors will also be allowed discount by his creditors. The effect will be the reverse of that relating to the discount he himself allows—it will reduce the amount he has to pay to his creditors and, because it reduces the amount he pays for his goods, it will increase his profit. To show the reduction in the amount of his debt, a debit entry will be made in the creditor's account. To show the increase in his profit, a 'Discounts Received Account' will be opened; this is a summarizing account which will be credited with each item of discount he is permitted to claim, and the total (_i.e.,_ the balance, since there will be no debit entries in that account) will be transferred to the credit side of the Profit and Loss Account, as an additional profit, at the end of the accounting period. These principles are illustrated in the examples given below:

I. DISCOUNTS ALLOWED

T. Smith owes a trader £100. He pays his debt by cheque but is allowed discount at the rate of 2 per cent.

T. SMITH ACCOUNT (1)

Dr.				£					Cr.
Balance	—	—	—	100	Bank (2)	...	..	...	£ 98
					Discount (3) ...	...	...	...	2
				£100					£100

CASH AT BANK ACCOUNT (2)

Dr.				£	Cr.
T. Smith (1) ...	...	...		98	

DISCOUNT ALLOWED ACCOUNT (3)

Dr.				£			Cr.
T. Smith (1) ..	...	...		2	Profit & Loss A/c. (4)	...	£ 2

PROFIT AND LOSS ACCOUNT (4)

		£	
Discount Allowed (3)	...	2	

II.   DISCOUNTS RECEIVED

A trader owes P. Bell £150. He pays by cheque, and is allowed discount at the rate of 2 per cent.

P. BELL ACCOUNT (1)

Dr.				£					Cr.
Bank (2)	..	...	...	147	Balance	—	—	—	£ 150
Discount (3) ..	...	...		3					
				£150					£150

CASH AT BANK ACCOUNT (2)

Dr.				Cr.
	P. Bell (1)	..	...	£ 147

DISCOUNT RECEIVED ACCOUNT (3)

Dr.			£					Cr.
Profit and Loss (4) ...	..		3	P. Bell (1)	...	...	...	£ 3
			£3					£3

PROFIT AND LOSS ACCOUNT (4)

Dr.			Cr.
	Discount Received (3)	..	£ 3

Trade Discount

Cash discount, which is allowed as an inducement to the customer to pay promptly, must not be confused with trade discount. Trade discount is allowed for one of the following reasons:

(a) As a correction of the price shown in the catalogue, if that price has changed since the catalogue was printed. If, for instance, the catalogue price of an article were £2 but the correct price only £1·50, a trade discount of £0·50 would be allowed. £0·50 is 25 per cent of the catalogue price, and therefore a trade discount of 25 per cent would be allowed.

If the correct price were to rise to £1·60, then a trade discount of 20 per cent would be allowed instead.

This device relieves the seller of the impossible task of reprinting his catalogue every time there is a price change in any of the articles listed.

If prices rise above the catalogue price, no discount, of course, will be allowed. Instead, a percentage increase will be added.

(b) A trader is sometimes charged the retail price for goods he buys from a manufacturer or wholesaler, but a trade discount is deducted which is equal to the difference between the wholesale price and the retail price. He sells the goods at the retail price and the discount is his profit on the sale.

(c) As a special discount to a trader buying a large quantity of goods.

Now the difference between trade discount and cash discount is that both seller and buyer know, at the time of giving the order, whether trade discount is to be allowed; but it is not until the account is paid that they can know with certainty whether it has been paid in time to qualify for cash discount. Trade discount therefore can be, and is, deducted in advance and the whole transaction goes through at the discounted price, which is the real price. No adjustments are called for later on. Cash discount, on the other hand, must be deducted when it is allowed, in the manner already shown.

Bad Debts

A debt is said to be bad when the debtor fails to pay either the whole, or part, of the debt. Whatever sum is not paid is a complete loss. To deal with it in the books, two entries are required:

(a) A debt is an asset. The debtor's account will therefore have a debit balance. To deduct the amount that has been lost through non-payment, a credit entry will be required in this account, showing the amount by which he has defaulted.

(b) The amount remaining unpaid is a loss and must be deducted from the profit made during the period (or added to the loss), by a debit entry in the Profit and Loss Account.

It is not, however, entered directly into the Profit and Loss Account because there may be a number of bad debts; and, as far as the Profit and Loss Account is concerned, only the total is significant. The bad debts are therefore summarized in a 'Bad Debts Account', on the debit side, and transferred to the debit of the Profit and Loss Account at the end of the accounting period.

This is known as 'writing off' a debt.

It should be noted that a bad debt is a serious thing, because the seller loses not only the profit on the sale, but also all or part of the cost of the goods he has sold.

A common arrangement is for a defaulting debtor to pay a proportion of his debts. This is known as a dividend or a composition, and is usually expressed as a payment of so many pence in the £. For example, if he pays three-quarters of each debt he owes, he is said to pay seventy-five pence in the £. The other twenty-five pence is a bad debt—a quarter of the amount owed.

Illustration: One of a trader's debtors, L. Broom, owes him £100, but is able to pay a composition of only 60p in the £, the remainder being a bad debt.

L. BROOM ACCOUNT (1)

Dr.				£					Cr. £
Balance	...	...	...	100	Cash (2)	..	..	..	60
					Bad Debts (3)		...	...	40
				£100					£100

CASH ACCOUNT (2)

Dr.			£		Cr.
L. Broom (1)	...	..	60		

BAD DEBTS ACCOUNT (3)

Dr.			£			Cr. £
L. Broom (1)	...	...	40	Profit & Loss A/c. (4)	...	40
			£40			£40

PROFIT AND LOSS ACCOUNT (4)

Dr.		£		Cr.
Bad Debts (3)		40		

Bad Debts Recovered

It may, and sometimes does, happen that a debt written off as bad is paid at a later date. For instance, L. Broom, in the example given above, may, after his account has been written off, pay the £40 which he still owes. If he does so, the Cash Account will be debited (or the Bank Account, if he pays by cheque) with the £40, but it cannot be entered against the debt in his account, because that has already been cancelled or written off. If it were now entered on the credit side of his account, it would be a credit balance. This would mean that it was a liability, which it certainly is not. The debt of £40 was transferred as a loss to the Profit and Loss Account, and it is this loss which must be cancelled. One method is to open a 'Bad Debts Recovered Account', to credit this account with the amount paid, and to carry the balance to the credit side of the Profit and Loss Account. The entries are shown below:

CASH ACCOUNT (1)

Dr.			Cr.
	£		
Bad Debts Recovered L. Broom (2)	40		

BAD DEBTS RECOVERED ACCOUNT (2)

	£		£
Profit & Loss A/c. (3) ..	40	Cash (1)	40
	£40		£40

PROFIT AND LOSS ACCOUNT (3)

Dr.		Cr.
		£
	Bad Debts Recovered (2) ...	40

A second method, and probably the better, is:

   (i) Debit the Cash Account and credit the debtor.
  (ii) Debit the debtor and credit Bad Debts Recovered Account.

The advantage of this method is that the debtor's account will show that he has paid his debt, and this will be in his favour should he subsequently seek more credit.

WRITTEN EXERCISES

1. The following account is shown in the books of J. Almond, a merchant:

K. COBB ACCOUNT

Dr.								Cr.
19—			£	19—				£
June 30	Goods	..	50	July 20	Bank	..	...	49
Aug. 15	„	.. ..	140	„ 20	Discount	..	..	1
Nov. 1	Legal Charges A/c.		5	Aug. 21	Returns	..	..	20
				Dec. 31	Bad Debts A/c.	..		125
			£195					£195

State concisely what is meant by each entry in this account.　　(*R.S.A.*)

2.　William Shaw appears in your books as a debtor for £46·80. On his becoming bankrupt, you receive a cheque for first and final dividend of 65½p in the £. Show William Shaw's account in your books.　　(*R.S.A., modified.*)

3.　From the following summaries prepare the Sundry Debtors Account, Sundry Creditors Account, Discount Accounts, Purchases Account, Sales Account, and Bad Debts Account, and show the transfers to the Trading and Profit and Loss Accounts.

					£
Jan. 1.	Total of Debtors	..	..	..	3,283
	Total of Creditors	..	..	..	1,825
Jan. 31.	Cheques received during month		..	2,100
	Cheques paid during month	..		..	1,300
	Discounts received	..	..	..	60
	Discounts allowed	..	..	..	95
	Bad Debts written off ..	..	..		40
	Purchases during month	..	..	600
	Sales during month	..	..	..	1,100

4.　On 31st December, 19—, a trader wrote off as a bad debt £25 owing to him by R. Kell since 10th July of that year. On 30th November in the following year R. Kell paid the debt in full. Open the necessary accounts and record these transactions, assuming the books to be closed annually on 31st December.

5.　On 1st January, 19—, L. Forbes had the following assets and liabilities:
　　Cash at bank £300. Stock £2,700. Leasehold premises £4,000. Debtor: R. Curry £500. Capital £7,500.
Show his Balance Sheet on that date, open accounts, and enter the following transactions:

Jan.	3.	Purchased goods on credit from W. Parr £1,000.
„	4.	Sold goods on credit to T. Ridley £200.
Jan.	7.	Sold goods on credit to A. Wine £400.
„	8.	T. Ridley returned goods £20.
„	10.	W. Parr agreed to allow £50 for goods damaged in transit.
„	14.	Cash sales to date £800 (banked).
„	15.	A. Wine reported that he had been overcharged by £60. This claim was allowed.
„	20.	Paid amount due to W. Parr less 4 per cent cash discount.
„	21.	Received cheque from R. Curry for £400. The balance of his account was written off as a bad debt.
„	25.	T. Ridley and A. Wine each paid his account by cheque less 5 per cent discount.
„	31.	Cash purchases for month (by cheque) £400. Cash sales to date £700 (banked). Paid wages by cheque £50. General expenses by cheque £30.

Take out a Trial Balance, a Trading Account, and a Profit and Loss Account. Balance off accounts and prepare a Balance Sheet as at 31st January, 19—, writing £10 off the value of the lease. Stock on that date was valued at £2,650.

6.   The following is the trial balance of M. Jones on 31st December, 19—:

	Dr. £	Cr. £
Cash at bank	400	
Sundry debtors and creditors	800	700
Stock (1st Jan., 19—)	2,500	
Discount allowed	20	
Discount received		10
Returns inwards and outwards	10	5
Purchases and sales	4,000	5,500
Wages	670	
Rent	200	
Rates	45	
Fixed assets	3,000	
Capital		5,430
	£11,645	£11,645

Open the above accounts and enter balances. Prepare a Trading Account and a Profit and Loss Account, allowing for the following:

(1) One quarter's rent £50, and rates £15, had been paid in advance.
(2) Depreciate fixed assets by 10 per cent.
(3) Stock, 31st Dec., 19—, was £2,800.

Show the Balance Sheet of M. Jones as it appeared at 31st December, 19—.

7.   Show the entries in the accounts, including the Trading and Profit and Loss Accounts, in the books of E. Kemp, recording the information given below:

Account	Balance, 1st Jan. Dr.	Cr.	Pur-chases	Sales	Returns	Cheques 10th Jan.	Cash Dis-count
C. Snow	320			100	20	380	20
R. Field	80			25		100	5
O. Wills		250	65		15	285	15
W. Laing	50			30		76	4
W. Gash		400	25		5	419	1
H. Foster		60			4	54	2
C. Lewis	70			10	3	66	4

15

REPAIRS, INTEREST, AND CARRIAGE

Repairs

LET us suppose that a machine worth £200 has suffered damage through accident or wear, and that the damage has been repaired at a cost of £50.

Because the machine must be repaired immediately, the damage has only a temporary effect upon its value. It is therefore not necessary to credit the Machinery Account with the damage.

Before the damage occurred, the machine was worth £200. After the damage had been repaired, it would still be worth £200, because the effect of repairing a machine is to restore its value, not to increase it. It is evident, therefore, that the cost of the repair should not be added to the value of the machine.

Thus no entry is necessary in the Machinery Account to record either the damage or the repair. If the amount of the damage and the cost of repair were entered, they would cancel out.

The amount of the damage is the cost of the repair. The damage is a loss, comparable to a sudden depreciation. The repair should therefore be debited to the Profit and Loss Account. As there may be many items of repairs during an accounting period, they are first collected in a 'Repairs Account', and only the total is transferred to the Profit and Loss Account.

If the repair is paid for at once, the credit entry will be in the Cash Account or the Bank Account. If it were not paid for at once, the credit entry would be in the account of the person to whom the money was owed.

The entries are shown below, assuming immediate payment:

BANK ACCOUNT (1)

Dr.				Cr.
	19—			£
	Repairs (2)	...	...	50

REPAIRS ACCOUNT (2)

Dr.					Cr.
19—			£	19—	£
Bank (1)	...	...	50	Profit and Loss (3) ...	50

PROFIT AND LOSS ACCOUNT (3)

Dr.				Cr.
19—			£	
Repairs (2)	..	..	50	

It is more likely that a firm of any considerable size would keep its own staff of maintenance engineers. In that case, any wages paid to that staff would be debited to a 'Maintenance and Repairs Account', instead of to the ordinary Wages Account. (The ordinary Wages Account would contain only the wages of people employed directly on goods for resale.) Similarly, any materials bought for purposes of repair would be debited to the same account. The total would be transferred to the debit of the Profit and Loss Account at the end of the accounting period—provided it had all been used. Any wages paid in advance, or any materials not consumed, would remain as a balance in the account and would appear as an asset in the Balance Sheet. An illustration is given below:

The X Manufacturing Co. had a debit balance of £400 in the Maintenance and Repairs Account on 1st December, 19—, for wages paid and materials bought to date. On 20th December, spare parts costing £115 were purchased on credit from J. Black, and a cheque was drawn for wages of maintenance staff, £40, on 31st December. Assuming the value of unused spares to be £80 on 31st December, show the Maintenance and Repairs Account, the Bank Account, the J. Black Account, and the Profit and Loss Account to record these matters on 31st December.

MAINTENANCE AND REPAIRS ACCOUNT (1)

Dr.							Cr.
19—			£	19—			£
Dec. 1	Balance b/d.	...	400	Dec. 31	Profit and Loss (4)		475
„ 20	J. Black (spare parts) (3)		115	31	Balance c/d. .. (materials in hand)		80
„ 31	Bank (Wages) (2)		40				
			£555				£555
19—							
Jan. 1	Balance b/d.	..	£80				

BANK ACCOUNT (2)

Dr.			Cr.
	19—		£
	Dec. 31	Maintenance and repairs (wages) (1)	40

J. BLACK ACCOUNT (3)

Dr.			Cr.
	19—		£
	Dec. 20	Maintenance and repairs (spares) (1)	115

PROFIT AND LOSS ACCOUNT (4)

Dr.   Cr.

	£	
Maintenance and Repairs (1)	475	

Interest

If a trader were to borrow a sum of money, the person from whom he borrowed it would be his creditor for that amount until it was repaid. But in lending the money, the creditor would be doing the trader a service, and in return he would expect not only to have the loan refunded, but to receive in addition some payment for the service. A payment made for the service of lending money is called interest. It is usually calculated at so much per hundred pounds of the loan per year, and is thus in proportion to the service rendered; for the larger the sum of money lent, and the longer the period, the greater is the help given.

Let us suppose a trader borrows on the 1st January, 19—, £1,000 from W. Lock at 4 per cent per annum, receiving the money by cheque.

(a) The loan would be recorded by a debit entry in the Bank Account, to show the receipt of money, and by a credit entry in W. Lock's Loan Account, to show the liability.

BANK ACCOUNT (1)

Dr.   Cr.

19—		£	
Jan. 1 W. Lock (loan) (2) ..		1,000	

W. LOCK (LOAN) ACCOUNT (2)

Dr.   Cr.

	19—		£
	Jan. 1 Bank (1)		1,000

(b) When the interest was paid on the following 31st December, there would be a credit entry in the Bank Account of £40. The debit entry would not be in the Loan Account because it does not reduce the amount of the loan. A special account called the 'Interest on Loan Account' would be opened. It represents an asset (i.e., services received) and so is debited. These two accounts would appear then as follows:

INTEREST ON LOAN ACCOUNT (3)

Dr.   Cr.

19—		£	
Dec. 31 Bank (1)		40	

BANK ACCOUNT (1)

Dr.			Cr.		
19—		£	19—		£
Jan. 1	W. Lock (loan) (2) ..	1,000	Dec. 31	Interest (3) ...	40

At 31st December, however, the service represented by the £40 in the Interest on Loan Account has been completely used up. That was a payment made for the loan of £1,000 for one year, and if he wants the service to continue he must make a fresh payment for any extension of the period. The £40 in the Interest on Loan Account is therefore written off to the Profit and Loss Account.

INTEREST ON LOAN ACCOUNT (3)

Dr.			Cr.		
19—		£	19—		£
Dec. 31	Bank (1)	40	Dec. 31	Profit & Loss A/c. (4)	40

PROFIT AND LOSS ACCOUNT (4)

Dr.		Cr.
	£	
Interest on Loan (3) ..	40	

If interest were paid in advance, only that part which had expired at the end of the accounting period would be transferred to the Profit and Loss Account.

If, on the other hand, interest were not paid until the loan had run for six months or a year, a certain amount of interest might be due at the end of the accounting period. The amount of interest to be debited to the Profit and Loss Account would be the total amount earned by the loan during the accounting period. Any sum due but unpaid at that time would be carried down as a credit balance in the Interest Account (see treatment of salaries due in Chapter 13).

Interest on Capital

Let us go back to the transaction with which this book began— A. Brown invested £10,000 in Eureka Motors. If he had preferred to do so, he could have invested it in Government Stock instead, and, assuming a rate of interest of 3 per cent, his income at the end of a year, without lifting a hand, would have been £300. And his money would have been perfectly safe.

Now let us suppose that, on taking out a Profit and Loss Account for Eureka Motors at the end of the first year, the net profit was found to be exactly £300. His net gain for undertaking the risks of running a business would have been nothing at all, because he could have obtained this sum without undertaking any risk. If his net profit had been only £250, he would actually have been £50 worse off than if he had simply lent his money. He cannot therefore be said to have made any profit at all until the earnings of the firm exceed the interest obtainable on his capital. For this reason, the profit is often divided into two parts: the one representing interest on capital; the other, the profit in the sense in which we have now defined it (*i.e.*, the return for undertaking the risks of running a business). These two parts are transferred to the Capital Account as separate figures. First the interest, which can be calculated, is debited to the Profit and Loss Account and credited to the Capital Account; then the remaining profit (or loss) is transferred in the ordinary way. This arrangement has the advantage of showing separately that part of the profit which represents the proprietor's income from running the business.

Below is an illustration assuming a capital of £10,000 and interest at the rate of 3 per cent.

PROFIT AND LOSS ACCOUNT OF . . .
FOR THE YEAR ENDED 31ST DECEMBER, 19—

Dr.			£				Cr. £
Amount of losses of various kinds..	..	..	.. 2,800	Gross Profit	...	...	... 4,000
Interest on Capital	..	..	300				
Net Profit	...	...	.. 900				
			£4,000				£4,000

CAPITAL ACCOUNT

Dr.				C.
19—			£	
Dec. 31	Balance c/d.		.. 11,200	
			£11,200	

19—				£
Jan. 1	Balance	...		.. 10,000
Dec. 31	Interest	...		.. 300
„ 31	Net Profit	...		.. 900
				£11,200
19—				
Jan. 1	Balance b/d			£11,200

Bank Loans and Overdrafts

It is the business of banks to lend money (that is their chief source of revenue), so most business men requiring money would apply to their bank.

There are two ways in which the bank may lend money—by bank loan or by overdraft. In both cases the bank would probably require security, *i.e.*, property that could be sold by the bank if the borrower defaulted when repayment was due, any money obtained for the sale in excess of the loan being returned to the borrower.

The entries required for a bank loan are similar to those for any other loan—debit the bank account, credit a bank loan account.

In the case of an overdraft, no entries are required. The bank merely gives permission to the trader to draw cheques up to a certain limit after his credit balance at the bank is exhausted. The result is that the Bank Account in the books of the trader shows a credit balance instead of a debit balance. This credit balance is the overdraft.

Whether the accommodation takes the form of a loan or of an overdraft, interest is charged by the bank. It will be credited to the Bank Account and debited either to the Interest Account or to the Bank Charges Account.

The rate of interest would be the same in each case, but the total amount of interest paid on a loan would exceed that paid for an overdraft unless the whole of the overdraft were taken on the first day. In the case of a loan interest is charged by the bank on the whole amount of the loan from the day it is given until the day it is repaid. In the case of an overdraft, the interest begins to run only from the day on which the account becomes overdrawn. It is then calculated daily, on the amount by which the account is overdrawn.

Carriage Inwards and Outwards

Carriage inwards is the service rendered by any carrying company (including railways, ships, etc.) in transporting to his place of business goods that a trader has bought. Carriage outwards is an exactly similar service, but is in respect of the goods the trader has sold to his customer.

In both cases the trader has received a service (*i.e.,* an asset) for which he must pay. And in both cases, the service has usually been rendered (and therefore used up) before it was paid for, and the whole cost must in consequence be deducted from profit when the Profit and Loss Account is drawn up.

Carriage inwards and outwards are not, however, treated in quite the same way. Carriage inwards must be regarded as part of the purchase price of the goods. Indeed, in many cases, the purchase price includes the cost of delivery to the buyer's place of business, no specific charge being made for carriage; and in those cases it is impossible to distinguish the amount paid for carriage. Because carriage inwards is part of the purchase price, it is deducted from the profit in the Trading Account.

Carriage outwards, on the other hand, is part of the cost of selling the goods, in the sense that the service would be quite unnecessary if no goods were sold. As selling expenses are entered in the Profit and Loss Account, the balance of the Carriage Outwards Account would be transferred to the Profit and Loss Account.

Illustration: A trader pays British Railways the sum £25, by cheque, for carriage of goods, of which £10 was in respect of goods bought and £15 in respect of goods sold.

BANK ACCOUNT (1)

Dr.			Cr.
			£
	Carriage Inwards (2) ..	..	10
	Carriage Outwards (3)	...	15

CARRIAGE INWARDS ACCOUNT (2)

Dr.					Cr.
	£				£
Bank (1)	10	Trading A/c. (4) ...	...		10

CARRIAGE OUTWARDS ACCOUNT (3)

Dr.					Cr.
	£				£
Bank (1)	15	Profit and Loss A/c. (5)	...		15

TRADING ACCOUNT (4)

Dr.			Cr.
	£		
Carriage Inwards (2)	10		

PROFIT AND LOSS ACCOUNT (5)

Dr.			Cr.
	£		
Carriage Outwards (3) ...	15		

WRITTEN EXERCISES

1. Prepare the Trading Account, Profit and Loss Account and Balance Sheet of J. Smith from the following:

			£	£
Office Equipment	...	...	136	
Purchases	..	...	7,854	
Salaries—Salesmen	..	...	1,615	
Rent	..	..	318	
Discount received	...	..		416
Insurance ..	...	...	45	
Bank	...	..		1,860
Sales	..	...		10,754
Debtors ..	..	..	3,750	
Discount allowed	..	..	128	
Stock, 1st July, 19–1 ..	..		1,653	
Creditors ..	..	..		1,817
Buildings ..	..	..	725	
Carriage Inwards	..	..	43	
Carriage Outwards	...	..	65	
Capital	...	...		1,485
			£16,332	£16,332

Adjustments
Insurance paid in advance £20.
Stock, 30th June, 19–2, £2,617.

2. From the following Trial Balance extracted from the books of Thomas Smith at 30th June, 19–2, prepare Trading Account, Profit and Loss Account, and Balance Sheet:

	£	£
Capital (1st July, 19–1) ..		2,500
Delivery Van (1st July, 19–1)	550	
Office Equipment (1st July, 19–1)	700	
Stock (1st July, 19–1).. ...	1,000	
Selling expenses	400	
Wages—salesmen	900	
Salaries..	375	
Carriage inwards	175	
Purchases	1,720	
Purchases returns		150
Sales		4,390
Sales returns	85	
Bad debts	80	
Rent	120	
Rates and taxes	40	
Interest..	25	
Insurance	10	
Sundry debtors	1,250	
Sundry creditors		680
Carriage outwards	130	
Cash in bank	160	
	£7,720	£7,720

Adjustments
Stock in hand, 30th June, 19–2, £870.
Insurance paid in advance £3.
Rent paid in advance £30.
Depreciate office equipment £70.

3. On 1st April, 19—, H. Mass borrowed £1,000 from K. Horne, at an agreed rate of interest of 4 per cent per annum, and twelve months' interest was paid on that date. On 30th September, £500 of the loan was repaid. Show (a) the Loan Account, (b) the Interest Account, as it would appear on 31st December of the same year, in the books of (a) H. Mass, (b) K. Horne.

4. The X Manufacturing Co. possesses machinery valued at £20,000 on 1st January, 19—. A maintenance staff is employed whose wages for the year were £750. Spare parts on hand on 1st January, 19—, were valued at £100. During the year, other parts, costing £120, were purchased, and the value of the unused spares on 31st December, 19—, was £80. New machinery was purchased on 30th June, 19—, at a cost of £5,000. Assuming depreciation, apart from repairs, to be at the rate of 15 per cent per annum, show

(a) The Machinery Account on 31st December, 19—.
(b) The Repairs Account on 31st December, 19—.

5. The following were the balances in the books of B. Abbot on 31st December, 19—:

	£ Dr.	£ Cr.
Cash at bank	300	
Purchases and sales ..	12,000	17,000
Purchases and sales returns	100	20
Stock, 1st Jan., 19–1 ..	4,000	
Carriage outwards	30	
Carriage inwards ..	10	
Loan: G. Murdie (1st Jan., 19–1)		2,000
Interest on loan	60	
Machinery (1st Jan., 19–1)	15,000	
Bad debts	120	
Repairs	600	
Drawings	1,200	
Sundry other expenses ..	400	
Wages and salaries ...	2,400	
Debtors and creditors ..	500	1,700
Capital (1st Jan., 19–1) ..		16,000
	£36,720	£36,720

Enter these balances in accounts and prepare a Trading Account and a Profit and Loss Account, allowing for the following:

(a) Depreciate machinery 10 per cent.
(b) The Repairs Account includes unused spare parts value £50.
(c) Stock, 31st Dec., 19–1, £4,800.
(d) Allow interest on capital at 4 per cent.

6. Show, in the correct accounts, the entries required to deal with the following matters:

(a) The writing off as bad debts of £55 due from A.; £19 from B.; and £27 from C.
(b) The transfer to Furniture and Fittings of £25, the cost of a typewriter, originally posted in error to the Office Expenses Account.
(c) The loss arising on the sale for £27 of a machine the book value of which is £55.   (R.S.A., modified.)

7. John William is a removal contractor. You examine his books and find that, during 19—, Repairs to Motor Vans Account had been wrongly debited with the cost of a new motor van £400; and with £15, being the cost of certain repairs to office premises.
In addition, you discover that a second-hand motor van, valued at £250, had been accepted from a debtor, Peters, in full settlement of his debt of £260, and that this transaction had not been recorded in William's books.
Open the necessary accounts, and show the entries required to record or correct these matters in the books of John William.   (Institute of Bankers, modified.)

8. A property-owning company employs an agent to collect rents, and to be responsible for repairs to the properties. He is paid for his services a commission of 5 per cent of the gross rents.
On 31st December, 19—, the agent sent the company a cheque for £4,150 representing rents collected £5,000, less cost of repairs £600, commission £250.
Open the necessary accounts and show the entries required to record these matters in the books of the company.   (Institute of Bankers, modified.)

9.   J. Whitehouse submits to you the following statement, compiled by his book-keeper, which purports to be a Trial Balance as at 31st March, 19–2. He instructs you to prepare Trading and Profit and Loss Accounts and Balance Sheet and informs you that the value of the Stock-in-Trade at 31st March, 19–2, was £2,166.

	Dr. £	Cr. £
Capital Account, Balance at 1st April, 19–1		4,100
Current Account, Balance at 1st April, 19–1		218
Cash at Bank, Balance at 31st Mar., 19–1	564	
Stock-in-Trade at 1st April, 19–2	1,896	
Purchases	2,550	
Sales		6,568
Rent and Rates	266	
Rates paid in advance at 31st Mar., 19–2		72
Wages	2,899	
Returns Outwards	93	
Office Salaries	256	
Bad Debts recovered	34	
Sundry Trade Expenses	458	
Plant and Machinery	1,260	
Discounts received	31	
Drawings during year	737	
Sundry Creditors	646	
Due from customers		732
	£11,690	£11,690

Carry out J. Whitehouse's instructions and state what comments, if any, you would make when sending him the accounts.
                    (*Association of Certified and Corporate Accountants.*)

16

PURCHASES, SALES, AND RETURNS JOURNALS

In the practical applications of the principles of accounts, two new considerations must be introduced. These two considerations are:

(a) The need for documentary evidence of the correctness of entries. Such documents are known as 'vouchers'.

(b) The system of account must be adapted to record very large numbers of transactions.

The Need for Documentary Evidence

This is required for the following reasons:

(i) As proof that the books provide an honest record of transactions.

(ii) To provide the book-keeper with information of the transactions that have taken place. Obviously he could not depend on oral instructions and his own memory.

Recording Large Numbers of Transactions

If the information given by an account is to be readily assimilated, the number of entries in the account must be kept to a minimum. This is achieved by substituting totals in place of details wherever possible.

The chief business of any trading concern must obviously be the purchase and sale of goods. It follows that transactions of this nature must be very numerous indeed, and the task of recording them may have to be spread over many people. The principles governing these entries have already been laid down in previous discussions, but the actual methods employed must now be examined.

Purchases

If goods are purchased on credit, the seller will send an invoice to the buyer. This invoice is the document from which the entry of the purchase is made by the buyer. An example of an invoice is given on the next page:

Tel.: ROTH. 49231

No. 1420
3 Coppice Road,
Rothwick.
15th March, 19—

MESSRS. CHUTER & LION,
   25, Easton Road,
      Barlow.

Bought of PARKDALE PUBLISHING CO. LTD.
TERMS: $2\frac{1}{2}\%$ for cash in month following delivery.

Order No.		Price	£	£
136	20 copies 'White Cliffs'..	£0·075	1·50	
	Less $12\frac{1}{2}\%$		0·19	1·31
140	36 copies Mathematical Tables ..	net £0·05		1·80
140	72 Atlases	net £0·20		14·40
				17·51
Carriage	— — — — —			0·27
				17·78

The record of this purchase in the books of Chuter & Lion would
be a debit entry in the Purchases Account and a credit entry in the
account of The Parkdale Publishing Co. Ltd. If Messrs. Chuter & Lion
made one hundred such purchases during a month, all from different
firms, there would be

(*a*) One hundred entries on the debit side of the Purchases
Account.

(*b*) One hundred entries on the credit side of the ledger; one, that
is, to the credit of each of one hundred firms.

The entries under (*b*) are unavoidable. Messrs. Chuter & Lion
require to know how much they owe to each individual creditor. The
Purchases Account, however, would be much more readily understood
if it contained only one entry consisting of the total value of the hundred
purchases. These invoices, therefore, are first listed in a book known
as the 'Purchases Journal', or the 'Purchases Day Book', or simply
the 'Purchases Book'. From this list the total of the purchases is
obtained, and this total is transferred to the Purchases Account in the
ledger. Each individual transaction (*i.e.,* the total of each invoice) is
credited to the account of the seller. In this way, the double entry
is completed with the minimum number of entries in the accounts. The
process is shown diagrammatically below:

ENTRIES FOR CREDIT PURCHASES

Debit side of Ledger	*Credit side of Ledger*
Enter total of credit purchases on debit side of Purchases Account.	Enter each credit purchase on credit side of seller's Account.

Form of Purchases Book

A Purchases Book is merely a list showing the name of the seller and the amount of the debt. The invoices are numbered consecutively as they are entered and filed in that order.

The Purchases Book of Messrs. Chuter & Lion is shown below. It should be studied in the light of the notes which follow.

PURCHASES BOOK

3

19—					Invoice No.	Ledger Folio	£
Mar.	15	Parkdale Publishing Co. Ltd.	...	...	136	46	17·78
„	20	Stockwell & Sons ..	...	..	137	112	12·50
„	25	E. Coldstone Ltd.	...	...	138	29	43·00
		Total to Purchases A/c. Dr.	...	...		6	73·28

PURCHASES ACCOUNT (6)

Dr.   Cr.

19—		£
Mar. 31	Sundries P.B.3	73·28

E. COLDSTONE LTD. (29)

Dr.   Cr.

	19—		£
	Mar. 25	Purchases P.B.3	43·00

PARKDALE PUBLISHING CO. LTD. (46)

Dr.   Cr.

	19—		£
	Mar. 15	Purchases P.B.3	17·78

STOCKWELL & SONS (112)

Dr.   Cr.

	19—		£
	Mar. 20	Purchase P.B.3	12·50

Notes
(i) Only credit transactions are entered in the Purchases Book. A cash purchase must be entered—

(1) On the credit side of the Cash Account or the Bank Account.
(2) On the debit side of the Purchases Account.

(Obviously if cash is paid, it must be entered in the Cash Account or Bank Account. It would be wrong to enter it in the Purchases Book also because then the same purchases would be included *twice* in the Purchases Account.)

(ii) The primary purpose of the Purchases Book is to collect totals for entry in the Purchases Account; therefore only purchases of 'merchandise' *i.e.,* goods bought for the purpose of resale, are entered in the Purchases Book.

(iii) The Purchases Book is usually totalled monthly. This reduces the number of entries in the Purchases Account for credit purchases to twelve per year. Clearly it could be totalled only once per year, but it is usually important to know, for purposes of comparison, the monthly variation in the amount.

(iv) Though the total of the Purchases Book is carried to the Purchases Account only once a month, the personal accounts of the sellers must be kept up to date through daily entries. The information may be wanted at a moment's notice.

(v) There are now three stages in the ascertainment of the amount of purchases:

(1) Each individual purchase is first entered in the Purchases Book or the Cash Account.
(2) The monthly totals of the Purchases Book of the Cash Purchases are 'collected' in the Purchases Account.
(3) The combined total is transferred from the Purchases Account to the Trading Account.

It will be seen later that there are the same three stages in the entry of sales and of returns (both inwards and outwards).

(vi) The figure entered in the Purchases Book is the net amount of the invoice *less* any trade discount *plus* any additions such as carriage purchase tax, etc. (see page 115 – concerning trade discount).

Purchases Returns (or Returns Outwards)

Let us suppose that the trader who bought the goods shown on the invoice on page 131 returned eight copies of 'White Cliffs' stating that only twelve were ordered. The price per copy was 7½p but it was subject to trade discount at the rate of 12½ per cent. The trader would therefore have been charged 60p ($8 \times 7\frac{1}{2}$p) for the books, less 7½p trade discount—that is, 52½p. When they were returned, all he could claim would be 52½p.

On receipt of the returned goods the seller would send a document called a 'Credit Note' to the buyer. It is always the seller who sends the documents in connection with the charge on a transaction. On a credit note (C/N), which is usually printed in red to prevent any possibility of its being mistaken for an invoice or a debit note, a full explanation of the reason for the allowance is given. An example is shown on page 134:

CREDIT NOTE

Tel. ROTH. 49231

No. 117
3 Coppice Road,
Rothwick.
28th March, 19—

MESSRS. CHUTER & LION,
25 Easton Road
Barlow.

Credit by PARKDALE PUBLISHING CO. LTD.

Order No. 136		£
8 copies 'White Cliffs' sent in excess of order.		
Invoiced 15 March No. 1420		0·60
Less Trade Discount 12½%		0·07
		0·53

The purpose of a credit note is to reduce the amount charged on the invoice; and there are many possible reasons, besides the return of goods, for this being done. The price charged, for instance, may be higher than the agreed price; trade discount may have been omitted; or there may be an arithmetical error on the invoice, resulting in an overcharge.

Whatever the reason for sending it, the buyer who received it would enter it in the same way. It would be listed in a book called the Purchases Returns Book (or Journal) or the Returns Outwards Book. As it was entered, it would be numbered, in the same way as the invoices were numbered, and filed in numerical order. At monthly intervals, the total of the Purchases Returns Book would be *credited* to the Purchases Returns Account. Each return (*i.e.*, the amount of each credit note), would be debited to the account of the seller.

An example of a Purchases Returns Book for Messrs. Chuter & Lion, with the entries in the ledger, is given below:

11   PURCHASES RETURNS BOOK

19—		C/N No.	Folio	£
Mar. 14	F. Wilson & Son	18	38	3·12
Mar. 20	D. Forbes & Co.	19	77	0·66
Mar. 28	Parkdale Publishing Co. Ltd.	20	46	0·53
Mar. 28	Total to Purchases Returns A/c. Cr. ...		15	4·31

PURCHASES RETURNS ACCOUNT (15)

Dr.		Cr.
	19—	£
	Mar. 31 Sundries P.R.B.11	4·31

PARKDALE PUBLISHING CO. LTD. (46)

Dr.			Cr.
19— Mar. 28	Returns P.R.B.11	£ 0·53	

F. WILSON & SON (38)

Dr.			Cr.
19— Mar. 14	Returns P.R.B.11	£ 3·12	

D. FORBES & CO. (77)

Dr.			Cr.
19— Mar. 20	Overcharge Purchase Tax Tax P.R.B.11	£ 0·66	

Sales and Sales Returns

When a sale takes place on credit, the seller sends an invoice to the buyer, from which the buyer enters his Purchases Book.

The invoice is made out in duplicate, and the seller retains a copy. This copy is the voucher from which a Sales Journal (or 'Sales Day Book', or simply 'Sales Book') is written up.

The Sales Book is identical in form with the Purchases Book, but the records in the ledger accounts are on the opposite sides:

(a) The total of the Sales Book is credited to the Sales Account, usually monthly.

(b) Each individual sale is debited in the account of the buyer, an individual sale being defined as the net total appearing on any one invoice.

In the same way, the seller retains a copy of each credit note he sends. From these copies, a Sales Returns Book (or Journal) is prepared; this, again, is simply a list in exactly the same form as the Purchases Returns Book already shown. In recording these in the ledger

(a) The total of the Sales Returns Book (or Returns Inwards Book) is debited at certain intervals, to the Sales Returns Account (or the Returns Inwards Account).

(b) Each separate allowance is credited in the account of the buyer when the credit note is sent.

The procedure outlined in this chapter is summarized in the table given on page 136:

PURCHASES, SALES AND RETURNS

Name of Book	Voucher	Ledger Postings	
		Debit	Credit
Purchases	Invoice	Total to Purchases Account	Items to accounts of sellers
Purchases Returns	Credit Note	Items to accounts of sellers	Total to Purchases Returns Account
Sales	Copy of Invoice	Items to accounts of buyers	Total to Sales Account
Sales Returns	Copy of Credit Note	Total to Sales Returns Account	Items to accounts of buyers

Illustrative Example No. 1

Enter the following information in the appropriate journals, post to the ledger and prepare a trial balance on 3rd July, 19—, for a business which has been operating for several years.

The account numbers for some accounts are:

Sales	1	Pace V.	32
Sales Returns	2	Paterson M.	34
Purchases	3	Percy P.	37
Purchases Returns	4		
Jackson T.	22		
James J.	23		
Jones M.	25		

The pages of the journals to be used are:

Sales Journal	64
Purchases Journal	72
Sales Returns Journal	27
Purchases Returns Journal	21

From carbon copies of invoices issued

19—				£
July 2	No. 730	James J.		100
	731	Jones M.		80
	732	Jackson T.		50

From invoices received

19—				£
July 1	No. 820	Percy P.		130
	821	Pace V.		20
2	822	Paterson M.		70

From carbon copies of credit notes issued

19—				£
July 3	No. 313	James J.		10
	314	Jones M.		5

From credit notes received

July 2	No. 211	Percy P.		15
3	212	Pace V.		5

SALES JOURNAL 64

Date 19—	Particulars	Invoice No.	L.F.	Amount £
July 2	James J.	730	23	100
	Jones M.	31	25	80
	Jackson T.	32	22	50
			1	230

PURCHASES JOURNAL 72

Date 19—	Particulars	Invoice No.	L.F.	Amount £
July 1	Percy P.	820	37	130
	Pace V.	21	32	20
2	Paterson M.	22	34	70
			3	220

PURCHASES RETURNS JOURNAL 21

Date 19—	Particulars	Credit Note No.	L.F.	Amount £
July 2	Percy P.	211	37	15
	Pace V.	12	32	5
			4	20

SALES RETURNS JOURNAL 27

Date 19—	Particulars	Credit Note No.	L.F.	Amount £
July 3	James J.	313	23	10
	Jones M.	14	25	5
			2	15

LEDGER SALES 1

	19— July	3	Debtors	S64	£ 230

SALES RETURNS 2

19— July	3	Debtors	SR27	£ 15	

PURCHASES   3

19— July	3	Creditors	P72	£ 220					

PURCHASES RETURNS   4

					19— July	3	Creditors	PR21	£ 20

JACKSON T.   22

19— July	2	Sales	S64	£ 50					

JAMES J.   23

19— July	2	Sales	S64	£ 100	19— July	3	Returns	SR27	£ 10

JONES M.   25

19— July	2	Sales	S64	£ 80	19— July	3	Returns	SR27	£ 5

PACE V.   32

19— July	2	Returns	PR21	£ 5	19— July	1	Purchases	P72	£ 20

PATERSON M.   34

					19— July	2	Purchases	P72	£ 70

PERCY P.   37

19— July	2	Returns	PR21	£ 15	19— July	1	Purchases	P72	£ 130

TRIAL BALANCE
AS AT 3RD JULY, 19—

Dr.	Account No.	£		Account No.	Cr. £
Sales Returns	2	15	Sales	1	230
Purchases	3	220	Purchases Returns	4	20
Jackson T.	22	50	Pace V.	32	15
James J.	23	90	Paterson M.	34	70
Jones M.	25	75	Percy P.	37	115
		£450			£450

Subsidiary Books

These four books are known as 'subsidiary books', as distinct from the ledger, the ledger being a book in which accounts are kept. The whole purpose for which subsidiary books are kept is to provide information in classified form preparatory to entry in the ledger.

They are also known as 'books of original entry', because the relevant documents are first entered in them (and then filed). *The entries in the ledger are made in all cases from the appropriate subsidiary books.*

Posting

The operation of transferring entries from a subsidiary book to the ledger is known as 'posting'.

Spreading the Work

Most businesses have more accounts than can be contained in a single ledger. The accounts may, in fact, be so numerous that many ledgers are required, and the responsibility for entering them is spread over a number of people. It is necessary then to classify the accounts and keep each group in a separate ledger. The following is a common classification, grouped according to the ledger used:

(a) *Nominal Ledger*

In this, the accounts of assets that have no tangible existence are kept. They are the accounts whose balances are transferred to the Profit and Loss Account. Examples are Wages, Rent, Commission, General Expenses, Heating and Lighting, etc.—all in the nature of services that cannot be stored. Such accounts are called Nominal Accounts.

(b) *General Ledger*

The accounts of other assets are kept in this ledger. Such accounts are called Real Accounts, because they represent tangible assets, such as Vans, Machinery, Furniture.

(c) *Private Ledger*

Accounts of a confidential nature, such as the Capital Account, Drawings Account, Trading Account, Profit and Loss Account, are kept in this ledger.

(d) *Bought Ledger*

This is used for the accounts of firms from whom purchases are made. It would be rare, obviously, for such an account to have a debit balance. Accounts showing how much is owed to, or by, specific people, are called Personal Accounts.

(e) *Sales Ledger (or Ledgers)*

These, again, contain personal accounts, usually debtors. As these accounts are numerous, there may be several Sales Ledgers, the customers being grouped alphabetically, geographically, or by some other classification.

Each ledger would commonly be entered by a different clerk. If there are several Sales Ledgers, one clerk might be responsible for two of them. For each Sales Ledger, there would probably be two Sales Books (kept by a different clerk), to enable the present day's sales to be entered in one Sales Book, whilst the Sales Book used on the previous day was being posted in the Sales Ledger.

The existence of a large number of ledgers raises difficulties in checking. These will be dealt with in a later chapter on Self-balancing Ledgers.

Statement of Account

The majority of sales in business, apart from sales over the counter in the retail trade, are made on credit. The credit terms—*i.e.*, the length of the period before payment is due, and the amount of cash discount (if any) allowed—vary considerably from trade to trade. A common arrangement is that all goods purchased in one month should be paid for before a fixed day in the following month. Before the due date, it is customary for the creditor to send a statement to the debtor showing the amount owed. It is a copy of the debtor's account as it appears in the ledger of the creditor, and is known as a 'Statement of Accounts' or more briefly a 'Statement'.

A statement must not be confused with an invoice. An invoice gives detailed information of a particular transaction, showing the nature, price, quantity, and quality of the goods bought. A statement gives the date, nature, and amount of every transaction that has taken place during the period for which payment is due; it gives, that is to say, just the information that is contained in the ledger account.

An example of an account and of the statement which would be prepared from it are shown below:

T. BROWN & CO. LTD. ACCOUNT

19—			£	19—			£
Feb. 1	Balance	...	150·52	Feb. 8	Cheque	...	100·00
„ 10	Sales	...	46·33	„ 15	Returns ...	...	6·12
„ 18	„	...	37·50				
„ 25	„	...	5·75				

Statement sent 3/3/19—
(to 25/2/19—)

STATEMENT

Tel. WHA. 2773

Fernley Mills,
Seatswood Road,
Wharton.
3rd March, 19—

Messrs. T. Brown & Co. Ltd.,
   Thorpe Street,
      Merrill.
Dr. to Angle & Bell Ltd.
   Terms: Net cash before 10th of month following purchase.

							£	£
								150·52
Feb. 1	Account Rendered	..	...	..	..			
„ 10	Goods ..	..	..	..	..		44·33	
„ 18	„ ..	..	..	..	..		37·50	
„ 25	„ ..	..	...	..	...		5·75	87·58
								238·10
Feb. 8	Cheque ..	..	...	...	..	..	100·00	
„ 15	Returns ..	...	...	...	...	...	6·12	106·12
								£131·98

Messrs. Angle & Bell Ltd. make a pencil note on the account in their ledger to the effect that the statement has been sent. This is for future guidance, in case the money is not received.

On receipt of the statement, Messrs. T. Brown & Co. Ltd. would check it against the account of Angle & Bell Ltd. in their own books. If it were correct they should return the statement with a remittance before 10th March. It would be receipted (probably with an adhesive receipt) by Angle & Bell Ltd., who would then return it to T. Brown & Co., by whom it would be retained as proof of payment.

Accounting Machines

A great deal of time can be saved by the use of accounting machines. These consist in essence of a machine similar to a typewriter combined with one or more mechanical adding 'registers' which enable totals and balances to be worked out automatically as the entries are typed. Clearly a bound ledger cannot be inserted in the machine, so a loose-leaf system must be adopted, but this has the advantage that several accounting records can be entered in one operation. For instance, when a sale is made a carbon copy of the invoice is retained. Instead of entering this in a Sales Journal and posting laboriously by hand, three sheets are inserted in the machine and typed simultaneously through carbon paper. These are:

(a) A Sales Posting Summary. This is retained in the machine, and as each invoice is entered on the Ledger Account it is reproduced on the Summary and the total of all invoices is automatically added. The Sales Posting Summary thus becomes the Sales Journal.

(b) The Ledger Account of the customer. The double entry is thus completed in the same operation and the possibility of a different figure being entered in the account is eliminated. At the same time one of the adding 'registers' which is linked to the typing keys, works out the resultant balance, which is inserted in an appropriate column on the account after each transaction.

(c) The Statement of Account. This is thus always ready when required and is an exact copy of the Ledger Account.

The adding 'register' on the accounting machine recording debit entries in all debtors' accounts and statements each day should produce a total which will agree with the total of the day's credit sales as summarized from the carbon copies of invoices. Similarly another register is used for recording credits and the total which it produces should agree with the total value of the carbon copies of receipts and credit notes, which will have been predetermined. With one type of accounting machine the typist reads the balance shown in a visible adding and subtracting register on the right hand side of the machine and types this balance on the statement and ledger account simultaneously. If copied correctly, a star will print after the balance figure and the amount in the register will return to nil. If the operator copies the balance incorrectly the star will not print and the keyboard will lock. More elaborate accounting machines will automatically print the balance after each posting. As accounting machines will type the date by depressing only one key, the words '3 MCH '75' illustrate this operation in the statement shown. At the commencement of work each day the machine must be re-set for the new date.

There is clearly a great saving of time when so many records are produced in one operation, and the risk of error is greatly reduced. It can be still further reduced by the introduction of a system of checks. For example, when invoices are typed on one of these machines, the total of the invoices is obtained at the same time. This should balance with the total of the Sales Posting Summary. Some risk, however, still remains. A wrong figure may be typed in the original invoice or an entry may be entirely omitted. These contingencies are usually met by a system of internal audit to ensure the accuracy and completeness of all prime records.

These machines can be used to cover all book-keeping procedures— Purchases Ledger posting, wages and salary records, cashiers' records, etc. When cash receipts are mechanically written, the receipt, the bank deposit slip, and the entry in the Cash Receipts Journal (see next chapter) are automatically printed and added at the same time.

It cannot be too strongly emphasized that the accounting principles employed are precisely the same whether the entry is done by machine or by hand.

An illustration of an account and statement prepared by the one mechanical operation is shown below:

Account No.	Sheet No.	NAME: T. BROWN & CO. LTD. Address: THORPE STREET, MENTONE.	KEY to Departments 1. Men's & Boys 2. Lingerie 3. Furnishings
924	7		

Date	Particulars	Ref.	Debit	Credit	Balance	Analysis of Balance: Month	Analysis of Balance: Acc'nt	Progressive Dept. Sales: Dept.	Progressive Dept. Sales: Amount
1 Mch '75	Bal/Fwd.				32·33*				
3 Mch '75	Men's	687	20·50*		52·83*				
6 Mch '75	Cash	6231		31·52	21·31*				
6 Mch '75	Disc.			0·81	20·50*				

ANGLE & BELL LTD.

SEATSWOOD ROAD,
BURNLEY,
P.O. Box 1976
Tel. 42.2773

MENTONE
T. BROWN & CO. LTD.
THORPE STREET.

STATEMENT FOR MONTH OF MARCH 1975

Details of Account Rendered					BALANCE DUE
Memo.	90 days and over	60 days overdue	30 days overdue	Last month	
				32·33	32·33*
Date	Particulars	Ref.	DEBIT	CREDIT	
3 Mch '75	Men's	687	20·50		52·83*
6 Mch '75	Cash	6231		31·52	21·31*
6 Mch '75	Disc.			0·81	20·50*

E. & O.E. This statement is made up to the end of the month.

Terms: Cash 30 days.

The last amount in this column is the sum owing.

WRITTEN EXERCISES

1. Enter into a suitable Sales Book, and post to the ledger accounts, the following transactions of L. Nelson, whose business is that of a wholesale clothing merchant:

19—
Mar. 13. Hawkins: Girls' boots £150.
" 14. Grenville: Men's velour hats £87·50.
" 15. Frobisher: Boys' coats £47·40.
" 16. Drake: Ladies' coats £189.
" 17. Woolf: Men's boots £6·85.
" 18. Kitchener: Jerseys £18·75.
" 19. Alexander: Ladies' hats £25.

When writing up the Sales Book you should bear in mind that trade discount should be allowed as follows:

Millinery	..	..	25%
Footwear	..	..	20%
General Clothing	..		10%

(Institute of Book-keepers, modified.)

2. Enter into a suitable Sales Book, and post to ledger accounts, the following transactions of J. Hammond, whose business is that of a clothing merchant:

19—
June 21. Sold to Beatty & Co.: 10 doz. boys' coats £385.
" 22. " Jellicoe Bros.: 4 doz. men's felt hats £71·20.
" 23. " Fishers Ltd.: 20 doz. pairs girls' boots £258.
" 23. " Somerville & Co.: 2 doz. ladies' hats £71·40.
" 25. " Beatty & Co.: 6 ladies' cloaks £33.
" 25. " Beatty & Co.: 60 pullovers £120.
" 26. " Somerville & Co.: 6 only boys' coats £16·20.

(Institute of Book-keepers, modified.)

3. On 1st March, 19—, William Addison, of 124 High Street, Westchurch, bought goods from John Langley, of 1005 Stamford Hill, London, as follows:

4 oak tables at £25 each
6 oak chairs at £4 each.
2 rugs at £18 each.
1 Axminster carpet, £60.
1 oak sideboard, £50.

The account is subject to 20 per cent trade discount and 5 per cent discount for cash, paid by the 15th of the following month.
Prepare:
(*a*) Invoice, dated 1st March, 19—
(*b*) Statement, dated 31st March, 19—.

(Institute of Book-keepers, modified.)

4. From the following information prepare the Purchases Book of N. Blank & Co., and post to the ledger:

Feb. 7. Purchased on credit from L. Morse—
job lot of ornaments £57·85
and 5 powder compacts at £2·50 each.
" 12. Purchased, on credit, from T. Warren & Co. Ltd.—
25 alarm clocks at £1·05 each.
5 pearl necklaces at £3·75 each.
All subject to 25 per cent trade discount.
Carriage £0·22.
" 18. Purchased, on credit, from F. Garvey—
10 cigarette cases at £2·50 each.
1 gross wristlet straps at £0·20
Trade discount 25 per cent.

5. The following credit notes were received by L. Beal & Co.:

Jan. 8. From Utility Trading Co.—
   36 yards printed cotton invoiced (No. 14) at 15p per yard, less 12½ per cent trade discount.
   Quality not up to sample.
  16. From D. Isaacs Ltd.—
   3 dresses, invoice No. 29, at £4 each.
   Stained in transit.

In which book would they be entered? Show and post this book.

6. The following credit notes were given by S. Lewis, hardware merchant:

Mar. 2. To Messrs. R. Court. 1 washing machine of unsuitable type returned.
   (Invoice No. 3341)   £38·62
  22. To S. Westman. Tools missing from consignment dispatched on March 15.
   (Invoice No. 3867)   £4·50
  23. To E. Coulthard. Allowance on price of 6 yards of linoleum, charged at £0·925 per yard, should be £0·875 per yard.
   (Invoice No. 4118)

Enter these credit notes in the appropriate subsidiary book and post to ledger accounts.

7. W. Park is in business as a tobacconist and has the following assets and liabilities on 1st January, 19—:

Cash at bank £400: stock £2,000; L. Clay (debtor) £200; R. Burns (creditor) £100; van £700; lease (10 years to run) £3,000; furniture and fittings £800; capital £7,000.

Open accounts and enter balances.

Jan. 1. Drew from bank for office cash £50.
  3. Paid rates for year by cheque £240.
  5. L. Clay paid his account by cheque and was allowed £5 discount.
  6. Paid R. Burns by cheque (balance allowed as discount) £98.
  8. Sold goods on credit to H. Wells £1,000.
  10. Purchased typewriter on credit from S. Lang £50.
  11. H. Wells returned goods (unsuitable) £15.
  12. Purchased goods on credit from R. Burns £200.
  15. Purchased goods by cheque £1,000.
  18. Sold goods on credit to L. Clay £500.
  20. General expenses paid in cash £10.
  24. Drawn by cheque for private expenses £50.
  31. Sales (banked) £1,400.

Enter these transactions, post to accounts, take out a Trial Balance, Trading Account, and Profit and Loss Account, and show the Balance Sheet of W. Park on 31st January, 19—. Make what transfers to the Profit and Loss Account you think necessary, and take note of the following:

(1) Stock, 31st January, 19—, £1,500.
(2) Depreciate van by £20 and the furniture and fittings by 5 per cent.

8. K. Kernow is in business as a merchant.
You are requested to—

(a) select those transactions necessary to write up his Sales Journal, Purchases Journal, and Returns Inwards Journal for the month; and
(b) indicate alongside the total of each journal the account and the side (debit or credit) to which the TOTAL will be posted.

			£
Mar.	1.	Sold goods on credit to L. Limp, Invoice No. 70 .. ---	75
„	4.	Part of these goods were returned, Credit Note No. 20 ..	15
„	7.	Received an invoice representing goods purchased on credit from M. Manley	56
„	11.	Drew cheque to purchase goods from D. Dwyer	27
„	17.	Sent invoice No. 71 to K. Kay for goods delivered today ..	48
„	19.	Forwarded Credit Note No. 21 to K. Kay for goods returned	11
„	22.	Purchased from B. Budge chairs and tables for the office	27
„	23.	Returned two damaged chairs to B. Budge	4
„	27.	Received cash for goods sold this day to H. Hopkins ..	37
„	30.	B. Bourke sold us goods on credit £45, less trade discount £5 net	40
„	31.	Sold a surplus typewriter to S. Snow	15

(Univ. of Melb. Inter. Cert.)

17

CASH RECEIPTS AND PAYMENTS JOURNALS

ALMOST every transaction results in the receipt or payment of money. From this it follows that the Cash and Bank Accounts would be extremely long. To reduce the detail appearing in these accounts, therefore, lists are made of money received in a Cash Receipts Journal and of money paid in a Cash Payments Journal. These lists are used, like the Purchases and Sales Journals, for the posting of the ledger, only the totals appearing in the Cash and Bank Accounts. A further advantage of this method is that, without access to the accounts, clerks entering these journals would not know the balances of cash, information which would usually be regarded as confidential.

Cash Discount

Cash discount for prompt payment is allowed at the time payment is made. It is therefore convenient that it should be listed in the cash journals, discount allowed in the Cash Receipts Journal and discount received in the Cash Payments Journal.

Vouchers for Receipts and Payments of Cash

I. *Cash Received*

For cash received from an outside source (*i.e.*, from debtors) a receipt is given. It is usually made out in duplicate in a receipt book. The top copy is gummed and perforated. It is torn out, attached to the statement which usually accompanies the remittance (see page 141) and sent to the payer. The other copy remains in the book as a permanent record, and it is from this copy that entries are made in the Cash Receipts Journal.

II. *Cheques received*

It is unusual to give receipts for money received by cheque unless asked for by the customer since the cheque itself is proof of payment. The statement commonly includes a tear-off portion which is returned with the cheque and which provides the voucher from which entries are made.

III. *Payments by Cheque*

When a cheque is drawn, a counterfoil, which remains in the cheque book and bears the same number as the cheque, is filled in, showing the full details of the payment. The bank column of the Cash Payments Journal is entered from these counterfoils.

IV. *Cash Payments*

When payment is made in cash a receipt will usually be obtained from the person to whom the payment is made. Alternatively a record will appear in a Wages Book or Petty Cash Book (see Chapter 18) or a note will be made (for such payments as tips).

V. *Payment of Office Cash into the Bank*

This is entered from the paying-in slip book (see page 168). The cash is entered in the cash column of the Cash Payments Journal and the bank column of the Cash Receipts Journal. The cheques, listed separately, are entered in the bank column of the Cash Receipts Journal when received and therefore no transfer is needed.

VI. *Bank Charges, Bank Interest, etc.*

When the bank makes a charge for its services, either for working the account or for lending money, the only intimation received from them is an entry in the pass book. It will usually appear at the end of June and December. At these times, therefore, an entry will be made in the Cash Payments Journal from the figures in the pass book.

Entering Cash Journals

The method of entering the cash journals is shown in the following example:

19—
Mar. 1. Cash in hand £30. Cash at Bank £200.
  „ 2. Cash sales £50.
  „ 2. Received cheque from S. Green £40. Allowed him discount £1.
  „ 3. Paid O. White cash £24 in settlement of a debt of £25.
  „ 4. Paid J. Black £83 by cheque, having deducted discount of £2.
  „ 5. Paid sundry expenses in cash £10.
  „ 5. Received cash £19 from T. Pink. Discount £1.
  „ 6. Paid £10 into the bank from office cash.

CASH RECEIPTS JOURNAL (fol. 101)

Date		Particulars	Receipt No.	Ledger Fol.	Discount Allowed	Cash	Bank
					£	£	£
19—							
March	2	Sales		5		50	
„	2	S. Green	232	6	1		40
„	5	T. Pink	233	7	1	19	
„	6	Cash		C			10
					£2	£69	£50
					fol. 3	fol. 1	fol. 2

CASH PAYMENTS JOURNAL (fol. 96)

Date		Particulars	Cheque No.	Ledger Fol.	Discount Received	Cash	Bank
					£	£	£
19—							
March	3	O. White		8	1	24	
,,	4	J. Black	1395	9	2		83
,,	5	Expenses		10		10	
,,	6	Bank		C		10	
					£3	£44	£83
					fol 4	fol. 1	fol. 2

Notes (to be read in conjunction with the accounts below)

(i) The balances in hand are the balances shown in the accounts in the ledger.

(ii) At certain intervals (*e.g.* daily or weekly) the totals of the columns of the Cash Receipts Journal are posted to the debit side of the accounts named, *i.e.*:

    (1) £2 on the debit side of the Discount Allowed Account.

    (2) £69 on the debit side of the Cash Account.

    (3) £50 on the debit side of the Bank Account.

(iii) The items in the Cash Receipts Journal, other than transfers of cash to bank or vice versa, would be posted to the credit side of the accounts named, *i.e.*:

    (1) The cash sales £50 on 2nd March would be credited to Sales Account.

    (2) The discount allowed £1 and the cheque £40 received from S. Green on 2nd March would be credited to his account.

    (3) Similarly, discount £1 and cash £19 would be credited in the account of T. Pink.

(iv) If cash is paid into the bank from office cash the Bank Account should be debited (because the amount in the bank is increased) and the Cash Account credited (because the amount of cash in the office is reduced). This happens automatically when the totals of the cash journals are posted, *i.e.*, the £50 posted to the debit side of the Bank Account and the £44 posted to the credit side of the Cash Account both include the £10 paid into the bank—and therefore no individual posting is made. The letter 'C' (an abbreviation of 'contra') indicates that no posting is to be made.

(v) It is important that in the particulars column the name of the account to which the posting is to be made should be shown.

(vi) The posting of the Cash Payments Journal is similar except that the sides are reversed, *i.e.*, totals are posted periodically to the credit side of the Discount Received Account, the Cash Account and the Bank Account, and the items to the debit side of the accounts named in the particulars column.

The postings are shown below:

CASH ACCOUNT (1)

Dr.							Cr.
19—			£	19—			£
Mar.	1	Balance b/d	30	Mar.	6	Sundries CPJ 96	44
,,	6	Sundries CRJ 101	69	,,	6	Balance c/d	55
			£99				£99
Mar.	7	Balance b/d	55				

BANK ACCOUNT (2)

Dr.								Cr.
19—			£	19—				£
Mar.	1	Balance b/d	200	Mar.	6	Sundries CPJ 96		83
,,	6	Sundries CRJ 101	50	,,	6	Balance c/d		167
			£250					£250
Mar.	7	Balance b/d	167					

DISCOUNT ALLOWED ACCOUNT (3)

Dr.							Cr.
19—			£				
Mar.	6	Sundries CRJ 101	2				

DISCOUNT RECEIVED ACCOUNT (4)

Dr.							Cr.
				19—			£
				Mar.	6	Sundries CPJ 96	3

SALES ACCOUNT (5)

Dr.							Cr.
				19—			£
				Mar.	2	Cash CRJ 101	50

S. GREEN ACCOUNT (6)

Dr.							Cr.
				19—			£
				Mar.	2	Cash CRJ 101	40
				,,	2	Discount CRJ 101	1

T. PINK ACCOUNT (7)

Dr.							Cr.
				19—			£
				Mar.	5	Cash CRJ 101	19
				,,	5	Discount CRJ 101	1

O. WHITE ACCOUNT (8)

Dr.							Cr.
19—			£				
Mar.	3	Cash CPJ 96	24				
,,	3	Discount CPJ 96	1				

J. BLACK ACCOUNT (9)

Dr.   Cr.

19—			£		
Mar.	4	Cash CPJ 96	83		
„	4	Discount CPJ 96	2		

EXPENSES ACCOUNT (10)

Dr.   Cr.

19—			£		
Mar.	5	Cash CPJ 96	10		

Use of Cash

It is usually a rule, in businesses of any size, that all payments should be made by cheque if possible, and not in cash, because cheques are safer and more convenient, and a record of the payment is made on the cheque counterfoil and in the books of the bank. Where cash must be used, as for wages (at present) or small items such as postage, a cheque is drawn to cover the total cost, and usually this cheque, and only this cheque, is entered in the Cash Payments Journal, the details of the actual cash payments being recorded in a Wages Book or Petty Cash Book (see next chapter). If then the cash column in the Cash Payments Journal is retained at all, it is only for the convenience, on occasion, of indicating the accounts affected when one cheque covers more than one payment (see Cash Payments Journal on page 162).

Whether the cash column should be retained in the Cash Receipts Journal depends upon circumstances. If much cash is received (*e.g.,* through retail sales) it is probably convenient to use this column as shown; if not, then all cash and cheques received may be entered in this column and transferred to the bank column when they are paid into the bank. The difference between the columns would then show what cheques and cash were in the office.

The Cash Book

In some small businesses a Cash Book is used instead of cash journals. An example, in which are recorded the transactions already entered in the cash journals, is shown on page 152. It will be noticed that the debit side is similar to the Cash Receipts Journal and the credit side to the Cash Payments Journal except that the initial balances are included.

If a Cash Book is kept, the cash columns and the bank columns respectively constitute the Cash Account and Bank Account. The totals, therefore, are not transferred to accounts in the ledger, and the balances brought down are included in the trial balance and the Balance Sheet. The items on the debit side are posted to the credit side of the accounts named in the particulars column (as with the Cash Receipts Journal)

CASH BOOK

Dr.

19—		Rec. No.	Fol.	Discount Allowed £	Cash £	Bank £
Mar. 1	Balances		b/d		30	200
" 2	Sales	232	5		50	
" 2	S. Green	233	6	1		40
" 5	T. Pink		7	1	19	10
" 6	Cash		C			
			3	£2	£99	£250
Mar. 7	Balances	b/d			55	167

Cr.

19—		Chq. No.	Fol.	Discount Received £	Cash £	Bank £
Mar. 3	O. White		8	1	24	
" 4	J. Black	1395	9	2		83
" 5	Expenses		10		10	
" 6	Bank		C		10	167
" 6	Balances		c/d		55	
			4	£3	£99	£250

and the items on the credit side to the debit side of the accounts named (as with the Cash Payments Journal).

The discount columns, however, do not provide the Discount Accounts. The discount column on the debit side shows the discount allowed, and that on the credit side the discount received. Thus only one side of each account is shown in the Cash Book. For this reason, these two columns are treated as lists for posting purposes, and the totals transferred to a Discount Allowed Account and a Discount Received Account in the ledger, to the debit and credit sides respectively, precisely as is done when cash journals are kept.

Dishonoured Cheques

As soon as a cheque is received, it is entered in the Cash Receipts Journal (or Cash Book) and credited to the account of the person who sent it.

If the cheque is not met, it is said to be dishonoured. In that case, the debtor still owes the money and the entries already made must be cancelled. This is done by entering the amount of the cheque in the Cash Payments Journal (or credit side of the Cash Book), which entry is posted to the debit side of the debtor's account.

If cash discount had been deducted, this also must be cancelled. Clearly an entry in the discount column of the Cash Payments Journal (where the cheque is entered) would increase the discount received instead of reducing the discount allowed, which is what must be done. The cancellation of the discount is therefore effected by debiting the debtor's account and crediting the Discount Allowed Account directly.

Example: L. Brown owes £100 and sends a cheque for £98 (deducting £2 discount) on 2nd February. On 5th February the cheque is returned dishonoured.

L. BROWN ACCOUNT

Dr.								Cr.
19—			£	19—				£
Feb.	1	Balance b/d	100	Feb.	2	Bank		98
	5	Dishonoured		,,	2	Discount Allowed		2
		cheque ..	98	,,	5	Balance c/d ..		100
,,	5	Discount Allowed	2					
			£200					£200
Feb.	6	Balance b/d	100					

DISCOUNT ALLOWED ACCOUNT

Dr.								Cr.
19—		(Sundries as per	£	19—				£
		Cash Receipts						
		Journal ...		Feb.	5	L. Brown —		2

CASH PAYMENTS JOURNAL

			Discount Received	Cash	Bank
19— Feb.	5	L. Brown (dishonoured cheque)			£ 98

WRITTEN EXERCISES

In the following exercises either a Cash Book or Cash Journals plus Cash and Bank Accounts may be shown.

1. Enter the following in the cash journals. All payments are by cheque and all receipts are banked daily.

19—		£
May 2.	Balance at bank	170·00
„ 3.	Cash Sales	30·50
	Cash Purchases..	23·75
	Paid rent	2·50
	Paid insurance ..	1·75
May 4.	Received cheque from R. Round	17·61
	Discount	0·49
	Paid S. Square ..	12·87
	Discount	0·13
	Paid O. Oval ..	14·97
	Discount	0·28
„ 5.	R. Round's cheque received on the 4th was dishonoured.	
	Bank debits our a/c with bank charge	1·50
	Bought machinery by cheque	27·50
„ 6.	Paid for repairs to office furniture ..	10·10
	Paid for stationery	1·52
	Received commission by cheque	10·52

2. Enter the following transactions in the cash journals. All cash was banked intact daily and all payments were made by cheque.

19—
Apr. 1. Cash in hand £85·43. Cash at bank £567·98. Cash sales £67·88. Cash purchases £54·26. Received from J. Johnah £56·99 (discount £1·53). Paid cartage £4·23.
„ 2. Drew one cheque for Stationery £0·28, Fares £0·38, Oil £0·42. Paid D. Dirt £34·43 (discount £1·49).
„ 3. Paid for typewriter £22·99. Paid for repairs to old typewriter £3·22. Received from F. Flea £24·45 (discount £0·98). Cash purchases £43·60.
„ 4. Paid for office equipment £55·32. Bought goods from F. Fly for cash £56·58.
„ 5. Cheque received from F. Flea on the 3rd was returned dishonoured. Cash sales £5·27. Paid W. Wasp £67·38.
„ 6. R. Rat paid into my bank account £500. Paid telephone £4·48. Bank debits my account with bank charge £1·50.

3. Prepare a Cash Payments Journal from the following information:

J. Jones who commenced business as a greengrocer on 1st April, 19— made the following payments for:

19—	Cheque No.		£
Apr. 1.	900	Shop premises	6,000·00
	901	Cash Register	110·00
		Cheque book	3·00
„ 2.	902	Erection of shop fixtures..	25·63
	903	Sundry equipment	30·28
	904	Second-hand Motor Truck	550·50
	905	Fruit and vegetables	53·18
	906	Fire Insurance	15·21
„ 3.	907	Fruit and vegetables	40·49
	908	Drawings ⎫	15·00
		Wages ⎬	13·35
	909	Petrol and Oil ⎫	2·38
		Repairs to truck ⎬	7·52
	910	Advertising	3·15

4. Enter the following transactions in the cash journals and post to the Cash at Bank Account. All cash received is banked daily in TOTAL and all payments are made by cheque drawn on the Safety Bank.

19—		£
Nov. 1.	A. Knight commenced a grocery business by paying £2,500 into the bank.	
	A. Knight advanced as Petty Cash	10·00
	A. Knight paid for goods bought	54·86
	A. Knight bought a delivery truck, paying	650·00
„ 2.	A. Knight sold goods for cash	64·48
	A. Knight received a settlement of F. Ford's account of £75, less 2½ per cent discount	
	A. Knight received a cheque £9·87 from A. Ferguson and allowed him discount	0·13
„ 3.	A. Knight drew for private purposes..	10·00
	A. Knight made a donation to charity from business ..	5·25
„ 4.	A. Knight sold part of Office Furniture for cash	35·00
„ 5.	A. Knight received commission due to date	25·18
	A. Knight drew a cheque to pay—	
	Salaries	35·98
	Sundries	4·82
„ 7.	A. Knight received cash for rent of premises sublet ..	2·00
	A. Knight settled his account of £45·50 with K. Norman, less 2½ per cent discount.	
	A. Knight paid cheque of £23·79 to settle T. Tyler's account of	25·00

(*Univ. of Melb. Inter. Cert., modified.*)

5. J. Chester is in business as a retail grocer. On 1st January, 19—, his Cash Book showed the following balances: Cash in hand, £23; Overdraft at bank, £72·42.

Record the above and the following transactions in a Cash Book with three columns and show against each item the name of the ledger account to which it would be posted.

Jan. 2. Cash sales (banked) £32.
„ 3. J. Holland sent a cheque for £24·38 which was banked, in settlement of his account. He had deducted £0·62 cash discount allowable.
„ 4. Received a loan of £650 from the bank.
„ 6. Bought from X. Garages Ltd. a delivery van for £350 and petrol and oil £2·79 (paid for by cheque).

F

Jan. 7.   Bought for cash: Stationery £3·25; Sundries for sale in shop £14·19; Paper bags £3·50.

,,   8.   Drew and cashed cheque £20, for use in office.

,,   9.   Settled the account of L. Smith, to whom £65 was owed, by cheque deducting 2½ per cent cash discount.

,,   10.   Paid from cash: Salaries £10 and private expenses £6·35.

Balance the Cash Book as on 10th January, 19—, and bring down the balances. No posting to ledger accounts is required.   (*R.S.A., modified.*)

6.   Record the following in a three-column Cash Book:

19—

June 30.   Cash in hand £93·24; Cash at bank £1,486·46.

July 2.   Notice was received from the bank that a cheque for £24·38 received from A. Blake and paid into the bank on June 30, had been returned marked 'no account'.

,,   3.   £56 of the cash in hand was banked.

,,   4.   A cheque for £30 was drawn for office cash. Wages £59·44 were paid from cash.

,,   5.   A cheque for £95 was received from H. Wilson and paid into the bank. He had deducted 5 per cent cash discount, which was allowed.

Balance the Cash Book as on 5th July and bring down the balances. No posting to the ledger is required.   (*R.S.A., modified.*)

7.   Open a three-column Cash Book, enter the following transactions in it, post to appropriate ledger accounts, and then extract a Trial Balance of Dexter:

19—		£
Sept. 1.	Paid into the bank, from private resources, as capital of the business	600
	Bank issued a cheque book, cost being	1
	Drew cheque for buying office furniture	150
	Drew cheque to purchase stationery	20
	Drew cash cheque, to provide cash for the office	50
,, 2.	Bought on credit from Bovey, goods valued	215
,, 3.	Sold goods on credit to Nicholls	109
,, 6.	Bought goods on credit from D. Einstein	56
	Returned to Bovey goods found to be defective	60
,, 8.	Paid from office cash:	
	Postages	2
	Travelling	3
	Small purchase of goods	10
		15
,, 9.	Drew a cheque to cover:	
	Salaries of staff	20
	State insurance	2
	Drawings, Dexter	15
		37
,, 11.	Paid M. Bovey by cheque the balance owing	
,, 12.	Sold goods for cash, and paid the proceeds into the bank	45
,, 16.	Drew a cheque to cover:	
	Salaries of staff	25
	State insurance	2
	Drawings, Dexter	20
		47
,, 19.	Bought goods on credit from Bovey	113
,, 19.	Received cheque from Nicholls, on account	50
,, 22.	Sold goods on credit to Nicholls	89
,, 25.	Bought goods on credit from Elliott	98
,, 29.	Received cheque from Nicholls	59

Sept. 30.	Drew cheque for:		
	Salaries	28	
	State insurance	2	
	Drawings, Dexter	20	
			50
„ 30.	Cash payments made:		
	Stationery	5	
	Postages	15	
	Travelling	6	
	Sundry expenses	2	
			28
„ 30.	Drew cheque to provide office cash		43

(Institute of Book-keepers.)

8.   Write up, from the following information, a Cash Book, with discount, cash, and bank columns, and balance at the end of the month.

19—			£
Jan. 1.	Cash balance		49·31
	Bank balance		1,150·84
„ 2.	Received cheque from Jameson & Co. (in settlement of account for £15·44)		14·44
„ 3.	Paid water rate by cash		3·25
„ 5.	John Towne pays his account, after deducting 5 per cent, by cheque		9·50
„ 9.	Bruce Brothers Ltd., paid cash on account		50·00
„ 12.	Salaries paid in cash		18·62
„ 13.	Cheque drawn for general rates		27·20
„ 15.	Cheque drawn for self		50·00
„ 16.	Jackson paid cash (£10 allowed for discount)		190·00
„ 19.	Evesham & Co.'s account of £58·50 paid by cheque, after deducting discount		55·65
„ 20.	Paid by cash to Roberts & Sons the amount due of £110 less 5 per cent discount		
„ 21.	Drew cash from bank		150·00
„ 25.	Newman & Co. paid in cash		69.00
„ 26.	Outram & Sons paid by cash their account, less 2½ per cent discount		48·75
„ 27.	Paid cash into bank		400·00
„ 28.	Cheque paid to Hall Bros. Ltd. (discount allowed £1·06)		15·44
„ 31.	Rent paid by cheque		25·00
	Salary paid to manager by cheque		75·00
	Faulkner settled their account for £25 by paying ..		23·75
	Paid Reece & Son's account by cheque		32·00
	Purchased machinery		450·00

(Institute of Book-keepers, modified.)

9.   H. Wilson commenced business on 1st January, 19—, with £3,000 in the bank. His transactions during January were as follows:

Jan. 1.	Purchased by cheque:	£
	Office furniture	250
	Van	450
	Stock	500
	Office supplies	50
„ 5.	Purchased goods on credit from N. Langley	1,000
„ 6.	Drew from bank for office use	25
„ 10.	Sold goods on credit to H. Bridge	700
„ 15.	H. Bridge paid his account by cheque, less 2 per cent discount	
„ 20.	H. Bridge returned goods	10
„ 31.	Wages for month	60
„ 31.	Cash sales for month (banked)	500
„ 31.	Drew by cheque for own use	50
„ 31.	Sundry expenses for month (paid in cash)	15

Enter the above transactions and post to the ledger. Make out a Trial Balance, and prepare a Trading Account, and Profit and Loss Account, assuming the following valuations of assets:

Stock, 31st Jan., 19—, £650.
Van was damaged in an accident and valued at £350.
Office supplies £38.

Balance the accounts and draw up a Balance Sheet as at 31st January, 19—.

18

THE PETTY CASH BOOK AND COLUMNAR BOOKS

Imprest System

THE vast majority of payments are made by cheque, and cash is used only for small items which could not conveniently be paid by cheque. To relieve the cashier of the detailed work of making and recording these small payments, this work is usually delegated to a junior clerk. An agreed amount is allocated to the junior clerk, larger than his probable requirements, out of which the payments are made. At the end of a week or a month, the sum he has expended is refunded to him, making his allocation (or 'float') up to the original amount. This system is known as the 'Imprest' system, and the sum allowed is called the imprest.

For every payment he makes, the junior cashier should, if possible, obtain a voucher, or receipt. At any time he may be called upon to produce his vouchers and his cash, which should together be equal to the imprest. In some cases, as in the purchase of postage stamps, he will have no receipt; but he should, of course, have the stamps and a record in the postage book of those that have been used.

The junior cashier keeps his records in a Petty Cash Book. When he receives money from the cashier it is credited in the Cash Payments Journal and debited in the Petty Cash Advance Account. When a Trial Balance is taken out, the Petty Cash Advance Account must be included.

Illustration: A petty cashier has a weekly imprest of £10. He has £3·24 in hand on Monday, 2nd May, 19—, and receives on that day £6·76 from the cashier. His payments during the week were:

					£
May 2.	Postage stamps	...	...	..	2·00
	Bus fares	..	...	...	...	0·11
	Telegram	..	...	...	...	0·09
„ 3.	Paper clips	..	...	...	..	0·23
	Gummed labels	...	...	...	0·13
„ 4.	Donation	..	..	...	..	0·10
„ 5.	J. Smith & Sons	...	...	..	1·47
	Directory	..	..	..	..	0·63
„ 6.	Cleaners' wages	..	..	...	..	3·13
	Cleaners' materials	..	..	..	0·39

Vouchers are numbered as received and filed in numerical order.

The first advance for petty cash will be debited to Petty Cash Advance account. In this case it would have been £10 and no further entries would be made unless the advance were increased or decreased.

PETTY CASH BOOK

Date	Details	Rec. No.	Receipts £	Total Payments £
19—May 2	Balance		3·24	
	Cash		6·76	
2	Stamps			2·00
	Bus fares			0·11
3	Telegram	16		0·09
	Paper clips	17		0·23
	Gummed labels	18		0·13
4	Donations			0·10
5	Smith & Sons	19		1·47
	Directory	20		0·63
6	Cleaners' wages	21		3·13
	Cleaners' materials	22		0·39
				8·28
7	Balance			1·72
			£10·00	10·00
9	Balance		1·72	
	Cash		8·28	

PETTY CASH BOOK

Date	Details	Rec. No.	Receipts £	Total Payments £	Postage £	Travelling £	Stationery £	Cleaning £	Sundries £	Ledger Account	Fol.	£
19—May 2	Balance		3·24									
	Cash		6·76									
	Stamps	16		2·00	2·00							
	Bus fares			0·11		0·11						
3	Telegram			0·09	0·09							
	Paper clips	17		0·23			0·23					
4	Gummed labels	18		0·13			0·13					
	Donations			0·10					0·10			
5	Smith & Sons	19		1·47						J. Smith & Sons	32	1·47
	Directory	20		0·63					0·63			
6	Cleaners' wages	21		3·13				3·13				
	Cleaners' materials	22		0·39				0·39				
7	Balance		£10·00	8·28	2·09	0·11	0·36	3·52	0·73			1·47
				1·72								
				10·00								
9	Balance		1·72									
	Cash		8·28									

The payments made from Petty Cash affect only a limited number of accounts, rarely more than five or six and it is usual to add a number of columns on the credit side, as shown in the illustration, one for each account affected. Payments made are classified in their appropriate columns, and the totals only of these columns entered in the Cash Payments Journal for posting to the ledger as shown below. The number of columns should be increased when a large account is shown in Sundries. They will be posted to the debit side of the accounts affected.

Occasionally there will be entered in the Petty Cash Book items for which no analysis columns are provided, because they are of an unusual or non-recurring nature. All such items are analysed in a column headed 'Ledger' and posted individually to the ledger accounts to which they respectively belong.

An example is that of J. Smith & Sons above. The Petty Cash Book, with the analysis columns completed, is shown.

As a check on accuracy, the totals of the analysis columns should together be equal to the total money spent.

The cashier would show the following entries in his Cash Payments Journal when giving the reimbursing cheque:

CASH PAYMENTS JOURNAL

Date		Particulars	Discount Received	Details	Bank
19— May	9	Postage Travelling Expenses Stationery Cleaning Sundries Smith J. and Sons		£ 2·09 0·11 0·36 3·52 0·73 1·47	£ 8·28

The ledger accounts for Postage, Travelling Expenses, Stationery, Cleaning, Sundries and Smith J. and Sons should be debited for the amounts shown. The Petty Cash Advance Account is NOT debited.

Further Uses of Columnar Books

The principle of employing additional columns in books, to facilitate posting to the ledger, is capable of extension.

For example, a trader may divide his business into departments and may wish to know the gross profit made in each department. This involves separate Purchases, Sales, and Stock Accounts for each department. An example of a Purchases Journal, ruled for two departments, is given below. The Sales Journal and the Returns Journals would be ruled in a similar manner, and an extra column might be added to the

Cash Receipts Journal and Cash Payments Journal for cash purchases and cash sales in each department.

PURCHASES JOURNAL

19—				Total	Woollens	Cottons
Mar.	28	Brought forward	—	24,800	12,800	12,000
	30	M. Kemp & Co.	27	200	50	150
		S. West	94	500		500
				£25,500	£12,850	£12,650
					Woollens Purchases —Dr.	Cottons Purchases —Dr.

Posting

(a) In the M. Kemp & Co. Account £200 is posted on the credit side.

(b) In the S. West Account £500 is posted on the credit side.
   (The individual amounts making up the £24,800 brought forward would similarly have been credited in the personal accounts of the sellers.)

(c) A Woollens Purchases Account would be opened and debited with £12,850.

(d) A Cottons Purchases Account would be debited with £12,650.
   (The total, £25,500, is not posted. It is used as a check on accuracy; i.e., £12,850+£12,650—£25,500. Failure of these totals to agree would indicate an error.)

Assuming no purchases were made for cash, the Trading Account would be arranged as follows:

TRADING ACCOUNT
FOR YEAR ENDED 31ST MARCH, 19—

	Woollens	Cottons	Total		Woollens	Cottons	Total
Stock 1/4/19—	2,700	3,300	6,000	Sales	18,400	14,600	33,000
Purchases	12,850	12,650	25,500	Stock 31/3/19–	3,500	3,000	6,500
Gross Profit	6,350	1,650	8,000				
	£21,900	£17,600	£39,500		£21,900	£17,600	£39,500

Sometimes only the total gross profit would be carried to the Profit and Loss Account because of the difficulty of allocating the Profit and Loss items as between the departments. When it is not possible to charge each department with the actual expenses incurred the allocation of expenses to departments in the Profit and Loss Account may be done by the following methods:

Selling and Administrative expenses—in proportion to sales of each department.

Finance expenses—in proportion to the credit sales of each department. Rates, Lighting, Rent, Insurance of Building—according to the floor space occupied by each department.

Purchases of Assets

It was stated earlier that only purchases of goods intended for resale should be included in the Purchases Account. Nevertheless, where a columnar Purchases Journal is kept, it is often convenient to have an additional column in which *assets* that have been purchased on credit may be entered. The total of this column is not posted to a purchases account. Instead, each item is double entered—

(*a*) on the debit side of the appropriate asset account;
(*b*) on the credit side of the appropriate personal account.

WRITTEN EXERCISES

1. Enter the following transactions in the Petty Cash Book of Messrs. Roberts & Co. Ltd., showing the analysis under the headings of Postage, Stationery, Carriage, Travelling Expenses, and Office Expenses:

19—
Feb. 1. Received £15 for petty cash float.
" 1. Bought postage stamps for £1·63.
" 5. Paid fares £0·68.
" 6. Paid £0·50 for cleaning office windows.
" 10. Paid £0·23 for tea.
" 11. Paid for carriage £0·74.
" 15. Bought postage stamps for £1·98.
" 18. Paid £0·37 for fares.
" 20. Paid £1·56 for stationery.
" 23. Paid £0·89 for carriage.
" 27. Bought postage stamps for £1·92.
" 28. Paid office milk bill £0·37.
Mar. 1. Received total amount of expenditure for February.
Post to the appropriate accounts in the ledger.   (*R.S.A., modified.*)

2. P. Gold is a coal and coke merchant. His credit purchases and sales during March, 19—, were:

19—
Mar. 3. Sold to G. Dickson 18 tons of coal for £67·50.
" 5. Bought from Best Coke Co. 78 tons of coke at a cost of £234.
" 8. Bought from Lass Colliery Co. Ltd. 50 tons of coal for £125.
" 11. Sold to H. Morse 22 tons of coal for £88 and 10 tons of coke for £40.
" 16. Bought from N. Lambert 25 tons of coal for £62·50 and 20 tons of coke for £60.
" 24. Sold to H. Bowles 53 tons of coke for £212.
You are required to:
(*a*) Enter the above transactions in P. Gold's Purchases and Sales Books, giving analysis columns for (1) coal, and (2) coke.

(b) Prepare separate Trading Accounts for coal and coke for the month of March to show the gross profit on each commodity. The stock valuations were:

	Coal	Coke
1st March, 19—	£178	£159
31st March, 19—	£260	£264

(R.S.A., modified.)

3. F. Williams divides his business into three departments, viz., (a) glass, (b) china, and (c) hardware. During February 19—, he made the following purchases:

Feb. 3. From P. Rowe:
    5 dozen kettles at £1·20 per dozen.
    4 dozen frying pans at £1·80 per dozen.
    10 water jugs at £3 per dozen.
    3 dozen china teapots at £2·40 per dozen.

Feb. 17. From R. Spence:
    1 gross table glasses at £0·90 per dozen.

Feb. 28. From M. Howe:
    6 china tea sets at £2·00 each.
    3 dozen galvanized buckets at £3·00 per dozen.
    18 glass bowls at £3·60 per dozen.

Enter the above in F. Williams' Purchases Book (tabular form) and show the totals for the month. Post to the ledger.   (R.S.A., modified.)

4. The transactions of H. Stephen for May, 19—, show the following:

			£	£
May 1.	Cash in hand (opening capital) paid into bank			500
	Office furniture purchased by cheque			25
	Purchased stationery by cheque			8
	Bank charged for cheque book			1
	Drew petty cash			25
„ 2.	Purchased goods from Duff on credit			200
„ 3.	Purchased goods on credit from Kent			320
„ 4.	Sold goods on credit to Roberts			100
„ 5.	Sold goods on credit to Dunn			140
„ 6.	Returned goods to Kent			10
„ 7.	Paid from petty cash:			
	Postages			2
	Stationery			3
	Travelling			5
„ 8.	Drew one cheque for:			
	Salaries		25	
	State insurance		2	
	Petty cash		10	
				37
„ 9.	Paid Duff on account			50
„ 12.	Paid travelling expenses from petty cash			7
„ 13.	Paid stationery from petty cash			4
„ 15.	Drew cheque for:			
	Salaries		26	
	State insurance		2	
	Petty cash		11	
				39
„ 16.	Paid Duff's balance of account less 2½ per cent discount on full amount of purchases.			
„ 17.	Dunn returned goods to the value of			30
„ 18.	Cash sales paid into bank			32
„ 19.	Petty cash payments:			
	Tips			1
	Postages			5
	Travelling			12
	Stationery			1

May 22.	Drew cheque for:						£	£
	Salaries	..	..	...	..	...	..	30	
	State insurance	..	..	..	..	..	3	
	Petty cash ..	..	..	..	..	..	19	
								52

,, 23.	Drew cheque to reimburse for purchases made in local market	..	..	..	..	..	..	50
,, 24.	Dunn settled his account but deducted £10 for discount							
,, 27.	Drew from petty cash for private purposes	..	..	10				
,, 28.	Petty cash payments:							
	Postages	..	..	..	..	..	..	5	
	Stationery ..	..	..	..	..	..	1	
	Travelling ..	..	..	..	..	..	8	
								14

May 29.	Draw cheque for:							
	Salaries	..	..	..	..	..	..	23	
	Self	..	..	..	..	..	..	25	
	Petty cash ..	..	..	..	..	..	24	
								72

,, 30.	Cash sales paid into bank	..	..	..	..	15
,, 31.	Roberts was adjudicated bankrupt with no assets, so that the account is written off as a bad debt.					

Set out the necessary entries in the books of H. Stephen (including a Petty Cash Book) to record the above transactions and extract a Trial Balance.

(Institute of Book-keepers.)

5.   M. Walker had the following balances in his books on 1st December, 19—:

Debit: Cash £40; Bank £750; Stock £9,000; Purchases £12,000; Insurance £360; Wages £1,500; Vans £1,000; Lease (8 years) £3,200; General Expenses £120; Furniture and Fittings £500; L. Burke £180; T. Finlay £62; Discount Allowed £18.

Credit: Sales £16,000; Discount Received £25; T. Hunt £260; Loan £2,000; Capital £10,445.
Open accounts and enter these balances.

Transactions:
Dec. 2.   Paid T. Hunt by cheque £250 and was allowed the balance as discount.
   ,, 4.   Purchased goods on credit from S. Tracy £450.
   ,, 6.   Sold goods on credit to L. Burke £120.
   ,, 7.   T. Finlay paid his account by cheque and was allowed £2 discount.
   ,, 10. S. Tracy sent C/N for £20 for goods, purchased on December 4, damaged in transit.
   ,, 11. L. Burke paid by cheque on account £150.
   ,, 12. Sold goods on credit to T. Finlay £50.
   ,, 15. Sent C/N to L. Burke for goods returned £10.
   ,, 18. Purchased goods on credit from T. Hunt £200.
   ,, 24. Cash sales to date £500.
   ,, 24. Paid into bank from office cash £520.
   ,, 31. M. Walker took goods for his own use £25.
   ,, 31. General expenses for month, in cash, £15.
   ,, 31. Paid interest on loan for year £80.

Enter transactions in the appropriate books, post to ledger, take out Trial Balance, prepare Trading Account, Profit and Loss Account, and Balance Sheet as on 31st December, 19—.

(a) Stock, 31st Dec., 19—, £4,845.
(b) Depreciate vans by 20 per cent; furniture and fittings by 10 per cent.
(c) £90 of the insurance was unexpired.
(d) Wages due but unpaid, £150.
(e) Make what other transfers to the Profit and Loss Account you think necessary.

6. K. Wheatley & Co. require the firm's expenditure to be recorded so as to show the total amount spent under the headings of (a) Postage and Telegrams, (b) Cleaning, (c) Stationery, (d) Travelling, and (e) Bought Ledger Accounts paid.

Draft a Petty Cash Book ruled to furnish the required information, record the following, and balance at 6th January, 19–1:

19–1

Jan. 1. Drew from bank for petty cash, £20.
   „ 1. Paid fares £0·08 and postage £0·36.
   „ 2. Paid for cleaning materials £0·43 and postage £0·44.
   „ 3. Paid for stationery £1·12 and postage £0·55.
   „ 4. Paid Chiswick & Co. £0·87 and postage £0·63.
   „ 5. Paid for envelopes £1·48, fares £0·15 and postage £0·39.
   „ 6. Paid cleaner £2·63, telegram £0·17 and postage £0·44.
   „ 6. Drew and cashed a cheque for the expenditure to date.

(R.S.A., modified.)

19

THE BANK ACCOUNT AND BANK RECONCILIATION STATEMENT

THERE are two main types of Account that may be opened with a bank.

I. Current Account

The purposes of opening a current account is to enable payments to be made by cheque and to avoid the dangers involved in keeping large sums of money in the office. Whenever the bank account has been mentioned in this book, the type of account referred to was the current account. No interest is paid by the bank on current accounts; on the contrary, it often makes a charge for 'working the account'.

When a current account is opened, the bank will provide a cheque book, charging 1p per cheque to cover the cost of the stamps; a paying-in slip book; and a wallet to hold bank statements which provide a copy of the customer's account as it appears in the books of the bank. This is used for checking purposes.

Paying-in Slip Book

When money or cheques are paid into the bank, a list showing exactly what is paid in is made out in the paying-in slip book. The list itemizes notes and coins of different denominations, cheques and postal orders.

The page is perforated down the centre, identical lists appearing on each half of the page. The right-hand side is torn out and retained by the bank. The left-hand portion, initialled by the bank cashier, remains in the book as a copy.

II. Deposit Account

This is an account which would be opened if a business had some spare money that could not be employed profitably in the business. Notice must be given before money can be withdrawn, the period depending on the arrangements made with the bank and the amount withdrawn. As very little interest is now paid on deposit accounts, it is usually better to invest unused funds in securities.

If money is placed on deposit with a bank, a Bank Deposit Account would be opened and debited in the ledger. If money is transferred to this account from the current account, a cheque would be drawn and an entry made in the Cash Payments Journal or on the credit side of the

Cash Book. It would be posted to the debit of a Bank Deposit Account in the ledger.

Bank Reconciliation Statement

When money is paid into a bank, the bank will debit its Cash Book and complete the double entry by crediting the customer. The customer, on the other hand, debits all money paid into the bank in the bank column of his own Cash Book.

Thus the bank statement, which gives a copy of the customer's account as it appears in the bank's books, will usually show the entries on the opposite sides to those in the Cash Book. It does sometimes happen, however, that in making out the bank statement, the bank reverses the sides to make the bank statement correspond with the customer's Cash Book.

Now it would appear, at first sight, that the balance shown in the bank statement should be exactly the same as the bank balance shown in the Cash Book, provided no mistake has been made on either side. In practice they seldom agree. The reason is that one or other (or both) is not up to date. The purpose of a Reconciliation Statement is to remove differences due to this cause. It can then be seen whether or not there is an error.

Usually it is the Bank Statement which is not up to date, because the customer has immediate knowledge of all cheques received and paid, but the bank has not. For example:

(a) When a cheque is received it is entered in the Cash Book immediately. If, however, it is not paid into the bank on or before the day on which the Bank Statement is made up, it will not be included in the Bank Statement.

(b) When a cheque is drawn, it is at once credited in the Cash Book. The bank, however, will have no knowledge of it (and therefore cannot enter it) until it is presented for payment. Before this can be done, it must usually be sent by post to the payee, be paid into his account, and pass through the clearing house. This takes time, and in the meantime there can be no record of it in the bank's books and, therefore, no record in the Bank Statement.

On the other hand, the bank has prior knowledge of the charges it makes for its services (e.g., for interest and working the account). The only indication it gives of these charges is an entry in the Bank Statement (from which the entry is made in the Cash Book), so in this respect the Cash Book must lag behind the Bank Statement.

As an illustration, the Bank Statement and the Cash Book of a hypothetical firm are given below. For the sake of simplicity, it is assumed that the balances of each were in agreement on 23rd June.

BANK ACCOUNT
(in books of V. Robins)

Dr.							Cr.
			£				£
June 23	Balance	...	600·00	June 25	C. Neil ..	...	40·00
„ 26	Cash ..	..	50·00	„ 27	D. Bradley	...	15·00
„ 28	H. Lucas	..	8·25	„ 28	S. Green	...	10·60
„ 30	T. Smith	..	22·50	„ 28	R. White	...	41·65
„ 30	M. Jones	...	15·75	„ 30	Balance ...	...	589·25
			£696·50				£696·50
July 1	Balance b/d.	...	589·25				

BANK STATEMENT

		Debit £	Credit £	Balance £
June 23	Balance forward			600·00
„ 25	C. Neil	40·00		560·00
„ 26	Cash		50·00	610·00
„ 27	D. Bradley	15·00		595·00
„ 28	H. Lucas		8·25	603·25
„ 30	Charges	5·25		598·00

It will be seen that the Cash Book includes, on the debit side, two cheques (received from Smith and Jones) that have not been credited in the Bank Statement; and, on the credit side, a further two cheques (paid to Green and White) that have not yet been presented. On the other hand, the Cash Book contains no record, as yet, of the bank charges.

A Bank Reconciliation Statement would now be drawn up to see whether, apart from these differences, the balances agreed. It could take two forms, depending on the starting point.

I. Starting with the balance shown in the Bank Statement—

    (*a*) add back the bank charges that have not been entered in the Cash Book;

    (*b*) add cheques that have been paid in but not credited (they are added because they were included in the Cash Book balance);

    (*c*) deduct unpresented cheques (they are deducted because they have been deducted from the Cash Book balance).

The resultant balance ought to be the same as the Cash Book balance.

II. If the Cash Book balance is taken as the starting point, the process is reversed—

    (*a*) deduct the bank charges (because they have been entered in the Bank Statement);

    (*b*) deduct the cheques that have been paid in but not credited by the bank;

    (*c*) add back unpresented cheques (because they have not yet been deducted by the bank).

The resultant balance should be the same as the balance shown in the Bank Statement.

If by these methods the balances cannot be reconciled, the difference may be due to error in one or other of the records, the loss of a cheque which has been received, or fraudulent conversion of funds.

A Bank Reconciliation Statement based on the figures already given, is shown below. The first method is adopted.

BANK RECONCILIATION STATEMENT
30TH JUNE, 19—

		£
Balance as per Bank Statement		598·00
Add bank charges		5·25
		£603·25
Add cheques not credited by bank—	£	
T. Smith	22·50	
M. Jones	15·75	
		38·25
		641·50
Deduct unpresented cheques—		
S. Green	10·60	
R. White	41·65	
		52·25
Balance as per Cash Book		£589·25

If a Reconciliation Statement begins with a bank overdraft the same principles apply but it must be remembered that—

  (i) Where a bank balance would be increased, an overdraft would be reduced.
  (ii) Where a bank balance would be reduced, an overdraft would be increased.

The illustration already given is reworked on the assumption that the Bank Statement showed an overdraft of £10.

BANK RECONCILIATION STATEMENT
30TH JUNE, 19—

		£
Overdraft as per Bank Statement		10·00
Add back bank charges		5·25
	Overdraft	£4·75(i)
Add cheques not credited by bank—	£	
T. Smith	22·50	
M. Jones	15·75	
		38·25
		33·50 (ii)
Deduct unpresented cheques—		
S. Green	10·60	
R. White	41·65	
		52·25 (iii)
Credit Balance (overdraft) as per Cash Book		£18·75

Notes
  (i) The overdraft would be decreased if the bank charges were not included.
  (ii) If these cheques were credited they would pay off the overdraft and create a balance in hand equal to the difference between the value of the cheques and the amount of the overdraft.
  (iii) When these cheques are met the balance at the bank will be absorbed and there will be an overdraft equal to the difference between the balance and the cheques paid.

In practice it is usual on receipt of the Bank Statement to bring the Cash Payments Journal up to date by the entry of bank charges, etc. All items would then be checked by ticking from the Bank Statement to the cash journals, and the unticked items in the cash journals, consisting entirely of unpresented cheques and cheques not paid in, should account for any difference that exists.

WRITTEN EXERCISES

1. Prepare a Reconciliation Statement as at 31st March, 19—, between the Bank Statement and the Cash Book, from the following figures:

CASH BOOK

Dr.								Cr.
19—			£	19—				£
Mar. 1	Balance..	..	110·00	Mar. 2	Brown	..	..	17·53
„ 10	Parkes ..	..	70·08	„ 12	Jones	..	..	1·56
„ 31	Hibble ..	▬	63·50	„ 15	Robinson ..		..	11·46

BANK STATEMENT

Dr.								Cr.
19—			£	19—				£
Mar. 1	Balance..	..	120·00	Mar. 2	Smith	..	..	10·00
„ 10	Lodged	..	70·08	„ 16	Robinson ..		..	11·46

Both Cash Book and Bank Statement have been written up to 31st March, 19—.
(*Institute of Book-keepers.*)

2. (*a*) What is the purpose of preparing a Bank Reconciliation Statement?
(*b*) Draw up a Bank Reconciliation Statement from the following information at 31st December, 19—:

	£
Cash at bank on 31st December, 19—, as shown by the Bank Statement	240·43
Cheques drawn and entered in Cash Book, but not presented for payment at the bank	58·52
Interest on 3½ per cent War Loan, paid direct to the bank on 1st December, but not entered in the Cash Book	35·00
Cheques received and paid to bank, but not credited to the account by the bank until 1st January of following year	73·64
Balance as shown by Cash Book, 31st December, 19—. (Dr.)	220·55

(*R.S.A., modified.*)

3. On 31st May, 19—, T. Knight's Cash Book showed a balance of £34·38 overdrawn on his bank account. On checking the cash book with the statement of

his account received from the bank, all the items were found to agree except the following:

- (a) Cheques drawn and entered in the Cash Book on 30th May, £28·52 in favour of P. Martin, and £17·25 in favour of F. Peck, had not been presented at the bank for payment.
- (b) The bank statement showed £5·40 interest charged by the bank which Knight had not entered in his Cash Book.
- (c) A cheque for £2·37 which Knight had entered as a receipt in his Cash Book and had sent to the bank on 31st May, 19—, was not credited to his account by the bank until 2nd June, 19—.

Draw up a statement showing the balance which appeared on the Bank Statement on 31st May 19—. (*R.S.A., modified.*)

4. On 31st December, 19—, the Cash Book of John Martin discloses a balance at bank amounting to £648.
An examination of the bank statement shows that:

- (i) A payment of £79 to Smith on 15th December, 19—— had been entered in the Cash Book as £99.
- (ii) Bank Charges of £2 (31st December, 19—), had not been entered in the Cash Book.
- (iii) A cheque for £125 drawn by Martin in favour of Roberts on 23rd December, 19—, was paid by the bank on 3rd January, following.
- (iv) A cheque for £100 received from Evans had been correctly entered in the Cash Book.
  This cheque had been dishonoured on 27th December, 19—, but no entry for the dishonour had been made in the Cash Book.
- (v) A cheque for £191 received from Jackson was paid into the bank on 31st December, 19—, but was not credited by the bank until 1st January, 19—.

You are required:

- (1) to prepare a statement showing the balance which should appear in the Cash Book on 31st December, 19—, after making all necessary corrections, and
- (2) to prepare a statement reconciling the corrected Cash Book balance with the balance shown by the bank statement. (*Institute of Bankers.*)

5. On 30th June, 19—, M. Dark's Cash Book showed a credit balance of £36·41 in the bank account. On checking the Cash Book with the Statement received from the bank all the items were found to agree except the following:

- (a) The following cheques drawn and entered in the Cash Book on 30th June had not been presented for payment:

  | R. Lescot | £21·19 |
  | S. Rock | £25·24 |

- (a) A cheque received from L. West £3·48 and paid into bank on 28th June was returned dishonoured on 30th June and had not been entered in the Cash Book.
- (c) The bank statement showed interest and charges £4·50 which were not yet entered in the Cash Book.
- (d) The bank had paid on Dark's behalf an annual insurance premium £12·50 and this was found to be not entered in the Cash Book.

Draw up a statement showing the balance which appeared on the Bank Statement on 30th June, 19—. (*L. Ch. C,. modified.*)

6. V. Goodfellow is a hotel-keeper. The following Trial Balance was extracted from his books on 31st December, 19—. The stock of provisions, wines, spirits linen, china and cutlery was valued on that date at £3,570.
Prepare Trading and Profit and Loss Accounts for the year ended 31st December, 19—, with a Balance Sheet on that date.

TRIAL BALANCE
31ST DECEMBER, 19—

	£	£
Stocks on hand 1st January, 19—:		
Provisions (wines, spirits, linen, china and		
cutlery)	4,052	
Receipts from Visitors		17,167
Fuel and Light	456	
Rent and Rates	590	
Advertising	175	
Purchases of provisions, wines and spirits	5,833	
Purchases of linen, china and cutlery ..	674	
Wages	3,210	
Carriages on purchases	129	
Salaries and General Expenses	1,877	
Interest paid on loan	200	
Loan: P. Henry		4,000
Repairs to Furniture and Premises ..	640	
Sundry Debtors and Creditors	204	147
Leasehold Premises	7,000	
Furniture and Fittings	3,600	
Bad Debts written off	216	
Capital Account, 1st January, 19— ..		10,461
Drawings during the year	2,000	
Cash at bank	828	
Cash in hand	91	
	£31,775	£31,775

(*a*) Depreciate furniture and fittings 5 per cent.

(*b*) Write £350 off the leasehold premises.

(*c*) Carry forward £25 of advertising and £90 of rent and rates.

(*R.S.A., modified.*)

20

THE JOURNAL

A SUBSIDIARY book or a book of prime entry is one in which a record of a transaction is made prior to its entry in the ledger.

The Purchase Book, Sales Book, and Returns Book are examples of subsidiary books. The main purpose of keeping them is to supply totals of the transactions entered in them and so to eliminate detail from the ledger.

There are, however, other advantages to be gained from the use of subsidiary books. These are:

(a) The risk of omission of one or both of the entries required for each transaction is reduced. This is particularly important when more than one ledger is kept, and one or both of those required is in use at the time it is wanted.

(b) More information can usually be given of the nature of the transaction in a subsidiary book than is possible in the ledger.

If there are sufficient transactions of a particular kind, a separate subsidiary book will be opened for them. This is the case, for instance, with Purchases and Sales. There may, however, be a considerable number of miscellaneous transactions that cannot be entered in any of the subsidiary books mentioned so far. Another book is therefore opened for these unclassified transactions. It is known as the Journal. Its use was once universal, but some firms at the present day, ignoring the advantages stated above, do not use it at all and enter miscellaneous transactions in the ledger directly.

In the Journal a memorandum is made, in the simplest possible terms, of the entries to be made in the ledger. The essential information consists of:

(a) the date;

(b) the name of the account to be debited;

(c) the name of the account to be credited;

(d) the amount of money;

(e) a brief description of the transaction (because they are not all of the same kind).

The ruling of the Journal and the method of entry are shown overleaf:

175

JOURNAL

(Date)	(A/c. to be debited) Dr. To (a/c. to be credited) Brief description of transaction	fol. fol.	Dr. amount	Cr. amount

Example: 1st Sept., 19—.   Purchased delivery van on credit from W. Brown for £400.

This would not be entered in the Purchases Book because the van is bought to use and not for re-sale (but see page 164).

19— Sept.	1	Vans A/c Dr. To W. Brown Purchase, on credit, of second-hand delivery van No. CRA62. Inv. No.		Dr. £ 400	Cr. £ 400

Notes

  (i) The account to be debited appears first in the Journal.

 (ii) The folio column would be entered when the transaction was posted to the ledger.

(iii) Note the use of the words 'Dr. . . . . to'.

(iv) The description of the transaction is called the 'narration'. In the narration, reference should be made to the voucher, or supporting evidence.

A Journal entry clearly presents no difficulties provided it is known which account is to be debited and which credited.

Uses of the Journal

The Journal is used for all transactions for which no other book of prime entry is suitable. (The Cash Book, though a part of the ledger, is to be regarded as a book of prime entry.)

The chief uses to which the Journal is usually put are the following:

I. *The purchase or sale on credit of capital instruments (i.e. things bought to keep and to use, and not for resale).* When such things are sold, a profit or a loss may result, if the price at which they are sold is different from the figure at which they appear in the ledger.

Example: On 1st September a lathe valued in the books at £50 is sold on credit to A. James for £75.

					Dr.	Cr.
19—					£	£
Sept.	1	A. James	Dr.		75	
		To Machinery A/c.				50
		„ Profit and Loss A/c.				25
		Sale of Lathe No. .... See Inv. No.... and correspondence Aug. 25 and 29.				

If the lathe in the above example had been sold for cash, the cash received would, of course, have been entered in the Cash Book and only the entry transferring profit would be shown in the Journal.

II. *The rectification of errors.* If an error is made in the books, wrong entries are not deleted. Instead, new entries, correcting or cancelling the old, are made.

Examples: (a) On 10th March, 19—, it was discovered that a cheque for £30, paid to M. Jones on 1st March, was posted in error to the account of T. Evans.

This cheque would have been wrongly debited in T. Evans account. To correct this, a credit entry in his account is required, and a debit entry is required in the account of M. Jones, thus:

					Dr.	Cr.
19—					£	£
Mar.	10	M. Jones A/c.	Dr.		30	
		To T. Evans A/c.				30
		Being cheque No. ...... paid to M. Jones on March 1, posted in error to T. Evans. C.B. Fol...				

(b) The Trial Balance may indicate that there is an error in the books, but it may be difficult to trace it without detailed search, which may take a long time. To enable work to go forward whilst search is being made, a 'Suspense Account' may be opened and debited or credited with the amount necessary to bring the Trial Balance into equilibrium. There is no double entry. When the mistake is discovered, a correcting entry is made through the Journal in the account which was wrong, the double entry being made in the Suspense Account, which is thus automatically closed.

The danger of employing this device is that a comparatively small discrepancy may mask a number of errors of considerable size, which almost cancel each other out.

Illustration: On 31st December, 19—, the Trial Balance of Messrs. George & Co. shows the debit side to be £5 greater than the credit. It is revealed on 10th January next that—

    (*a*) the Sales Journal has been undercast by £110;
    (*b*) a cheque for £105, paid to W. Smith, has not been posted to his account.

Show the Suspense Account and the Journal entries to correct the errors.

(i) *Before correction of errors*

SUSPENSE ACCOUNT

Fo. 19

19—				19— Dec. 31	Diff. in books	–	£ 5

(ii) *After correction of errors*

JOURNAL

Fo. 12

19— Jan. 10		Dr.		£ Dr.	£ Cr.
	Suspense A/c. Dr.		19	110	
	To Sales A/c.		27		110
	Error in casting on Fol. 214				
Jan. 10	W. Smith A/c. Dr.		161	105	
	To Suspense A/c.		19		105
	Cheque paid 18/12/19— not posted to Smith A/c. C.B. Fol. 92				

SUSPENSE ACCOUNT

Fo. 19

19— Jan. 10	Sales A/c.	J.12	£ 110	Dec. 31	Diff. in books		£ 5
				19— Jan. 10	W. Smith A/c.	J.12	105
			£110				£110

If no Suspense Account were opened, errors of the kind shown above would be entered in the Journal as follows, when they were discovered.

JOURNAL

19—			Dr.	Cr.
			£	£
Jan. 10	.... Dr.	—		110
	To Sales A/c.	27		
	Error in casting Sales Book on Fol. 214			
Jan. 10	W. Smith A/c. Dr.	161	105	
	To...................	—		
	Cheque paid 18/12/19—not posted to Smith's A/c. C.B. Fol. 92			

III. *Transfers from one account to another in the ledger.*

Examples: (a) The proprietor of a business had a bookcase made in his workshop and took it home for his own use. The cost was £8 (wages £5, materials £3). (*R.S.A., modified.*)

In a sense, this was an error in book-keeping, since the cost of the bookcase, if known before the payments were made, should have been treated as drawings. The £5 paid as wages must therefore be taken from the Wages Account (where it would have been debited) by a credit entry, and the £3 paid for materials subtracted from purchases by a credit entry in the Purchases Account. The £8 is then debited to Drawings.

JOURNAL

19—			Fo. 12	
			Dr.	Cr.
			£	£
	Drawings A/c. Dr.		8	
	To Wages			5
	„ Purchases			3
	Being cost of bookcase made for proprietor.			

(b) At the end of each accounting period, a considerable number of transfers take place. For example, Purchases, Sales, Returns, and Stock (and possibly Manufacturing Costs) must be transferred to the Trading Account, and the amounts by which assets have depreciated, or used up, transferred to the Profit and Loss Account. Such entries are known as 'Closing Entries' and, if they are to appear in a book of first entry, the only possible book is the Journal. The entries necessary for the transference of opening and closing stock, and certain items to the Profit and Loss Account, are shown in the following:

JOURNAL

19—			Fo. ..	Dr. £	Cr. £
Dec. 31	Trading A/c. To Stock A/c. Being stock as at 1/1/19—	Dr.		3,000	3,000
Dec. 31	Stock A/c. To Trading A/c. Being stock as at 31/12/19—	Dr.		3,200	3,200
Dec. 31	Trading A/c. To Profit and Loss A/c. Being gross profit transferred to Profit and Loss A/c.	Dr.		4,000	4,000
Dec. 31	Profit and Loss A/c. To Depreciation (plant) „ Rent A/c. „ Interest A/c. „ General Expenses A/c. Being transfers of losses to Profit and Loss A/c.	Dr.		645	325 200 40 80

IV. *Opening Entries.* When a new set of books is opened, the balances from the old books must be entered in the new. They are frequently journalized first, the Journal entries being described as 'Opening Entries'. An example, adapted from a Royal Society of Arts question, is given below:

JOURNAL
(Opening Entries)

19—			Dr. £	Cr. £
Mar. 1	Cash in hand	Dr.	29·50	
	Cash at bank	„	483·62	
	Sundry Debtors:	„		
	P. Rogers		42·00	
	F. Shirt		94·00	
	Stock	„	720·22	
	Furniture and Fittings	„	200·00	
	To Rent due			75·00
	„ *Sundry Creditors:*			
	N. South			126·75
	W. Wills & Son			110·50
	„ Capital			1,257·09
	Being assets and liabilities on this date.			
			£1,569·34	£1,569·34

Though opening entries are totalled, the totals are not ruled off because other Journal entries will probably follow.

If the debtors and creditors are very numerous, they would be included as a total in the opening entries and a separate list attached.

Obviously, the occasions when opening entries are needed are very infrequent. They are not required, for example, at the beginning of each accounting period, because the balances from the previous period are brought down. They would usually serve little purpose in the case of a new business, which would probably have only one asset, cash, and no liabilities except capital. On the other hand, they would be an advantage if a business were bought as a 'going concern', or if a new partnership were formed, each partner contributing various assets and liabilities.

In examination work, the examination exercise is frequently treated as a new set of books and opening entries are asked for.

V. The Journal is used as a book of first entry for transactions in connection with the issue of shares by a joint stock company (see Chapter 31), and by a partnership for such transactions as the admission of a new partner, the winding-up of the partnership, etc. (see Chapter 30).

These are the main purposes served by the Journal. The form taken by a Journal entry, however, is the most concise way of indicating the ledger entries necessary for *any* transaction, even though it would not normally be passed through the Journal. For instance, the entries necessary to record a credit purchase of merchandise could be shown in the Journal as follows:

JOURNAL

19—		Fo. ..	
		Dr.	Cr.
....	Purchases A/c. Dr.	£ 100	£
	To A. Creditor		100
	Being goods purchased on credit, Inv. No.		

This is a useful device in answering examination questions, and one which, in fact, the examinee is frequently asked to employ.

WRITTEN EXERCISES

1. Prepare the opening Journal entry of David Williams, who is about to open a set of books. His position is:

		£
Stock on hand		500
Furniture and fittings		160
Sundry debtors		210
Sundry creditors		70
He owes J. Richards		100

(*Institute of Book-keepers.*)

2.   William Shenley is in business as a jeweller. On 1st January, 19—, he decides to put his books on a double-entry basis. His position then was:

		£
Cash in hand	.. ..	23
Fixtures and fittings, at cost	.. ..	600
Bank overdraft	.. ..	500
Investment in 3 per cent Government Stock	.. ..	1,000
Stock in trade	.. ..	1,450
Sundry debtors:		
James Hay	.. ..	52
John Bee	.. ..	42
Maxim See	.. ..	10
Sundry creditors:		
Jewellers' Supply Co.	.. ..	200
Timepieces Ltd.	.. ..	50

On the 30th June you ascertain that his total assets less liabilities amount to £3,600, and during the half-year he withdrew £250; you are required to:

(a) Set out the Journal entry required for the opening of the books.
(b) Give your computation showing the net profit of the business for the six months to 30th June, 19—.   (*Institute of Book-keepers.*)

3.   By mean of Journal entries show how you would record the following:
19—
May 31.   Received a letter from A. Archer stating that he cannot allow the £5 cash discount you had deducted when paying his account.
June 4.   The correction for £28 cash purchases debited in error to Wages Account.
,,   10.   Goods for resale worth (at cost) £63, and shop fittings valued at £37 received in settlement of £100 owing to you by B. Good.
,,   30.   Write 5 per cent depreciation off machinery at present standing in your ledger at £2,100.   (*R.S.A.*)

4.   Show, by means of Journal entries, how the following transactions of B. Richards, a house builder, should be dealt with in his books:
19—
Apr. 5.   B. Richards received a credit note for £28 from Timber Suppliers Ltd., for timber short delivered.
,,   7.   B. Richards bought a motor lorry for £500 from C. Ford who took his old lorry and allowed him £200 for it. B. Richards paid the balance in cash.
,,   30.   B. Richards wrote 5 per cent depreciation off his plant and machines, standing in his books at £2,500.   (*R.S.A.*)

5.   The Trial Balance of a trading company, extracted as at 31st December, 19—, failed to agree. The Trading and Profit and Loss Account and Balance Sheet were prepared on the basis of the figures shown in the Trial Balance, and the difference on the Trial Balance was shown in the Balance Sheet as a Suspense Account. The net profit shown was £5,000.

Subsequent investigation disclosed the following errors:
(a) Part of the company's premises were let, as from 1st December, 19—, to a sub-tenant, at a rent of £5 per calendar month. The sub-tenant paid, on 1st December, three months' rent in advance. This amount had been entered in the Cash Book, but the double entry had not been completed, and no other entry had been made in respect of the rent.
(b) The Purchases Journal was undercast by £100.
(c) A credit balance of £24 on the account of Thomas, a customer, had been omitted from the Trial Balance.
(d) A payment of £38 for repairs to motor vans had been credited in the Cash Book and debited to Motor Vans Account.
(e) Discounts shown as £140 on the credit side of the Cash Book had been posted to the wrong side of the Discounts Account.

(f) On 31st December, 19—, goods valued at £50 (selling price) were returned by a customer. No entry had been made in the books and these goods had not been included in the closing stock. The cost of these goods was £32.

You are required to state by how much the Trial Balance was out of balance by reason of each error, and also which side of the Trial Balance was in excess by reason of each error.

Tabulate your answer in the following form:

Debit Excess	Credit Excess
(a)	

and so on for items (b) to (f).

You are also required to prepare a statement showing the correct net profit after the adjustment of the above errors.

(*Note:* You are required to show the Suspense Account and any journal entries.)

(*Institute of Bankers.*)

6. A book-keeper, having been unable to balance his Trial Balance at 31st December, 19—, opened up a Suspense Account and entered in it the amount he was out of balance.

The following errors were subsequently discovered:

(a) An allowance of £6·25 to a customer was entered in his account as £0·65.

(b) The total of the discount received column in the Cash Book for the month of December, £37·89, had inadvertently not been posted.

(c) £50, representing the sale proceeds of a machine scrapped, had been passed through the Sales Account.

(d) A balance of £97·40 owing by a customer had been omitted from the Schedule of Debtors at 31st December.

(e) The Bank Overdraft at £313·85 had been entered in the Trial Balance at £385·13.

(f) A cheque for £75, received from A. Robinson's Trustee in Bankruptcy, had been credited to Robinson's account. The debt had been written off at the end of the preceding financial year.

(g) Commission of £37·88 due to an agent in respect of goods sold by him had been passed through his account but no other entry made.

You are required:

(i) To set out—where necessary—the Journal entries rectifying the foregoing errors.

(ii) To show the Suspense Account after the rectification of all errors, bringing out the original difference in the books. (*L. Ch. C., modified.*)

7. When preparing the trial balance of L. Bromsgrove, it is found that the totals differ.

On checking the transactions in the books, the following errors are found:

(1) Bank charges amounting to £10·13 have been entered in the Cash Book but not posted to a Ledger.

(2) The sales journal has been undercast by £10.

(3) A cheque received from J. Green for £21·50 has been posted to the Ledger Account of A. Green.

(4) F. White requested a further copy of the invoice for a sale to him amounting to £24·53 and this duplicated copy was entered in the sales journal and posted to White's account in error.

The difference on the trial balance drawn up previously had been placed in a Suspense Account. What was the balance in the Suspense Account?

Draft the entries in the journal to correct these errors and show the Suspense Account. (*R.S.A., modified.*)

8. A trial balance was extracted from the books of Z. Moloney and failed to balance. The following errors were later found in the books and after their correction the trial balance agreed:

(1) The Sales Day Book was overcast by £100.

(2) £25 received from P. Peters was entered correctly in the cash book but posted as £52 to the credit of Peters' account.

(3) £10 allowed to a debtor, K. Bennet (for faulty goods sold to him) was included in the Returns Inwards and Allowances Book but debited to Bennet's account.

State the effect of each error on the balancing of the books and the amount of the difference on the trial balance extracted before they were corrected.   (*R.S.A.*)

9. (*a*) State how *each* of the following errors, made during the year ending 31st December, 19—, would affect the Net Profit of M. Martyn for that period:

(i) Stock at 1st January, 19—, under-valued by £176.

(ii) Interest on Martyn's bank deposit, £28, debited to his Profit and Loss Account.

(iii) The omission of credit purchases of £180 from the Purchase Day Book.

(iv) Discounts Received, £370, debited to Profit and Loss Account.

(v) A loan of £1,000 made to Martyn during 19— was credited to his Profit and Loss Account.

(*b*) If the incorrect Net Profit obtained after committing these errors was £2,000, calculate what the correct amount should be.   (*R.S.A.*)

10. L. Holland is a wholesale tobacconist. On 1st January, 19— his position was as follows: Warehouse fixtures and fittings £444; Cash in hand £15·38; Cash at bank £598·54; Stock £3,000; Sundry debtors, F. Marks £125·50, A. Pearce £348; Sundry creditors, Tabac Co. Ltd., £415.

Open, by Journal entry, the accounts necessary to record the above position in L. Holland's books, and post thereto, using the proper subsidiary books, the following transactions:

(*Note:* All cheques received are paid direct to bank.)

19—

Jan. 2.   Received from F. Marks a cheque for £122·36 in settlement of his account, 2½ per cent cash discount allowable having been deducted by him. Sold goods for cash (not banked) £98·28.

„ 3.   Bought on credit from Tabac Co. Ltd.: 50,000 Virginia cigarettes at £8·00 per thousand and 20,000 Turkish cigarettes at £9·00 per thousand, both less 10 per cent trade discount.
Sent a credit note for £5·11 to A. Pearce for goods returned by him.

„ 5.   Paid Tabac Co. Ltd., by cheque, the amount due on 1st January, deducting 2½ per cent cash discount.
Received a cheque from A. Pearce for the balance due from him.

„ 6.   Bought two delivery vans and paid for them £650, by cheque.
Sold goods for cash (not banked) £287·33.

„ 7.   Sold on credit to A. Pearce: Cigarettes £86, tobacco mixture £45 and snuff £20, less 5 per cent trade discount on cigarettes only.

„ 8.   Paid £370 cash into bank.
Sold on credit to F. Marks, fancy goods £280.

„ 9.   L. Holland took £5 from cash and cigarettes valued at cost at £12 for his own use.
Sold goods for cash (not banked) £53·75.

„ 10.   Bought and paid for from cash: packing materials £18·38, petrol for van £1·10.
The cheque received from A. Pearce on 5th January was returned by the bank 'unpaid'.

„ 12.   Bought, on credit, from X.Y. Co. Ltd., one case of briar pipes £72.
Returned 1,000 Virginia cigarettes to Tabac Co. Ltd. and received a credit note for them at the invoiced price of 3rd January.

„ 13.   Received a cheque from F. Marks for £140 on account.
Paid X.Y. Co. Ltd., by cheque, the amount due to them less 2½ per cent cash discount.

„ 14.   Received a cheque from A. Pearce for the whole amount due from him less £11·79 cash discount allowable.
Sold some of the warehouse fittings for £24 cash, which was banked.

Balance the ledger accounts and Cash Book, bring down the balances and extract a Trial Balance as on 14th January, 19—. (*N.B.* No Trading Account, Profit and Loss Account, or Balance Sheet is to be prepared.)   (*R.S.A., modified.*)

11.   The financial position of C. Ross, a stationer, on 1st April, 19—, was as follows:

> Fixtures and fittings, £185·50; Stock, £725·75; Cash at bank, £346·63; Cash in hand, £29·88; Creditors: J. King, £52·75, L. Derby, £24; Rent payable £15; Debtor: S. Miller £38.

19—
Apr. 2.   Purchased from G. Wood, 6 gross pencils at £1·80 per gross. Paid by cheque.
 „ 3.   Paid from cash: Wages, £7·90; Advertising, £5·60.
 „ 5.   Sold on credit to S. Miller: 12 reams foolscap at £0·90 per ream; 6 clip files at £0·50 each; 2½ dozen bottles of ink at £0·10 each. The whole invoice subject to 10 per cent discount.
 „ 6.   Paid L. Derby, by cheque, the amount due to him, less 2½ per cent cash discount.
 „ 7.   Paid £15 rent by cheque.
        Cash sales (banked) £27·64.
 „ 8.   Purchased, on credit, from L. Derby: 6 sets of account books at £8 per set, and one parcel of blotting paper costing £5.
 „ 9.   Received from S. Miller a cheque (banked) for £37·05. He had deducted £0·95 cash discount allowable.
 „ 10.   Drew and cashed cheque £20 for office cash.
        C. Ross took £5 cash for private expenses.
 „ 12.   S. Miller's account was credited with the invoiced price of 15 bottles of ink broken in transit.
Apr. 13. Sold sundry fixtures for £12 (paid into office cash).
 „ 14.   Paid J. King £25 on account, by cheque.

Balance the Cash Book and ledger accounts, bring down the balances and extract a Trial Balance as on 14th April, 19—.
(*N.B.*   No Trading Account, Profit and Loss Account, or Balance Sheet is to be prepared.)   (*R.S.A., modified.*)

12.   On 1st March, 19—, the assets of F. Smith were: Cash in hand £6·11; Cash at bank £188·15; Stock £546·99; Furniture and fittings £250. His liabilities were: £18·50 due to G. Davis, and £16 due to P. Allen.
Open, by Journal entry, the accounts necessary to record the above in F. Smith's books and post thereto, using the proper subsidiary books, the following transactions:

19—
Mar. 3.   Sold, on credit, to H. Miller, goods to the value of £50 subject to 25 per cent trade discount.
        Paid G. Davis, by cheque, the amount owing, less 2½ per cent cash discount.
        Cashed a cheque for £20 out of which F. Smith took £5, the balance being paid into office cash.
 „ 4.   Cash sales were £18·87 (paid to bank).
        Bought a safe for the office from D. Peel and paid for it by cheque £32. Sold, on credit, to H. Miller, goods to the value of £85, not subject to trade discount. He returned half the goods sold to him on 3rd March, and was given a credit note for them.
 „ 5.   Cash sales £27·90 (paid to bank).
        Sent P. Allen a cheque for £10 on account and purchased from him, on credit, goods to the value of £22.
        Purchased, on credit, from G. Davis goods valued at £38·75.
 „ 6.   Received a cheque (paid to bank) for £78 from H. Miller, and allowed £2 cash discount due to him.

Mar. 7. Paid out of office cash: Wages £7·60; Stationery £2·50; and private expenses £7·90.
Paid to P. Allen by cheque the balance due to him, less £0·95 cash discount.

„   8. Sold for £5 cash, which was banked, an old desk out of the office.

Balance the Cash Book and ledger accounts as on 8th March, 19—, carry down the balances and extract a Trial Balance.   (*R.S.A.*, *modified*.)

13.   F. Parker and M. Jones are in partnership as house furnishers. On 1st May, 19—, the partnership capital belonged: two-thirds to F. Parker, one-third to M. Jones.

On the above date the financial position of the partnership was: Cash at bank £925; Cash in hand £27; Stock £2,323; Shop fixtures and fittings £350; Sundry debtors: B. Franks £168, P. Masters £70; Creditor; N. Rose £113.

Open, by Journal entry, the accounts necessary to record the above in the partnership books and post thereto, using the proper subsidiary books, the following transactions:

19—
May   2. Sold to P. Masters, on credit, 6 kitchen cabinets at £25 each and 4 cupboards at £15 each The whole invoice subject to 20 per cent trade discount.
Paid N. Rose, by cheque, the amount due to him less 2½ per cent cash discount, which he allowed.

„   5. B. Franks sent a cheque (which was banked) for £163·80 to settle his account; he had deducted £4·20 cash discount which could not, however, be allowed as the payment was overdue.
Cash sales (paid into office cash) £83.

„   6. Purchased, on credit, from N. Rose: 20 carpets at £32 each; 1 bedroom suite at £85; and 9 dozen stair rods at £8 per gross.
B. Franks paid the balance due from him in cash, which was not banked.

„   7. F. Parker and M. Jones each took £20 out of office cash for private purposes.

„   8. Sold to B. Franks, on credit: 8 chairs at £4 each, 4 bookcases at £12 each, and 10 electric lamps at £1·25 each.

„   9. Paid from office cash: £15 for purchase and fixing of shelves in the shop and £14·75 for linoleum purchased for resale.

„ 10. P. Masters sent a cheque, which was banked, for the amount due from him on 1st May, less 2½ per cent cash discount allowable.

„ 12. M. Jones paid £1,250 into the partnership bank account as additional capital.
Cash sales (not banked) £55.

„ 14. Parker and Jones bought the freehold of the shop in which they were carrying on business and paid their landlord, by cheque, £2,020 (£2,000 for the freehold and £20 rent due to date).

„ 15. P. Masters returned one of the kitchen cabinets sold to him on 2nd May, and a credit note was sent to him for the invoice value of it.

„ 16. £70 of the cash in hand was paid to bank.
Paid N. Rose, by cheque, £300 on account.

Balance the Cash Book and ledger accounts, bring down the balances and extract a Trial Balance as on 16th May, 19—.

(*N.B.*   No Trading Account, Profit and Loss Account, or Balance Sheet is to be prepared.)   (*R.S.A.*, *modified*.)

14.   Miller & Hodges are the proprietors of the *Blankshire Weekly News*. The following Trial Balance was extracted from the books of the firm on 31st December, 19—.

On that date the stock of paper, etc. was valued at £640.

You are required to prepare Trading and Profit and Loss Accounts for the year ended 31st December, 19—, and a Balance Sheet as on that date. Show also the closing entries in the journal.

TRIAL BALANCE
31st December, 19—

	£	£
Capital Accounts Jan. 1, 19—:		
Miller		1,725
Hodges		1,414
Drawings during year:		
Miller	585	
Hodges	520	
Cash at bank	577	
Cash in hand	58	
Sales of newspapers		2,222
Received for advertisements		4,510
Insurances	80	
Carriage on purchases	38	
Purchases: paper	823	
Purchases: ink, blocks, etc.	132	
Rent and rates	275	
Office salaries	365	
General expenses	419	
Compositors' and reporters' wages	3,108	
Repairs to machinery	78	
Sundry debtors and creditors	289	313
Stock (paper, etc.), Jan. 1, 19—	750	
Plant and machinery	1,575	
Motor cars	512	
	£10,184	£10,184

(a) Value of blocks on hand 31st December, 19—, was £52.
(b) Carry forward: Insurance £20; Rent and rates £100.
(c) Depreciate plant and machinery by £120.   (*R.S.A., modified.*)

ILLUSTRATION TO SHOW USE OF SUBSIDIARY BOOKS CONCURRENTLY

On 1st February 19—, J. Overend went into business as a retailer. You are asked to record the following transactions in the proper subsidiary books, posting them to the necessary ledger accounts.

(*Note.*—A petty cash book having two analysis columns, (1) Wages, (2) Sundry Expenses, is to be used for recording payments in cash. Cheques and cash received are banked on the day of receipt, and no 'cash' column is therefore required in the main cash book.)

19—

Feb. 1. J. Overend paid to the business bank account a personal cheque for £500 as his capital; he also brought in a motor van, value £300, for the use of the business.
Received by cheque a loan of £250 from L. Tubbs.
Paid by cheque, rent £20.
Drew and cashed cheque for £25 for petty cash imprest.
Purchased on credit from N. Fish goods valued at £120, less 10 per cent trade discount.

„ 2. Bought furniture for use in the business from L. Brown, invoice price £65, paying £20 on account, balance due on 31st March.
Paid from Petty Cash—Wages £5, Sundry Expenses £1·90.

„ 4. Purchased on credit from T. Crabbe goods for £60.
Received for shop sales £30.

„ 5. Sold goods on credit to K. Smith for £19 and to Y. Netherby £26.
Purchased a job lot of goods for £120, paying for them by cheque.

„ 6. Returned to N. Fish one fourth of the goods purchased from him and sent cheque for balance due, less 5 per cent cash discount.

„ 7. K. Smith sent cheque in payment of his account, deducting 2½ per cent cash discount.

„ 8. It was agreed this day that L. Tubbs should become a partner in the business; the amount received from him on 1st February to be transferred to his capital account. L. Tubbs also contributed, as part of his capital, goods (stock) costing £150 for future sale by the firm.

„ 9. Paid from Petty Cash—Wages £5·50. Sundry Expenses £4·30.
Received for shop sales £35.
Paid by cheque to O. Ormerod £75 for shop furniture.

„ 11. Purchased on credit from L. Bodkin goods invoiced at £25.

„ 12. N. Fish wrote that he was unable to allow the cash discount from the payment of 6th as it was contrary to terms, and that the amount deducted was being carried forward as outstanding.
Received for shop sales £42.

„ 13. Drew and cashed cheque for petty cash purposes to restore imprest.
(*R.S.A., modified.*)

188

CASH BOOK

Dr.

Feb.	Particulars	Fo.	£	£
1	Balance	J		500·00
,, 1	Loan a/c. (L. Tubbs)	6		250·00
,, 4	Sales	8		30·00
,, 7	K. Smith	14	0·47	18·53
,, 9	Sales	8		35·00
,, 12	Sales	8		42·00
	Total to Dis. Alld. a/c. Dr.	17	0·47	875·53
				875·53
Feb. 14	Balance	b/d		521·88

Cr.

Feb.	Particulars	Fo.	£	£
1	Rent	16		20·00
,, 1	Petty Cash	PCB		25·00
,, 2	L. Brown	5		20·00
,, 5	Purchases	7		120·00
,, 6	N. Fish	11	4·05	76·95
,, 9	Furniture	4		75·00
,, 13	Petty Cash	PCB		16·70
,, 13	Balance	c/d		521·88
				875·53
	Total to Dis. Rec'd a/c. Cr.	10	4·05	
			4·05	

PETTY CASH BOOK

Dr.

Amount	Fo.	Particulars	Date
£25·00	CB	Bank	Feb. 1
25·00			
8·30	b/d	Balance	Feb. 13
16·70	CB	Bank	,, 13

Cr.

Date	Particulars	Rec. No.	Amount	Wages	Sundries
			£	£	£
Feb. 2	Wages	1	5·00	5·00	
,, 2	Expenses		1·90		1·90
,, 9	Wages	2	5·50	5·50	
,, 9	Expenses		4·30		4·30
			16·70	10·50	6·20
Feb. 13	Balance	c/d	8·30	(18)	(19)
			25·00		

JOURNAL

			Dr. £	Cr. £
19—				
Feb. 1	Cash at Bank .. .. Dr. Motor Van .. .. „ to Capital a/c. (J. Overend) .. Being assets brought into business by proprietor.	CB 3 1	500·00 300·00	800·00
			800·00	800·00
Feb. 2	Furniture a/c. .. .. Dr. to L. Brown .. .. .. See Invoice No..... and Agreement of this date.	4 5	65·00	65·00
Feb. 8	Loan (L. Tubbs) a/c. .. Dr. Purchases a/c. .. .. „ to Capital a/c. (L. Tubbs) .. Being Capital contribution of L. Tubbs who became partner this day.	6 7 2	250·00 150·00	400·00
Feb. 12	Discount Received a/c. .. Dr. to N. Fish .. .. .. Discount not allowed by N. Fish on payment made Feb. 6th	10 11	4·05	4·05
			£1,269·05	£1,269·05

PURCHASES JOURNAL

								£
Feb.	1	N. Fish					11	108·00
„	4	T. Crabbe					12	60·00
„	11	L. Bodkin					13	25·00
		Total to Purchases a/c. Dr.					7	£193·00

SALES JOURNAL

								£
Feb.	5	K. Smith					14	19·00
„	5	Y. Netherby					15	26·00
		Total to Sales a/c. Cr.					8	£45·00

PURCHASES RETURNS JOURNAL

								£
Feb.	6	N. Fish					11	27·00
		Total to Purchases Returns a/c. Cr. ...					9	£27·00

LEDGER
CAPITAL ACCOUNT (J. OVEREND) (1)

Dr.				Cr.
	Feb.1	Balance	J	£ 800·00

Dr.   CAPITAL ACCOUNT (L. TUBBS) (2)   Cr

			£
Feb. 8	Sundries	J	400·00

Dr.   MOTOR VAN ACCOUNT (3)   Cr.

			£	
Feb. 1	Balance	J	300·00	

Dr.   FURNITURE ACCOUNT (4)   Cr.

			£	
Feb. 2	L. Brown	J	65·00	
„ 9	Bank	CB	75·00	

Dr.   L. BROWN ACCOUNT (5)   Cr.

			£				£
Feb. 2	Bank	CB	20·00	Feb. 1	Furniture	J	65·00

Dr.   LOAN ACCOUNT (L. TUBBS) (6)   Cr.

			£				£
Feb. 8	Capital a/c. (L. Tubbs)	J	250·00	Feb. 1	Bank	CB	250·00

Dr.   PURCHASES ACCOUNT (7)   Cr.

			£	
Feb. 5	Bank	CB	120·00	
„ 8	Capital a/c. (L. Tubbs)	J	150·00	
„ 13	Sundries	PJ	193·00	

Dr.   SALES ACCOUNT (8)   Cr.

						£
			Feb. 4	Bank	CB	30·00
			„ 9	„	CB	35·00
			„ 12	„	CB	42·00
			„ 13	Sundries	SJ	45·00

Dr.   PURCHASES RETURNS ACCOUNT (9)   Cr.

			£
Feb. 6	Sundries	PRJ	27·00

Dr.   DISCOUNT RECEIVED ACCOUNT (10)   Cr.

			£				£
Feb. 12	N. Fish	J	4·05	Feb. 13	Sundries	CB	4·05

Dr.   N. FISH ACCOUNT (11)   Cr.

			£				£
Feb. 6	Returns	PRJ	27·00	Feb. 1	Purchases	PB	108·00
„ 6	Bank & Dis.	CB	81·00	„ 12	Disc. Recd. a/c.	J	4·05

Dr.   T. CRABBE ACCOUNT (12)   Cr.

					£
			Feb. 4	Purchases	PJ	60·00

Dr.   L. BODKIN ACCOUNT (13)   Cr.

			Feb. 11	Purchases	PJ	£ 25·00

Dr.   K. SMITH ACCOUNT (14)   Cr.

Feb. 5	Sales	SJ	£ 19·00	Feb. 7	Bank & Dis.	CB	£ 19·00

Dr.   Y. NETHERBY ACCOUNT (15)   Cr.

Feb. 5	Sales	SJ	£ 26·00

Dr.   RENT ACCOUNT (16)   Cr.

Feb. 1	Bank	CB	£ 20·00

Dr.   DISCOUNT ALLOWED ACCOUNT (17)   Cr.

Feb. 13	Sundries	CB	£ 0·47

Dr.   WAGES ACCOUNT (18)   Cr.

Feb. 13	Sundries	PCB	£ 10·50

Dr.   SUNDRY EXPENSES (19)   Cr.

Feb. 13	Sundries	PCB	£ 6·20

TRIAL BALANCE

	Dr.	Cr.
	£	£
Cash at Bank	521·88	
Cash in hand	25·00	
Capital (J. Overend)		800·00
Capital (L. Tubbs)		400·00
Motor Vans	300·00	
Furniture	140·00	
L. Brown		45·00
Purchases	463·00	
Sales		152·00
Purchases Returns		27·00
N. Fish		4·05
T. Crabbe		60·00
L. Bodkin		25·00
Y. Netherby	26·00	
Rent	20·00	
Discount allowed	0·47	
Wages	10·50	
Sundry Expenses	6·20	
	£1,513·05	£1,513·05

21

INCOME AND EXPENDITURE ACCOUNTS

THE financial records of institutions such as sports clubs, societies and charitable organizations, which are formed not to make a profit but to pursue certain activities, are dictated by the size and nature of the organization and by the form of the final accounts. In place of the Trading and Profit and Loss Accounts the treasurer is usually called upon to provide:

1. A Receipts and Payments Account.
2. An Income and Expenditure Account.
3. A Balance Sheet.

Receipts and Payments Account

This is a classified summary of the Cash Book, showing, as in the Cash Book, receipts on the debit side and payments on the credit side. The compilation of this account is greatly facilitated if a cash book with analysis columns (particularly on the credit side on which items are usually more numerous) is kept.

Income and Expenditure Account

As the main object of a club or society is not to make a profit, a Profit and Loss Account is not prepared. Nevertheless, most organizations will have some capital (*i.e.,* assets in excess of liabilities) and this capital may either increase or diminish, depending largely on the level of subscriptions in relation to expenditure. To ascertain the nature and size of any such changes, an Income and Expenditure (or Revenue) Account is compiled.

The Income and Expenditure Account is similar in form to the Profit and Loss Account. All income (*i.e.,* additions to Capital) will be shown on the credit side and all expenses (which reduce Capital) on the debit side.

Unlike the Receipts and Payments Account, which shows only money actually received or paid, the Income and Expenditure Account will include income due but not received, and expenses due but not paid, up to the date on which it is drawn up. Again the Receipts and Payments Account will include all income received and all expenses paid whether they refer to the period under review or not. The income and expenses entered in the Income and Expenditure Account will be those for the current financial period only.

The Income and Expenditure Account is usually prepared from the Receipts and Payments Account. An example is given on page 194:

RECEIPTS AND PAYMENTS ACCOUNT OF
THE ALBION SOCIAL CLUB
FOR YEAR ENDED 31ST DECEMBER, 19—

	£				£
Balance (1st Jan., 19—) ..	70	Affiliation Fees			10
Subscriptions	240	Prizes			12
Profit on dances	148	Games Equipment			20
Collections (Matches) ..	25	Rent			105
Competition fees	18	Rates			30
Sales of Refreshments ..	82	Printing..			16
		Stationery			22
		Postages			19
		Secretaries Expenses			14
		Repairs (Equipment)			27
		Wages			120
		Refreshments			51
		Balance			137
	£583				£583

The Income and Expenditure Account is shown below (allowance being made for the following matters):

	£			£
Accounts Outstanding 31/12/19—		Rent paid in advance		15
Printing	4	Subscriptions due		12
Refreshments	7	Subscriptions in advance ..		5

Fixed assets owned on 1st Jan., 19— (Furniture and fittings £50 and Games Equipment £200) to be depreciated 10 per cent.
Capital 1st Jan., 19—, £420

INCOME AND EXPENDITURE ACCOUNT
FOR YEAR ENDED 31ST DECEMBER, 19—

	£	£	£		£	£	£
Affiliation Fees ..			10	Subscriptions			
Prizes			12	received		240	
Rent	105			Add subs. in			
Less rent in				arrear		12	
advance ..	15					252	
			90	Less subs. in			
Rates			30	advance ..		5	
Printing	16						247
Add A/cs. out-				Profit on Dances			148
standing ..	4			Collections at			
			20	matches ..			25
Stationery ..			22	Competition fees			18
Postages ..			19	Sales of Refresh-			
Secretaries expenses			14	ments ..		82	
Repairs (equipment)			27	Cost of Refresh-			
Wages			120	ments	51		
Depreciation:				Add outstanding			
Furniture and				A/cs.	7		
Fittings ..	15					58	
Equipment ...	20						24
		35					
Surplus of Income							
over Expenditure			63				
			£462				£462

Notes: 1. It is unlikely that accounts would be kept of the fixed assets included in the above list. Probably an inventory would be kept.

2. A separate Profit and Loss Account would probably be prepared for each dance.

BALANCE SHEET OF THE ALBION SOCIAL CLUB
AS AT 31ST DECEMBER, 19—

	£	£		£	£
Accounts outstanding:			Cash at Bank		137
Printing	4		Furniture and Fittings ..	150	
Refreshments.. ..	7		*Less* Depreciation ..	·15	
	—	11		—	135
Subscriptions in advance		5	Games Equipment ..	200	
Capital	420		additions during year	20	
Add surplus of income				—	
over expenditure ..	63			220	
	—	483	*Less* depreciation ..	20	
				—	200
			Rent in advance ..		15
			Subscriptions due ...		12
		£499			£499

SOME ADVICE TO CLUB TREASURERS

1.   Open a bank account. The Bank Statement, besides being a check on your accounts, will show that the funds of the club have not been tampered with.

2.   Pay accounts by cheque when possible.

3.   Draw sufficient cash out of the bank for petty cash expenses. To run out of petty cash and pay out of your own pocket is to run on a deficit. A deficit cannot be checked.

4.   On the last day of the financial year, pay all cash into the bank, even if some must be withdrawn the following day.

5.   Issue a receipt, keeping a carbon copy, for all money received.

6.   Obtain a receipt for all money paid (if possible).

7.   Number and file receipts in the order in which they are entered in the cash book.

8.   To reduce detail in the cash book enter subscriptions as received in separate book. Transfer in totals to the Cash Book as and when the money is banked.

9.   Pay accounts promptly. It will probably then be unnecessary to keep personal accounts for creditors. Instead invoices due can be kept in a file until paid and receipted.

10.   Keep a Cash Book with cash and bank columns and analysis columns on the credit side.

11.   Keep an inventory of equipment in a card index or in a loose-leaf book.

12.   When you pay or receive money, make a note at the time—do not depend on memory.

13.   Check the cash every day cash is received or paid.

WRITTEN EXERCISES

1.   In a school of 360 pupils it is decided to issue a magazine at 3p per copy. All the students except 30, purchase the magazine. Each member of the staff, 10 in all, pays 5p for his copy. Two local firms insert advertisements for which they each pay £0·75. Two and a half gross copies are printed at a cost of 2p per copy and there are incidental expenses amounting to £2·50 that have not been paid.

(a) Prepare the Receipts and Payments, and Income and Expenditure Accounts for the venture.

(b) State the nature of the balances obtained in the two accounts.

(R.S.A., modified.)

2.　The Secretary of the Southwell Tennis Club at the end of its first year's existence 31st March 19–7 asks you to prepare a financial statement to be presented to club members—48 in all. You find that the Secretary holds £8 in petty cash, there is a bank account with a balance of £25, a portable typewriter worth £18, and sporting material worth £45. Accounts amounting to £24 are owing to suppliers of canteen goods and subscriptions for the first year still owing, amount to £4. Five members have paid in advance the annual subscription of £1 for the year beginning 1st April, 19–7. A levy at the rate of £0·05 a member has yet to be paid to the Central Tennis Association.

Canteen stocks on hand are valued at £10.

Show the statement of Assets and Liabilities as at 31st March, 19–7. (Club Funds £78·60.)　　　　　　　　　　　　(<i>Univ. of Melb., Leaving Cert, modified.</i>)

3.　The honorary treasurer of a tennis club presented the following statement at the annual meeting of members:

Balance Sheet Year Ended 31st August, 19–8

19–7		£	19–8		£
Sept. 1	Cash at Bank　...	102	Aug. 31	Purchases of Balls	40
19–8				Refreshments　..	220
Aug. 31	Subscriptions　..	240		Marking and Repair-	
	Sales of Refreshments	305		ing Courts..　...	38
	Court Hire　..	27		Construction of New	
	Sales of Balls　...	37		Court　..　..	250
				General Expenses ..	31
				Cash at Bank　...	132
		£711			£711

In presenting the statement he remarked: 'The balance sheet shows a surplus for the year of £30.' In reply to questions he gave the following information:

Tennis balls on hand at 1/9/19–7 cost £4.
Tennis balls on hand at 31/8/19–8 cost £9.
Creditors for refreshments at 1/9/19–7, £40, at 31/8/19–8, £30.
Subscriptions owing at 1/9/19–7, £20, at 31/8/19–8, £35.
The club's courts were valued at 1/9/19–7 at £600.

Prepare statements of (a) income and expenditure, and (b) assets and liabilities as you think they should have been presented to the members.
(Club Funds £996. Surplus £30.)

(Univ. of Melb., Leaving Cert., modified.)

4.　The Riverview Golf Club had the following balances at 1st July, 19–1:

Subscriptions paid in advance by members £10; Cash at Bank £400; Land and Buildings £4,500; Stock of refreshments £65; Furniture £240; Tractor and equipment £1,070.

Receipts and payments for the year ended 30th June, 19–2, were:

Receipts—					£
Total subscriptions　..	..	...	...	...	4,500
Donations　..	..	...	...	...	40
Sale of part of the Golf Course	...	...	...	300
Sale of refreshments ..	...	...	...	220
					£5,060

Payments—						£
Wages ..	..	...	...	—	...	.. 3,255
Rates and taxes	..	..	...	...	..	26
Electricity	..	..	...	...	...	... 12
New furniture	..	...	...	...	..	100
Water rates	..	..	...	...	..	.. 32
Refreshments ..	..	..	..	..	..	140
Sundry expenses	..	..	..	..	..	46
Secretary's honorarium		..	...	..	..	52
						£3,663

On 30th June, 19–2, you are supplied with the following:

(a) The committee requires the following depreciation provision: Land and Building £300; Furniture £20; Tractor and Equipment £200.

(b) Subscriptions paid in advance by members for year ended 30th June, 19–2, totalled £25, whilst subscriptions in arrears on this date were £32.

(c) Stock of refreshments at 30th June, 19–2, £75.

The committee requests you to prepare an Income and Expenditure account for the year ended 30th June, 19–2, and a Balance Sheet as at 30th June, 19–2. (Club Funds £6,969. Surplus £704.)

5. Prepare statements showing (a) income and expenditure; and (b) assets and liabilities, from the following information relating to a club:

(i) Summary of cash transactions for year ended 30th September, 19–9.

Receipts—						£
Balance 1st October, 19–8	..	...	..	...	..	346
Subscriptions	..	..	..	...	...	... 632
Interest ..	..	..	...	...	...	... 15
Donations	..	..	...	..	..	.. 110
Card Parties and Social Functions		..	...	...	..	247
						£1,350

Payments—						£
Printing ..	..	..	...	...	—	.. 140
Books for Library	..	..	..	..	..	.. 88
Rent ..	..	..	..	..	..	... 624
Refreshments and Expenses for Social Functions			..	..	230
Purchase of Typewriter (1st October, 19–8)	..	...	..		60
Balance, 30th September, 19–9 ..	..	...	—	..		208
						£1,350

(ii) Assets at 1st October, 19–8

						£
Furniture and Office Equipment	...	—	...	...		400
Library ..	..	...	...	...	..	342
Commonwealth Bonds ..	...	...	...	...	..	500
Subscriptions in Arrear	..	..	..	..	..	26

(iii) Depreciation to be charged on furniture and equipment (including type-writer) at 5 per cent per annum on value at 1st October, 19–8, and on library, £65.

(iv) Subscriptions in arrear at 30th September, 19–9, £18.
(Deficit £86.) *(Univ. of Melb., Leaving Cert., modified.)*

6. The following details relate to the catering activities of 'Ye Ancient Golf Club' for the year ended 30th June, 19–2.

Stock of Foodstuffs: £

1st July, 19–1		567
30th June, 19–2		680
Creditors for catering stocks:		
1st July, 19–1		123
30th June, 19–2		135
Cash paid to suppliers during year ended 30th June, 19–2		6,789
Catering receipts		10,012
Staff wages paid		2,345
Staff wages outstanding:		
1st July, 19–1		100
30th June, 19–2		75
Sundry direct expenses		250
Proportion establishment charges		625

You are required to set out in good style the Catering Account for the year ended 30th June, 19–2, bringing out the profit or loss on the working for the year.

(*L. Ch. C.*)

7. Prepare, from the following Trial Balance (*a*) the Refreshments Trading Account and (*b*) the Income and Expenditure Account, of the Stamford Club for the year ended 31st December, 19—, and Balance Sheet as at that date.

TRIAL BALANCE

31st December, 19—

	£		£
Stock-takers' fees	6	Refreshment creditors	102
Accountancy	5	Expenses creditors	154
Cash register	20	Bank loan, secured on Free-	
Refreshments stock at		hold	1,625
1/1/19—	54	Refreshments takings	1,693
Purchases of refreshments	1,125	Members' subscriptions	71
Light and heat	76	Playing fees	27
Telephone	9	Rents received	13
Insurance	13	Sundry receipts	2
Games accessories	8	Capital account, accumulated	
Papers and periodicals	9	balance at 1st January, 19—	717
Printing and stationery	21		
Cash at bank	287		
Cash in hand	2		
Steward's float	5		
Property tax	16		
Rates and water	64		
Secretary's honorarium	30		
Furniture, at 1/1/19—	25		
Additions to furniture	67		
Wages	206		
Repairs	40		
Freehold premises	2,000		
Additions thereto	200		
Donation	2		
Bank interest and charges	68		
Cleaning	27		
Sundry expenses	19		
	£4,404		£4,404

You are required to make the following adjustments:

1. Subscriptions receivable but unpaid amount to £9.

2. Refreshments Stock at 31st December, 19—, is valued at £190.

3. Write off:

    (*a*) £5 depreciation of Cash Register.
    (*b*) £42 depreciation of Furniture.
    (*c*) £100 from value of Freehold Premises.

4. Insurance, £4, should be treated as a payment in advance.
                               (*Institute of Book-keepers, modified.*)

8. From the following particulars prepare the Income and Expenditure Account for the year ended 31st December, 19—, and the Balance Sheet as at that date, of a Professional Body:

TRIAL BALANCE
31ST DECEMBER, 19—

	£		£
Salaries and wages	9,280	Accumulated Fund: Balance	
Printing and stationery ..	1,257	at 1st Jan., 19—	55,933
Sundry expenses	549	Reserve funds, at 1st Jan.,	
Annual conference	655	19—	10,000
Audit fees	105	Sundry creditors	3,338
Parliamentary expenses ..	488	Subscriptions	21,569
Travelling expenses	2,239	Entrance fees	1,332
Post and telephones ..	558	Examination fees	9,618
Publicity expenditure ..	1,788	Interest and dividends ..	2,359
Grants to Branches, etc. ..	3,828	Subscriptions in advance ..	505
Cost of Year Book	2,466	Students' registration fees	
Production of Journal ..	2,050	(income)	4,041
Rent and light	855	Examinees' fees in advance	724
Cleaning	234	Sundry receipts	687
Repairs and renewals ..	217		
Amortization of lease ..	330		
Expenses of conducting exam-			
inations	11,118		
Leasehold premises	3,213		
Furniture, fittings and library	569		
Sundry debtors	527		
Payments in advance ..	490		
Cash at bank: Current ..	680		
Deposit ..	1,500		
Grants to various schemes ..	540		
Investments, at cost	62,347		
Cash in hand	25		
Expenses of joint committees	578		
Superannuation contribution	666		
Income tax and corporation			
duty	954		
	£110,106		£110,106

There are no adjustments to be made, but you should note the following:

    (*a*) The value of Leasehold Premises shown above is arrived at after deducting amortization of £3,300, which sum includes the amount written off already in the current year.

    (*b*) The Furniture, Fittings and Library, shown at £569 above, includes additions of £200 made during the year.   (*Institute of Book-keepers.*)

9. A well-known English County Cricket Club has just produced its Accounts for the year ended 31st December, 19—. You are required to prepare, from the following list of balances, the Income and Expenditure Account for that year and the Balance Sheet at the closing date:

	£
Gate receipts	28,904
Match expenses	27,803
Repairs to grounds	9,827
Rent received for Test Trial	150
Subscriptions received from supporters	16,478
Sundry wages, grants and other payments	5,886
Sundry receipts from Test Matches	1,759
Sale of tickets for reserved seats	386
Printing, postages and stationery	2,151
Office rent, rates, etc.	2,207
Interest and dividends received	749
Sundry interest received	148
Income-tax recovered	845
Insurances (paid)	217
Income-tax paid	278
Accumulated fund at 1st Jan., 19—	25,058
Life Membership fund	1,974
General reserve	19,000
Investments, at cost	36,731
Cash at bank and in hand	5,646
Loans made to other cricket clubs	5,816
Sundry creditors and reserve for income-tax ..	1,532
Sundry debtors	221
Office furniture	200

(Institute of Book-keepers.)

22

RESERVES AND PROVISIONS

LET us suppose that the following is the Balance Sheet of a trader at the end of an accounting period:

BALANCE SHEET

				£					£
Creditors	...	...	...	1,000	Bank ..	..	...	...	2,000
Capital	...	...	...	35,000	Debtors	..	..	..	10,000
					Stock	..	..	..	5,000
					Fixed Assets..		...	...	19,000
				£36,000					£36,000

His capital is £35,000; but this is on the assumption that the fixed assets would sell for £19,000 and that the whole sum, £10,000, will be collected from the debtors.

These are both questionable assumptions. As shown in Chapter Twelve, the value of the fixed assets is an estimate—one which may be far from the truth. Again, some of his debtors may be, or may become, insolvent. It follows that the amount shown as capital is open to doubt.

In consequence of this, the capital is often divided into two parts. One part, still called the capital, is the amount which may be regarded as 'safe'. The rest, about which there is doubt, is called a 'reserve' or a 'provision'. It would be called a provision if it were set aside to meet losses arising from a specific cause, such as bad debts. If it is intended as a margin of safety against unspecified risks, it is called a reserve.

It must be understood that the setting aside of a reserve or provision is simply a division of capital. It does not mean that money has been put in the bank for a 'rainy day'. Capital is not usually money, except on the day the business opens; it is the excess of all the assets over all liabilities. A reserve therefore is not necessarily money either—it is part of the excess of assets over liabilities.

In the example shown above there might be created a reserve for contingencies, and also a provision for bad debts. These will be shown separately.

Creation of Reserve

Let us suppose that it is decided to create a reserve of £1,500. The entries would be:

(*a*) Debit Profit and Loss Account £1,500 (to deduct the amount from Capital).

(*b*) Credit Reserve Account £1,500 (to transfer the amount to Reserve).

The Reserve Account will thus show a credit balance of £1,500, which would appear on the liabilities side of the Balance Sheet. The capital would be £1,500 less.

Provision for Bad Debts

The purpose of a provision is to anticipate losses arising from a specific cause—in this case, failure of debtors to pay the full sum due from them. The amount provided should bear a relation to the probable loss, and experience will give some guidance as to how big this provision should be. Let us assume that 5 per cent of the sum due is felt to be a safe allowance. The amount to be set aside this year in the example given would then be 5 per cent of £10,000, that is, £500. The entries would be:

(*a*) Debit Profit and Loss Accounts £500.

(*b*) Credit Provision for Bad Debts Account £500.

In any year, therefore, there will be two deductions from capital (in the Profit and Loss Account) in respect of bad debts:

(1) The bad debts actually incurred during the year.

(2) Provision for the bad probable debts amongst the sums still outstanding from debtors.

These deductions are usually shown independently.

Adjustment of Provision for Bad Debts

Once a provision has been created, all that is required in future years is to adjust the amount so that it bears the desired relation (say 5 per cent) to the book-value of the debtors. In the example given, the debtors stood at £10,000 and a 5 per cent provision amounted to £500. If in the next year the debtors rose to £11,000 it would be necessary to increase the provision to £550 by adding a further £50 in order to maintain the same percentage and the entries then would be:

(*a*) Debit Profit and Loss Account £50.

(*b*) Credit Provision for Bad Debts Account £50.

If, on the other hand, the debtors fell to £9,000, the provision would be £50 too big. This would be corrected by transferring £50 from the provision back to the Profit and Loss Account, the entries being:

(*a*) Debit Provision for Bad Debts Account £50.

(*b*) Credit Profit and Loss Account £50.

Illustration: The following is the Trial Balance (after ascertaining gross profit) of A. Trader, on 31st December, 19—:

	Dr. £	Cr. £
Sundry debtors ...	10,000	
Bad debts	450	
Provision for bad debts		300
Gross profit		7,500
Expenses	4,000	
Assets	12,000	
Liabilities		6,000
Capital		12,650
	£26,450	£26,450

The provision for bad debts is to be raised to an amount equal to 5 per cent of the 'sundry debtors'.

(A) Show the Profit and Loss Account, Bad Debts Account, Provision for Bad Debts Account, and the Balance Sheet on 31st December, 19—.

PROFIT AND LOSS ACCOUNT OF A. TRADER
FOR YEAR ENDED 31ST DECEMBER, 19—

Dr.			Cr.	
		£		£
Expenses		4,000	Gross Profit	7,500
Bad Debts		450		
Provision for Bad Debts				
5% of £10,000	500			
Less Provision	300			
		200		
Net Profit		2,850		
		£7,500		£7,500

BAD DEBTS ACCOUNT

Dr.			Cr.	
		£		£
Sundry Debtors		450	Profit and Loss A/c.	450

PROVISION FOR BAD DEBTS ACCOUNT

Dr.			Cr.	
		£		£
Balance ... ... c/d		500	Balance	300
			Profit and Loss A/c. ...	200
		£500		£500
			Balance ... ... b/d	£500

BALANCE SHEET OF A. TRADER
AS AT 31ST DECEMBER, 19—

Liabilities			£ 6,000	Other Assets			£ 12,000
Capital	..	.. 12,650		Sundry Debtors	.. 10,000		
Add Net Profit	..	2,850		*Less* Provision	..	500	
			15,500				9,500
			£21,500				£21,500

(B) Some firms prefer to combine the Bad Debts Account and the Provision for Bad Debts Account, which would then appear as follows:

PROVISION FOR BAD DEBTS ACCOUNT

Dr.   Cr.

Bad Debts	..	..	..	£ 450	Balance	..	...	...	£ 300
Balance	...	...	c/d	500	Profit and Loss A/c		...		650
				£950					£950
					Balance	...	...	b/d	£500

PROFIT AND LOSS ACCOUNT

	£	£	
Prov. for Bad Debts	500		
(5% of Debtors)			
Add Bad Debts	450		
	950		
Less Amt. in Pro-			
vision	300		
		650	

The first method has the advantage of giving a clearer statement, with less complication.

Provision for Discount Allowed

If it is the custom in the trade to allow discount for prompt payment, then in valuing the sundry debtors total for Balance Sheet purposes, provision must be made for the probable amount of discount to be allowed. As in the case of bad debts, the amount is usually determined as a percentage of the debtors but, before calculating the percentage, the provision for bad debts must be deducted. Clearly no allowance would be made for discount on accounts which were not expected to be paid.

Thus, proceeding with the example with which we started, if the debtors were £10,000 and provision for bad debts £500, the amount to be provided against discount at the rate of 5 per cent would be 5 per cent of £9,500, which is £475. The final estimated value of the debtors would then be £10,000 less £975, which is £9,025.

The entries and later adjustments for provision for discount would be similar to those for bad debts:

(a) Debit Profit and Loss Account £475.

(b) Credit Provision for Discount Allowed Account £475.

Provision for Discount Received

Some firms adjust the book-values not only of their debtors, but of their creditors also, by making an allowance for the discount they expect to receive, on the assumption that they themselves will pay their accounts in time and will be allowed discount.

The entries, though similar in nature, are on the opposite sides, because a reduction in creditors would increase the capital. For example, if the creditors stand at £5,000 and the discount expected is 5 per cent of this amount (*i.e.,* £250) the entries would be:

(a) Debit Provision for Discount Received Account £250.

(b) Credit Profit and Loss Account £250.

This deduction from the creditors would be shown in the Balance Sheet in the same way as deductions from debtors.

WRITTEN EXERCISES

1. The sundry debtors on 31st December, 19—, are £5,720. A bad debts provision of 5 per cent is to be made. The bad debts provision at 1st January, 19—, was £270 and the bad debts during the year amounted to £240. Show the Journal Ledger, Profit and Loss Account, and Balance Sheet entries for the above. (*U.E.I.*)

2. P. Ltd finds that the amount spent on repairs to machinery varies greatly from year to year. In order to equalize the charge against profits, a provision is built up commencing in 19–1 and credited with £800 each year, actual repairs being charged against this.

The actual amounts spent were as follows:

			£
Year to 31st December,	19–1	...	312
ditto	19–2	...	946
ditto	19–3	...	1,353
ditto	19–4	..	227

Write up the Provision Account, bringing down a balance each year and state how the balances would be shown in the successive Balance Sheets of the business. (*R.S.A., modified.*)

3. You are accountant to a firm which prepares accounts annually to 31st December. All routine entries and postings have been made up to 31st December, 19—, and an agreed Trial Balance has been drawn up which has served as the basis for preparation of accounts for the year.

It is the practice of this company to transfer all outstandings to an Outstanding Expenses Account or Payments in Advance Account as the case may be.

You are to imagine that you are engaged in 'closing the books' and to set out in Journal form the following adjustments which have been made in preparing the Profit and Loss Account:

(1) The allocation of wages. The debit in the Trial Balance is £29,373, and the amount outstanding £285, representing the wages for 29th–31st December.

Of the total, £80 had been spent on the erection of new plant, £158 on repairs to existing plant, £105 on repairs to buildings; £980 represents wages of lorry drivers; and the balance represents manufacturing wages.

(2) The provision of depreciation as follows: £3,170 on plant and machinery, £450 on motor lorries, and £100 on furniture and fittings.

(3) The bringing into account of the following payments in advance: Insurance (fire, etc., unexpired) £47, insurance on motor lorries, £31, and rates £190.

(4) The writing off as bad of the three following debtors' balances: A. Brown £170, C. Dickens £31, and E. Fenson £28.

(5) The provision for the firm's contribution for the year, £385, to the staff superannuation fund.

4. The sundry debtors of H. Foster & Co. stood at £8,400 on 31st December, 19—. On the same date the provision for bad debts was £150. Of the debtors £300 was considered to be bad and was written off. It was decided that provision for bad debts should be made equal to 2 per cent of the outstanding accounts and provision at the same rate for discount.

On 31st December in the following year the sundry debtors had fallen to £6,100 of which £200 was considered bad. Provision for bad debts and for discount was to be maintained at the same rates as in the previous year.

Show the Provision for Bad Debts Account, the Provision for Discount Account and the relevant entries in the Profit and Loss Account for both years.

5. On 1st January, 19—, the books of A. Trader show a credit balance on Provision for Doubtful Debts Account amounting to £270. This sum was made up as to £40 for an estimated loss on the account of G. Taylor, who owed £80, and as to the balance for general risks. During the year Taylor paid £60 but was clearly unable to make any further payment, and Clark, whose debt had been written off previously as wholly bad, paid £75. On 31st December, 19—, A. Trader decides that further debts to the extent of £340 are bad. The total debtors now remaining on his books amount to £8,920, but he fears that John Williams, whose debt is included in that figure, would be unable to pay £120 due from him. In addition he decides that the general provision for doubtful debts should amount to 5 per cent of the balance. It is brought to his notice that as he allows a discount of 2½ per cent for early payment, and most of his debtors take advantage of this allowance, he should make provision for it in his annual accounts. He has not previously done this, but decides to accept the advice given to him. The total discounts already allowed by A. Trader during 19— amount to £730.

You are asked to prepare the accounts in the books of A. Trader for the year to 31st December, 19—, recording these matters and to show the relevant entries in the Profit and Loss Account for the year to 31st December, 19—. Personal accounts of debtors are not required.   (*Institute of Bankers—Part* 1.)

23

THE WORK SHEET OR FOUR-COLUMN TRIAL BALANCE

IF a business man were presented with a Trial Balance by his book-keeper, it would be quite possible for him to prepare a Trading Account, a Profit and Loss Account, and a Balance Sheet from the figures contained in it. This would not relieve the book-keeper of the need to complete and balance the accounts in the ledger, which would naturally have to be kept up to date in order to provide similar information at the end of the next accounting period. But it would enable the business man to discover how he stood with the least possible delay, and would be of considerable assistance in making the necessary transfers in the accounts. An example is shown below, based on a Balance Sheet modified from one used in a Royal Society of Arts examination.

Example: N. Senior carries on the business of retail stationer and lending library. From the following Trial Balance, prepare his Trading and Profit and Loss Accounts for the year ended 31st March, 19—, and a Balance Sheet as on the date.

TRIAL BALANCE
31ST MARCH, 19—

	Dr. £	Cr. £
Opening stock of stationery and library books	3,020	
Insurance (annual premium to 31/12/19—)..	400	
Shop rent and rates (at £240 p.a.) to 30/6/19—	300	
House rent and rates (to 31/3/19—)	75	
Sales		8,694
Sundry debtors	22	
Sundry creditors		350
Furniture and fittings..	1,750	
Cash at bank ..	835	
Loan from M. Junior		1,000
N. Senior Capital Account ..		4,500
Bad debts written off	15	
Wages of shop assistants	1,420	
Office salaries ..	480	
Heating and lighting ..	690	
Repairs to furniture and fittings	226	
Purchases: Stationery	4,682	
Books for library	860	
Receipts from lending library		322
Returns outwards		303
Drawings during year	416	
Discount received		32
Carriage inwards	10	
	£15,201	£15,201

207

Adjustments:

1. House rent and rates are chargeable to the proprietor.
2. Furniture and fittings are estimated to have depreciated by 8 per cent.
3. Interest on capital is to be charged at 4 per cent.
4. Wages due and unpaid on 31st March, 19—, amounted to £20.
5. Interest is due on the loan from M. Junior for one year at 4 per cent.
6. Stock of stationery and books at 31st March, 19—, was £4,022.

Method

Step I. In preparing a Trading Account, Profit and Loss Account, and Balance Sheet from a Trial Balance, it is of great assistance to analyse the Trial Balance first. This is done by separating the balances which would appear in the Trading Account and Profit and Loss Account from those which would appear in the Balance Sheet. The Trial Balance is therefore drawn up again. The debit side is divided into two columns, the first containing the items which would be put in the Balance Sheet as assets, and the second containing the items which would be entered on the debit side of the Trading Account or Profit and Loss Account. The credit side of the Trial Balance is similarly divided into two columns, the first of these containing the items which would be entered on the credit side of the Trading Account and Profit and Loss Account, and the second containing the items which would appear on the Balance Sheet as liabilities.

The Trial Balance set out in this way is usually called a Work Sheet.

Step II. It is next necessary to deal with the matters referred to at the end of the original Trial Balance. No entries for these adjustments have yet been made in the books, from which it follows that each will require a double entry, one on the debit side and one on the credit side. The principles governing these entries have been discussed in detail in previous chapters, but it should be noted that each adjustment affects one asset or liability only; consequently each will increase, or diminish, capital. From this it is clear that:

(*a*) One entry will be in the Balance Sheet columns (*i.e.,* in the assets or liabilities columns).

(*b*) The double entry will be in the Trading Account or Profit and Loss Account columns.

If the first of these entries is on the debit side, the second will be on the credit side, and vice versa.

The four-column Trial Balance (or Work Sheet) is now set out as follows:

WORK SHEET

Account	DR. Balance Sheet (Assets) £	DR. Trading and P.& L. A/cs. (Debit side) £	CR. Trading and P.& L. A/cs. (Credit side) £	CR. Balance Sheet (Liabilities) £	Notes
Stock, 1/4/19—		3,020			Opening Stock
Insurance	300	100			(a)
Rent & Rates, Shop	60	240			(b) £60 in advance
House	75				(c) Add to Drawings
Sales			8,694		
Debtors	22				
Creditors				350	
Furniture & Fittings	1,750				Deduct Deprecia- tion
Bank	835				
Loan (Junior)				1,000	
Capital				4,500	Net Profit. Interest —Drawings
Bad Debts		15			(d)
Wages		1,420			(e) Add Wages due
Salaries		480			
Heating & Lighting		690			
Repairs		226			
Purchases (Stat.)		4,682			
(Books)		860			
Receipts (Library)			322		(f)
Returns Outwards			303		
Drawings	416				
Discount Received			32		
Carriage Inwards		10			
Adjustments					
Depreciate Furni- ture & Fittings		140		140	Deduct from Furn. & Fittings
Interest on Capital		180		180	Add to Capital
Wages Due		20		20	Add to Wages
Interest Due		40		40	
Stock 31/3/19	4,022		4,022		Closing Stock
	7,480	12,123	13,373	6,230	
	12,123			13,373	
	£19,603			£19,603	
			12,123		
Net Profit			£1,250		
	(1)	(2)	(3)	(4)	

For notes (a)—(f) see next page

Columns (1) and (2) added together should be equal to columns (3) and (4) added together, because when this is done we have reverted to the original Trial Balance *plus* the double entry for the adjustments.

The difference between columns (2) and (3) shows the net profit or loss because these columns contain the items for the Trading Account and the Profit and Loss Account.

In most cases the reasons for the distribution of items will be self-evident, but the following notes are given to explain the less obvious items. The letters refer to those in the final column of the Work Sheet.

(a) If the insurance premium of £400 gives cover for the whole year, at the end of March only one quarter of it will have expired. The rest is an asset.

(b) As the annual rent of the shop is £240, this sum must be regarded as having been consumed. The remaining £60 is payment for a service still owed by the landlord—the use of the premises for another three months—and is therefore an asset.

(c) The proprietor apparently lives in the house. Consequently the rent and rates paid for the house are a contribution to his private expenses. They are thus a form of drawings. The position is the same as if he had withdrawn the money to pay the rent.

(d) The bad debts written off during the year have already been deducted from the £22 still owing by debtors. Had they not been written off, the debtors would have been £37.

(e) It is assumed, in the absence of other information, that this and the following three items have been completely consumed. In the case of wages, the £20 still due must be added (see adjustments).

(f) The receipts from the library are equivalent to Sales and will be included with Sales in the Trading Account.

Step III. From this work sheet the Trading Account and the Profit and Loss Account and the Balance Sheet are prepared. The items in columns (2) and (3) make up the Trading Account and Profit and Loss Account. The Balance Sheet items are in columns (1) and (4), but to these must be added the net profit.

Notes may be made in the final column of items which should be grouped together (as wages and wages due).

The final accounts and Balance Sheet are shown on page 211.

The order of the assets and liabilities in the Trial Balance was not the correct order for a Balance Sheet, so they have been rearranged.

The Manufacturing Account

Gross profit is the difference between the cost of goods and the amount for which they are sold. It is simple to find this amount in the

TRADING ACCOUNT OF N. SENIOR
FOR YEAR ENDED 31ST MARCH, 19—

Dr.				Cr
	£	£		£	£
Opening Stock ..		3,020	Sales	8,694	
Purchases: Stationery	4,682		Receipts from Library	322	
Books ..	860				9,016
	5,542		Stock 31/3/19—		4,022
Less Returns Outwards	303				
		5,239			
Carriage Inwards ..		10			
Gross Profit ...		4,769			
		£13,038			£13,038

PROFIT AND LOSS ACCOUNT OF N. SENIOR
FOR YEAR ENDED 31ST MARCH, 19—

Dr.				Cr.
	£	£		£
Insurance		100	Gross Profit	4,769
Rent		240	Discount	32
Bad Debts ..		15		
Wages	1,420			
Add Wages due ..	20			
		1,440		
Office Salaries ..		480		
Heating and Lighting		690		
Repairs to Furniture and				
Fittings		226		
Depreciation ..		140		
Interest due on Loan		40		
Interest on Capital ..		180		
Net Profit		1,250		
		£4,801		£4,801

BALANCE SHEET OF N. SENIOR
AS AT 31ST MARCH, 19—

	£	£		£	£
Capital: N. Senior	4,500		*Fixed Assets*		
Add Interest ..	180		Furniture and Fittings	1,750	
Add Profit ..	1,250		Less Depreciation	140	
	5,930				1,610
Less Drawings..	491				
		5,439	*Current Assets*		
Loan: M. Junior		1,000	Rent and Rates prepaid	60	
Current Liabilities			Insurance prepaid	300	
Wages due ..	20		Stock	4,022	
Interest due on loan	40		Debtors	22	
Creditors ..	350		Cash at Bank ...	835	
		410			5,239
		£6,849			£6,849

case of a trader, because the cost of the goods is what he pays for them, and he is equally clear as to the amount for which they are sold. This is not true, however, of the manufacturer. He buys, not finished articles, ready for sale, but raw materials, labour, coal or electricity for power, etc. The cost of obtaining goods is, to the manufacturer, the cost of making them. And it is this cost which must be deducted from the sales in order to discover his gross profit.

Now the cost of manufacturing goods is divided into two parts— 'Prime Cost' and 'Oncost'. By prime cost is meant those costs which vary directly with the amount produced. It comprises those expenses, like wages and raw material, which would be avoided if the goods were not produced. Oncost, on the other hand, consists of expenses such as rent, salaries, interest on loans, etc., on which there would be no immediate saving if output were reduced. In the long run, of course, all expenses bear a relation to the amount produced. If, for instance, output were curtailed for a sufficiently long period of time, it would pay the business to take smaller premises and thus reduce the rent. In a similar way, the salary bill would have to be cut down. But the relation between such costs and output is not immediate and direct.

In a manufacturing business, it is the prime cost which takes the place of purchases in the Trading Account. The Trading Account is renamed the Manufacturing Account. The prime costs of a trading business, of course, are all included in purchases and carriage inwards.

It is difficult to give the student clear-cut rules to distinguish between the costs which are entered in the Manufacturing Account and those which would be entered in the Profit and Loss Account, because the decision would frequently depend on an intimate knowledge of the particular industry concerned. Some guidance, however, is possible.

(a) All selling expenses will be put in the Profit and Loss Account. They are not incurred until after the goods are in a saleable condition. These will include advertising expenses, commissions to travellers, carriage outwards, etc. It would also include packing material such as crates used purely for transport purposes, but not the containers in which the goods must be sold to the consumer, such as packets for soap powders, tins for paint, etc.

(b) Wages present a problem. If separate accounts are kept for manufacturing wages, these would be put in the Manufacturing Account and other wages in the Profit and Loss Account. If separate accounts are not kept, wages for lack of more precise information would usually be put into the Profit and Loss Account; but, if they are large in relation to turnover, it might be more correct to assume that they represent a manufacturing cost and that they should therefore appear in the Manufacturing Account.

(c) Salaries, again, may be differentiated between manufacturing and other salaries. It is, however, certain that some salaries will be in the nature of oncost. If there is no clear indication that they are factory costs, they should be charged in the Profit and Loss Account.

(d) General expenses, rent and rates, heating and lighting, and similar costs should be entered in the Profit and Loss Account unless they are specifically stated to be manufacturing costs.

(e) Fuel and power is almost certainly a prime cost and as such would appear in the Manufacturing Account.

(f) Depreciation, which includes both wear and tear and obsolescence, cannot be related directly to output. Machinery, buildings, etc., would depreciate even if they were not used, and it is not always clear that depreciation is hastened by use. Depreciation, therefore, is usually entered in the Profit and Loss Account.

(g) Repairs and renewals are made necessary through wear and tear over a considerable period. They are thus part of the cost of producing goods throughout the whole of that period. They cannot, therefore, be the cost of making goods only in the accounting period in which the repair was done. For this reason they are usually entered in the Profit and Loss Account.

An example of the Final Accounts of a company, divided into Manufacturing, Selling, and Profit and Loss Accounts, is shown on page 295, and should be carefully studied.

It will be noticed that a manufacturer divides his stock into a number of small stocks—raw materials, partly-finished goods, work in progress, finished goods, etc. A Stock Account for each of these is kept, similar to a trader's Stock Account, which consists entirely of saleable goods. Sometimes, as in the example given, only the amounts consumed are shown in the Revenue Accounts (*i.e.*, the accounts devoted to the ascertainment of profit). In this example, note also that Unfinished Assemblies, Finished Parts, and Work in Progress are shown as the difference between opening and closing stocks; and that the increase in stocks, being a deduction from the debit side of the Manufacturing Account, is equivalent to an addition to the credit side, increasing the gross profit.

WRITTEN EXERCISES

1. H. Henry is proprietor of the Regis Café and the following is the Trial Balance extracted from the books of the business at 30th June, 19—:

	£	£
Capital		2,285
Lease and goodwill	1,000	
Café change float	5	
Equipment and furniture	560	
China and utensils	96	
„ „ renewals (Profit & Loss)	66	
Motor van	240	
Opening stock	165	
Sales		3,142
Purchases	1,302	
Rent and rates	200	
Wages and insurance	586	
Light and heat, etc.	104	
Motor van expenses	105	
Postages and telephone	18	
Stationery and advertising	17	
Repairs	67	
General expenses	105	
Income Tax, Schedule 'D'	29	
Drawings	352	
Cash at bank	449	
Creditors		39
	£5,466	£5,466

H. Henry tells you the closing stock at 30th June, 19—, was £195 and that he estimates that £104 included in Purchases represents private consumptions by himself and his family. You are to adjust for this and prepare a Trading and Profit and Loss Account for the year to 30th June, 19—, and a Balance Sheet as at that date after allowing for: (1) Depreciation at 10 per cent per annum on the equipment and furniture and the motor van, (2) Rent and rates prepaid £8, (3) Outstanding light and heat £9, and (4) Accountancy expenses due £23.

(Incorporated Sales Managers' Association, modified.)

2. B. Evans and D. Gray are partners in a manufacturing business. They share profits and losses equally.

You are required to prepare their Trading and Profit and Loss Account for the year ended 31st March, 19—, with a Balance Sheet as on that date, from the following Trial Balance:

TRIAL BALANCE
31ST MARCH, 19-2

	Dr. £	Cr. £
B. Evans: Capital Account, 1st April, 19-1		8,220
Drawings during the year	633	
D. Gray: Capital Account, 1st April, 19-1		8,104
Drawings during the year	633	
Freehold land and buildings	5,000	
Rent received		150
Sundry debtors	1,852	
Sundry creditors		1,264
Loan Account		1,500
Stock of materials and finished goods as on 1st		
April, 19-1	2,422	
Factory wages	11,525	
Office salaries	793	
Carriage on purchases	304	
Carriage on sales	656	
Factory expenses	1,810	
Office expenses	188	
Purchases	6,775	
Sales		22,380
Returns inwards	110	
Returns outwards		234
Discount	552	
Interest on loan	75	
Advertising	78	
Dispatch expenses	104	
Office furniture	368	
Plant and machinery	8,500	
Cash in hand	272	
Bank overdraft ... ... — ...		798
	£42,650	£42,650

On 31st March, 19-2, the stock of materials and goods on hand was valued at £4,786.

  (1) Factory wages due but unpaid £136.

  (2) Make provision for bad debts £152.

  (3) Provide for discount:
        (a) 2 per cent of net debtors.
        (b) £64 on creditors.

  (4) Allocate £1,000 to general reserve.

  (5) Depreciation:
        Office furniture £18.
        Machinery and plant 10 per cent.

  (6) The Office Expenses Account includes an annual payment of which £18 is unexpired. *(R.S.A., modified.)*

3. From the following Trial Balance you are required to prepare a Trading and Profit and Loss Account for the year ended 31st May, 19—, and a Balance Sheet as at that date.

TRIAL BALANCE
AS AT 31ST MAY, 19—

	£			£
Salaries	250	Capital, W. Knott ...	..	4,496
Freehold Premises, at cost	3,300	Bank Overdraft ..	..	1,800
Purchases	416	Sundry Creditors ..	..	20
Wages	1,532	Sales	..	3,075
Debtors	400			
Opening Stock ..	540			
Rates and Water ..	120			
Power	45			
Light and Heat ..	35			
Bank Charges	88			
Sundry Expenses ..	165			
Type	500			
Plant and Machinery ...	2,000			
	£9,391			**£9,391**

The following adjustments must be made:
(*a*) Stock at 31st May, 19—, was valued at £1,214.
(*b*) Depreciate plant and machinery by 10 per cent per annum.
(*c*) Write £100 off the value of the type.
(*d*) Make provision for bad debts of 5 per cent on debtors.
(*e*) An invoice for £100 has not been received, and this purchase has not been put through the books, although the goods represented by it have been included in stock at 31st May, 19—.   (*Institute of Book-keepers.*)

4.   T. Jones and A. Roberts are in partnership and on 31st December, 19—, the following Trial Balance was extracted from their books:

	£	£
T. Jones: Capital		4,500
A. Roberts: Capital		4,500
Cash at bank	100	
Cash in hand	45	
Repairs and renewals	250	
Commission..	63	
Plant and machinery	850	
Fixtures and fittings	380	
Sales		19,910
Sales returns	720	
Rates and taxes	128	
Opening stock	2,720	
Bad debts	90	
Sundry debtors	5,800	
Carriage inwards	1,420	
Sundry creditors		1,050
Travelling expenses	160	
Discount		6
Purchases	13,750	
Purchases returns		750
General expenses	210	
Bills receivable	950	
Insurance	55	
Wages	1,650	
Provision for bad debts		160
Salaries	355	
T. Jones: Drawings	550	
A. Roberts: Drawings	350	
Heating and lighting	130	
Rent	150	
	£30,876	**£30,876**

You are required to prepare a Trading and Profit and Loss Account for the year ended 31st December, 19—, and a Balance Sheet as on that date. Before preparing these accounts it is necessary to take the following matters into consideration:

(a) Profits and losses are shared equally.
(b) The value of stock in hand at 31st December, 19—, was agreed at £3,000.
(c) The bad debts provision is to be made up to £400.
(d) Depreciation is to be charged as follows:
    Plant and machinery 10 per cent per annum.
    Fixtures and fittings 5 per cent per annum.
(e) Interest at 5 per cent per annum is to be charged on capital but not on drawings.
(f) Only three quarters' rent has been paid on 31st December, 19—, and no provision had been passed through the books for the quarter owing.
(g) £5 insurance is to be carried forward.

(*Note.* Bills receivable appear in the Balance Sheet as an asset.)

(*U.E.I., modified.*)

5. George Cave and William Sinclair commenced business as manufacturers on 1st January, 19—, and agreed to share profits and losses—G. Cave three-fifths and W. Sinclair two-fifths. On 31st December, 19—, the following Trial Balance was extracted from their books:

TRIAL BALANCE
31ST DECEMBER, 19—

	Dr. £	Cr. £
Capital: G. Cave ..		4,000
W. Sinclair		2,000
Drawings: G. Cave	360	
W. Sinclair	240	
Freehold premises ..	2,250	
Plant and machinery	2,010	
Loan Account, R. Barker		1,000
General expenses ..	360	
Purchases and sales	6,427	8,714
Debtors and creditors	1,524	1,392
Discount		74
Carriage on purchases	247	
Bad debts ..	124	
Interest on loan ..	60	
Manufacturing wages	1,927	
Office salaries ..	245	
Returns inwards and outwards	212	169
Cash in hand ..	37	
Cash at bank	1,326	
	£17,349	£17,349

On 31st December, 19—, the stock on hand was valued at £1,570.

You are required to prepare Trading and Profit and Loss Accounts for the year ended 31st December, 19—, and a Balance Sheet as on that date.

Provisions:
    (i) Bad and doubtful debts £75.
    (ii) Discount on debtors £44.
    (iii) Discount on creditors £26.
    (iv) General reserve £100.

Rates outstanding £32.
Wages due £17.

(*R.S.A., modified.*)

6.   C. Testout is in business as a sole trader. On 31st December, 19—, the following Trial Balance was extracted from his books:

TRIAL BALANCE

	Dr. £	Cr. £
C. Testout: Capital Account		6,000
Drawings Account	720	
Purchases and sales	9,285	16,807
Purchases and sales returns	324	218
Machinery and plant	3,680	
Sundry debtors and creditors	3,276	4,684
Telephone	19	
Bank overdraft		1,729
Bank charges	36	
Stock, 1st January, 19—	3,874	
Bills payable		1,000
Discount account	121	
Office expenses	214	
Trade expenses	874	
Carriage outwards	274	
Carriage inwards	196	
Eldorado 5 per cent Bonds	3,000	
Office salaries	1,424	
Office furniture	340	
Rent, rates and taxes—		
(Warehouse four-fifths; Office one-fifth) ..	705	
Cash in hand	96	
Heating and lighting—		
(Warehouse four-fifths; Office one-fifth) ..	225	
Provision for bad debts (1st January, 19—) ..		320
Insurance (Warehouse £156; Office £40) ..	196	
Travellers' salaries and expenses	1,984	
Interest Account		105
	£30,863	£30,863

(*Note.*   Bills payable are a liability.)

You are requested to prepare Trading and Profit and Loss Accounts for the year ended 31st December, 19—, and a Balance Sheet as on that date.

When preparing these accounts the following must be taken into consideration:

(*a*) One quarter's rent (£100) is outstanding.

(*b*) Half-year's interest is due on the Eldorado Bonds but has not yet been received.

(*c*) Depreciation is to be provided as follows:
Machinery and plant 15 per cent.
Office furniture 10 per cent.

(*d*) The provision for bad debts is to be increased by £200.

(*e*) Stock, as on 31st December, 19—, was valued at £4,296.

(*f*) Provide for 5 per cent interest on Testout's Capital Account.

(*R.S.A.*)

7.   J. Carey and B. Bailey were in partnership, sharing profits in the proportion of three-fourths and one-fourth. On 30th June, 19—, the following balances stood in the books of the firm:

	Dr. £	Cr. £
Purchases and sales	2,656	4,985
Sales and purchases returns	103	86
Freehold premises	2,100	
Rates and taxes	46	
Fixtures and fittings	240	
Sundry debtors and creditors	540	444
J. Carey: Capital Account		1,800
B. Bailey: Capital Account		600
Premises Repairs Reserve Account		150
Advertising	104	
J. Carey: Drawings Account	74	
B. Bailey: Drawings Account	38	
Traveller's salary and commission	395	
Cash at bank	123	
Cash in hand	12	
Office salaries	558	
Lighting and heating	57	
Loan to C. Lawrence	200	
Interest on loan		5
Bad debt reserve		40
Office expenses	158	
Opening stock	932	
Carriage inwards	27	
Carriage outwards	54	
Insurance	30	
Bills payable		298
Discount Account (balance)		39
	£8,447	£8,447

You are required to prepare a Trading and Profit and Loss Account for the year ended 30th June, 19—, and a Balance Sheet as on that date.

When preparing these accounts the following matters must be taken into consideration:

(a) B. Bailey is to be credited with a partnership salary of £250.
(b) The premises repairs reserve is to be increased to £200.
(c) Interest at 4 per cent per annum is to be allowed on capital.
(d) The bad debts reserve is to be adjusted to 5 per cent of the trade debtors.
(e) £6 of the charge for insurance is in respect of the three months to 30th September.
(f) Depreciation at 7½ per cent is to be charged on fixtures and fittings.
(g) £13 is owing in respect of lighting for the June quarter.
(h) Stock as on 30th June, 19—, was valued at £825.
(*Note.* Bills payable are a liability.)   (*R.S.A., modified.*)

8.   F. Wilton is a manufacturer. From the following balances extracted from his books at 31st December, 19–2, you are required to prepare Trading and Profit and Loss Accounts for the year ended 31st December 19–2, and a Balance Sheet, at that date.

	Dr. £	Cr. £
Capital 1st Jan., 19–2		113,886
Drawings	4,000	
Sales		197,684
Sales returns and allowances	164	
Stock and work progress 1st Jan., 19–2	8,509	
Purchases	81,916	
Purchases returns and allowances		76
Petty cash	20	
	Fwd. £94,609	£311,646

	£	£
Fwd.	94,609	311,646
Bank overdraft		5,809
Sundry creditors		8,401
Freehold land and buildings	30,000	
Mortgage on freehold land and buildings, 1st Jan., 19–2		14,875
Factory wages and salaries	73,265	
Factory wages and salaries accrued at 31st Dec., 19–1		1,435
Office wages and salaries	8,400	
Manufacturing expenses	873	
Factory power	1,628	
Factory rates and taxes	496	
Office rates and taxes	125	
Rates and taxes unexpired at 31st Dec., 19–1	116	
Lighting and heating (factory 4/5, office 1/5) ...	295	
Sundry debtors	17,474	
Bad debts	302	
Discounts	2,803	
Carriage on purchases	198	
Carriage on sales	3,479	
Plant and machinery (cost £150,000)	105,000	
Fixtures and fittings	700	
Office expenses	531	
Mortgage Repayment Account	1,740	
Bank interest	132	
	£342,166	£342,166

In preparing the Accounts the following adjustments are to be incorporated:
  (i) Stock and Work in Progress at 31st December, 19–2, £7,997.
  (ii) The Mortgage Repayment Account is to be apportioned as to £660 interest, and the remainder to reduction of the amount outstanding at 1st January, 19–3.
  (iii) Bank interest due at 31st December, 19–2, and not entered in the books, £128.
  (iv) Depreciation to be allowed as follows:
        Plant and machinery, 10 per cent on cost.
        Fixtures and fittings, £70.
(*Note.—Closing Journal Entries are not required.*) (*L. Ch. C.*)

9. Prepare Manufacturing and Trading Accounts from the following information:

Stocks at beginning:		£
Iron ore		1,700
Coal and coke		4,000
Limestone		500
Pig iron .. .. — —		40,000
Purchases during the year:		
Coal and coke .. ... — —		45,000
Limestone		4,200
Iron ore		34,500
Expenses:		
Furnace wages		9,000
Furnace repairs and maintenance		3,000
Furnace overhead expenses		2,500
Carriage outwards		3,750
Stocks at end:		
Iron ore ... . —		3,600
Coal and coke		3,200
Limestone		700
Pig iron		47,000
Sales for the year		142,000

(*Institute of Book-keepers.*)

24

SINGLE ENTRY

THE method of keeping books which we have described is known as Double Entry Book-keeping because the double effect of each transaction is recorded.

The only alternative is not to complete the double entry in every case, or to omit some entries altogether. Books are then said to be kept by Single Entry. This course is never followed by a firm of any standing.

Usually in single entry, the only accounts that are kept are a Cash Account and the accounts of the persons or firms with whom the business has had dealings on a credit basis. As a result—

(a) There is no complete record of the assets owned, or of their depreciation.

(b) The only records of expenses like rent and wages (for assets purchased and used up) are scattered throughout the Cash Account.

(c) There is no clear record of purchases and sales. Such information must be sought (but may not be found) as individual entries in the accounts already named.

It is clear that the omission of this information must greatly reduce the value of the books. In particular, profit must usually be assessed by comparing the capital at the beginning with the capital at the end of the accounting period, as described in Chapter Seven, with no guarantee that either figure of capital is correct. The result, when known, is the net profit only. The advantages of completing the double entry in all cases are:

(a) The present book-value of each asset is recorded.

(b) Both gross and net profit can be ascertained.

(c) There is detailed information of all losses.

(d) There is a check on the accuracy of the books through the correspondence of the debit and credit totals, or the balances, in the Trial Balance and Balance Sheet.

In some cases, as in the following example, it is possible to obtain sufficient information from sources external to the books, from which the necessary accounts can be opened. The first step is to post the Cash and Bank Accounts, and the second to double enter the rest of the information given. The amount of the credit purchases and sales is obtained from the accounts of the debtors and the creditors, which are shown to demonstrate the method employed.

Illustration: A. Slowcoach has been requested by the Inland Revenue to submit accounts showing his profit for the year ended 31st December, 19—. He approaches you and asks for your assistance. On inquiry you find that Mr. Slowcoach has not kept a complete set of books, but is able to supply you with information regarding his cash transactions, from which you prepare the following summary:

CASH SUMMARY FOR 19—

	£		£
Balance in hand on Jan. 1, 19—	30	Goods purchased for cash ..	1,340
Cash taken in the shop ..	8,420	Expenses paid in cash ..	320
Cash drawn from bank ..	1,470	Cash paid into bank	7,320
		Cash used for private purposes	560
		Loan to a friend	300
		Balance in hand Dec. 31, 19—	80
	£9,920		£9,920

You obtain his bank statement for the year, which you summarize as follows:

	£		£
Balance Jan. 1, 19—	1,420	Cash drawn from bank ..	1,470
Customers' cheques banked ..	4,390	Cheques drawn for private pur-	
Cash paid in from till ..	7,320	poses	640
Dividends on investments ..	85	Investment purchased.. ..	1,200
Amount received from Insur-		Customers' cheques returned	
ance Company in respect of		(re-presented and cleared) ..	100
goods destroyed by fire		Purchase of delivery van (on	
(valued at cost of purchase)	150	July 1, 19—) ..	500
		Bank charges	15
		Cheques for purchase of goods	7,940
		Expenses	950
		Balance, Dec. 31, 19— ..	550
	£13,365		£13,365

You obtain the following information regarding the business:

	Jan. 1	Dec. 31
	£	£
Stock in trade	1,050	1,420
Debtors for goods sold	740	520
Creditors for goods purchased	830	950
Creditors for expenses	90	110
Value of shop fittings	300	250

Cost of goods used for private purposes was £100. It is agreed to depreciate the motor van at the rate of 20 per cent per annum.

You are required to prepare a Trading and Profit and Loss Account for the year and a Balance Sheet at 31st December, 19—.

(*Note.* It may assist you in your workings to prepare ledger accounts, but they are not required by the terms of the question.)

(*Institute of Bankers.*)

SUNDRY CREDITORS ACCOUNT

Dr.				£					Cr. £
Bank	...	..	..	7,940	Balance	..	...	b/f	830
Balance	...	..	c/d	950	Purchases A/c	...	..		8,060
				£8,890					£8,890
					Balance	...	...	b/d	£950

PURCHASES ACCOUNT

Dr.				£				Cr. £
Cash	..	...	...	1,340	Trading A/c.	...	...	9,400
Creditors A/c	...	...		8,060				
				£9,400				£9,400

SUNDRY DEBTORS ACCOUNT

Dr.				£					Cr. £
Balance	..	..	b/d	740	Bank	...	...	..	4,390
Returned Cheques		..		100	Balance	...	...	c/d	520
Sales A/c	..	...	..	4,070					
				£4,910					£4,910
Balance	...	...	b/d	£520					

SALES ACCOUNT

Dr.				£				Cr. £
Trading A/c.	...	...		12,490	Cash	..	..	...	8,420
					Sundry Debtors A/c.		...	4,070
				£12,490				£12,490

CREDITORS (EXPENSES) ACCOUNT

Dr.				£					Cr. £
Bank	...	..	..	950	Balance	..	...	b/d	90
Balance	...	...	c/d	110	Expenses A/c.	...	..		970
				£1,060					£1,060
					Balance	...	...	b/d	£110

EXPENSES ACCOUNT

Dr.				£			Cr. £
Cash	..	..	..	320	Profit and Loss A/c.	...	1,290
Creditors (Expenses) A/c				970			
				£1,290			£1,290

TRADING ACCOUNT OF A. SLOWCOACH
FOR YEAR ENDED 31ST DECEMBER, 19—

Dr.			£				Cr. £
Stock, 1/1/19—	..	...	1,050	Sales	..	.. ..	12,490
Purchases ..	..	..	9,400	Drawings ..	..	..	100
Gross Profit	...	...	3,560	Stock, 31/12/19— ..		..	1,420
			£14,010				£14,010

PROFIT AND LOSS ACCOUNT OF A. SLOWCOACH
FOR YEAR ENDED 31ST DECEMBER, 19—

Dr.				£					Cr. £
Expenses	..	..		1,290	Gross Profit	..	..		3,560
Depreciation—					Dividends ..	..	..		85
Fittings ..	..	50			Insurance ...	...	...		150
Van	..	...	100						
				150					
Bank Charges	..	..		15					
Net Profit ..	..	..		2,340					
				£3,795					£3,795

BALANCE SHEET OF A. SLOWCOACH
AS AT 31ST DECEMBER, 19—

	£	£		£	£
Capital: A. Slowcoach	2,620		*Fixed Assets*		
Add Profit ..	2,340		Van	500	
	4,960		*Less* Depreciation	100	
Less Drawings..	1,300				400
		3,660	Furniture and Fittings	300	
			Less Depreciation	50	
Current Liabilities					250
Sundry Creditors		1,060			650
			Loan		300
			Investment ..		1,200
			Current Assets		
			Stock	1,420	
			Sundry Debtors ..	520	
			Bank	550	
			Cash	80	2,570
		£4,720			£4,720

WRITTEN EXERCISES

1. The books of A.B., a sole trader, are not kept by double entry, and his position at 1st January, 19—, was:

						£
Plant	...	..	..	..	..	1,000
Stock	..	..	..	..	..	2,000
Debtors	..	..	..	..	..	500
Cash	..	..	..	..	...	200
Creditors	...	..	...	...	...	800

On the following 31st December his position was:

						£
Plant	..	...	...	...	...	800
Stock	..	...	...	...	...	3,000
Debtors	...	...	...	...	..	600
Cash	...	...	...	...	...	100
Creditors	...	..	..	..	..	500

During the year he withdrew £300 in cash for weekly personal expenditure, and introduced further capital amounting to £500. What was his net profit or loss for the year? Show your workings.   (*Corporation of Certified Secretaries.*)

2.   On 1st July, 19—, X. Serviceman invested his accumulated savings and gratuity, amounting to £500, all in a garage. The fixed assets were acquired for £400 and the remaining £100 was left in the business as working capital. Towards the end of the following year it was clear that, as a result of petrol restrictions, the business was not paying; and, at the end of the year, Serviceman closed it down, having collected the debts due to him and paid all his creditors. He sold the fixed assets for £300; the petrol and oil had all been sold already.

An analysis of the cash book disclosed the following figures:

			First year's trading 19—	Following six months 19—
			£	£
Receipts:	From sales of petrol and oil		960	320
	From repairs, etc.	..	800	320
Payments:	Wages ..	..	390	210
	Drawings	..	260	100
	Purchases, petrol and oil		535	220
	spare parts ..	...	475	175
	Rent ..	..	104	52
	Sundry expenses	..	50	27

At 30th June, after one year, the petrol and oil on hand was valued at £40; there was no stock of spare parts. On the same date, £65 was owing from customers for repair jobs, while £35 was owing by Serviceman to the suppliers of petrol and oil and £10 for spare parts.

You are required to draw up:
   (*a*) Profit and Loss Accounts for the year to 30th June, 19—, and the six months to 31st December, 19—.
   (*b*) A Balance Sheet as on 30th June, 19—; and
   (*c*) Serviceman's Capital Account for the six months ended 31st December.
                                                (*R.S.A., modified.*)

3.   From the following particulars write up the Advertising Account as it would appear after the accounts of a business for the year ended 30th September, 19–2, had been closed.

			£
Payments during year for advertising materials supplied and work done ..	..	..	2,794
Cost of own goods given away at exhibitions		..	369
Receipts from sales of old materials		..	67
Stock of materials:			
30th September, 19–1	...	...	287
30th September, 19–2	..	..	243
Creditors (for advertising materials)	..	..	198
			(*R.S.A.*)

4.   X sets up in practice as a doctor on 1st January, 19–1. During 19–1 he received fees amounting to £545, and at the end of the year £237 was owing to him. During 19–2 the fees received amounted to £831 and at the end of the year £364 was owing to him. His expenses amounted to £265 in 19–1 and £320 in 19–2, there being no liabilities outstanding at the end of either year.

Ascertain his profit for each of these years.

5.   John Brown, a retail trader, had not kept a complete double entry record.
   During the year 19—, Brown took £350 in cash from the shop takings; out of this sum, he paid general business expenses amounting to £50 and used the remainder for private purposes.
   Brown prepares the following summary of his Bank Account for the year:

BANK SUMMARY FOR 19—

	£		£
Balance, January 1st	130	Payments to creditors for goods	4,800
Shop takings	6,200	Payments for business expenses	1,060
Sale of motor van	250	Payments for private purposes	315
		Purchase of new motor van	
		(December 31st)	400
		Balance, December 31st ..	5
	£6,580		£6,580

A comparison of the above with the Bank Statement shows that Brown has omitted bank charges of £10 from the summary; in all other respects, the summary is correct.
   The following information is also provided:

				Jan. 1st	Dec. 31st
				£	£
Stock in trade ..	..	...	..	650	800
Debtors for goods sold		..	..	550	850
Creditors for goods purchased			..	400	600
Creditors for expenses		..	..	60	40
Furniture and fittings..		..	..	100	100

The motor van, which was sold during the year for £250, was valued on 1st January at £320.
   You are required to prepare a Trading and Profit and Loss Account for the year 19— and a Balance Sheet at 31st December, 19—.   (*Institute of Bankers.*)

6.   J. Penn commenced trading on 1st July, 19—. A summary of his bank transactions during the year to 30th June, 19—, is as follows:

				£
Payments into bank:				
Capital introduced ..	..	...	..	3,500
Receipts from credit customers		..	..	1,764
Cash sales (balance) ..	..	..	—	2,472
Cheque payments:				
Purchase of business premises	...	—		1,690
Purchase of fixtures and fittings	...	...		640
To suppliers of goods	..	...	—	4,137
For general business expenses		..	..	277

The amount of cash sales shown above is the remainder after deducting from such sales J. Penn's personal drawings during the year, amounting to £646, and £2·25 per week for petty cash expenses.
   Goods invoiced out at £100 have been returned by credit customers during the year, and, similarly, goods costing £80 have been returned to suppliers. Discounts allowed for cash to credit customers and by suppliers averaged 2 per cent and 1½ per cent respectively, and during the year debts totalling £74 have been written off as bad.
   On 30th June, 19—, the amount owing by credit customers was £361, and £540 was owing to suppliers.
   Depreciation at 10 per cent per annum is to be written off Fixtures and Fittings and it can be assumed that the rate of gross profit on sales was a uniform 30 per cent.
   Give the necessary accounts to show how you arrive at any figures required but not given above, and prepare Trading and Profit and Loss Account for the year ended 30th June, 19—, and draw up the Balance Sheet as at that date.
   (*Association of Certified and Corporate Accountants.*)

7.   The Balance Sheet of William Hamilton, a trader, on 1st January, 19—, is as under:

BALANCE SHEET

	£		£
Capital	2,500	Furniture and fittings, at cost	450
Trade creditors	1,600	Stock-in-Trade, at cost ..	1,480
Creditors for expenses ..	120	Trade debtors	1,830
		Balance at bank	460
	£4,220		£4,220

Hamilton pays all business takings into his bank account, and all business payments are made by cheque.

His transactions during 19— are as follows:

	£
Purchases per day book for year	15,250
Sales per day book for year	20,970
Business expenses paid by cheque ..	2,340
Drawn from bank for private purposes ..	4,800

All purchases and all sales have been recorded in the day books.

There were no returns inwards or outwards and no bad debts. No discounts were allowed or received.

In July, 19—, Hamilton took over a motor van, valued at £300, in satisfaction of a debt for that amount due to him from a customer.

On 31st December, 19—, trade debtors amounted to £1,725, trade creditors amounted to £1,560, and creditors for expenses were £200; stock-in-trade amounted to £760.

You are required to prepare:

(a) A summary of Hamilton's Bank Account for the year 19—.
(b) Trading and Profit and Loss Account for the year 19—, and Balance Sheet at 31st December, 19—.

Notes:

(i) You may take it that there are no entries in the Bank Account other than those which may be ascertained from the information given above.
(ii) Ignore depreciation.
(iii) Show your workings.

(*Institute of Bankers.*)

8.   A.B., a trader, makes up his accounts to 31st December in each year. On the night of 31st December, 19—, his stock-in-trade is totally destroyed by fire, and some of his accounting records are lost. The following figures are available:

	£
Stock-in-trade, 1st Jan., 19—, at cost	5,400
Total cost of goods purchased during 19—	47,800
Debtors for goods, 1st Jan., 19—	4,000
Cash received from debtors for goods (including cash sales) 19—	70,000
Discounts allowed during 19—	340
Debtors for goods, 31st Dec., 19—	2,660
Goods taken by A.B. for his own personal use during 19—, at cost	200

The destruction of the stock by fire is covered by insurance, and it may be assumed that the whole cost of the stock will be recovered from the insurance company.

There were no transactions in bills of exchange during 19—, and there were no bad debts.

You may take it that A.B.'s gross profit is at a uniform rate of $33\frac{1}{3}$ per cent of selling price.

You are required to prepare A.B.'s Trading Account for the year 19—.

(*Institute of Bankers.*)

25

TRADING RESULTS

A CERTAIN amount of the information recorded in a set of books is in daily use in the running of a business—for example, the records of transactions with debtors and creditors, and the receipt and payment of cash. The function of the accountant, however, goes far beyond this. It is his business to present this information in a form that will help the management to reach decisions. Clearly he cannot give all the information required, for he is limited to facts that can be stated in financial terms. In addition the manager has to know a great deal about his products, about the processes of manufacture, about market possibilities and sources of supply, about labour relations, the capabilities of his staff and many other matters which may affect the problems that arise. Nor can the accountant give the answers—a figure may seem larger or smaller than it should be but the financial records do not often show why this should be so or what should be done. The manager, not the accountant as such, must discover the reasons and devise a course of action to correct what is wrong. But the accountant can do a great deal to indicate areas in which investigations should be made.

The Examination of the Final Accounts and Balance Sheet

The following are the Trading and Profit and Loss Accounts and Balance Sheet of J. Dunne.

TRADING ACCOUNT OF J. DUNNE

Dr.   FOR YEAR ENDED 31ST DECEMBER, 19—   Cr.

	£			£
Purchases	1,950	Net Sales	2,500
Gross Profit	1,000	Stock, 31/12/19—	450
	£2,950		£2,950

PROFIT AND LOSS ACCOUNT OF J. DUNNE

Dr.   FOR YEAR ENDED 31ST DECEMBER, 19—   Cr.

	£		£
Interest on Loan	20	Gross Profit	1,000
Upkeep of Car	75		
Rent and Rates	100		
Wages	250		
Salaries	350		
Office Expenses	55		
Selling Expenses	50		
Net Profit	100		
	£1,000		£1,000

BALANCE SHEET OF J. DUNNE
AS AT 31ST DECEMBER, 19-1

	£	£		£	£
Capital	260		*Fixed Assets*		
Add Profit ...	100		Furniture and Fittings	250	
	—		Car	350	
	360			—	600
Less Drawings..	350		*Current Assets*		
	—	10	Stock ...	450	
Loan (A. Wills) ...		400	Debtors	180	
			Bank	55	
Current Liabilities			Cash	25	
Creditors		900		—	710
		£1,310			£1,310

Two points are immediately obvious:

(*a*) The business is only just solvent, the proprietor having consumed all his capital except £10.

(*b*) The total current assets, including stock, are insufficient to pay the current liabilities.

Tests Applied to Final Accounts

Before examining in detail the Trading Account and the Profit and Loss Account of J. Dunne, it is necessary to show the kind of tests that would be applied to them.

(*a*) *Sales.* The governing factor is the size of the net sales. If these are small, the net profit must be small.

(*b*) *Stock.* Sufficient stock must be held to meet probable demand without undue delay, but the amount should be kept to a minimum because it represents capital that could earn interest if it were invested outside the business. The actual amount held will depend on—

   (i) The nature of the business. A furniture dealer, for example, will require a larger stock than a fishmonger.

   (ii) The amount of the sales. The higher the sales, the greater the amount of stock that must be held.

As the amount of stock to be held in a given business depends on the amount of the sales, it is usual to express its value as a ratio of the sales. This ratio is known as the *Rate of Turnover*. It is found by dividing the average stock (*valued at selling price*) held during the accounting period into the sales. The average stock is ascertained by adding the opening stock to the closing stock and dividing by two. For example:

(i) *Average stock.* If the opening stock (valued at selling price) were £2,000, and the closing stock (again valued at selling price) were £3,000, the average stock would be $\dfrac{£2,000+3,000}{2}$ =£2,500.

(ii) *Rate of Turnover.* If the sales during that period were £10,000, the rate of turnover would be $\dfrac{10,000}{2,500}$ =4. If the accounting period is one year, a rate of turnover of 4 means that stock is held, *on the average,* for three months before being sold. This is obviously too long for a fishmonger, but would probably be unusually short for a furniture dealer.

(*c*) *Expenses.* Each individual expense (such as advertising, salaries, etc.) is then calculated as a percentage of the sales. This facilitates comparison between one year and another. Moreover, since all expenses must be met out of the proceeds of the sales, they should bear a relation to the sales. An expense that appeared excessive with sales at a certain figure might be reasonable if the sales were much bigger.

These percentage figures may be reduced in two ways—

(i) By reducing the amount actually spent on each item.

(ii) By increasing the sales without a proportionate increase in the expense.

The business man will attempt to do both of these things. Each expense must be examined in detail to see if a saving is possible. Every change in the ratio and in the amount must be accounted for. The examination of such changes is a fruitful source of ideas for further economies.

(*d*) *Total Expenses in relation to Sales and Gross Profit.* As pointed out on page 68, the gross profit varies roughly in proportion to the sales. If more goods are sold, more must be bought, and if both the cost price and the selling price remain the same, the gross profit will rise in the same proportion as the sales. For example:

Let us assume that cars are bought at £500 each and sold at £750, and that these prices remain constant:

No. of cars sold	Cost	Sales	Gross Profit
	£	£	£
1	500	750	250
2	1,000	1,500	500
3	1,500	2,250	750

On the other hand, the oncost (*i.e.* the total expenses in the Profit and Loss Account) is more or less fixed. An increase in the sales does not necessarily mean a proportionate increase in the oncost.

Assuming, in the example given above, that the oncost is fixed at £400, the net profit (or loss) in the three cases given would be as follows:

No. of cars sold	Gross Profit	Oncost	Net Profit
	£	£	£
1	250	400	—150
2	500	400	100
3	750	400	350

It is therefore possible to calculate how great the sales must be to cover any given sum of fixed charges (*i.e.* oncost) and leave a given margin of profit.

For example, if, in the above case, the proprietor wanted a minimum net profit of £600, and his oncost remained at £400, the gross profit would have to be £600+£400=£1,000.

The gross profit is $33\frac{1}{3}$ per cent of the sales (£250 on a car sold for £750).

£1,000 would therefore be $33\frac{1}{3}$ per cent of the sales.

The sales, therefore, would be $\dfrac{100}{33\frac{1}{3}} \times 1,000 = £3,000$, and the number of cars to be sold $\dfrac{3,000}{750} = 4$ cars.

It should be noted, however, that the oncost is not rigidly fixed. As a business increases in size, expenses do increase, larger premises must be obtained, increasing the rent; more staff must be employed, increasing the salaries bill, and so on. These expenses tend to increase in 'jumps'.

Examination of Trading and Profit and Loss Accounts of J. Dunne

We are now in a position to analyse the Trading and Profit and Loss Accounts of J. Dunne, applying the methods shown in the previous section.

(*a*) *Sales.* This will be dealt with in paragraph (*d*) below.

(*b*) *Stock.* As there was no stock at the beginning of the year, it may be assumed that the business has been in existence for one year only. It is probable that most of the stock was bought very soon after the business was opened. It is shown in section (*d*) below that the gross profit is 40 per cent of the sales, which means that goods bought for £60 are sold for £100. The selling price of the closing stock, valued at cost price at £450, is therefore $£450 \times \dfrac{10}{6} = £750$. Assuming the average stock to be the same as the closing stock (it may easily have been larger if purchases were curtailed towards the end of the year) the rate of turnover would be $\frac{2,500}{750}=3\frac{1}{3}$. In the absence of further information it is impossible to say whether this is good or bad.

(c) *Expenses*. Each of the expenses, and the gross profit, are shown below as a percentage of the sales (£2,500):

			£	%
Interest on loan	..	..	20	$\frac{4}{5}$
Upkeep of car	..	..	75	3
Rent and rates	..	..	100	4
Wages	..	..	250	10
Salaries	..	..	350	14
Office expenses	..	..	55	$2\frac{1}{5}$
Selling expenses	..	..	50	2
Gross profit	..	..	£1,000	40

These figures, like the rate of turnover, cannot be judged without further information.

(d) *Total Expenses in relation to Sales and Gross Profit*. The gross profit of £1,000 is, as shown above, 40 per cent of the sales.

Dunne's total expenses (shown in the Profit and Loss Account) are £900. His drawings are £350 (shown in the Balance Sheet). The gross profit must therefore be raised from £1,000 to £1,250, to cover both of these sums, if he is to remain solvent.

The gross profit is 40 per cent of the sales. To earn a gross profit of £1,250, his sales must be raised to $\frac{1,250}{40}\times100=£3,125$.

(e) *Policy*. The sales will not rise to this figure automatically. It will be necessary for J. Dunne to work out how it can be done, bearing in mind his present position. Two points that must be borne in mind are—

(i) That he is short of stock and deeply in debt. If his sales are to be £3,125, the goods he sells will cost him 60 per cent of this, that is £1,875. How is he to persuade his creditors to supply him with goods to this value when he cannot pay them the £900 he already owes?

(ii) If his sales are increased, his oncost, though it may not rise in the same proportion, will almost certainly be higher. In other words, it is not rigidly fixed.

Let us assume then that his solution is to obtain a further loan of £2,000, at 5 per cent per annum interest. This would pay off the creditors in full and leave him £1,100 plus his current assets as working capital. He then comes to the following decisions:

(i) To spend £250 on advertising.

(ii) To allocate £150 for the salaries of the additional staff that might be necessary if sales were to be greatly increased.

(iii) To reduce his gross margin (*i.e.* the percentage of gross profit on sales) from 40 per cent to 25 per cent, by reducing his selling prices, in an attempt to undercut his competitors.

His oncost for the next year would now be as follows:

	£
Fixed charges as previous year (which include £350 net profit to cover his drawings) ..	1,250
Add interest on loan	100
Add advertising expenses	250
Add additional staff	150
Add depreciation on car	80
Add depreciation furniture and fittings ..	20
Add allowance for contingencies (*e.g.* more office supplies, petrol, etc.)	50
Total ..	£1,900

As this sum, at the new prices he is to charge, is equal to 25 per cent of the sales, the sales must during the following year reach a minimum figure of:

£1,900 × 4 = £7,600

Every £100 increase in his sales above that figure will represent £25 more net profit until the point is reached at which he must make additions to his oncost, through engaging more staff, taking larger premises, etc.

Budgeted Final Accounts and Balance Sheet

Having come to the decisions outlined in the previous section, J. Dunne would project his Final Accounts and Balance Sheet to show how he would expect to stand at the end of the following year.

TRADING ACCOUNT OF J. DUNNE
FOR YEAR ENDED 31ST DECEMBER 19–2

	£		£
Stock 1/1/19–2	450	Sales	7,600
Purchases	6,250	Stock 31/12/19–2	1,000
Gross Profit	1,900		
	£8,600		£8,600

PROFIT AND LOSS ACCOUNT OF J. DUNNE
FOR YEAR ENDED 31ST DECEMBER 19–2

	£		£
Wages	400	Gross Profit	1,900
Salaries	350		
Car expenses	75		
Depreciation Car	80		
„ Furniture & Fittings ..	20		
Selling Expenses	50		
Advertising	250		
Office Expenses	55		
Interest	120		
Rent	100		
Sundries	50		
Net Profit	350		
	£1,900		£1,900

BALANCE SHEET OF J. DUNNE
AS AT 31ST DECEMBER 19–2

	£	£			£	£
Capital	10		*Fixed Assets*			
Add Profit ...	350		Car		350	
	360		*Less* Depreciation	80		270
Less Drawings ..	350	10	Furniture and Fittings	250		230
			Less Depreciation	20		
						500
Loans		2,400				
			Current Assets			
Current Liabilities			Stock		1,000	
Creditors		520	Debtors		560	
			Cash		870	2,430
		£2,930				£2,930

Notes

(a) Purchases. Cost of goods sold 75% of £7,600 = 5,700
Additional stock = 550

£6,250

(b) Debtors and Creditors are approximately equal to one month's sales (less cash sales) and purchases respectively.

(c) Note the following ratios:

1. Turnover of stock (assuming stock to be raised to £1,000 immediately) = 5·7
2. Cash to creditors = 1·67
3. Cash plus debtors to creditors = 2·75
   (This is high. Dunne might consider increasing stock or paying off loan to Wills—£400—thus saving interest.)
4. Profit to capital employed = $\frac{350}{2,930}$ = 11·94%

(d) Dunne would probably prepare similar projected Final Accounts and Balance Sheets for each month and check against actual monthly figures, even if these were in some cases only approximately correct. This would enable him to take action if he were not meeting his budget or if he saw the possibility of improving on it. It would be too late to do anything if he waited until the end of the year before measuring his progress.

WRITTEN EXERCISES

1. Q. Ltd. is a company engaged in retail trade. All the goods it handles are sold at a gross profit equal to 25 per cent of the *cost* price.

An analysis of the expenses shows that they may be divided into (a) fixed charges amounting to £4,500 per annum, and (b) expenses varying in direct proportion to turnover equal to 15 per cent of sales.

You are required to ascertain what should be the monthly amount of sales in order that:

(1) The business shall just cover expenses, *i.e.*, make neither net profit nor loss.
(2) What *additional* monthly turnover would be necessary to arrive at the same position if the rent payable were to be increased by £600 per annum.

(*R.S.A.*)

2. From the undermentioned figures, which were extracted from the books of a manufacturer, you are asked to prepare an account or statement in a form that will give the proprietor the maximum information as to his trading results, including the percentages of the various items to turnover, and to state what conclusions can be drawn from the figures:

	Year ended 30th September:	
	19–1	19–2
	£	£
Purchases of material	5,823	6,494
Wages:		
Productive	5,064	6,768
Non-productive	620	984
Return inwards	472	1,903
Discount received	180	36
Salaries	1,560	1,584
Selling expenses	1,720	2,784
Discount allowed	420	492
Works expenses	3,176	3,456
Office expenses	370	420
Stock at commencement of year ..	2,189	2,876
Sales	20,472	25,903

The stock of material at 30th September, 19–2, was valued at £1,882.

(R.S.A.)

3. The records of Herbert Bishop disclose:

Year			Turnover £	Gross Profit £	Net Profit £
1949	..	...	8,000	1,200	700
1950	..	..	7,000	1,300	750
1951	..	..	8,000	1,100	600

Prepare a statement in tabular form showing the percentages for each year of gross profit, overhead expenses, and net profit, based on turnover.

(*Institute of Book-keepers.*)

4. You ascertain the following facts:

		Sales	Gross Profit	Net Profit	Capital Employed
19–1	..	£100,000	£25,000	£15,000	£150,000
19–2	..	£175,000	£35,000	£23,000	£160,000
19–3	..	£120,000	£36,000	£24,000	£180,000
19–4	..	£250,000	£60,000	£40,000	£200,000

Show by mean of a simple statistical statement the main facts shown by these results.   (*Institute of Book-keepers.*)

26

BILLS OF EXCHANGE

IF Smith owes Adams £100, he could pay by means of a cheque. Alternatively, if Adams agrees, he could give a Bill of Exchange.

A Bill of Exchange (B/E) is drawn up in the following form:

No. 1325	£100	1st April, 19—
Stamp £0·05	One month after date pay to me or my order the sum of £100, value received.	
To T. Smith, Joyce Road, Nottingham.		J. Adams.

Notice that the bill is drawn by J. Adams, the creditor.

The period before payment fell due (called the 'tenor' of the bill) could be of any duration agreed upon between the parties.

Acceptance

The bill, as shown above, is an order to pay, signed by Adams. As such, it is not binding upon Smith until Smith has signified his acceptance; this he does by crossing the bill like a cheque and writing, in the space between the two lines, the word 'Accepted' above his signature, adding perhaps the name of his banker. Until the bill has been accepted in this way, it is known as a 'draft'; afterwards it is an 'acceptance'.

Advantages of Bills

The advantage to Smith is that he is granted credit during the tenor of the bill.

The advantages to Adams are:

(*a*) It is itself a proof of debt irrespective of the circumstances that gave rise to the debt.

(*b*) A date is fixed for payment, and failure to pay when the bill 'matured' would be extremely damaging to the credit of the acceptor.

(*c*) It can usually be turned into ready cash by 'discounting' it at the bank.

Discounting a Bill

Provided that the credit of the parties to the bill is good enough, the bank is usually prepared to advance the money to the holder of the bill. In other words, they lend the money until the bill falls due.

For this service they make a charge. The charge is calculated as simple interest on the face value of the bill for the period during which the bank has to wait for payment (*i.e.,* from the date of discounting until the due date).

The interest is known as 'discount', hence the term 'discounting a bill'. The bill would be paid into the bank like a cheque, and the amount of discount charged might not be known until the pass book was next made up (see page 169).

Due Date

If the tenor of the bill is reckoned in months, it is calendar months that are referred to. Thus one month from 28th February, the last day in February, is 31st March, the last day in March. One month from 27th February is 27th March.

To the period stated on the bill there must *always be added three 'Days of Grace'*. The student is expected to know this, and to make allowance for it, whether the days of grace are mentioned or not in an examination question.

The due date on the bills mentioned above would therefore be 31st March plus three days=3rd April, and 27th March plus three days =30th March.

Parties to the Bill

    (1) Drawer.   The creditor who draws up the bill.
    (2) Drawee.   The person on whom the bill is drawn.
    (3) Acceptor.   The drawee after acceptance.
    (4) Payee.   The person in whose favour the bill is drawn. It may be the drawer, or the drawee may be instructed to pay somebody else.
    (5) Endorser.   A B/E, like an order cheque, must be endorsed (*i.e.,* signed on the back) before payment into the bank. Similarly, if it is passed from hand to hand in settlement of debts (again like a cheque) it must be endorsed by the person giving it.
    (6) Holder.   The person who possesses the bill. If it came into the possession of the acceptor, he would, of course, file it.

Bills of Exchange and Cheques

Legally, a cheque is a Bill of Exchange, with the following distinguishing features:

(1) It is always drawn on a banker.
(2) The acceptance of the banker is taken for granted (if the drawer has sufficient funds in the bank).
(3) It is always payable on demand on and after the date under which it is drawn, and there are no 'Days of Grace'.

It is very rarely that B/Es. are used in the home trade. Their chief use is in international trade when complications arise over rates of exchange, etc., that are outside the scope of the present book.

The Book-keeping of B/Es.

There are two aspects to every bill. To the creditor who holds it, it is an asset; to the debtor who accepts it, it is a liability. The records are similar in both sets of books but they will be on opposite sides of the ledger. The creditor, who will receive the money, regards the bill as a Bill Receivable; the debtor, who pays, calls it a Bill Payable.

Treatment of Bills Receivable

I. *When the Bill is accepted.* If a creditor receives a cheque, he will credit the person from whom he receives it and debit the Bank Account. If, instead, he receives a B/E he will again—

(*a*) Credit the person from whom he received it;

(*b*) debit, not the Bank Account (since the money is not yet in the bank) but a Bills Receivable Account.

If at this stage a Balance Sheet is prepared, the bill will be included amongst his assets. It will have taken the place of the debtor whose indebtedness has been cancelled by it.

The accounts in Adams' books (see B/E at the beginning of the chapter) are shown below:

SMITH ACCOUNT

Dr.						Cr.
			£			£
Mar. 31	Balance	..	100	Apr. 1	Bill Receivable (No. 25) ..	100

BILLS RECEIVABLE ACCOUNT

Dr.						Cr.
			£			
Apr. 1	J. Smith (No. 25)	.. ..	100			

The holder of the bill, Adams, has three courses open to him. He may keep it until maturity, discount it at a bank, or pass it to a third person to whom he owes money. Taking these in order, the entries would be.

II (*a*). *Receipt of Payment on Maturity.* The day before the bill became due it would be paid into the bank like a cheque (and entered on the paying-in slip). It would then be (i) debited in the Bank Account with the money received; (ii) credited in the Bills Receivable Account because the bill has been replaced by cash and must therefore be cancelled.

BILLS RECEIVABLE ACCOUNT

Dr.					Cr.
		£			£
Apr. 1	Smith (No. 25)	100	May 4	Bank (No. 25)	100

BANK ACCOUNT

Dr.					Cr.
		£			
May 4	B/R (No. 25)	100			

It should be noted that when the bill is paid, no entry is made in the account of the acceptor. He has already been credited with the amount of the bill and obviously should not be credited with the payment of it as well.

II (*b*) *Discounting the Bill.* There are two stages in recording the discounting of a bill:

Stage 1. The bill is paid into the bank like a cheque.

    (i) The Bank Account is debited.

    (ii) The Bills Receivable Account credited with the full amount of the bill. (The entry is the same as that made when a bill is paid on maturity.)

Stage 2. The bank makes a charge for discount. If the amount of the charge is not known accurately until the pass book is made up, then when it is known

    (i) the Bank Account is credited;

    (ii) the Bank Charges Account or Discount Charges Account is debited.

Bank charges are later transferred to Profit and Loss Account.

If the bill already referred to in section II (*a*) had been discounted on 2nd April, the entries would be as under (assuming the bank charges to be £1):

BILLS RECEIVABLE ACCOUNT

Dr.					Cr.
		£			£
Apr. 1	Smith (No. 25)	100	Apr. 2	Bank (No. 25)	100

BANK ACCOUNT

Dr.						Cr.
		£				£
Apr. 2	Discounted Bill (No. 25) ..	100		Apr. 6	Charges (Discount on B/E No. 25) ..	1

DISCOUNT CHARGES ACCOUNT

Dr.				Cr.
		£		
Apr. 6	Bank (Discount Bill No. 25)	1	(Transferred to Profit & Loss A/c. at end of accounting period)	

II (c). *Passing Bill to Third Party.* If the bill is passed to a third party in payment of a debt the entries would be:

(i) Credit the Bills Receivable Account because the asset is no longer held.

(ii) Debit the person to whom it has been given, because the debt to him has been cancelled to the amount of the bill.

For example, if Adams were to pass Smith's bill to T. Roth, to whom he owed £150, the entries would be as follows:

BILLS RECEIVABLE ACCOUNT

Dr.						Cr.
		£				£
Apr. 1	Smith (No. 25)	100		Apr. 10	T. Roth (No. 25) ...	100

T. ROTH ACCOUNT

Dr.						Cr.
		£				£
Apr. 10	B/R No. 25	100		Apr. 1	Balance b/d ...	150

III. *Rebated Bills.* The acceptor may pay the bill before maturity, *i.e.,* before the full period for which he is allowed credit. In that case he may receive interest for the unexpired term, similar to the discount allowed by the bank.

If the bill used in previous illustrations were rebated on 15th April and £1 interest were allowed, the necessary entries are indicated in the Journal.

JOURNAL

		£	£
Apr. 15	Bank A/c. .. .. .. Dr.	99	
	Interest and Discount Charges A/c. Dr.	1	
	To Bills Receivable A/c.		100
	Being B/R No. 25 (Smith) Rebated April 15th.		

IV. *Dishonoured Bill.* If a bill is not met on maturity it is said to be 'dishonoured'. In that case, the original debt is restored; so the entries made when the bill was given must be reversed. When the bill was given, the Bills Receivable Account was debited and the acceptor's account credited. Now—

(*a*) The acceptor's account is debited.

(*b*) The Bills Receivable Account is credited.

J. SMITH ACCOUNT

Dr.							Cr.
			£				£
Mar. 31	Balance	...	100	Apr. 1	B/R (No. 25)		100
May 4	Dis. B/R		100				
	(No. 25)	...					

BILLS RECEIVABLE ACCOUNT

Dr.							Cr.
			£				£
Apr. 1	J. Smith			May 4	J. Smith,		
	(No. 25)	...	100		Dishonour		
					(No. 25)	...	100

If the bill had been discounted, the credit entry would be in the Bank Account instead of the Bills Receivable Account.

If legal action is contemplated to recover the money, the dishonour of the bill should be 'noted' by a notary public, as proof of the dishonour. The notary public makes a small charge which is usually claimed from the defaulting acceptor. The entry for the charge would be—

(*a*) Credit Cash Account.

(*b*) Debit the acceptor's account.

Retiring or Renewing a Bill

One of the alternatives open to the drawer of a bill that has been dishonoured is to draw a second bill, payable at a later date. The bill that has been dishonoured is then said to be 'retired' or 'renewed'. In that event, he would probably charge interest for the extended period of credit, since this was longer than the period originally agreed. Assuming that this was done in the example of dishonour given in the previous section, and that the interest charged was £1 and the noting charges were £1, the accounts would appear as under:

J. SMITH ACCOUNT

Dr.						Cr.
			£			£
Mar. 31	Balance	..	100	Apr. 1	B/R (No. 25)	100
May 4	Dis. B/R (No. 25)		100	May 4	B/R (No. 30)	102
" 4	Noting Chgs.	...	1			
" 4	Interest	...	1			

BILLS RECEIVABLE ACCOUNT

Dr.						Cr.
			£			£
Apr. 1	J. Smith (No. 25)		100	May 4	J. Smith, Dishonour (No. 25)	
May 4	J. Smith (No. 30)		102			100

CASH ACCOUNT
(in Cash Book)

Dr.						Cr.
						£
				May 4	J. Smith (Noting Chgs.)	1

INTEREST ACCOUNT

Dr.					Cr.
					£
			May 4	J. Smith	1

Bills Payable

In the books of the debtor, any bills he accepts are Bills Payable. The original debt must be cancelled by a debit entry in the creditor's account, because that liability has been replaced by another one, owed to whatever person holds the bill when it matures. The new liability, on the bill, is recorded by a credit entry in the Bills Payable Account. This is shown below as a Journal entry in the books of J. Smith. A narration, of course, would be required. (The bill illustrated at the beginning of the chapter is the basis of the entry.)

JOURNAL

		Dr.	Cr.
		£	£
Apr. 1	Adams A/c. .. .. .. Dr.	100	
	To Bills Payable A/c.		100

The transactions recorded in the books of Adams, to whom the bill was a Bill Receivable, are now shown, in Journal form, in the books of J. Smith.

I. *Payment on Maturity*

		Dr.	Cr.
		£	£
May 4	Bills Payable A/c. .. .. .. Dr.	100	
	To Bank A/c		100

II. *Rebating a B/P*

		Dr.	Cr.
		£	£
Apr. 15	Bills Payable A/c. .. .. .. Dr.	100	
	To Bank A/c...		99
	„ Interest and Discount Chgs. A/c.		1

III. *Dishonour of B/P*

		Dr.	Cr.
		£	£
May 4	Bills Payable A/c. ... ... Dr.	100	
	To T. Adams		100

IV. *Noting Charges*

		Dr.	Cr.
		£	£
May 4	Interest and Disc. Charges A/c. ... Dr.	1	
	To T. Adams		1
	Being Noting Chgs.... ... . etc.		

V. *Interest Charges (on Renewed Bill)*

		Dr.	Cr.
		£	£
May 4	Interest A/c. ... ... Dr.	1	
	To T. Adams		1

VI. *Renewed B/P (including Interest and Noting Charges)*

		Dr.	Cr.
		£	
	To Adams A/c. .. .. .. Dr.	102	
	To Bills Payable A/c. ...		102

Subsidiary Books

If the number of bills dealt in is small, the first entries would be made in the Journal (as illustrated in dealing with Bills Payable). As soon as the numbers become important, however, there are advantages in recording them in books ruled for the purpose. The advantages are:

(1) Only the total need be entered in the Bills Receivable Account or the Bills Payable Account.

(2) As much information as is desired can be recorded in these books.

Examples of simple rulings, giving the minimum of information required, are given below:

BILLS RECEIVABLE BOOK

Date	From Whom Received	Tenor	Due Date	Amount
	(Items posted to personal a/cs. of debtors, on credit side; total to Bills Receivable A/c., debit side)			

BILLS PAYABLE BOOK

Date	To Whom Given	Tenor	Due Date	Amount
	(Items posted to personal a/cs. of creditors, on debit side; total to Bills Payable A/c., credit side)			

Bills of Exchange and the Balance Sheet

Bills Receivable are assets and Bills Payable are liabilities. The balances of the accounts in which their value is recorded (the Bills Receivable Account and the Bills Payable Account) should therefore be included in the Balance Sheet.

WRITTEN EXERCISES

1. The Old Copper Co. Ltd. owes John Pixley the sum of £600, and gives him its acceptance at six months for this amount and £15 for interest, payable 31st December, 19—. The Old Copper Co. Ltd. takes up the bill on 1st October, 19—, by a cash payment of £400 and a bill at three months for the balance for £215, which bill John Pixley discounts with his bankers at 4 per cent.

Make the necessary entries in John Pixley's books embodying these transactions.
(Institute of Book-keepers.)

2. Record the following matters in ledger accounts (including Bank) to be kept by B:

On 1st January, 19—, A. owes B. £300, and B. owes C. £500.

On that day A. accepts a bill at three months, in favour of B. for £300. On 4th January, B. endorses the bill over to C. in part settlement of his indebtedness. On 31st January, B. hands C. a cheque for the balance of his account less 5 per cent discount on that balance. On presentation of the bill on the date due by C. against A., it is dishonoured, whereupon B. pays C. a cheque for £300. On 31st May, A. (who has been declared bankrupt) pays a first and final dividend of 50p in the pound. *(R.S.A., modified.)*

3. On 1st May, 19—, A. Lion received from L. Jones his acceptance for two months for £500 for goods supplied on that date. He at once discounted the bill with his bankers for £495. On the due date his bankers notified him that Jones had dishonoured the bill on presentation. Show the necessary entries in the books of A. Lion. *(U.E.I.)*

4. On 3rd January, Q. purchased from P. goods to the value of £600 and settled the account by means of three Bills of Exchange for £200 each, due respectively in two, three, and four months. A week later P. discounted the first of the three with his bank, receiving £199; the others he held.

The first two bills were paid at maturity. The third Q. was unable to meet and it was retired by arrangement, Q. paying £50 in cash and giving P. a fresh bill for three months to cover the balance with interest at the rate of 5 per cent per annum. P. discounted this on 10th May for £150.

Set out the entries recording the above in P's ledger. (The Cash Book is not required.) *(R.S.A., modified.)*

5. On 1st January, 19—, A. sells goods to B. for £800. On the same date, B. sells goods to C. for £500.

Subsequent transactions are:

19—

Jan. 2.   A. draws a bill (No. 1) at three months on B. for £300, which B. accepts.

  „   3.   B. draws a bill (No. 2) at three months on C. for £400, which C. accepts. C. draws a bill (No. 3) at three months for £100 in his favour on D., D. accepts and C. endorses this bill over to B.

  „   4.   B. endorses both bills (No. 2 and No. 3) over to A.

Apr. 6.   A. notifies B. that C's acceptance for £400 (No. 2) was presented by A. and dishonoured.

          B. immediately pays £400 to A.

The other bills are paid on the due dates.

Show how these transactions would appear in the ledger of B.

Purchases and Sales Accounts need not be shown and Journal entries are not required. *(Institute of Bankers.)*

27

CONTROL ACCOUNTS AND
SELF-BALANCING LEDGERS

IN most business houses, the largest group of accounts consists of the accounts of customers. For this reason, and to facilitate posting, these accounts are usually kept in a separate ledger known as the Sales Ledger.

Even if only one Sales Ledger is kept it would be a laborious task to ascertain the total value of the book debts on any particular date. The figure, however, can be arrived at if the totals of the amounts posted to this ledger are known.

For example, if a business commences operations on 1st September, and it is known (from the Sales Book or Journal) that the total sales for September are £3,000 whilst the total cash receipts from customers during the same period (according to the Cash Book) were £1,800, then the value of the book debts on 30th September would be the difference, £1,200, assuming there were no other items to allow for, such as goods returned.

This could be shown in the form of an account as follows:

Dr.						Cr.
19—			£	19—		£
Sept. 30	Total Sales as per Sales Journal	..	3,000	Sept. 30	Total Cash Received as per Cash Book	1,800
				„ 30	Balance c/d	1,200
			£3,000			£3,000
Oct. 1	Balance	b/d	£1,200			

An account such as this is called a 'Control Account'. There are two advantages in keeping a Control Account:

(a) It shows at a glance the total value of the debts contained in the ledger to which it refers. This should be equal to the total obtained by adding the separate balances in the accounts in that ledger. A failure to correspond would indicate an error in either the ledger or the Control Account.

(b) If the Control Account is entered in the General Ledger (together with a similar Control Account for every other ledger, including the Purchases Ledger), the General Ledger will contain a summary of all the accounts and will therefore be self-balancing. That is to say that if a Trial Balance were taken out to include all the balances in the General Ledger (including the Control Accounts) plus the Cash Book, plus the Private Ledger, that Trial Balance would balance.

Both of these advantages become very much more important if the number of customers is such that thirty or forty Sales Ledgers have to be kept. If a mistake occurred and there were no indication as to which ledger contained the mistake, all thirty or forty would have to be checked—a laborious and costly process.

Double Entry of Control Account

It should be stated emphatically that the Control Account, as shown in the above illustration, is *not* part of the double-entry system. The double entry for sales is: debit Personal Account, credit Sales Account; *not* credit Control Account. This Control Account involves, in fact, a third entry, made for convenience only, and not included in the Balance Sheet.

A double entry for it, however, can be completed by opening two Control or Adjustment Accounts for each Sales Ledger—one in the Sales Ledger itself, and one in the General Ledger. The one in the Sales Ledger would show the same totals, but on the opposite sides. Using the same figures as in the previous illustration, the two accounts would appear as under. (Notice that when this is done the accounts are now called Adjustment Accounts.)

(1) *In the Sales Ledger*

GENERAL LEDGER ADJUSTMENT ACCOUNT

Dr.					Cr.
19— Sept. 30	Total Cash Re- ceived as per Cash Book	£ 1,800	19— Sept. 30	Total Sales as per Sales Journal ..	£ 3,000
,, 30	Balance c/d	1,200			
		£3,000			£3,000
			Oct. 1	Balance b/d	£1,200

(2) *In the General Ledger*

SALES LEDGER ADJUSTMENT ACCOUNT

Dr.					Cr.
19— Sept. 30	Total Sales as per Sales Journal ..	£ 3,000	19— Sept. 30	Total Cash Re- ceived as per Cash Book	£ 1,800
			,, 30	Balance .. c/d	1,200
		£3,000			£3,000
Oct. 1	Balance ..b/d	£1,200			

Modern Practice

Although at one time it was usual to double-enter the Adjustment Accounts, it is becoming increasingly the practice in modern business to omit the Adjustment Accounts in the personal ledgers and to retain only the Control Accounts in the General Ledger. No advantage is sacrificed through this omission. As a separate Control Account is kept for each personal ledger, the total amount of the balances in each ledger is known and a mistake can thus be traced to the ledger in which it occurs. Moreover, there is no valid reason why both Adjustment Accounts should be kept, since neither forms part of the double-entry system. They are both shown in this chapter because both still appear in examination papers.

Totals included in the Adjustment Accounts

The example given of a Control Account was simplified for purposes of illustration. In practice, the following totals would have to appear in the account, on the sides shown.

GENERAL LEDGER
SALES LEDGER ADJUSTMENT ACCOUNT

Dr.	Cr.
Balances of all personal a/cs. (brought down from previous period).	Total cash paid by customers.
Total sales.	Total discount allowed.
Dishonoured cheques.	Total returns from customers.
	Total of Bills Receivable from customers.
	Total of bad debts.
	(Balance c/d. to debit side)

In the Adjustment Account in the Sales Ledger, the same information would be given, but on the opposite sides. This means that the entries in the General Ledger Adjustment Account in the Sales Ledger would be on the opposite sides to those on which the entries had been made in the personal accounts.

Books of First Entry

The information for the Adjustment or Control Account is obtained from the books of prime entry—Sales Book, Returns Book, Cash Book, etc. This presents no difficulty if only one Sales Ledger is kept. If, on the other hand, there are a number of Sales Ledgers, the figures given in the books of prime entry will have to be analysed. This will be accomplished in the Sales Book by the addition of a column for each Sales Ledger.

Suppose, for example, two Sales Ledgers are kept, divided alphabetically A–M and N–Z. A ruling for the Sales Journal would be as shown on page 248:

SALES BOOK

Date	Name	Total	Ledger A—M	Ledger N—Z
		(1)	(2)	(3)

Col. 1. The items in this column would be debited in the usual way in the personal accounts of the purchasers, in whatever Sales Ledger their accounts appeared.

The total of the column would be credited in the Sales Account in the General Ledger.

This completes the double-entry.

Columns (2) and (3) are used only for the Control or Adjustment Accounts.

Col. 2. The total of this column would be posted to the debit of 'Sales Ledger A–M Adjustment Account' in the General Ledger, and to the credit of the Adjustment Account in Sales Ledger A–M.

Col. 3. Debit total in 'Sales Ledger N–Z Adjustment Account' in the General Ledger. Credit total in General Ledger Adjustment Account in the Sales Ledger N–Z.

The Cash Book, Sales Returns Book, etc., would also have similar analysis columns.

Sundry Items

Those items for which there is no specific subsidiary book would be entered first in the Journal. A Journal with analysis columns could be devised; but only a small number of entries would be required, and it is doubtful whether they would justify the practical difficulties that would be incurred. Probably the simplest solution is to make a monthly analysis of Journal entries.

The kind of item that would be entered in the Journal would include the following:

(*a*) A customer may also be a supplier of goods of a different kind, and in that case an account would be opened for him in both the Sales Ledger and the Bought Ledger. At balancing time, the smaller balance would probably be transferred to the account containing the larger balance.

(*b*) Interest on overdue accounts.

(*c*) Bad debts.

For example, if W. Terry were unable to pay £100 due to you for goods sold to him, the bad debt would be recorded in the following manner:

(i) Debit Bad Debts Account (in the General Ledger).

(ii) Credit the W. Terry Account (in the Sales Ledger).

The above entries would be recorded first in the Journal. The Journal would be used as a book of prime entry for the Adjustment Accounts also. The Journal entry for the Adjustment Accounts is shown below:

				Dr. £	Cr. £
(Date)	General Ledger Adjustment A/c.	Dr.	SL	100	
	To Sales Ledger Adjustment A/c.	..	GL		100
	Bad debt, W. Terry, written off.				

It should be noted that:

(a) The General Ledger Adjustment Account is in the Sales Ledger, and the Sales Ledger Adjustment Account is in the General Ledger.

(b) The entry in the W. Terry Account in the Sales Ledger is on the *credit* side. The entry in the General Ledger Adjustment Account in the Sales Ledger is therefore on the debit side.

Similarly, the entry in the Sales Ledger Adjustment Account in the General Ledger is on the opposite side to the entry in the Bad Debts Account, which is also in the General Ledger.

WRITTEN EXERCISES

1.   J. Younger, a merchant, keeps his books so that a Bought Ledger Adjustment or Control Account and a Sales Ledger Adjustment or Control Account are shown in his General Ledger and balanced each month.

From the details given below, show how these accounts would appear in his General Ledger for the month of January, 19—.

19—				£
Jan. 1.	Balances brought forward in Bought Ledger	...		2,296
„ 1.	Balances brought forward in Sales Ledger ..	..		3,574
„ 31.	Total sales	..	...	3,812
„ 31.	Total purchases	..	..	2,935
„ 31.	Sales returns and allowances	..	..	56
„ 31.	Purchases returns and allowances ..	..	..	97
„ 31.	Discounts received	..	...	186
„ 31.	Discounts allowed	..	...	29
„ 31.	Cash paid to creditors	..	..	3,011
„ 31.	Cash received from debtors .:	..	..	3,565
„ 31.	Transfers to Bad Debts Account ..	..	..	28
„ 31.	Legal expenses paid and charged to debtor ..		..	13

(R.S.A.)

2.   Draw up and balance off in the books of X. the Sold Ledger and Bought Ledger Control (or Adjustment) Accounts to appear in his General Ledger, from the following particulars:

19—					£
Jan. 1.	Debit balances in Sold Ledger	..	..	..	3,456
„ 1.	Credit balances in Sold Ledger	..	..	..	27
„ 1.	Debit balances in Bought Ledger	..	..	..	35
„ 1.	Credit balances in Bought Ledger	...	...	...	1,234

			£
Jan. 31.	Sales	... ...	7,219
,, 31.	Purchases	... .	2,619
,, 31.	Cash received	.. ..	5,864
,, 31.	Discounts received	.. ..	69
,, 31.	Discounts allowed	.. ..	537
,, 31.	Bad debts written off	.. ..	96
,, 31.	Sales returns	.. ..	156
,, 31.	Purchases returns	.. ..	115
,, 31.	Sold Ledger debits transferred to Bought Ledger	..	84
,, 31.	Cash paid	.. ..	1,640
,, 31.	Credit balances in Sold Ledger	.. .. ..	89
,, 31.	Debit balances in Bought Ledger	.. .. ..	90

(*R.S.A.*)

3. On 31st May, 19—, the balances in the Bought Ledger of Thomas Church & Co. were £6,570.

During the half-year ending 30th November, 19—, transactions had taken place which resulted as follows:

		£
Purchases	.. ..	29,505
Cash paid to creditors	... .	29,664
Discount receivable	... .	1,236
Returns outwards	.. ..	465
Acceptances given to creditors	.. ..	2,055
Interest charged by creditors	.. ..	75
Transfers to credit of accounts in Sales Ledger	.. .. ..	110
Transfers to Nominal Ledger to wipe off old debit balances	..	40
Cash overpaid returned	.. ..	10

Prepare the Bought Ledger Control Account for the half-year.

What are the reasons for keeping such an account?

(*Association of Certified and Corporate Accountants.*)

4. Retailers, Ltd. keep two sales ledgers A–K and L–Z and one Purchases Ledger, for which Control Accounts are kept.

On 31st March, 19—, the following errors and omissions came to light.

You are required to show what entries would be required in the ledger account and in the control accounts to make the necessary corrections.

(a) The L–Z column of the Sales Returns Book was undercast by £10 on 10th March, 19—.

(b) An amount received from John White in payment of his account of £300 was received gross on 20th March, 19—, and entered in the Cash Book. White was entitled to discount of 3 per cent.

(c) A cheque for £60 was received from James Black & Sons. This was in full settlement of a debt which had previously been written off as irrecoverable. The amount received was entered in the Cash Book, extended to the appropriate Sales Ledger column and posted.

(d) An invoice for goods invoiced at £170 supplied to William Hall & Son, was entered in the Sales Day Book but was extended into the L–Z column.

(*L. Ch. C.*)

28

PURCHASING A BUSINESS: GOODWILL

If a man wishes to start in business he has two courses open to him. He may set up a completely new business and gradually build it up, or he may purchase as a going concern an already established business.

If he adopts the first alternative he may have to establish himself in the face of competition, there is some risk that the business may not suit the district, and in any case he must wait some considerable time before he begins to earn profit. These difficulties are overcome if he buys a flourishing business of proved value.

It is thus an advantage to buy an established business. The name given to this advantage is 'Goodwill'. Goodwill has been defined as 'the benefit arising from connection and reputation'; it exists because of the probability that customers who have been used to dealing with a particular business will continue to do so.

A person buying a business will have to pay for goodwill. The price is usually a number of years' purchase of the profits, the number of years varying with the nature of the business. It will be smaller where the business depends largely upon the personal characteristics of the proprietor (as in the case of a dentist), and greater in the case of a business of a more impersonal nature.

Example: B purchases a business from A and agrees to pay for the goodwill an amount equal to two years' purchase of the average profits —the average to be calculated over the previous four years. The profits during the previous four years were £800, £700, £900, £1,000, a total of £3,400.

$$\text{Average Annual Profits} = \frac{£3,400}{4} = £850$$

Goodwill (two years' purchase) = £850 × 2 = £1,700

Purchase of a Business

The purchaser of a business will pay not only for the goodwill (which is an asset) but also for the other assets that he acquires. The process is best shown by means of an example:

B agrees to purchase the business of A for the sum of £7,000, which is to include goodwill. A's Balance Sheet was:

	£			£
Sundry Creditors	300	Cash at Bank	1,000
Capital	7,000	Sundry Debtors	200
		Stock	1,800
		Premises and Fixtures ..	4,300
	£7,300		£7,300

For the purpose of the sale, stock has been revalued at £1,900 and premises and fixtures at £4,000.

The cost of the assets would be:

	£
Sundry debtors	200
Stock	1,900
Premises and fixtures	4,000
	6,100
Less creditors	300
	£5,800

B, of course, would not buy the cash. As he has arranged to pay £7,000 for the business, the difference between that sum and the net value of the assets (£5,800) is the payment for goodwill, £1,200.

No man buying a business would ascertain the value of goodwill in this way. It would be calculated as shown in the previous example. But in examination questions, it is frequently left to the student to find goodwill in this way.

It would now be necessary for B to start a set of books, by opening an account for each asset and liability. The debtors and creditors would each have a separate account. Assuming he had £10,000 and had not at that date paid the vendor (A), the opening entries in the Journal would appear as follows:

OPENING ENTRIES

		Folio 1	
		Dr.	Cr.
19—		£	£
Cash at Bank .. .. Dr.		10,000	
Sundry Debtors .. .. .. ,,		200	
Stock .. .. ,,		1,900	
Premises and Fixtures .. .. ,,		4,000	
Goodwill .. .. ,,		1,200	
To Sundry Creditors			300
,, A (Vendor)			7,000
,, Capital			10,000
Being assets and liabilities taken over at valuation from A.			
		£17,300	£17,300

Depreciation of Goodwill

Goodwill rarely appears in a set of books unless it has been bought and paid for. There is no necessary reason why it should depreciate in value. In a period of good trade it may even appreciate. On the other hand, a series of bad years may wipe it out altogether. If no profits have been made for a number of years, there is clearly no goodwill. Its value, therefore, is problematical.

Moreover, it is an intangible asset. It could not normally be used as security for a loan, because it could not be sold on the market unless the business itself were sold.

As a matter of common prudence, therefore, most traders prefer to write it off. If it is likely to disappear in bad times, it is better to write it off when times are good, rather than suffer the loss when the business is least able to bear it.

There is no reason, however, why it should all be written off in a single year. It is usually spread over a number of years. If, for instance, in the illustration given in the previous section, A decided to write off the goodwill in four years, then £300 would be taken off each year. The Goodwill Account would be credited with this sum, and the Profit and Loss Account debited (thus reducing capital). A Journal entry would be necessary. This, and the Goodwill Account at the end of the first year, are shown below:

JOURNAL

| | | | Folio.. | |
			Dr.	Cr.
19— Dec. 31	Profit and Loss A/c. .. .. Dr. To Goodwill A/c. .. .. .. Being one quarter of the goodwill written off.		£ 300	£ 300

GOODWILL ACCOUNT

Dr.							Folio.. Cr.	
Jan. 1	Balance ..		£ 1,200	19— Dec. 31 „ 31	Profit and Loss A/c. Balance ..	c/d	£ 300 900	
			——— £1,200				——— £1,200	
19— Jan. 1	Balance ...	b/d	£900					

WRITTEN EXERCISES

1.   1st February, 19—, Albert Lane purchased a business from Fred Hibble. He
paid £2,500. The assets and liabilities taken over were:

		£
Book debts (including £50 estimated to be bad)	..	500
Sundry creditors	..	100
Stock	..	800
Plant and machinery	..	700
Motor van	..	150

You are required to show, in the books of Albert Lane:
(a) Journal entries to record the purchase.
(b) The Account of the vendor.   (*Institute of Book-keepers, modified.*)

2.   X Ltd. purchased a freehold factory on 1st December, 19—, and the following is a complete statement of the transaction:

		£	£
Purchase price			5,000
Add Proportion of general rates paid in advance at 1st December, 19—			40
Proportion of water rate paid in advance at 1st December, 19—			10
			5,050
Less Proportion of Property Tax owing at 1st December, 19—		60	
Deposit paid 1st September, 19—		500	
			560
Cheque in settlement, paid 1st December, 19— ...			£4,490

Make all the entries necessary to record the above in the books of the company.
(*R.S.A.*)

3.   E. Rhodes decides to purchase the business of W. Nash on 1st January, 19—,
when W. Nash's Balance Sheet stood as follows:

				£					£
Creditors	...	...	...	560	Cash at Bank ..	..	..	480
Capital ...	...	...	...	5,850	Stock ..	..	..	1,250
					Debtors..	..	..	320
					Fixtures	..	..	860
					Premises	...	...	3,500
				£6,410				£6,410

E. Rhodes was to take all assets and liabilities except cash at bank, but the assets,
were revalued as follows:
   5 per cent was to be deducted from Debtors for possible bad debts.
   Fixtures were depreciated to £800.
   Premises were revalued at £4,500.
In addition, E. Rhodes was to pay, as goodwill, three year's purchase of the
average profits for the last five years. These were: £715, £620, £840, £765, £985.
   The transaction was duly carried out, payment being made to W. Nash by
cheque. Show the accounts in E. Rhodes's books, and his Balance Sheet on 1st
January, 19—, after the transaction.

29

PARTNERSHIPS

A PARTNERSHIP is an association from two to twenty persons (ten is the upper limit in the case of banking) carrying on a business in common with a view to profit.

The main advantages enjoyed by a partnership over a sole trader are:

(a) It has access to more capital, since up to twenty people may contribute.

(b) It can command a wider range of experience and ability.

A partnership, however, is an association that requires a high degree of trust between the partners because—

(a) Each partner is liable to the full extent of his private possessions for all debts incurred by the partnership if it should become insolvent. It is to be expected, of course, that each partner would pay his share. If any partner were unable to do so, the other partners would be called upon to make up the deficiency.

(b) A partner commits the partnership by any agreements he makes in the ordinary course of partnership business (unless his powers are specifically limited; but, even then, the outside party must be aware of the limitation).

Under the Partnership Act of 1907, a partner may limit his liability to the amount of capital he contributes, but in that case, he is forbidden by the Act to take any share in the management of the business. He is then known as a 'Limited Partner', but every partnership must include at least one member who is fully liable.

Partners may, in general, make what arrangements they please as between themselves; but it is wise to record the arrangements in an agreement in the form of a deed. If there is no satisfactory evidence of the nature of their arrangements and a dispute occurs, it will be settled according to the rules laid down in the Act of 1890.

Amongst the provisions of this Act are—

(a) Partners share profits and losses equally.

(b) Partners are entitled neither to interest on capital before profits are ascertained nor to remuneration for acting in the partnership business.

Where partners contribute unequal amounts of capital and where some partners do much more work than others, they will usually prefer to make different arrangements. The reasons for allowing interest on capital have already been discussed in Chapter Fifteen in relation to a sole trader. These reasons are equally valid for a partnership, but in addition it is necessary for partners to make an equitable division of the earnings of the firm. The fairest way to recompense those who contribute most capital is to allow interest, just as the fairest way of remunerating those partners who do more work than others is to pay them a salary. The profit remaining after these charges have been made can then be shared as the partners think fit. They may agree that it should not be divided equally.

Book-keeping of Partnerships

The obvious point has already been made that a separate Capital Account must be opened for each partner. (See illustration on page 85.)

These Capital Accounts can be treated like the Capital Account of a sole trader, being credited with profits, interest, etc., and debited with the total amount of drawings (from the Drawings Account). If this is done, the Capital Accounts will show different balances at different times. It is, however, a common practice for partners to agree to provide a fixed amount of capital, not to be varied except by agreement; so it is usual to divide the Capital Account of each partner into two parts—one part, known as the Capital Account, to show the fixed contribution; the other to show the additions (through profits etc.) and deductions (through drawings). The second part is called the Current Account. If the Current Account shows a credit balance the partner is a creditor of the firm and is entitled to withdraw this balance. If, on the other hand, it shows a debit balance, he has not maintained his original contribution of capital and can be required to make the deficiency good. Until this is done, he is a debtor to the firm. The amount shown in the Capital Account does not vary.

The method just described is known as the 'Fixed Capital' method. An illustration is given below:

A and B are in partnership, sharing profits and losses equally, A's capital being £5,000 and B's £10,000. On 1st January, 19—, A's Current Account shows a debit balance of £150 and B's Current Account a credit balance of £250. Partners are to receive interest on capital at the rate of 3 per cent and B is entitled to a salary of £200 per annum. The profit for the year, before making allowance for interest on capital or salary, was £2,250. During the year each partner had drawn £500.

Show the partners' Capital Accounts and Current Accounts on 31st December of that year and the necessary Journal entries.

CAPITAL ACCOUNT: A.

Fo. 1

Dr.							Cr.
				19—			£
				Jan. 1	Balance ...	b/d	5,000

CURRENT ACCOUNT: A.

Fo. 2

Dr.							Cr.
19—			£	19—			[£
Jan. 1	Balance ...	b/d	150	Dec. 31	Interest on		
Dec. 31	Drawings	C.B	500		Capital	J.20	150
„ 31	Balance ...	c/d	300	„ 31	Profit ...		800
			£950				£950
				19—			
				Jan. 1	Balance ...	b/d	£300

CAPITAL ACCOUNT: B.

Fo. 3

Dr.							Cr.
				19—			£
				Jan. 1	Balance ...	b/d	10,000

CURRENT ACCOUNT: B.

Fo. 4

Dr.							Cr.
19—			£	19—			£
Dec. 31	Drawings	C.B	500	Jan. 1	Balance ..	b/d	250
„ 31	Balance ...	c/d	1,050	Dec. 31	Interest	J.20	300
				„ 31	Salary ..	J.20	200
				„ 31	Profit ...		800
			£1,550				£1,550
				19—			
				Jan. 1	Balance ...	b/d	£1,050

INTEREST ON CAPITAL ACCOUNT

Fo. 5

Dr.						Cr.
19—			£	19—		£
Dec. 31	Current			Dec. 31	Profit and	
	A/cs.	J.20	450		Loss A/c.	450

PARTNERSHIP SALARIES ACCOUNT

Fo. 6

Dr.						Cr.
19—			£			£
Dec. 31	Current			Dec. 31	Profit and	
	A/c.:B	J.20	200		Loss A/c.	200

JOURNAL

						Fo. 20	
						Dr.	Cr.
						£	£
Dec. 31	Interest on Capital A/c. ... .. Dr.				5	450	
	To Current A/c.: A				2		150
	„ Current A/c.: B				4		300
	Being interest on capital at 3 per cent p.a.						
Dec. 31	Partnership Salaries A/c. .. .. Dr.				6	200	
	To Current A/c.: B				4		200
	Being salary at £200 p.a. payable to B.						

Notes
  (i) If a partnership salary is allowed, there are two ways in which it may be
       treated:
       (*a*) The salary may be paid at intervals (*e.g.*, monthly) by cheque. In
              that case the Cash Book will be credited and the Partnership
              Salaries Account debited, the total of this account being transferred
              to the Profit and Loss Account at the end of the accounting period.
              No entry will appear in the Current Account if this method is
              adopted.
       (*b*) The more usual method is to debit the Partnership Salaries Account
              and credit the Current Account, thus increasing the amount the
              partner may draw in the same way as his share of profit. No dis-
              tinction is made on the debit side between drawings against profit
              and drawings against salaries. This was the method adopted in the
              Illustration.
  (ii) If no allowance had been made for interest on capital, and no salary
       given for special services, the division of profits would have been A,
       £1,125; B, £1,125. The actual division of profit was—
              A: £800 (profit)+£150 (interest)=£950.
              B: £800 (profit)+£300 (interest)+£200 (salary)=£1,300.
       B thus gained £175 (*i.e.*, £1,300—£1,125) through this arrangement.
 (iii) If the 'Fixed Capital' method had not been employed, Current Accounts
       would not have been opened, and the Capital Accounts and Drawings
       Accounts would have been the same as those of a sole trader. The account
       of B, drawn up in this way, is shown below:

CAPITAL ACCOUNT: B.

Dr.				£					Fo. 3 Cr.
19—					19—				£
Dec. 31	Drawings				Jan. 1	Balance	b/d	10,250	
	(as per				Dec. 31	Interest	J.20	300	
	Drawings				„ 31	Salary	J.20	200	
	A/c.)	4	500		„ 31	Profit		800	
„ 31	Balance	c/d	11,050						
			£11,550					£11,550	
					19—				
					Jan. 1	Balance	b/d	£11,050	

The 'Fixed Capital' method, however, is the one usually employed.

Interest on Drawings

Interest is sometimes charged on partners' drawings for the following
reasons:

(a) The business loses the use of money so withdrawn.

(b) This loss is greater if big withdrawals are made at the beginning of the trading period. It is therefore fairest as between partners that those whose drawings are greatest at the beginning of the period should suffer the greatest penalty, and this result is obtained by charging interest on drawings.

The effect is a partial cancellation of interest on capital, which in turn leaves a larger amount to be divided as profit.

Obviously, if partners have a credit balance in their Current Accounts, against which they are entitled to draw, the case for charging interest on drawings disappears. A better arrangement is clearly to charge interest on debit balances instead.

Example: A and B are in partnership, sharing profits and losses equally. Interest is allowed on capital, and is charged on drawings, at 5 per cent. A's capital is £10,000, B's £8,000, and neither has a balance in his Current Account. B withdraws £1,200 on 28th February, and A £1,200 on 30th November. Profit at the end of the year, before charging interest, is £3,045.

Interest on capital, A=5 per cent of £10,000=£500.
Interest on capital, B=5 per cent of £8,000=£400.

Interest on drawings is charged for the period between the withdrawal of the money and the end of the year—the period during which the business is deprived of its use. The calculation for interest on drawings would therefore be:

$$A. \ \frac{5}{100} \times £1,200 \times \frac{1}{12} = £5$$

$$B. \ \frac{5}{100} \times £1,200 \times \frac{10}{12} = £50$$

The net profit at the end of the accounting period would be allocated between the partners in an Appropriation Account, which is an extension of the Profit and Loss Account:

APPROPRIATION ACCOUNT

Dr.					Cr.
		£			£
Interest on Capital: A	...	500	Net Profit	...	3,045
B	..	400	Interest on Drawings: A	...	5
Net Profit: A	...	1,100	B	...	50
B	...	1,100			
		£3,100			£3,100

The partners' Current Accounts would then be:

CURRENT ACCOUNT: A.

Dr.   Cr.

	£		£
Drawings	1,200	Interest on Capital ...	500
Interest on Drawings ..	5	Net Profit	1,100
Balance c/d.	395		
	£1,600		£1,600
		Balance b/d.	£395

CURRENT ACCOUNT: B.

Dr.   Cr.

	£		£
Drawings	1,200	Interest on Capital ...	400
Interest on Drawings ..	50	Profit	1,100
Balance c/d.	250		
	£1,500		£1,500
		Balance b/d.	£250

A would thus receive £1,100+£500—£5=£1,595

B would receive £1,100+£400—£50   =£1,450

If interest were not charged on drawings the Appropriation Account would appear:

	£		£
Interest on Capital:		Net Profit	3,045
A	500·00		
B	400·00		
Profit: A	1,072·50		
B	1,072·50		
	£3,045·00		£3,045

Under this arrangement, profit would be shared as under:

A: £1,072·50+£500=£1,572·50.

B: £1,072·50+£400=£1,472·50.

The effect of charging interest on drawings is therefore to increase A's share of the profit by £22·50 and to reduce B's share by a similar amount.

Loans

A partner may make a loan to the partnership, over and above his contribution of capital. Such a loan would bear interest at an agreed rate, irrespective of profits. In the absence of an agreement, the Partnership Act lays down a rate of 5 per cent. A Loan Account would be opened in the usual way. It would be credited with the amount of the loan, the debit entry being in the Cash Book (if the loan were in the form of money). When interest became due, a Loan Interest Account would be opened, the interest being debited to this account (from which it would be transferred to Profit and Loss Account), and credited in the Partners' Current Account. In the event of dissolution of the partnership, the loan would be repayable in full, whether or not there was sufficient money to repay the capital. No entry is made in the Capital Account or the Current Account of the partner in respect of such a loan.

The Appropriation Account

The division of the profits as between partners is usually shown in an extension of the Profit and Loss Account known as the Appropriation Account. Strictly speaking, one would not expect to see interest on capital and partners' salaries in this part of the account, because such payments are not part of the profit they earn. But, because they are not expenses in the sense of being necessary payments to people outside the firm, in practice they are shown in the Appropriation Account. Interest on a loan from a partner would, however, normally appear in the body of the Profit and Loss Account and not in the Appropriation Account. The Appropriation Account relating to the example on page 256 is shown below, assuming, for purposes of illustration, that A had made a loan to the firm of £1,000 at 5 per cent, and that the interest on this loan (£50) had been deducted before the profit (£2,250) had been ascertained.

PROFIT AND LOSS ACCOUNT

Dr.					Cr.
			£		£
Interest on Loan	..	..	50	Profit (before deduction of	
Net Profit	...	c/d	2,250	Interest)	2,300
			2,300		2,300

APPROPRIATION ACCOUNT

				£				£
Interest on Capital: A		..		150	Net Profit ..	...	..	2,250
	B	..		300				
Salary: B	..	..	...	200				
Profit: A	..	...	..	800				
	B	..	...	...	800			
				£2,250				£2,250

The Balance Sheet

It is usual on the Balance Sheet to set out the Current Accounts and the Capital Accounts in full. The liabilities side of the Balance Sheet is shown on page 262, assuming sundry liabilities of £4,000.

LIABILITIES

							£	£
Capital A/c.: A ..	...	...	...	...	...	...		5,000
B ..	...	...	...	...	...	..		10,000
Current A/c.: A—								
Share of profit	..	...	...	...	...	...	800	
Interest on capital		..	...	...	...	...	150	
							950	
Less Debit balance 1/1/19—			..	...	..	150		
Drawings	..	..	...	...	...	500		
							650	
								300
Current A/c.: B—								
Balance 1/1/19	..	..	..	...	..	..	250	
Share of profit	..	..	..	..	..	..	800	
Interest on capital		..	..	..	..	..	300	
Salary	..	..	..	..	..	..	200	
Interest on loan	..	..	...	...	..	..	50	
							1,600	
Less Drawings	...	...	...	...	...	...	500	
								1,100
Sundry liabilities	..	..	..	...	..	..		4,000
Loan A/c.: A	..	...	...	...	...	...	..		1,000
								£21,400

WRITTEN EXERCISES

1. Brown and Green are in partnership. They have fixed Capital Accounts (Brown £5,000 and Green £3,000), and share profits equally. On 1st January, 19—, Brown's Current Account showed a credit balance of £300; there was no balance on Green's Current Account. Prepare their Current Accounts for the year 19— from the foregoing information and the following particulars:

(a) Interest is to be credited to the partners at 4 per cent per annum on their capitals, but is not chargeable on drawings.
(b) Green is to be credited with a salary of £200 for the year.
(c) The net profit for the year was £2,920 before charging the above interest and salary.
(d) Drawings during the year were:
Brown £1,200; Green £1,100.   (R.S.A.)

2. J. Turpin and W. Diamond are partners in a business and their partnership agreement provided that:

(1) The partners' Capital Accounts remain constant.
(2) The partners are entitled to interest on their Capital Accounts at the rate of 4 per cent per annum.
(3) The partners are to be charged with interest at the rate of 5 per cent per annum on their Drawings Accounts (calculated in months).
(4) Turpin is entitled to two-thirds and Diamond one-third of the profits and losses.

On 1st April, 19—, the balances on the Partners' Capital Accounts were: Turpin Cr. £10,000 and Diamond Cr. £6,000. There were no balances on the Partners' Current Accounts.

During the year ending 31st March, 19—, Turpin drew £60 and Diamond £50 on the last day of each month.

The firm's profit for the year, before making any adjustment required by the agreement, amounted to £2,672.

Prepare the Current Accounts of each partner for the year ending 31st March, 19—.   (*R.S.A.*)

3. John Cooper and James Martin are trading as general merchants and the following Trial Balance is extracted from their books at 31st December, 19—:

	£	£
Capital Accounts:		
Cooper		5,000
Martin ..		5,000
Loan Account: Cooper as at 1/1/19— ..		2,000
Purchases ..	20,000	
Trade creditors		3,700
Sales ..		27,000
Trade debtors	5,100	
Carriage inwards ..	360	
Carriage outwards ..	430	
Discounts received ..		410
Balance at bankers	1,100	
Rent ..	750	
Rates ..	400	
Salesmen's salaries	1,200	
General expenses ..	400	
Wages ..	570	
Delivery vans	1,400	
Insurances ..	200	
Fixtures and fittings	1,500	
Bad debts ..	800	
Provision for doubtful debts		500
Stock at 1st January 19—	5,000	
Drawings:		
Cooper	2,400	
Martin ...	2,000	
	£43,610	£43,610

You are asked to prepare Trading and Profit and Loss Accounts for 19—, together with a Balance Sheet at 31st December, 19—.

The following matters are to be taken into account:

(1) Profits are to be divided according to the provisions of the Partnership Act, 1890.

(2) Rent accrued at 31st December, 19—, £250.

(3) Insurance paid in advance at 31st December, 19—, £50.

(4) Rates paid in advance at 31st December, 19—, £80.

(5) Depreciation is to be written off the delivery vans at the rate of 20 per cent per annum.

(6) Stock at 31st December, 19—, £4,500.

(7) Provision for doubtful debts to be increased to 10 per cent of trade debtors.
  (*Institute of Bankers.*)

4. J. Baxter and D. Dexter carry on business as partners in boot and shoe retailers and repairers.

The following balances were shown by the books at 31st December, 19—:

		£	£
J. Baxter: Capital Account			1,009
Drawings Account		816	
D. Dexter: Capital Account			658
Drawings Account		816	
Sales (Retail £4,794; Repairs £3,307) ..			8,101
Purchases (Retail £3,215; Repairs £1,612)		4,827	
Shop fixtures and fittings (Retail) at 1st January, 19—		300	
Rent (Retail £208; Repairs £104) ..		312	
Wages: Sales staff		569	
Repairers		695	
Creditors			28
Tools		81	
Repairs to premises		98	
Rates and Water (Retail £41; Repairs £21)		62	
Bank balance		672	
Advertising (Retail £123; Repairs £41) ..		164	
General expenses (Retail £75; Repairs £102)		177	
Machinery at 1st January, 19—		260	
Cash in hand		72	
Loan Account, J. Baxter, at 1st January, 19—			600
Opening stock on hand at 1st January, 19— (Retail £341; Repairs £58) ..		399	
Lighting and heating (Retail £38; Repairs £38)		76	
		£10,396	£10,396

You are required to prepare the Trading and Profit and Loss Account for the year ending 31st December, 19—, showing the profit of each department and Balance Sheet at that date after making adjustments for the following:

(1) The stock on hand at 31st December, 19—, was valued at: Retail £124, and Repairs £29.
(2) Depreciate shop fixtures and fittings at 10 per cent per annum.
(3) Depreciate machinery which was used in Repairs Departments at 20 per cent per annum.
(4) Provide for interest on the loan at 5 per cent for the year.
(5) The expenditure on repairs to premises is recoverable in full from the War Damage Commission.
(6) J. Baxter and D. Dexter share profits and losses in the proportions of two-thirds and one-third respectively.   (R.S.A.)

5.   The following accounts appear in the annual trial balance of the books of Messrs. Herring and Company as at 30th September, 19—:

			£	£
Loan Account	...	... Albert Herring		4,750
Capital Accounts	...	... Albert Herring		18,000
		John Herring		10,000
		William Herring		5,000
Current Accounts as at 1st Oct., 19— ..	..	... ... Albert Herring		2,470
		John Herring		4,960
		William Herring	1,790	
Drawing Accounts	...	... Albert Herring	2,400	
		John Herring	2,000	
		William Herring	1,000	
Profit and Loss Accounts	...	Hoxton Branch		8,920
		Hayling Branch		6,790
		General	7,183	

For managing the Hoxton Branch, John Herring should be credited with a salary of £750, plus 5 per cent of the Branch profits after charging his salary. For managing the Hayling Branch, William Herring should be credited with commission of 15 per cent of Branch profits remaining after charging his commission. Interest on loan at 6 per cent has not been provided for. The loan is repaid quarterly in cash at the rate of £500 per annum. Profits after charging interest on capital of 8 per cent are shared as follows:

Albert Herring, one-half.
John Herring, one-third.
William Herring, one-sixth.

Show the adjustments to the accounts in the form of journal entries, the Appropriation Account and the appropriate sections of the Balance Sheet as at 30th September, 19—.   (*Institute of Cost and Works Accountants.*)

30

PARTNERSHIPS

(*continued*)

Admission of New Partner

IF a new partner is admitted into an existing partnership, he gets the benefit of entry into an established business. In addition therefore to making a contribution of capital, he will usually be expected to agree to arrangements under which existing partners gain advantage from the goodwill they have already created. The commonest arrangements are:

I. A Goodwill Account is opened and debited with the agreed amount. This is credited to the Capital Accounts of the existing partners, in the proportion in which profits are shared. No money in respect of goodwill is paid by the incoming partner.

The existing partners will thereafter receive a larger sum as interest on capital.

There are other possible advantages; for example:

(*a*) If the goodwill is not written off and the business is sold as a going concern, the existing partners will receive the whole amount of the goodwill if it is sold at the figure appearing in the books.

(*b*) If the goodwill is written off out of profits, part of the cost will be borne by the new partner. The Capital Accounts of the existing partners (which include the Current Accounts) will not therefore be reduced to the level at which they stood before the goodwill was created.

II. The new partner may pay into the business an agreed sum in respect of goodwill in addition to his contribution of capital. The amount he pays as goodwill would be credited to the Capital Accounts of the existing partners in the proportion in which they share profits, no Goodwill Account being opened. The debit entry would be in the Cash Book.

III. A premium for entering the business may be paid privately to the existing partners, no entries appearing in the firm's books.

Example: A and B are in partnership, sharing profits in the proportion of two-thirds to A and one-third to B. They agreed to admit C as a partner on the following conditions:

(*a*) C to have one-quarter of the profits, and A and B to share the remainder in the same proportion as before.

(b) A Goodwill Account to be opened and debited with £1,800, which should be credited to A and B in the proportion in which they share profits.

(c) C to contribute capital equal to one-quarter of the combined capitals of A and B after the addition of goodwill.

The following is the Balance Sheet of A and B (before admitting C):

	£			£
Sundry Liabilities	1,300	Sundry Assets		7,000
Capital Accounts: A	4,800	Cash at Bank		1,500
B	2,400			
	£8,500			£8,500

Show the Journal entry to open the Goodwill Account; show the Capital Account of each partner, the Goodwill Account, the Cash Account and the Balance Sheet after these arrangements have been put into effect.

JOURNAL

	Dr. £	Cr. £
Goodwill A/c. .. .. Dr.	1,800	
To Capital A/c.: A		1,200
„ Capital A/c.: B		600
Being Goodwill A/c. created on admission of C to partnership.		

CAPITAL ACCOUNT: A.
Dr.   Cr.

	£		£
Balance c/d.	6,000	Balance	4,800
		Goodwill	1,200
	£6,000		£6,000
		Balance b/d.	£6,000

CAPITAL ACCOUNT: B.
Dr.   Cr.

	£		£
Balance c/d.	3,000	Balance	2,400
		Goodwill	600
	£3,000		£3,000
		Balance b/d.	£3,000

CAPITAL ACCOUNT: C.
Dr.   Cr.

			£
		Cash	2,250

GOODWILL ACCOUNT

Dr.			£				Cr. £
Capital A/c.: A	..	..	1,200	Balance c/d. ...	...	..	1,800
Capital A/c.: B	...	..	600				
			£1,800				£1,800
Balance	...	...	£1,800				

CASH ACCOUNT

Dr.			£				Cr. £
Balance	..	...	1,500	Balance c/d. ...	...	...	3,750
Capital A/c.: C	..	...	2,250				
			£3,750				£3,750
Balance	...	...	£3,750				

BALANCE SHEET OF A, B, AND C

		£				£
Sundry Liabilities	...	1,300	Sundry Assets	...	...	7,000
Capital A/c.: A ..	..	6,000	Goodwill	..	...	..	1,800
B ..	..	3,000	Cash at Bank	...	...	3,750
C ...	..	2,250				
		£12,550				£12,550

C. would receive $\frac{1}{4}$ of the profit.
B. would receive $\frac{1}{3}$ of $\frac{3}{4}=\frac{1}{4}$ of the profit.
A. would receive $\frac{2}{3}$ of $\frac{3}{4}=\frac{1}{2}$ of the profit.

Dissolution of Partnership

If a partnership is dissolved, it will be necessary to sell all the assets of the firm. The money received for them will then be apportioned in the following order of priority, each class being paid in full before the claims of succeeding groups are considered:

(a) In paying debts due to persons who are not partners in the firm (e.g., sundry creditors). If there were insufficient money for this, partners would be required to contribute additional funds in the same proportion as their capitals. If any partner were unable to do so, the remaining partners would be liable for his share.

(b) In repayment of loans made by partners over and above their capital contribution. If there were insufficient to repay the whole amount, and there were more than one loan, each partner would receive the same proportion of what was due to him under this heading.

(c) In paying back the capital contributions of the partners. The money available, if insufficient to pay the whole amount, would be shared in proportion to capital.

(d) The residue, if any, is divided amongst partners in the proportion in which they share profits.

The creditors of the firm must always be paid first, but the arrangements for repayment of partners' loans, and capital, and the distribution of profit are subject to variation by agreement amongst the partners. The above are the provisions of the Partnership Act of 1890, which would apply in the absence of an agreement to the contrary.

Method. 1. The Current Accounts of partners would be made up to date (*e.g.,* by adding undistributed trading profits) and the balance transferred to the Capital Accounts.

2. The assets would be transferred to a Realization Account (on the debit side, of course). This account would be credited with the proceeds of the sale of the assets and debited with any expenses incurred in the selling.

If the assets realize more than their book value, there will be a profit. If they realize less, there will be a loss. This profit or loss is transferred to the Capital Accounts in the proportion in which profits or losses are shared.

The advantage of the Realization Account is that it saves the trouble of finding the profit (or loss) on each separate asset, and of transferring those profits (or losses) individually.

3. When this is completed, the only asset held will be cash. It will be appropriated as described in the previous section.

Example: X and Y have been trading in partnership on terms that profits and losses are shared as to three-fifths to X and two-fifths to Y. On 31st December, 19—, they agree to dissolve, when their Balance Sheet was as under:

BALANCE SHEET
31ST DECEMBER, 19—

	£	£			£	£
Capital:			Freehold Premises ...			4,000
X	4,000		Machinery			2,000
Y	3,000		Debtors..		750	
		7,000	*Less* Provision for Bad			
Current A/c.: X ...		600	Debts		100	
Creditors		800				650
Bank Overdraft ...		250	Stock			1,500
			Current A/c.: Y ...			500
		£8,650				£8,650

X takes over the Stock at book value as part of his share. Freehold premises are sold for £3,500 and machinery for £2,100. Debtors realize

£500 and creditors (other than bank overdraft) are settled for cash £720. Prepare the accounts necessary to record the dissolution.   (*R.S.A.*)

CAPITAL ACCOUNT: X.

Dr.				£					Cr.
				£					£
Stock	..	...	...	1,500	Balance	..	...	...	4,000
Loss on Realization		..		282	Current A/c.		...	...	600
Cash ..	..	...	..	2,818					
				£4,600					£4,600

CURRENT ACCOUNT: X.

Dr.				£					Cr.
				£					£
Capital A/c.: X	...	...		600	Balance	...	...	...	600

CAPITAL ACCOUNT: Y.

Dr.				£					Cr.
				£					£
Current A/c.		...	...	500	Balance	...	...	...	3,000
Loss on Realization		..		188					
Cash ...	...	...	...	2,312					
				£3,000					£3,000

CURRENT ACCOUNT: Y.

Dr.				£					Cr.
				£					£
Balance	...	...	...	500	Capital A/c.: Y	...	...	500

CREDITORS ACCOUNT

Dr.				£					Cr.
				£					£
Cash ..	..	...	...	720	Sundries	...	...	...	800
Realization A/c.		...	...	80					
				£800					£800

BANK ACCOUNT

Dr.				£					Cr.
				£					£
Premises	..	...	...	3,500	Balance	..	...	...	250
Machinery	..	..	..	2,100	Creditors	..	...	...	720
Debtors	...	...	...	500	Capital A/c.: X	...	...	2,818
					Capital A/c.: Y	...	...	2,312
				£6,100					£6,100

FREEHOLD PREMISES ACCOUNT

Dr.			£			Cr. £
Balance	...	...	4,000	Realization A/c. ...	...	4,000

MACHINERY ACCOUNT

Dr.			£			Cr. £
Balance	...	...	2,000	Realization A/c. ...	...	2,000

SUNDRY DEBTORS ACCOUNT

Dr.			£			Cr. £
Balance	...	...	750	Provision for Bad Debts		100
				Realization A/c. ..	..	650
			£750			£750

STOCK ACCOUNT

Dr.			£			Cr. £
Balance	...	...	1,500	Capital A/c.: X ...	...	1,500

REALIZATION ACCOUNT

Dr.			£			Cr. £
Freehold Premises	..	..	4,000	Cash—Premises ..	..	3,500
Machinery	..	..	2,000	do. —Machinery	..	2,100
Sundry Debtors	...	..	650	do. —Debtors ..	..	500
				Discount (creditors)	..	80
				Loss on Realization	..	
				Capital A/c.: X	..	282
				Capital A/c.: Y	...	188
			£6,650			£6,650

WRITTEN EXERCISES

1. (i) A. and B. are trading in partnership, preparing accounts annually to 31st March. Interest on capital is allowed at 5 per cent per annum, and A. and B. share profits in the proportion of 3 to 2. On 31st March, 19—, A's capital stood at £8,000, B's at £6,000, and no Goodwill Account appeared in the books.

On 1st April, 19—, C. joined the firm as a partner on the terms that (a) he was to receive one-sixth of the profit, A. and B. as between themselves sharing the remaining five-sixths in the same proportion as before; (b) he was to pay into the firm's bank account a cheque for £2,500, of which £2,000 was to be credited to his Capital Account and £500 was to be credited to Goodwill Account, which was forthwith to be transferred to A's and B's capital accounts in their profit-sharing proportion.

(ii) D. and E. are also trading in partnership on the same terms as, and having the same capitals as, A. and B. respectively.

On 1st April, 19—, F. joined the firm, on the same terms as those on which C.

joined the first firm, with the exception that £3,000 was to be debited to Goodwill Account immediately before F's entry, and the whole of the £2,500 paid in by F. was to be credited to his Capital Account.

For the year ended 31st March, 19—, both firms made a profit of £4,985 before charging interest.

Show how this profit would be shared among the partners in each of the two firms; compare the corresponding figures, and explain the comparative results.

(*R.S.A.*)

2.   P., a sole trader, who had built up his business himself, took Q. into partnership on 1st January, 19–1, Q. taking one-third of the profits. Immediately prior to Q's entry a Goodwill Account for £3,000 was raised in the books, and it was agreed that this should be written off against profits at the rate of £500 per annum, the firm's accounts being prepared annually as on 31st December.

On 31st March, 19–4, the business was sold for cash to a limited company, the amount paid for the goodwill being £5,000.

Write up the Goodwill Account in the firm's books, and prepare a statement showing the actual amount of profit derived by P. and Q. respectively from goodwill over the whole period of carrying on the business.   (*R.S.A.*)

3.   The following is the Balance Sheet of a sole trader, William Brown, as at 1st January, 19—. An agreement is made admitting J. Smith to partnership at that date on payment of £5,000 in cash, and providing that goodwill £3,000 shall be credited to Brown; the value of premises will also be revalued at £3,800 and the difference credited to Brown.

You are required to redraw the Balance Sheet showing the result of this arrangement to the new partnership.

BALANCE SHEET OF WILLIAM BROWN
AS AT 1ST JANUARY, 19—

Liabilities		£	*Assets*				£
Creditors	... ...	.. 14,000	Cash ..	..	...	...	800
Capital	... ...	.. 6,000	Debtors..	..	...	...	6,400
			Stock ..	...	...	..	10,000
			Premises	...	...	..	2,800
		£20,000					£20,000

(*Institute of Cost and Works Accountants.*)

4.   X. and Y. are equal partners, and on 31st December, 19—, agree to admit Z. having one-third share of profits. The Balance Sheet of X. and Y. at this date is as follows:

Liabilities			£	*Assets*				£
Creditors	... ...	...	750	Stock ..	...	...	...	1,750
Capital: X	... ...	...	1,250	Debtors..	..	...	..	750
Capital: Y	... ...	..	1,000	Cash ..	...	...	..	500
			£3,000					£3,000

X. and Y. value their goodwill at £500 and agree to reserve 10 per cent on debtors for bad debts.

Z. brings in stock £300, debtors £200, and sufficient cash to make his capital equal to that of Y. X. withdraws sufficient cash to make his capital equal to that of Y. and Z.

You are required to write up the ledger and cash account of X. and Y. to give effect to the above agreement and prepare a Balance Sheet of the new firm. (*N.B.* No journal entries are required.) (*U.E.I.*)

5. A. and B. are in partnership and share profits and losses in the proportions: A. two-thirds and B. one-third. At the 1st January the balances on their Capital Accounts are: A. £10,000 (Cr.) and B. £7,000 (Cr.). There is no Goodwill Account on the books. C. is admitted as a partner on this date and profits and losses will be shared in future as follows: A. one-half, B. one-quarter and C. one-quarter. C. contributes £5,000 in cash as capital and a further £1,500 in cash in respect of his share in the goodwill. Show the Capital Accounts of all three partners and state the reasons for the entries you make. (*C.C.S.*)

6. (*a*) A partnership consists of three partners with capital and sharing profits as follows:

			Capital £	Profit	Drawings £
X ..	...	...	15,000	50%	1,500
Y ...	...	...	10,000	30%	1,000
Z ..	..	..	5,000	20%	1,000

Capital is chargeable with 5 per cent per annum interest.
Y. and Z. each receive a salary of £750 per annum, capital to remain fixed.
X. has loaned a further £10,000 to the partnership at 4 per cent per annum interest.
Profit for the year, before charging partners' salaries and interest on capital and loans, £10,000. You are required to prepare Drawings Accounts for the partners.
(*b*) X. dies at the end of the year, and Y. and Z. in accordance with agreement, take over his share. Total goodwill is valued at £12,500. Itemize the total sum due to the representatives of X. (*Institute of Cost and Works Accountants.*)

7. J. Brown and A. Green, partners in a manufacturing business sharing profits and losses as to three-quarters and one-quarter respectively, decided to close down on 31st December, 19—.

The Balance Sheet of the firm at the date of cessation was as follows:

		£				£
Capital Accounts:			Freehold Premises	...	...	10,295
J. Brown ..	...	... 10,720	Machinery	..	...	... 6,341
A. Green ..	..	... 6,004	Debtors...	...	...	... 2,693
Loan Account: J. Brown		.. 1,000	Stock	...	...	... 1,762
Creditors	...	.. 2,568				
Bank overdraft	...	.. 799				
		£21,091				£21,091

The assets were sold on 28th January of the next year, and the following amounts were realized:
Premises £12,750, machinery £6,191, and stock £1,798.

The book debts were received except for the sum of £93 which was irrecoverable. On 18th February, 19—, the creditors and the loan were paid, together with the expenses of the dissolution amounting to £120, and the bank balance was distributed.
Prepare the Realization, Cash, and Capital Accounts to show the dissolution. (*R.S.A.*)

8. A, B and C are in partnership, sharing profits and losses in the ratio A one-half, B one-third and C one-sixth. The Balance Sheet of the firm on 31st December, 19—, is as follows:

Capital Accounts:	£	£		£
A	8,000		Freehold property ...	6,000
B	6,000		Plant and machinery ...	4,000
C	4,000		Furniture and fittings ...	700
		18,000	Stock-in-trade	7,400
Creditors		5,000	Debtors	4,600
			Balance at Bank	300
		£23,000		£23,000

The partnership is dissolved as from the date of this Balance Sheet.

A took over the Freehold Property at a valuation of £5,000. The debtors realized £4,500, and the remaining assets were sold for cash as follows:

Plant and machinery £6,200,   Furniture and fittings £850,   Stock £7,500

It is agreed that B is to be credited with £150 as remuneration for his services in connection with the realization of the assets.

The Creditors are paid off in full, and each partner is paid the amount found to be due to him.

You are required to show the Realization Account, the Cash Account and the Capital Accounts of the Partners. No other ledger accounts are required.

(*Institute of Bankers.*)

9.   On 1st February, 19—, Alpha and Beta, who were trading in partnership, sharing profits and losses in the proportions of two-thirds and one-third respectively, decided to wind-up their business.

On the cessation of trading, the Balance Sheet was as follows:

BALANCE SHEET, 1ST FEBRUARY, 19—

	£			£
Alpha Capital Account ..	3,500	Freehold factory	4,218
Beta Capital Account . ..	1,500	Machinery	1,707
Alpha Current Account ..	276	Debtors	625
Creditors	1,592	Stock	458
Bank overdraft	402	Beta Current Account ...	262
	£7,270		£7,270

The assets realized the following: Freehold factory, £8,438; Machinery, £1,026; Debtors, £600; and Stock, £456. The expenses of realization amounted to £275.

Show how the Realization, Bank and Partners' Accounts would appear after the amounts due to the partners have been paid out.   (*R.S.A.*)

10.   L, S and D were partners in a firm sharing profits and losses in the proportions of one-half, one-third and one-sixth respectively.

On 30th June, 19—, L retired from the firm and it was agreed that in order to ascertain the balance due to him certain of the assets should be revalued.

The original Balance Sheet at 30th June, 19—, was:

	£			£
L Capital Account	20,000	Freehold Premises	10,500
S Capital Account	17,000	Plant	16,000
D Capital Account ...	7,000	Equipment	2,100
Creditors	3,200	Investment	10,000
		Debtors	2,700
		Bank	5,900
	£47,200		£47,200

It was agreed to revalue the Premises at £21,000, Plant at £14,000 and Equipment at £1,800, and to value Goodwill at £5,600. The investment was transferred to L at book value in part payment of his capital of which the balance was left on loan account.

Draw up the initial Balance Sheet of the new firm immediately after L's retirement.   (*R.S.A.*)

31

COMPANY ACCOUNTS—ISSUE
OF SHARES, ETC.

THE amount of capital a sole trader can command is limited to his own resources and to what he can borrow. A trading partnership can combine the resources of a maximum of twenty people. In neither case can sufficient capital be accumulated to operate the gigantic companies made necessary by modern industrial developments. Hence there has arisen the device of the 'Joint Stock Company', whereby the public can be invited to lend their money to a concern, the size of which is limited only by its power and ability to borrow.

Limited Liability

If people are to lend their money to complete strangers, they must know the extent of the liability they undertake. This is fixed by the amount they agree to subscribe, *i.e.,* the number of shares they agree to take. They may be called upon to pay the company the full value of the shares they agree to take, and if the company is unsuccessful they may lose the whole amount; but, unlike a sole trader or a member of a partnership, they cannot be called upon to contribute anything more in the event of the company's becoming insolvent. Such loss would fall upon the creditors, who would be compelled to accept a proportion of what was owed to them.

Formation of a Company

The usual method of forming a Joint Stock Company is by registration. A minimum of seven people is required by law. Certain stamped documents, which include the Memorandum of Association, the List of Directors, and the Articles of Association, are filed with the Registrar of Joint Stock Companies. If these documents conform to legal requirements, a Certificate of Incorporation is issued by the Registrar; the company has then been formed, and may commence business.

Broadly speaking, the *Memorandum of Association* defines the company in relation to the outside world. It states:

1. The name of the proposed company (with the word 'Limited' at the end).
2. The address of the Registered Office (if it is known—the county at least must be shown).
3. The objects for which the company is being formed (these are widely interpreted to allow for expansion of the business in the future).

4. A declaration that the liability of members is limited.
5. The amount of capital the company takes power to acquire and the shares into which it is to be divided. (An *ad valorem* stamp duty is payable on this, but the amount is usually made big enough to allow for expansion.)

The *Articles of Association*, on the other hand, define the relations of the shareholders as between themselves. It is their agreement with one another. If no Articles of Association are drawn up, the company is governed (with regard to meetings, election of directors, etc.) by Table A, which is an appendix to the Companies Act, and is, in effect, a model set of Articles.

A Joint Stock Company is a legal entity, or person, apart from the particular people who form it. If all the shareholders in a given company were to die simultaneously, and their shares were to pass to their legatees, it would still be exactly the same company in the eyes of the law. It may own property, sue or be sued, and carry on a trade or business. But whereas a natural (as distinct from a legal) person may do anything that is not against the law, what a given company may do is defined and restricted by its Memorandum of Association.

Control of the Company

The shareholders, who have subscribed the capital, are in ultimate control of the company. As there are probably many of them, they elect from their number a body known as the Board of Directors, who manage the company on their behalf. The voting strength of a shareholder is in proportion to his holding of shares. At the Annual General Meeting the directors must make a report on their stewardship.

Issue of Shares

The first step in commencing business is to raise the capital by the issue of shares. The process is the same whether it is a newly-formed company issuing shares for the first time, or an established company asking for more capital to extend its operations.

(a) A prospectus is drawn up giving all essential information concerning the company and its activities. The directors are personally responsible for the accuracy of all statements made in the prospectus.

It is not usual for a company to demand the whole of the purchase money for the shares at once. A certain amount is due on application. The amount due is stated in the prospectus, together with the closing date for applications. The name of the company's banker is also stated. Usually an application form is attached to the prospectus.

(b) Those desiring shares fill in the application form and send it with the application money to the bankers named on the prospectus.

(*c*) After the closing date, the bank sends the application forms to the company.

(*d*) The directors proceed to the allotment of the shares.

If all the shares have not been taken up, the underwriters will be called upon to take the balance. Underwriters are members of Lloyd's who agree in advance to buy such shares, in return for a commission.

If the issue is over-subscribed (more being applied for than are offered), the directors are free to allot shares as they think fit. Some applicants may receive no shares at all, in which case they will be sent a 'Letter of Regret' and their application money will be refunded. The others may be allotted all the shares they asked for, or only a proportion. They receive a 'Letter of Allotment'; but, even if they are allotted only a proportion of the shares asked for, no money is returned. This is because a second instalment of the purchase price becomes due on allotment, and the balance of the application money is retained as part payment of this.

(*e*) The allotment money (or the balance of it) is paid into the company's bank by the shareholders to whom shares have been allotted.

(*f*) The company is now in a position to call in the balance of the purchase money as and when the directors deem necessary. The whole amount may be called in at once by what is known as a 'First and Final Call'; it may be asked for in a further series of instalments known as 'First Call', 'Second Call', etc.; or part of it may be left 'uncalled' for an indefinite period, as a reserve in case of emergency. In the last case, the holder of the shares is liable for the balance due whenever it is requested by the company.

Sale of Shares

If a shareholder wishes to realize on his shares, he cannot for obvious reasons demand his money back from the company. His only course is to sell his shares privately, or on the Stock Exchange, to another person for the best price he can obtain. It is a purely private bargain between him and the purchaser, and the price he obtains is of no direct concern to the company except in so far as it is an indication of the view taken by investors of the company's prospective earning power, which in turn might affect its power to borrow.

A Joint Stock Company is required to keep a Register of Shareholders, wherein any such change of ownership must be recorded. Dividends, of course, are receivable by the holder whose name appears in the register.

If shares, not fully paid, are sold, the new buyer takes, with the shares, the liability to pay to the company any balance due on the shares.

An illustration of a Share Register is given on the next page.

REGISTER OF MEMBERS

Name........................

Address........................

Date of Entry as Member............ ....

Date of Ceasing to be a Member............

AMOUNT DUE			AMOUNT PAID			SHARES ACQUIRED						SHARES TRANSFERRED						BALANCE	
Dates	Particulars	Amount	Dates	Particulars	Amount	Dates	No. of Allotment or Transfer	No. of Shares	Distinctive Nos. From	To	No. of Share Cert.	Dates	No. of Transfer	No. of Shares	Distinctive Nos. From	To	No. of Share Cert.	No. of Shares	Amt.

Types of Shares

There are two main types of shares: Preference Shares and Ordinary Shares.

Whatever profit is available for distribution is applied first to the payment of a fixed rate of dividend on the Preference Shares. The balance, if any, is then distributed amongst the Ordinary Shareholders. Preference Shareholders have thus a greater degree of security than the Ordinary Shareholders; but the Ordinary Shareholders, who accept the main burden of risk of success or failure, may obtain a higher return where good profits are made, because they are not limited to a fixed rate of dividend.

There are, of course, various types of preference shares. Examples are First and Second Preference (which explain themselves) and Cumulative Preference Shares. Cumulative Preference Shares carry the right to have arrears of dividends made up at a later date if, in any year, the company is unable to pay the agreed rate.

An important legal consideration is that no dividends of any kind may be paid except out of profits or reserves; and, if dividends are paid out of reserves, this fact must be clearly stated.

Another type of share is the Deferred or Founders' Share. Holders of these shares are paid no dividends until after the Ordinary Shareholders have received an agreed rate. The effect of issuing such shares is to convert the Ordinary Shares into a type of Second Preference Shares.

Debentures

A debenture is not a share. It represents a loan made to the company on the security of the assets generally, or of some specified assets. The holders draw, not dividends, but interest; and this is payable whether profits are made or not. So long as the interest is paid, the debenture holders exercise no control over the company. Such loans may be for an indefinite time, in which case they are 'Perpetual', or they may be repayable on a specified date, in which case they are 'Redeemable'. The method of issue of debentures (usually in the form of certificates for a round sum such as £100) is identical with that for shares, and so are the book-keeping records.

Company Accounts

These are precisely similar to those of any other business except that:

- (a) They include accounts showing the issue of shares.
- (b) Certain legal requirements must be observed in drawing up the Final Accounts and Balance Sheet, which must be published annually and filed with the Registrar of Joint Stock Companies.

A copy may be obtained by anyone on payment of a small fee. These requirements are dealt with in the next chapter.

Book-keeping Records of the Issue of Shares

The principles followed are fairly simple.

(a) Instead of having one Capital Account, a separate Share Capital Account is opened for each type of Preference Share, or Ordinary Share, etc., issued, because different types of share carry different legal rights.

These accounts are credited with the amounts due from the holders of the shares as they become due.

(b) Having agreed to take the shares, the shareholders are liable to the company for the purchase price whenever it is demanded by the company. The shareholders are therefore debtors of the company until they have paid the amounts demanded. An account is opened for them and debited with the amounts due from them. This completes the double entry in the Share Capital Account referred to in the previous parargaph.

It should be noted that—

    (i) There are usually very many shareholders. The individual amounts due from them are recorded in the Register of Shareholders. It is not necessary therefore to open a separate account for each shareholder. Instead the sums due from them are shown in total in a single account similar in principle to the Sundry Debtors Account used in an earlier chapter of this book.

    (ii) The purchase price is payable in a series of instalments. An instalment is not treated as being due until the company asks for it. Thus the account for the shareholders becomes a series of accounts called the Application Account, the Allotment Account, First Call Account, and so on until the shares are fully paid. The Application Account and the Allotment Account may be, and usually are, combined into one.

(c) When the shareholders pay the various calls, the Cash Book will be debited and the Shareholders Account (i.e., Application and Allotment Account, or First Call Account, etc.) will be credited.

These principles are illustrated in the following example:

The XY Engineering Co. issue 50,000 6% Preference Shares of £1 each. The last date for application, which must be accompanied by £0·10 per share application money, is 5th March. On 15th March all shares were allotted and the allotment money, £0·25 per share, was all received by 25th March.

The First Call of £0·30 per share was made on 1st June, and a Second and Final Call on 30th July. All money was received.

PREFERENCE SHARE CAPITAL ACCOUNT

Dr.		£				Cr. £
July 31	Balance c/d.	50,000	Mar. 5	Application A/c. ..		5,000
			„ 15	Allotment A/c.		12,500
			June 1	First Call A/c.		15,000
			July 30	Final Call A/c.		17,500
		£50,000				£50,000
			Aug. 1	Balance b/d. ...		£50,000

APPLICATION ACCOUNT
(6% PREF. SHARES)

Dr.		£				Cr. £
Mar. 5	Pref. Share Capital A/c.	5,000	Mar. 5	Cash		5,000

ALLOTMENT ACCOUNT
(6% PREF. SHARES)

Dr.		£				Cr. £
Mar. 15	Pref. Share Capital A/c.	12,500	Mar. 25	Cash		12,500

FIRST CALL ACCOUNT
(6% PREF. SHARES)

Dr.		£				Cr. £
June 1	Pref. Share Capital A/c.	15,000	June 1	Cash		15,000

FINAL CALL ACCOUNT
(6% PREF. SHARES)

Dr.		£				Cr. £
July 30	Pref. Share Capital A/c.	17,500	July 30	Cash		17,500

The sale of shares to the public is treated as a credit transaction. That is to say, it is divided into two stages, the first stage recording that the money is due, and the second stage recording the payment of the money. The reason for this is that the money received may not correspond exactly with the face value of the shares, which is the amount that must be entered in the appropriate Share Capital Account.

The money received may be either greater or less than the face value of the shares. It would be greater if more shares were applied for (and the application money sent) than were to be issued—in other words, if the issue were over-subscribed. Again the shares might be issued at a premium (i.e., for more than the face value), the premium being in the nature of a profit.

On the other hand, less will be received if some shareholders default on one of the calls, or if the shares are issued at a discount (*i.e.,* for less than their face value).

Shares Over-subscribed

Let us suppose that in the illustration just given, 60,000 shares were applied for, though only 50,000 were being issued.

The application money received would be £6,000 instead of £5,000 and the Application Account would read:

APPLICATION ACCOUNT

Dr.				Cr.
19—		£	19—	£
Mar. 5	6% Pref. Share Cap. A/c. ..	5,000	Mar. 5 Cash	6,000

Some of this money may have been received from people to whom no shares were allotted. This would be returned to them. If it amounted to £200, and was returned on 10th March, the Application Account would now read:

APPLICATION ACCOUNT

Dr.				Cr.
19—		£	19—	£
Mar. 5	6% Pref. Share Cap. A/c. ..	5,000	Mar. 5 Cash	6,000
„ 10	Cash	200		

This still leaves a balance of £800 received from people who will be allotted only a proportion of the shares they asked for. It could be returned to them, but almost immediately afterwards they would be called upon to pay the allotment money. The most sensible course, therefore, is that the company should hold this money as part payment of the sum due on allotment. It would accordingly be transferred to the Allotment Account by (*a*) a debit entry in the Application Account and (*b*) a credit entry in the Allotment Account.

These accounts, at this stage, are shown below:

APPLICATION ACCOUNT

Dr.				Cr.
Mar. 5	6% Pref. Share Cap. A/c. ..	£ 5,000	19— Mar. 5 Cash	£ 6,000
„ 10	Cash	200		
„ 10	Allotment A/c.	800		
		£6,000		£6,000

ALLOTMENT ACCOUNT

	19—			£
	Mar. 10	App. A/c.	—	800

On 15th March the Allotment Account will be debited with the sum due (£12,500). On 25th March the balance of the allotment money (£12,500 less £800, *i.e.,* £11,700) would be debited in the Cash Book and credited in the Allotment Account.

This difficulty does not arise if, as usually happens, the Application Account and the Allotment Account are combined into a single Application and Allotment Account. The above transactions would then be entered as follows:

APPLICATION AND ALLOTMENT ACCOUNT

Dr.						Cr.
19—		£	19—			£
Mar. 5	6% Pref. Share Capital A/c. ..	5,000	Mar. 5	Cash		6,000
„ 10	Cash	200	„ 25	Cash		11,700
„ 15	6% Pref. Share Capital A/c.	12,500				
		£17,700				£17,700

Shares Issued at a Premium

If a prosperous company issues a new block of shares, these are likely to be in great demand. Any person who was allotted such shares, paying only the face value, would be able to make a profit by selling them privately at an enhanced price. When this is likely to happen, a company sometimes intercepts part of the profit by issuing the shares at a premium—that is, issuing them at a higher price than the face value.

The premium is a profit to the company; but, as it is not a trading profit, it is not distributed amongst the shareholders. Nor is it credited to the Share Capital Account, which shows the value of the shares at par (*i.e.,* face value). Instead it is credited to a separate account called the Share Premium Account, where it remains as a kind of reserve. It may be used for writing off preliminary expenses (see page 292).

Let us suppose that the 50,000 6 per cent Preference Shares in the previous illustrations had been issued at a premium of £0·05 per share, payable on allotment. Of the accounts already shown on page 281 only the Allotment Account would be different. It is shown together with the Share Premium Account, on the next page.

K

ALLOTMENT ACCOUNT

Dr.		(6% PREF. SHARES)					Cr.
		£					£
Mar. 15	Pref. Share Cap. A/c	12,500	Mar. 25	Cash			15,000
„ 15	Share Premium A/c. ..	2,500					
		£15,000					£15,000

SHARE PREMIUM ACCOUNT

Dr.		(6% PREF. SHARES)				Cr.
						£
			Mar. 15	Allotment A/c. ..		2,500

The shares rank for dividend at their face value—in the above example, £1. A Preference Shareholder who had 1,000 £1 shares would receive as dividend 6 per cent of £1,000 (£60), not 6 per cent of the £1,050 he paid for the shares.

The balance of the Share Premium Account appears as a liability on the Balance Sheet.

Shares Issued at a Discount

If a company needs fresh capital but it is felt that the public would be unwilling to buy the shares at their face value, they may be issued at a discount; that is, at less than their face value. If the shares were entered in the Share Capital Account at the price at which they were issued, no record of the discount would be necessary. But they are not entered at this price. They are entered at face value; and, assuming that 80,000 £1 Ordinary Shares were issued at a discount of £0·125, the following position would arise:

ORDINARY SHARE CAPITAL ACCOUNT

			£
	App. and Allot. A/c. ..	..	40,000
	First and Final Call ..	..	40,000

APPLICATION AND ALLOTMENT ACCOUNT

	£				
Ord. Share Cap. A/c.	.. 40,000	Cash ..	..	...	.. 30,000

FIRST AND FINAL CALL ACCOUNT

	£				
Ord. Share Cap. A/c.	.. 40,000	Cash ..	..	..	.. 40,000

The Application and Allotment Account shows a debit balance of £10,000. This would suggest that the shareholders owe the company £10,000. In fact they do not. The balance represents the discount they have been allowed; and, like any other discount, it must be written off in the Profit and Loss Account.

The point, however, arises that the loss was incurred in order to raise capital, which will be used by the company over a number of years. The loss, therefore, is also spread over a number of years (but not necessarily the same number). For this reason it is transferred to a Share Discount Account and written off at the discretion of the directors.

It should be noted that a company is not permitted to issue shares at a discount unless the following conditions are all fulfilled: it has been in existence for at least a year, shares of the same class have already been issued, the shareholders have agreed, and legal sanction has been obtained. The shares rank for dividend at their full face value. Thus, if £0·05 discount is allowed on a £1 share, it is a £1 share which is bought and not a £0·95 share.

Forfeited Shares

If a shareholder defaults on a call, the company has the right, in certain conditions, to declare his shares forfeit. If the company avails itself of that right, the defaulting shareholder loses his shares and forfeits whatever he has already paid. If not, the unpaid calls are a debt to the company, and figure amongst the assets or 'Calls in arrear'. They are credited to the appropriate Call Account and debited to a Calls in Arrear Account.

The entries necessary to record a forfeiture will be most clearly seen from an illustration:

A shareholder holds 1,000 £1 Ordinary Shares, part of an issue of £100,000 shares, on which he has already paid £600 on Application and Allotment and a First Call. He fails to pay the Second Call of £200 (£0·20 per share) and forfeits his shares.

(a) The forfeited shares cease to be part of the share capital of the company. The Ordinary Share Capital Account must therefore be debited with the amount with which it has already been credited; *i.e.,* the £600 which has been paid and the £200 which is due, £800 in all.

(b) The Second Call Account must be credited with the amount of the default, £200, because this will not be paid.

(c) To complete the double entry, the £600 already paid must be credited to the Forfeited Shares Account.

The accounts would now appear:

ORDINARY SHARE CAPITAL ACCOUNT

	£		£
Forfeited Shares	800	Balance	60,000
		Second Call A/c.	20,000

SECOND CALL ACCOUNT

	£					£
Ord. Share Capital A/c.	20,000	Cash				19,800
		Forfeited Shares				200

FORFEITED SHARES ACCOUNT

			£
		Share Capital A/c.	600

JOURNAL

							Dr.	Cr.
							£	£
Ord. Share Capital A/c.	..	...	...	...	..	..	800	
Second Call A/c.	..	..	...	..	..	..		200
Forfeited Shares A/c.	..	..	..	..	..	..		600

The balance of the Forfeited Shares Account, representing the money already paid and forfeited, is a capital profit to the company. It could therefore be transferred to the credit side of the Premium on Shares Account. More often, the shares are sold again at a price such that the company eventually obtains in all at least £1 for each £1 share—they cannot be sold at a discount, but part of the profit is sacrificed.

Suppose in the illustration already given the forfeited shares were resold. The minimum price at which they could be resold would be £200, the amount of the unpaid call. With the £600 already paid and £200 to be called later, the company would then obtain the full face value of the shares. But this would be to sacrifice the whole of the profit. Let us therefore assume that the shares were resold for £400, this price to include the second call. Thus £200 of the £600 profit is retained in the Forfeited Shares Account and the other £400 put back into capital. The entries to record this would be as follows:

(a) Credit the Ordinary Share Capital Account with the paid-up value of the share; i.e., £800.

(b) Debit the Cash Book with the £400 received on resale.

(c) Debit the Forfeited Shares Account with the difference between the paid-up value of the share £800, and the cash received, £400, when the shares were resold (i.e., the paid-up value of the shares when they are resold is £800. Only £400 is received from the new shareholder, so the balance, £400, is taken from the Forfeited Shares Account by a debit entry therein).

The accounts are now shown on the next page.

ORDINARY SHARE CAPITAL ACCOUNT

Dr.					Cr.
	£				£
Forfeited Shares A/c. ..	800	Balance			60,000
Balance .. .. c/d	80,000	Second Call A/c.			20,000
		Forfeited Shares Reissued			800
	£80,800				£80,800
		Balance ... ... b/d			£80,000

FORFEITED SHARES ACCOUNT

Dr.				Cr.
	£			£
Ord. Share Capital A/c. ..	400	Share Capital A/c. ...		600
Premium on Shares A/c. ..	200			
	£600			£600

CASH ACCOUNT

Dr.			Cr.
	£		
A. Shareholder	400		

SHARE PREMIUM ACCOUNT

Dr.			Cr.
			£
		Forfeited Shares A/c. ...	200

JOURNAL

							Dr.	Cr.
							£	£
Cash							400	
Forfeited Shares A/c.							400	
Ord. Share Capital A/c.								800
Forfeited Shares A/c.							200	
Share Premium A/c.								200

WRITTEN EXERCISES

1. A limited company was registered with a nominal capital of £150,000, divided into 50,000 6 per cent Preference Shares of £1 each and 100,000 Ordinary Shares of £1 each. The shares were offered for subscription at par. On 1st February, 19—, the public subscribed for 45,000 Preference Shares and 80,000 Ordinary Shares, payable as follows:

On application £0·15 per share.
On allotment (10th February) £0·25 per share.
On 15th March £0·60 per share.

On 20th March, all moneys due on the shares had been received except the final call on 100 Preference Shares, which remained outstanding.

Submit the entries necessary to record the above issue in the books of the company. (*R.S.A., modified.*)

2. On 1st January, 19—, the balance on the Share Capital Account in the ledger of a limited company is £30,000, representing 40,000 Ordinary Shares of £1 each, upon which £0·75 per share has been called up.

On 1st March, 19—, the directors make a Final Call of £0·25 per share, and on 5th March all call moneys were received by the company, with the exception of £100 due from John Short, the holder of 400 shares.

On 15th April the shares held by Short were declared forfeited, and, on 1st May, 19—, these shares were re-issued to James Long as fully paid, in consideration of £360 paid in cash by Long.

You are required to show the entries in the ledger of the company to record the above transactions. Ledger accounts should be closed off, and any balances brought down. Journal entries are not required.

(Institute of Bankers, Part 1, modified.)

3. J. Tisbury applied for, and was allotted, 500 shares of £1 each in the St. Helens Co. Ltd. After paying £0·10 a share on application and £0·35 a share on allotment, he failed to pay the call of £0·55 made by the directors. The directors subsequently resolved to forfeit the shares allotted to Tisbury. Later still they re-issued them to Norbury as fully paid on receiving £0·70 a share from him.

You are required to set out Journal entries recording these transactions.

(Institute of Book-keepers, modified.)

4. Boom Ltd. decided to make an issue of 100,000 Ordinary Shares of £1 each, payable as to £0·25 per share on application, £0·25 per share on allotment, and the balance two months after allotment.

On 25th June, 110,000 shares were applied for and the deposits thereon received. On 1st July following, applications for 70,000 shares were accepted in full, while applicants for the remaining 40,000 shares were allotted 75 per cent of the number they had respectively applied for. The excess application moneys went in reduction of the amount due on allotment, and the balance of the allotment moneys was received on 3rd July. The final instalment was received on 1st September.

You are asked to record the above matters in the company's Cash Book and ledger. *(Institute of Bankers, Part 1, modified.)*

5. Draw up Journal entries, in proper commercial form, to record the following matters.

(a) A company issues twenty debentures of £100 each at the price of £98 each for cash.

(b) The company decides to reduce its provision for bad debts from £500 to £400.

(c) The company finds that its net profit for the year is £1,100, and decides to grant Mr. A. B., the managing director, a commission of 10 per cent of the amount of profit that will remain after the commission has been granted. *(R.S.A.)*

6. Draw up Journal entries, in proper commercial form, to record in the books of a company the following matters:

(a) The directors make a first call of £0·25 per share on 10,000 shares.

(b) The company issues fifty Debentures of £100 each at the cash price of £98 each.

(c) The directors forfeit 100 shares of £1 each held by A. B. who has already paid £0·25 per share on application, and £0·50 per share on allotment, but has allowed a call of £0·10 per share to remain unpaid.

(d) The company decides to carry £1,000 to Reserve out of accumulated profits. *(R.S.A., modified.)*

7. A.B., Ltd., issued a prospectus inviting applications for 50,000 Ordinary Shares of £1 each, at a premium of £0·10 per share. £0·25 per share is payable on application, £0·35 (including the premium) on allotment, and the balance three months after allotment.

On 1st May, 19—, applications were received for 60,000 shares. On 6th May, applications for 42,000 shares were accepted in full, and applicants for 16,000 shares were allotted one-half of the number for which they had applied, excess application moneys being applied in reduction of the amount due on allotment. On the same date, deposits were returned to applicants for 2,000 shares.

On 9th May, all amounts due on allotment were received.

The final instalment due on 6th August, 19—, was received on that date from all shareholders, with the exception of Henry Wilson, the holder of 500 shares.

You are required to show the entries to record the above matters in the Cash Book and Ledger of the Company.

Journal entries are not required.   (*Institute of Bankers, modified.*)

32

COMPANY ACCOUNTS—FINAL ACCOUNTS, ETC.

Appropriation Account

THE capital of a Joint Stock Company is held entirely in the form of shares. It cannot be increased except through the issue of new shares. The profit, therefore, is not added to the Capital Account. Instead, it is transferred in the first place from the Profit and Loss Account to an account called the Appropriation Account, in which the allocations to general reserves and the distribution to the shareholders are shown. Any profit not specifically allocated remains as a balance in the Appropriation Account. It appears as a liability in the Balance Sheet, and will be added to the profit made in the following year. It is the duty of the directors to make proposals for the appropriation of the profit, but their proposals must receive the assent of the shareholders at the Annual General Meeting before being put into effect.

Illustration: Let us suppose that a company with a share capital consisting of 100,000 6 per cent £1 Preference Shares and 500,000 £1 Ordinary Shares makes a profit of £52,000 and had undistributed profits amounting to £1,250 from the previous year.

Assuming that the shareholders agreed to the allocation of £5,000 to reserve, and that the Preference Share dividend would absorb £6,000, there would be left a sum of £42,250 for distribution amongst the Ordinary Shareholders. The maximum percentage payable, if nothing were carried forward, would be $8\frac{9}{20}$ per cent. Such a fractional figure would not normally be taken as a basis on which to distribute dividends. An even 8 per cent dividend would absorb £40,000 and leave £2,250 to carry forward. If this were decided upon, the Appropriation Account would appear as follows:

APPROPRIATION ACCOUNT

	£				£
Reserve..	.. 5,000	Balance	..	..	.. 1,250
Pref. Share Dividend ..	.. 6,000	Profit ..	...	...	.. 52,000
Ord. Share Dividend ..	.. 40,000				
Balance c/d.	.. 2,250				
	£53,250				£53,250
		Balance b/d. ..	...		.. £2,250

The double entry in the Ordinary Share Dividend Account would not be completed until the assent of the shareholders was obtained. This does not apply to the Preference Share dividend, or to an Interim dividend, which the directors have power to pay without the consent of the shareholders.

There are usually further steps necessary to complete the book-keeping entries relating to dividends.

(a) As the profit is not carried to the Capital Accounts, a separate Dividend Account is opened for each Share Capital Account. The dividend is credited there; and, after the reserve is credited in the Reserve Account, the double entry for the items in the Appropriation Account is complete. The accounts at this stage are shown below:

6% PREFERENCE SHARE DIVIDEND ACCOUNT

	£
Appropriation A/c.	6,000

ORDINARY SHARE DIVIDEND ACCOUNT

	£
Appropriation A/c.	40,000

RESERVE ACCOUNT

	£
Appropriation A/c.	5,000

(b) Ignoring Income Tax, which is outside the scope of this book, the Dividend Accounts would be closed when the dividends were paid. The entries would be:
  (i) Credit Cash
  (ii) Debit Dividend Accounts.

Purchase of a Business

The book-keeping entries necessary to record the purchase of a business have already been explained (Chapter 28). The only difference that would appear if the purchase were made by a company, would be that part of the purchase price would probably be paid by the issue of shares to the vendor (or seller). An illustration is appended.

The A.B. Manufacturing Co. Ltd. acquired the business of R. Dale on 1st January, 19—, his Balance Sheet on that date being as follows:

BALANCE SHEET OF R. DALE
1ST JANUARY, 19—

	£		£
Creditors	7,000	Cash in Hand	100
Capital	27,000	Cash at Bank	1,900
		Sundry Debtors	5,000
		Stock	8,000
		Fixed Assets	15,000
		Goodwill	4,000
	£34,000		£34,000

R. Dale was to retain the cash in hand and at bank, the other assets and liabilities being taken over at the valuations shown. The purchase price was to be satisfied by a payment in cash of £5,000 and by the issue to Dale of 18,000 Ordinary Shares of £1 each, treated as fully paid.

Show by means of Journal entries how the transaction would be recorded in the books of the A.B. Manufacturing Co. Ltd.

(*Note.* The purchase price of the business was £25,000, consisting of assets £32,000 less creditors £7,000. The amount paid was £23,000— £5,000 in cash and £18,000 in shares. The difference, £2,000, would represent a premium on shares.)

JOURNAL

		£	£
Jan. 1	Sundries .. .. Dr.		
	To Sundries		
	Debtors	5,000	
	Stock	8,000	
	Fixed Assets	15,000	
	Goodwill	4,000	
	To Creditors		7,000
	„ R. Dale (Vendor)		25,000
	For Assets and Liabilities taken over on purchase of business, Agreement dated		
		32,000	32,000
Jan. 1	R. Dale (Vendor) .. .. Dr.	25,000	
	To Bank		5,000
	„ Ord. Share Capital A/c.		18,000
	„ Share Premium A/c.		2,000
	Payment made to Vendor on purchase of business, Agreement dated		
		£57,000	£57,000

Preliminary Expenses

These are the costs incurred in the formation of the company, for such items as solicitors' and accountants' fees, printing, stamp duties, advertising, etc. They must be written off in the Profit and Loss Account, because clearly the services rendered have been used up.

In some cases, however, when such expenses are large, it is felt to be better to spread the loss over a number of years, a proportion being transferred to Profit and Loss Account each year.

The balance remaining must appear in the Balance Sheet as an asset though, in fact, it has been used up. Such debit balances, which must be treated as assets though it is known that their value has been exhausted, are called 'Fictitious Assets'.

The expenses incurred in the issue of Debentures are also included under this heading.

Final Accounts of Companies

The Balance Sheet of a limited company is in its nature exactly the same as every other Balance Sheet, but it must be presented to conform with legal requirements. Further, the profit clearly cannot be added to the share capital.

The main requirements of the Companies Act of 1948 are as follows:

1. The Final Accounts and the Balance Sheet must be filed annually with the Registrar of Joint Stock Companies and may be inspected by anyone wishing to do so on payment of a small fee. It is not necessary, however, to show the whole of the Profit and Loss Account as this might contain information of value to a competitor. The following must be disclosed:

(a) The provisions for depreciation and renewals.
(b) Interest on debentures and loans.
(c) The charge for income tax and profits tax.
(d) Income from investments separately stated.
(e) Directors' fees.
(f) The amounts placed to, or withdrawn from, reserves.
(g) The amount of dividends paid or proposed. These must be shown net, that is, after deduction of tax.

To conform to these requirements the Profit and Loss Account is divided into two sections. The first section, which is not published, contains all losses and expenses not listed above. The second section, which is published, contains the balance of the first section plus items (a), (b), (c), (d) and (e) above. The balance of the second section is then carried to the Appropriation Account which is also published. Items (f) and (g) above are shown in the Appropriation Account.

2. In both the Profit and Loss Account and the Balance Sheet, the corresponding amounts at the end of the immediately preceding financial year must be shown for purposes of comparison.

3. In the Balance Sheet a statement of Authorized Capital must be given. Some notes on Capital are appended.

Authorized Capital. This is the amount that the company takes power to issue in the Memorandum of Association, and is probably in excess of immediate requirements.

Issued or Subscribed Capital. The amount offered and actually taken up by the public.

Called-up Capital. The holder of shares is asked to pay in a series of 'calls'. The Called-up Capital is the amount that shareholders have been asked to pay to date.

Paid-up Capital. This will be equal to the Called-up Capital, less any Calls in Arrear

4. The method of setting out the Balance Sheet is illustrated on page 296. It should be noted that fixed and current assets are separately

distinguished and totalled, and are so arranged that it is easy to compare fixed assets with fixed liabilities (mainly the claims of shareholders) and current assets with current liabilities. It is also easy to determine the degree to which the current assets are liquid.

5. The basis of valuation of the fixed assets must be shown. This means that the original value, the provision for depreciation, and the method of computation of that provision must be given. The Institute of Chartered Accountants recommends that the fixed instalment method should be adopted.

6. Reserves, provisions, and investments must be separately stated. Goodwill, patents and trade-marks may be shown as one composite total. Preliminary expenses and underwriting commission must be separately stated.

7. The market valuation of quoted investments at the time of drawing up the Balance Sheet must be shown.

8. Contingent liabilities must be referred to as a note on the Balance Sheet. A contingent liability is a liability to pay a sum of money only upon the occurrence of a specified event, which may or may not occur. For example, if the drawer of a Bill of Exchange passes it, after acceptance, to a third party in payment of a debt, he will be liable to pay the amount of the bill to the holder if, but only if, the bill is dishonoured. His liability is thus contingent upon the dishonour of the bill.

Example of Final Accounts of a Company

The following is a Trial Balance of C.S.C. Ltd. for the year 19—. The accounts are shown in the form in which they would be presented to the shareholders, as laid down by the Companies Act of 1948, no details of a trading character being required by the Act.

	£	£
Share Capital, £1 shares, authorized and fully paid ...		80,000
5 per cent Debentures		20,000
Profit and Loss Account, b/f.		8,900
General reserve		10,000
Sinking fund investments ..	11,000	
Sinking fund		11,000
Sales ..		152,000
Purchases	110,000	
Returns inwards	2,000	
Stock, 1st January ..	7,300	
Salaries and wages ..	9,200	
Office expenses	3,600	
Selling expenses	7,400	
Legal and accountancy	500	
Dividend (interim) ...	2,400	
Bad debts	300	
Discounts (net), Cr.		200
Lease	29,000	
Plant and machinery: 1st January	48,000	
bought 1st October	6,000	
Creditors		13,600
Fwd.	£236,700	£295,700

		£	£
	Fwd.	236,700	295,700
Debtors		12,500	
Payments in advance		150	
Debenture interest, paid 30th June		500	
Bank balance		20,850	
Goodwill		25,000	
		£295,700	£295,700

Provide for:

    (a) Closing stock £13,500.

    (b) Provide for bad debts, 6 per cent on debtors.

    (c) Provide for discounts, 4 per cent on debtors, 2 per cent on creditors.

    (d) Depreciation of lease £1,000; depreciation of plant, etc., 10 per cent per annum.

    (e) Directors' fees £2,000.

    (f) Final dividend to be recommended to the Annual General Meeting of 5 per cent.

    (g) Sinking fund instalment for the year £900.

Ignore taxation.   (C.C.S.)

PROFIT AND LOSS ACCOUNT OF C.S.C. LTD.
FOR YEAR ENDED 31ST DECEMBER, 19—

	£	£			£
Debenture Interest ..	500		Trading Profit ... —		... 24,452
Add Interest due	500				
		1,000			
Directors' Fees ...		2,000			
Depreciation—					
Lease	1,000				
Plant (10%) ..	4,950				
		5,950			
Profit c/d... ...		15,502			
		£24,452			£24,452
Sinking Fund Instal-			Net Profit b/d. —		.. 15,502
ment		900	Balance b/fwd... ...		... 8,900
Dividends—					
Interim	2,400				
Proposed Final ..	4,000				
		6,400			
Balance c/fwd. ...		17,102			
		£24,402			£24,402

(The trading profit £24,452 was arrived at as shown on page 297. This would not form part of the published accounts.)

BALANCE SHEET OF C.S.C. LTD.
AS AT 31ST DECEMBER, 19—

	£	£			£	£
Share Capital:			**Fixed Assets:**			
Authorized and Issued—			Lease		29,000	
Shares of £1, fully paid ..		80,000	*Less* Depreciation		1,000	28,000
Reserves and Undistributed Profits:			Plant, 31st December, 19—		48,000	
Debenture Sinking Fund	11,900		Additions		6,000	
General Reserve	10,000				54,000	
Profit and Loss A/c. ..	17,102	39,002	*Less* Depreciation		4,950	49,050
		119,002	Sinking Fund Investment ..			11,000
5% Debentures		20,000	Goodwill			25,000
Current Liabilities:						113,050
Creditors	13,600		**Current Assets:**			
Reserve for Discount at 2%	272		Stock		13,500	
	13,328		Debtors	12,500		
Directors' Fees	2,000		*Less* Provision for Bad Debts 750			
Debenture Interest due ..	500		Provision for Discount 470	1,220	11,280	
Proposed Dividend.. ..	4,000	19,828	Bank		20,850	
			Prepayments		150	45,780
		£158,830				£158,830

TRADING AND PROFIT AND LOSS ACCOUNI OF C.S.C. LTD. FOR YEAR ENDED 31ST DECEMBER, 19—

	£	£		£	£
Stock, 1st Jan., 19—		7,300	Sales ..	152,000	
Purchases ..	110,000		*Less* Returns	2,000	
Less Stock, 31st					150,000
Dec., 19—	13,500				
		96,500			
Gross Profit c/d. ..		46,200			
		£150,000			£150,000
Salaries and Wages ..		9,200	Gross Profit b/d.		46,200
Office Expenses		3,600	Discount Received		200
Selling Expenses		7,400	Provision for Discount on		
Legal and Accounting Fees		500	Creditors at 2% ...		272
Bad Debts written off ..		300			
Provision for Bad Debts 6% of Debtors		750			
Provision for Discount on Debtors at 4%		470			
Trading Profit		24,452			
		£46,672			£46,672

Manufacturing Company—Final Accounts

An example is also given of the Final Accounts of a Manufacturing Company to show the form of the Revenue Accounts, divided into Manufacturing Account, Selling Account, and Profit and Loss Account.

The following is the Trial Balance and data extracted from the books of Messrs. Enterprise Ltd. for the year ended 31st December, 19—. You are required to prepare:

(a) Manufacturing Account.
(b) Selling Account.
(c) Profit and Loss Account.
(d) Balance Sheet.

No Journal entries required.

TRIAL BALANCE

	£	£
Capital Account—Ordinary Shares		100,000
Preference Shares		100,000
Mortgage Debenture Account		15,000
General reserve, 1st Jan., 19—		30,000
Stock of finished assemblies, 1st Jan., 19—	35,678	
unfinished assemblies, 1st Jan., 19—	46,000	
finished parts, 1st Jan., 19—	12,347	
other work in progress, 1st Jan., 19—	20,502	
raw materials, 1st Jan., 19—	35,408	
Leasehold buildings at cost	20,000	
Plant and machinery at cost	55,000	
Motor vehicles	5,000	
Loose tools and equipment, 1st Jan., 19—	3,729	
Buildings in course of erection	715	
Plant in course of construction	1,036	
Cash in hand	512	
Cash at bank		7,342
Profit and Loss Account, 1st Jan., 19—		14,387
Customers' Accounts (Debtors)	97,845	
Suppliers' Accounts (Creditors)		37,014
Raw materials purchased	305,888	
Investments at cost	12,000	
Fuel and power purchased	7,500	
Sales office expenses	5,025	
Delivery expenses (outwards)	6,718	
Repairs and renewals	30,000	
Sales		557,212
Stationery and printing	917	
Telephone and stamps	520	
Insurances	340	
Rates	350	
Depreciation, 1st Jan., 19—: Plant and machinery		27,825
Motor vehicles		2,000
Building lease		10,000
Salaries—Administrative	10,000	
Manufacturing	8,000	
Travellers	9,000	
Manufacturing wages	170,750	
	£900,780	£900,780

The capital of the company is:
Authorized: 200,000 Ordinary Shares of £1 each.
100,000 5% Cum. Pref. Shares of £1 each.
Issued: 100,000 Ordinary Shares, fully paid.
100,000 Preference Shares, fully paid.

The Mortgage Debentures bear interest at 5% per annum.
Stock values at 31st Dec., 19—, were:

	£
Finished assemblies	43,729
Unfinished assemblies	65,413
Finished parts	15,712
Other work in progress	23,202
Raw materials	33,415

Provision is required for the following: £
   Bad and doubtful debts   2,037
   Depreciation on original values—

       Plant and machinery $7\frac{1}{2}\%$ per annum.
       Motor vehicles 20% per annum.
       Buildings leased for 20 years, 5% per annum.

   Valuation of loose tools and equipment at 31st Dec., 19—, £3,246.
   Taxation: £9,000 (net).
   Prepayments: Rates £57; Raw materials in transit £2,500.
   Accrued Accounts: Legal expenses £157; Audit fees £200; Directors'
     fees. £800.

It is proposed to add £5,000 to General Reserve and to pay the Preference
   Dividend and an Ordinary Dividend of 10%, both less Income Tax at
   £0·45 in the £.

Market value of investments at 31st Dec., 19—, is £13,546.

(Association of Cost and Works Accountants, Inter.)

MANUFACTURING ACCOUNT

	£		£
Raw Materials—		Transfer to Selling A/c.	500,761
Stock, 1st Jan., 19—	35,408		
Purchases	305,888		
	341,296		
Less Stock, 31st Dec.,			
19— 33,415			
Goods in transit 2,500			
	35,915		
	305,381		
Wages	170,750		
Salaries	8,000		
	484,131		
Less Increase in Stocks—			
Unfinished As-			
semblies .. 19,413			
Finished Parts .. 3,365			
Work in Pro-			
gress 2,700			
	25,478		
	458,653		
Fuel and Power ..	7,500		
Prime Cost	466,153		
Dep. of Machinery			
$7\frac{1}{2}\%$ of original			
value 4,125			
Repairs 30,000			
Reduction in			
Loose Tools ... 483			
	34,608		
	£500,761		£500,761

L

SELLING ACCOUNT

	£		£
Stock, 1st Jan., 19— ..	35,678	Sales ... — — ...	557,212
Manufg. A/c.	500,761		
	536,439		
Less Stock, 31st Dec., 19—	43,729		
Cost of Sales	492,710		
Sales Office Expenses ..	5,025		
Travellers' Salaries ..	9,000		
Delivery Expenses	6,718		
Gross Profit	43,759		
	£557,212		£557,212

PROFIT AND LOSS ACCOUNT
FOR YEAR ENDED 31ST DECEMBER, 19—

		£		£
Stationery and Printing ..		917	Gross Profit — ...	43,759
Telephone and Stamps ..		520		
Insurance		340		
Rates	350			
Less prepayments	57			
		293		
Salaries		10,000		
Accrued Accounts—				
Legal..	157			
Audit fees	200			
		357		
Trading Profit c/d. ..		31,332		
		£43,759		£43,759

Published Accounts

PROFIT AND LOSS ACCOUNT OF ENTERPRISE LTD.
FOR YEAR ENDED 31ST DECEMBER, 19—

		£		£
Depreciation			Trading Profit b/d.	35,457
Motor Vehicles (20% original value)	1,000			
Buildings	1,000		*(N.B. Depreciation on machinery*	
Machinery ..	4,125		*properly shown in manufacturing*	
		6,125	*account is added back to trading*	
Debenture Interest due ..		750	*profit because it must be shown in*	
Provision for Bad and Doubt-			*published accounts.)*	
ful Debts		2,037		
Directors' Fees due ...		800		
Net Profit c/d.		25,745		
		£35,457		£35,457

BALANCE SHEET OF ENTERPRISE LTD.
AS AT 31ST DECEMBER, 19—

	£	£	£
Authorized Capital:			
200,000 Ordinary Shares of £1 each			200,000
100,000 5% Cum. Pref. Shares of £1 each			100,000
Issued Capital:			
100,000 Ordinary Shares of £1 each, fully paid		100,000	
100,000 5% Cum. Pref. Shares of £1 each, fully paid		100,000	
			200,000
Reserves and Undistributed Profits:			
General Reserve		35,000	
Taxation Reserve		9,000	
Profit and Loss A/c.		15,132	
			59,132
Long-term Liabilities:			
5% Mortgage Debentures			15,000
Current Liabilities:			
Bank Overdraft		7,342	
Creditors	37,014		
Accrued Accounts	357	37,371	
Mortgage Interest due		750	
Directors' Fees due		800	
Proposed Dividends	20,000		
Less Tax	9,000	11,000	
			57,263
			£331,395

	£	£	£	£
Fixed Assets:				
Buildings		20,000		
Add in course of erection		715		
		20,715		
Depreciation to 1st January, 19—	10,000			
Add 5% of original value	1,000	11,000		
			9,715	
Plant		55,000		
Add in course of erection		1,036		
		56,036		
Depreciation to 1st January, 19—	27,825			
Add 7½% of original value	4,125	31,950		
			24,086	
Motor Vehicles		5,000		
Depreciation to 1st January, 19—	2,000			
Add 20% of original value	1,000	3,000		
			2,000	
Loose Tools (at valuation)			3,246	
				39,047
Current Assets:				
Stocks: Finished Assemblies		43,729		
Unfinished Assemblies		65,413		
Finished Parts		15,712		
Work in Progress		23,202		
Raw Materials		33,415		
Goods in Transit		2,500		
			183,971	
Debtors		97,845		
Less Provision for Bad Debts		2,037	95,808	
Investments at cost (Market value £13,546.)			12,000	
Rates Prepaid			57	
Cash			512	
				292,348
				£331,395

ELEMENTS OF ACCOUNTS

APPROPRIATION ACCOUNT

	£	£				£
Taxation Reserve ..		9,000	Balance b/f. ..	..	..	14,387
General Reserve ..		5,000	Net Profit ...	...	..	25,745
Proposed Dividend ..	20,000					
Less Income Tax ..	9,000					
		11,000				
Balance c/f. ...	...	.. 15,132				
		£40,132				£40,132

WRITTEN EXERCISES

1. Beta Gamma Ltd. was formed to take over as from 31st March, 19—, the business of a private trader whose Balance Sheet on that date was as follows:

	£			£
Capital	46,000	Plant and Machinery	..	17,300
Sundry Creditors	5,471	Vans and Lorries ..	..	3,940
		Fixtures and Fittings	..	600
		Stock	..	19,731
		Debtors	..	7,978
		Cash	..	1,922
	£51,471			£51,471

The company took over all the assets, including cash, at the book values and assumed responsibility for the liabilities. The goodwill was valued at £9,000.

The Authorized Capital of Beta Gamma Ltd. consisted of 40,000 6 per cent Preference Shares of £1 each; 236,000 Ordinary Shares of £0·25 each; and 20,000 Deferred Shares of £0·05 each. The vendor took the whole of the Deferred Shares and the balance of the purchase consideration in Ordinary Shares, all at par; and on 30th April, 19—, 20,000 of the Preference Shares were subscribed privately at a premium of £0·05 per share and fully paid. £15,000 was spent on new machinery, the balance being retained as working capital.

Six months' dividend on the Preference Shares was paid on 31st October, 19—.

On closing the books on 31st December, 19—, £3,000 was provided for depreciation of plant and machinery, £440 for depreciation of vans and lorries, and £30 for depreciation of fixtures and fittings, and £620 was provided for bad and doubtful debts. The remaining balances, after closing the Profit and Loss Account, in addition to those already indicated, were:

				£
Sundry creditors ..	..	..		4,597
Stock, 31st December, 19—	..	..		29,388
Sundry debtors ..	..	..	...	11,396
Cash	..	..		5,605
Net profit for the period	..	..		8,142

You are required to draw up the company's Balance Sheet as on 31st December, 19—. (*R.S.A., modified.*)

2. A. Alpha carried on business as a manufacturer and his position at 31st December, 19—, was as follows: Freehold Property, £5,000; Loan from J. Alpha, £1,200; Machinery, £3,250; Debtors, £3,786; Creditors, £1,100; Balance at Bank, £254; and Cash in Hand, £10.

It had been arranged that a limited company should be formed to take over all the assets and liabilities of the business as shown for the purchase price of £15,000 and the price was to be satisfied by the issue of 15,000 shares of £1 each.

A. Alpha Limited was duly formed with an authorized capital of £20,000 divided into shares of £1 each, and the transfer took place on 1st January, 19—, when the remaining 5,000 shares were allotted to J. Alpha, as to £3,800 in consideration of cash and as to the balance in consideration of the cancellation of his loan.

Draft the Balance Sheet of the Company on the completion of these transactions.

(*R.S.A.*)

3. Black and Blue are in partnership sharing profits and losses equally and on 31st December, 19—, the position was as follows:

Capital Accounts:	£		Freehold Premises	£ 4,000
Black	3,615		Machinery ..	1,800
Blue ..	2,685		Patents	550
Creditors ..	1,760		Stock	2,250
Bank Overdraft ..	540			
	£8,600			£8,600

On this date, the whole of the assets and liabilities of the firm were purchased by Takeover Ltd. The Machinery was taken over for £1,500, the Patents £1, the Stock £1,649, and the Premises £5,300. The purchase price was satisfied by the issue of fully paid shares of £1 each in Takeover Ltd. at a valuation of £1·50 per share.

Prepare the Realization Account, Purchasers' Account and the Partners' Capital Accounts in the books of the firm, showing the settlement, and state the number of shares allotted to each partner. (*R.S.A.*, *modified.*)

4. From the following Trial Balance and additional information, you are required to prepare the Trading and Profit and Loss Account of X.Y.Z. Ltd. for the year to 31st December, 19—, and Balance Sheet at 31st December, 19—.

TRIAL BALANCE

	£	£
Share Capital, Authorized and Issued—		
40,000 Ordinary Shares of £1 each		40,000
Purchases	80,000	
Stock in trade, 1st January, 19—	5,000	
Wages and salaries	6,165	
Rent	500	
Sales		97,000
Calls in arrear	200	
5 per cent Debentures (issued in previous year)		10,000
Debtors ..	6,000	
Motor vans	14,000	
Discounts	750	1,050
Insurances	280	
Telephone	120	
Printing and stationery ..	340	
Cash at bank	10,735	
Trade creditors		5,100
Freehold land and buildings	30,000	
Debenture interest	250	
General expenses	270	
Rates	400	
Profit and Loss Account, 1st January, 19— ..		1,500
Provision for bad debts, 1st January, 19—		350
Bills receivable ..	1,000	
Interim Dividend paid 1st July, 19— ..	2,000	
General reserve		5,000
Bad debts	490	
Directors' fees	1,500	
	£160,000	£160,000

The following matters are to be taken into account:

	£
Stock in trade, 31st December, 19—	6,000
Rent accrued, due 31st December, 19—	100
Rates paid in advance, 31st December, 19—	60
Insurances paid in advance, 31st December, 19—	80
Provide depreciation on motor vans	2,800
Provision for bad debts to be decreased to	325
Transfer to General Reserve an additional	1,000
Bills Receivable discounted but not due at 31st December, 19—	300

Notes
(a) Taxation is to be ignored.
(b) No provision is to be made for any final dividend for the current year.
(c) The auditor's report is not required.   (*Institute of Bankers, Part 1.*)

5. Y Ltd. has an Authorized Capital of £100,000 divided into 50,000 Preference Shares (6 per cent) and 50,000 Ordinary Shares, all £1 each. From the subjoined Trial Balance, and notes appended thereto, prepare annual accounts for submission to the members.

TRIAL BALANCE
31ST DECEMBER, 19—

	£	£
Issued Capital—		
40,00 Preference Shares, £0·80 called per share		32,000
30,000 Ordinary Shares, £0·75 called per share		22,500
Bills Receivable (see Note 1)	12,000	
General reserve (see Note 2)		5,000
Purchases (see Note 3)	70,000	
Sales returns	5,000	
Bad debts	500	
Calls in arrear (Ordinary Shares)	300	
Sales		100,000
Rent (see Note 4)	750	
Purchases returns		2,000
Directors' fees	1,000	
Stock, 1st January, 19— (see Note 5)	13,000	
Carriage outwards	750	
Carriage inwards	3,000	
Plant (see Note 6)	30,000	
Rates (see Note 7)	900	
Dividends paid (ignore tax)—		
Ordinary, interim, on 1st July	10,000	
Preference, half-year, on 1st July (see Note 8) ..	960	
Bank	14,840	
Salesmen's salaries	2,000	
Trade debtors	7,500	
Bills payable		1,000
Profit and Loss Account, 1st January, 19—		3,000
Discounts	700	800
Trade creditors		6,000
Provision for bad debts (see Note 9)		900
	£173,200	£173,200

Notes

	£
(1) Bills Receivable discounted but not yet due	500
(2) Carry to general reserve an additional	2,000

(3) Invoices received from suppliers, not yet entered in books   2,000
(4) Rent accrued due   250
(5) Stock, 31st December, 19—   10,000
(6) Depreciate plant by   1,500
(7) Rates paid in advance   300
(8) Preference Dividend for half-year was declared on 31st December but is not yet paid (ignore tax)
(9) Raise provision for bad debts to   1,000

(Institute of Bankers, Part 1, modified.)

6. Prepare a Trading and Profit and Loss Account of ABC Ltd. for the year ended 31st December, 19—, and Balance Sheet as at that date from the following information (ignore taxation):

	Authorized £	Issued £
Share Capital—		
6% Preference Shares of £1 each	10,000	10,000
Ordinary Shares of £0·05 each	90,000	70,000
Other balances—		
Premium on shares..		5,000
5% Mortgage Debentures		50,000
Discount on Debentures		5,000
Freehold land and buildings (at cost)		20,000
Fixtures and fittings (at cost, *less* depreciation)		2,000
Stock, 1st January, 19—		50,600
Purchases		400,000
Sales ..		600,500
Investments in government securities		30,000
Interest on investments		900
Returns inwards		12,300
Salaries and wages ..		70,000
Rent and rates		10,000
Insurances ..		2,000
Discounts received ..		10,000
Debenture interest to 30th June, 19—		1,250
Directors' salaries and fees		9,000
Sundry expenses		19,000
Travellers' commission		40,400
Travelling expenses		7,390
Sales Ledger balances		78,580
Bought Ledger balances		34,470
Bank balance		26,325
Petty cash balance ..		15
Profit and Loss Account, 1st January, 19— (Cr.)		3,590
Preference Dividend		600

Take into account:
(1) Stock, 31st December, 19—   57,800
(2) Rates prepaid   700
(3) Provide depreciation—
  Freehold land and buildings   500
  Fixtures and fittings   200
(4) Provide for interest accrued on Debentures.
(5) Write off £1,000 from Discount on Debentures Account.
(6) Create a provision for bad debts of 5 per cent on sundry debtors.

(C.C.S., modified.)

7. The following figures relate to a company carrying on business as engineers and contractors, and were extracted at 30th June, 19—:

	£	£
Share Capital Authorized, Issued and Fully Paid—		
100,000 6% Cumulative Preference Shares of £1 each		100,000
100,000 Ordinary Shares of £1 each		100,000
General trade charges	9,703	
Income tax	16,412	
Bad debts	4,065	
Fuel and power	5,163	
Royalties	4,941	
Salaries	33,466	
Wages	129,781	
Discounts received		2,846
Freehold land and buildings	66,556	
Machinery and plant	36,120	
Loose tools (opening stock)	5,194	
Additions during year	3,140	
Stock	16,300	
Works expenses	3,830	
Motor vehicles	2,547	
Purchases	249,765	
Work in progress	40,140	
Preference Dividend for half-year to 31st December, 19—	3,000	
Profit and Loss Appropriation Account—		
Balance b/d.		3,465
Sales		515,825
Cash at bank and in hand	42,493	
Cash received on account of work in progress ..		13,600
Sundry debtors	52,644	
Sundry creditors		29,524
Goodwill	40,000	
	£765,260	£765,260

You are required to prepare Manufacturing and Profit and Loss Accounts for the year ended 30th June, 19—, and Balance Sheet at the latter date, when stock was valued at £19,183, loose tools at £5,604, and work in progress at £70,807. Provide £1,130 for bad and doubtful debts and depreciate machinery and plant by £3,600 and motor vehicles by £510. Fees due to directors amounted to £675.

Provide for the half-year's dividend and for a proposed dividend of 6 per cent on the Ordinary Shares, free of tax.

(*Association of Certified and Corporate Accounts.*)

8. From the undernoted Trial Balance of the Utility Trading Co. Ltd., as at 31st December, 19—, you are required to prepare Profit and Loss Account and Balance Sheet giving effect to the following adjustments:

(a) The capital of the company is £80,000 divided into 40,000 Ordinary Shares of £1 each, all issued and paid-up to the extent of £0·75 per share, and 40,000 6 per cent Preference Shares of £1 each, of which 30,000 have been issued and fully paid-up.

(b) Provide 10 per cent depreciation on furniture and fittings, £600 for bad debts and 2 per cent on the debtors for discounts.

(c) The market value of investments at 31st December is £9,000 and provision is to be made for depreciation in value.

(d) Stocks at 31st December are valued at £11,360.

TRIAL BALANCE

	£	£
Ordinary Share Capital		30,000
Preference Share Capital		30,000
Stocks at 1st January	9,000	
Purchases	136,000	
Sales		200,000
Sundry debtors	46,000	
Bills receivable	10,000	
Sundry creditors		24,000
Bills payable		3,000
Office furniture and fixtures	2,160	
Rent, rates and insurances	3,600	
Marine insurance	4,800	
Travellers' salaries and expenses	10,800	
Office salaries	3,600	
Agents' commission	2,400	
Advertising	9,600	
Stationery and printing	5,400	
Telephones and stamps	1,200	
Bank charges	240	
Discounts allowed	4,800	
Directors' renumeration	6,000	
Investments at cost	12,000	
Bank balance	19,100	
Income tax		600
Dividend Account—half-year's Dividend on Preference		
Shares, 30th June	900	
	£287,600	£287,600

Note. No journal entries required.

(Institute of Cost and Works Accountants, modified.)

9. The Westover Trading Co. Ltd. has an Authorized Capital of £200,000 divided into 100,000 Ordinary Shares of £1 each and 100,000 7 per cent Cumulative Preference Shares of £1 each. The following Trial Balance was extracted from the books of the company on 31st December, 19—:

TRIAL BALANCE

	£	£
Gross Profit Trading Account, 31st December, 19—		43,860
Rates and insurance (office)	4,205	
Salaries	6,160	
Directors' fees .. .. — — ...	9,500	
Discounts allowed and received	1,768	2,639
Bad debts written off	740	
Provision for bad debts		3,400
Interest on bank overdraft	140	
Profit and Loss Account balance, 1st January, 19—		1,030
12,000 shares, £1 each, fully paid, in subsidiary com-		
pany at cost	8,300	
Loan to subsidiary company and interest thereon ..	4,000	146
General reserve		1,500
Dividends on Preference Shares:		
Year to 30th September, previous year (*less* tax)	3,500	
Year to 30th September, current year (*less* tax)	3,850	
	Fwd. 42,163	52,575

		£	£
	Fwd.	42,163	52,575
Repairs to property		1,680	
Stock, 31st December, 19—		31,760	
Bank overdraft			8,630
Sundry debtors and creditors		76,500	44,163
Plant and machinery at cost, *less* depreciation, 1st January, 19—		61,500	
Depreciation plant and machinery (charged to Manufacturing Account)			5,162
General office expenses		2,981	
Bills receivable		3,000	
Freehold premises at cost		26,773	
Goodwill at cost		10,000	
Preliminary expenses (balance)		225	
Fixtures and fittings at cost, *less* depreciation, 1st January, 19—		6,000	
Income tax reserve			500
Rates and insurance in advance, 31st December, 19—		238	
Factory wages owing, 31st December, 19—			1,672
7 per cent Preference Share Capital, 100,000 Shares, £1 each, fully called and paid-up			100,000
Ordinary Share Capital, 100,000 Shares, £1 each, £0·50 called up			50,000
Calls in arrear and in advance		70	188
		£262,890	£262,890

You are asked to prepare Profit and Loss Account for the year ended 31st December, 19—, and a Balance Sheet on that date, taking into consideration the following:

(1) Income tax provision to be increased to £6,000 as a provision for taxation on current profits.
(2) Sundry debtors include £500 due from the subsidiary company for goods supplied.
(3) The provision for bad debts is to be increased to an amount equal to 5 per cent of the sundry debtors (other than subsidiary company).
(4) The directors were paid a bonus of £2,500 in February of the following year, in respect of the year to 31st December, 19—. The amount is to be provided for in the Appropriation Account for that year.
(5) Fixtures and fittings to be depreciated by 5 per cent.
(6) The balance of preliminary expenses is to be written off.

(*C.I.S., modified.*)

10. The Trojan Manufacturing Co. Ltd. has a Nominal Capital of £100,000 divided into 75,000 Ordinary Shares of £1 each and 5,000 6 per cent Preference Shares of £5 each. The whole of the Ordinary Shares have been subscribed for and allotted to the public and £1·00 per share called up. The whole of the Preference Shares have been issued and fully paid up.

Six months before the end of the financial year the company issued 100 5 per cent Debentures of £100 each at 95.

Apart from the accounts required to record the transactions shown above, the balances on the books at the 31st December, 19—, are as follows:

	£	£
Plant and machinery	18,382	
Plant and machinery additions	5,228	
Leasehold property	48,421	
Manufacturing wages	40,484	

Profit and Loss Account ..	...	...	...		4,792	
Leasehold redemption fund	...	...	..			4,500
Sundry debtors ..	..	..	..	...	6,258	
Sundry creditors ..	..	...	..	...		18,248
Raw materials stock 31/12/—	..	..	..		2,687	
Finished goods stock 31/12/—	..	..	..		15,023	
Factory power, light and heat	..	..	..		2,569	
Rates and insurances ..	..	..	...	..	1,003	
Sundry factory expenses ..	..	..	...	..	659	
Raw material purchases ..	..	..	...	..	33,963	
Work-in-progress 31/12/—		...	...	..	7,211	
Unpaid calls ..	..	...	...	..	300	
Sales returns ..	..	...	..	..	263	
Purchases returns ..	...	..	..			2,128
Loose tools ..	..	..	...	...	1,629	
Plant and machinery sales..		...	..	..		2,000
Management salaries ..	..	...	..	...	1,750	
Repairs to machinery ..	..	...	..	..	863	
Office salaries ..	..	..	...	..	2,035	
Directors' fees ..	..	..	..	..	1,000	
Office furniture ..	..	..	..	..	1,425	
Discounts received	...	...	...	...		163
Discounts allowed ..	..	..	...	...	239	
Bad debts reserve ..	..	..	..	..		200
Travellers' salaries and commission		..	...		3,002	
Carriage inwards ..	..	..	...	...	796	
Carriage outwards ..	..	..	..	..	1,374	
Transfer fees ..	..	..	..	...		69
Sales ..	..	..	..	..	..	95,626
Cash at bank ..	..	..	..	..	8,903	
Cash in hand ..	..	..	...	..	175	
Goodwill ..	..	ʹ..	..	..	10,000	
Patents ..	..	..	..	..	7,500	
Leasehold Redemption Fund Investment Account					4,500	

You are required to prepare a Manufacturing and Profit and Loss Account for the year ended 31st December, 19—, and a Balance Sheet as at that date.

The undermentioned matters must be taken into consideration when preparing the accounts:

(a) No provision has been made for the Debenture Interest due on the 31st December.

(b) The following items had accrued due but had not been recorded in the books: £

   (i) Wages 863
   (ii) Office salaries 252
   (iii) Management salaries 175

(c) Manufacturing wages amounting to £369 had been expended on making Loose Tools.

(d) The value of Stock at 31st December, 19—, was certified at: £

   Raw material 2,963
   Finished goods 12,739
   Work-in-progress 9,365

(e) Depreciation to be charged at the following rates:

   Plant and machinery .. .. .. 10 per cent
   Loose tools .. .. 20 per cent
   Office furniture .. .. .. 7½ per cent

(f) Bad debts reserve is to be made equal to 5 per cent of Sundry Debtors.

(g) It has been decided to transfer £1,500 to the Leasehold Redemption Fund.

(*Institute of Cost and Works Accountants, modified.*)

11. The capital of the Amenbury Company Limited was 50,000 Ordinary Shares of £1 each and 60,000 7 per cent Cumulative Preference Shares of £1 each. For the year 19–6 the profit available for dividend and other purposes was, after extinguishing a debit balance on Appropriation Account of £16,000, the sum of £50,000. The Preference Shareholders had received no dividend since that for the year 19–1. At the Annual General Meeting held on 13th July, 19–7, it was resolved:

1. To pay the dividend on the Preference Shares for the five years 19–2 to 19–6 inclusive;
2. To pay a dividend of 6 per cent on the Ordinary Shares;
3. To transfer £8,000 to a Dividend Equalization Reserve;
4. To provide for Taxation, £27,000; and
5. To carry forward the balance.

You are required to show the entries in the books of the company brought about by the resolution and by the payment of the dividends. Take into account Income Tax at the rate of £0·45 in the £.   (*Institute of Book-keepers, modified.*)

12. Thomas Oliver and Co. Ltd., was formed to take over the business of T. Oliver as a going concern as from 1st February, 19—. Oliver's Balance Sheet as at 31st January, 19—, on which the purchase price was to be based, was as follows:

Liabilities		£	Assets		£
Sundry creditors	..	2,900	Freehold land and build-		
Bills payable	.. ..	550	ings		3,000
Capital ..	... ...	16,000	Plant and machinery ..		4,200
			Office furniture, fixtures,		
			etc.		650
			Stock-in-trade		6,800
			Sundry debtors		3,600
			Cash at bank		1,200
		£19,450			£19,450

The purchase price was agreed at £22,000 and was to be discharged as to £2,000 in cash and as to £20,000 in fully paid Ordinary Shares of £1 each. Oliver was to guarantee the debtors and assume responsibility for any liabilities not appearing in the books. It was agreed that he should retain the cash at the bank. The nominal capital of the company was fixed at £35,000 in 35,000 shares of £1 each. On 15th April, 19—, the directors proceeded to allot 10,000 shares upon which £0·25 per share had been paid on application, the balance due on allotment being duly received. Formation expenses were £650 and were borne by the company. The purchase price was discharged on 30th April, 19—.

(i) Show how you would record the above transactions when opening the books of the company and draw up a Balance Sheet as at 30th April, 19—.
(ii) Give the Journal entries closing the books of T. Oliver.
(*Association of Certified and Corporate Accountants, modified.*)

13. George and Peter are in partnership, sharing profits and losses in the ratio, George two-thirds and Peter one-third. The Balance Sheet of the firm on 31st December, 19—, is as follows:

Capital Accounts:			£			£
George ..	£10,000			Freehold property ..	..	5,000
Peter ..	7,500			Motor vans	..	3,500
			17,500	Furniture and fittings	..	600
Creditors	.. .. ..		6,500	Stock-in-trade ..	..	5,300
(*Note*: there is a contin-				Debtors ..	.. ..	8,400
gent liability on a dis-				Balance at bank ..	..	1,200
counted bill, £300,						
accepted by John Smith.)						
			£24,000			£24,000

The partnership is dissolved as from the date of this Balance Sheet, and the business is taken over by a company, G.P. Ltd., which was incorporated on the same date.

G.P. Ltd. acquires all the assets of the firm, except the balance at bank, but accepts no responsibility for the liabilities of the partners. For purposes of the transfer, the assets are valued at the amount shown in the above Balance Sheet.

The purchase consideration is £30,000, and is satisfied as to £12,000 in cash and as to £18,000 by the issue of 15,000 ordinary shares of £1 each in G.P. Ltd., at a premium of £0·20 each.

The above matters were completed on 1st January, 19—, and, on the same day the company issued a further 20,000 ordinary shares of £1 each, at a premium of £0·20 to other subscribers and these shares were immediately paid up in cash.

John Smith becomes insolvent and is unable to meet the bill accepted by him and the bill is met by the partnership; there is no possibility of recovering anything from Smith. The creditors of the partnership are paid off in full. The shares in the company and the remaining cash are then distributed to the partners, and the books of the partnership are closed.

You are required:

(a) to show the Realization Account, the Cash Account, the Account with G.P. Ltd., and the partners' Capital Accounts as they would appear in the books of the partnership after the above transactions have been completed. No other Ledger Accounts are required.

(b) to show, in summarized form, the Balance Sheet of G.P. Ltd., on 1st January, 19—.

You are not required to show any ledger accounts in the books of the company.

(Institute of Bankers, modified.)

14. It has been the practice of Manufacturers Ltd., to maintain its fixed assets in the books at cost, and to deal with the depreciation element in Depreciation Provision Accounts—one for each type of asset.

Depreciation has been regularly provided for at the rate of 10 per cent per annum for plant, and 20 per cent per annum for motor vehicles—on the fixed instalment system—in respect of assets in existence at the end of each financial year, proportionate charges on assets held for only part of a year being avoided.

At 31st March, 19–4, the books reflected the following position:

	Aggregate cost to date.	Aggregate depreciation to date.
Plant	£35,720	£22,375
Motor Vehicles	£7,450	£3,040

During the year ended 31st March, 19–5, there were additions as follows: Plant £6,250, Motor Vehicles £525.

The additional expenditure on Motor Vehicles was consequent upon the sale of an old vehicle bought originally in September, 19–1, for £750, and now sold for £250.

You are required to write up: (1) The Plant Account; (2) The Motor Vehicles Account; (3) The Depreciation Provision Accounts for the year ended 31st March, 19–5, and show how these accounts would appear in the Balance Sheet of the Company as on 31st March, 19–5.

(L.Ch.C.)

33

DEPRECIATION AND SINKING FUNDS

THERE are various methods by which the annual depreciation to be deducted from fixed assets is calculated. They are designed to:
- (*a*) reduce the value of the asset in the books to the estimated sum the asset will fetch when it is discarded;
- (*b*) spread the burden fairly over the years during which the asset is in use.

Straight Line (or Fixed Instalment) Method

The estimated scrap value is deducted from the purchase price, and the difference divided by the estimated life of the asset. This is the annual amount of depreciation—the same amount each year.

Example:

				£
Purchase price of machine	...	...	..	500
Estimated scrap value	..	...	...	..	20
		Net Cost	...	£480

Estimated life 10 years.
Annual depreciation $£\frac{480}{10} = £48$

The advantage of the method is that the cost of the asset is completely written off within a definite period. The disadvantage is that a separate calculation is required for each item (*e.g.*, for each machine in a machine shop) because of differences in their 'life' and in their scrap value.

Reducing Instalment Method

The value of the asset is depreciated each year by a given percentage of the value of the asset at the beginning of that year. As this value diminishes the depreciation diminishes also.

Example:

				£
Purchase price of machine	..	..	...	500·00
Depreciation first year at (say) 10 per cent				50·00
				450·00
Depreciation second year	...	...	...	45·00
				405·00
Depreciation third year	...	...	...	40·50
				364·50

and so on.

The advantages are:
- (*a*) Simplicity. All items, including additions, are lumped together and depreciated at the same rate.

(b) It is the method adopted by the Inland Revenue Authorities in making allowances for wear and tear.

(c) The cost of an asset is made up of depreciation plus repairs. By this method the depreciation, charged annually to Profit and Loss Account, becomes progressively smaller towards the end of the life of the asset, when repairs become (usually) heavier. The combined cost is thus evened out.

The disadvantages are:

(a) An asset cannot be completely written off by this method.

(b) If the life is short, the burden thrown on the early years is excessive. Compare the following figures, to write off an asset in three years.

	Reducing Instalment £	Straight Line £
New value	300·00	300
Depreciation first year ..	270·00 (90%)	100 (33⅓%)
	30·00	200
Depreciation second year ...	27·00	100
	3·00	100
Depreciation third year ...	2·70	100
	0·30	

The Reducing Instalment method is thus best suited to assets, like buildings or heavy plants, which depreciate slowly.

Revaluation

Assets like loose tools, which are replaced at frequent intervals and consist of a large number of individual items on which it would be difficult to calculate depreciation, are usually revalued at the end of each accounting period.

Example: A firm possesses loose tools valued at £2,500 on 1st January, 19—. During the year, additional tools are bought at a cost of £600. On 31st December, 19—, the loose tools were valued at £2,700. Show the Loose Tools Account.

LOOSE TOOLS ACCOUNT

Dr.							Cr.
19— Jan. 1	Balance ... ... Bank		£ 2,500 600	19— Dec. 31	Stock c/d Profit & Loss A/c. ..		£ 2,700 400
			£3,100				£3,100
19— Jan. 1	Balance b/d		£2,700				

If the new tools had been made in the works the cost (£600) might be included in the items Wages Paid and Materials Used, and would have the effect of reducing the profit in the Profit and Loss Account by £600. There would have been no entry, of course, for the £600 on the debit side of the Loose Tools Account. The revaluation of loose tools at £2,700 would, in consequence, show a credit balance of £200 on Loose Tools Account, which would be transferred to the Profit and Loss Account as shown below:

LOOSE TOOLS ACCOUNT

Dr.							Cr.
19—			£	19—			£
Jan. 1	Balance	..	2,500	Dec. 31	Balance	c/d	2,700
Dec. 31	Profit & Loss A/c.	..	200				
			£2,700				£2,700
19—							
Jan. 1	Balance	b/d	£2,700				

Set off against the £600 for wages and materials, the net effect of transferring the balance of this account to the credit of Profit and Loss Account would be a debit of £400 in the Profit and Loss Account. Thus the resultant charge against profits on account of the depreciation of the tools would be the same as if the additional tools had been bought outside and not made in the works.

Sinking Funds

The methods already described ensure that the fixed assets owned by a business will appear in the books at a reasonable valuation. They do not ensure that, when the time comes to replace them, the assets will include sufficient cash to purchase new ones. In order that the means to do this may be available, it is necessary to earmark the money. The method adopted, known as the 'Depreciation Fund', is as follows.

When (say) a new machine is bought, a certain sum is invested each year throughout its life, such that, with interest, the total investment will amount to the cost of replacing the machine. At the end of the time, the investment is sold to provide the money.

As an illustration let us suppose that a machine bought for £3,000 is to be written off in three years and the amounts written off are to be invested at $3\frac{1}{2}$ per cent compound interest to produce £3,000 to replace the machine. Reference to Sinking Fund tables shows that £0·321933 invested annually will produce £1 in three years at $3\frac{1}{2}$ per cent compound interest, assuming the first investment to be made at the end of the first year. To produce £3,000, therefore, the annual investment would be £965·80 (3,000 times £0·321933).

The method is described below. It should be studied step by step in conjunction with the illustration which follows.

I. The annual provision £965·80 is debited each year to the Profit and Loss Account, and credited, not to the Machinery Account, but to an account called the Depreciation Fund Account. Throughout the period during which the money is being raised, therefore, the machinery remains in the books at its full value, the depreciation being shown in the Depreciation Fund Account. Both Accounts would appear in the Balance Sheet—Machinery as an asset, the Depreciation Fund as a liability.

II. This money will be invested (see Step III) and interest will be received. The interest will be—

    (*a*)   debited in the Bank Account;
    (*b*)   credited in the Depreciation Fund Account.

III. Each year, an amount equal to that added to the Depreciation Fund Account (the annual instalment plus interest) is invested. The investment will be—

    (*a*)   credited in the Bank Account;
    (*b*)   debited in the Depreciation Fund Investment Account.

This account must not be confused with the Depreciation Fund Account. The investment account will be shown as an asset in the Balance Sheet.

IV. At the end of the three years, the Depreciation Fund Account would amount to £3,000—the value of the machine to be replaced. It is transferred to the Machinery Account by—

    (*a*)   a debit entry in the Depreciation Fund Account;
    (*b*)   a credit entry in the Machinery Account, which is thereby balanced.

The last instalment, at the end of the third year, is needed at once for the purchase of the new machine, and will not therefore be invested. The investment already made is sold for what it will fetch, any difference between the book value and the realized value being transferred to the Profit and Loss Account. No difference is assumed in the present example. The entries are—

    (*a*)   debit Bank Account with the amount received;
    (*b*)   credit Depreciation Fund Investment Account, balancing the account.

This money, together with the third instalment and the interest earned during the third year, will provide the £3,000 required.

PROFIT AND LOSS ACCOUNT

Dr.   Cr.

			£
Year 1.	Depreciation Fund		965·80
„ 2.	Do.	..	965·80
„ 3.	Do.	..	965·80

DEPRECIATION FUND ACCOUNT

Dr.   Cr.

			£			£
Year 1	Balance c/d.	..	965·80	Profit and Loss A/c.		965·80
Year 2	Balance c/d.	..	1,965·40	Balance b/d. ..		965·80
				Cash (Interest at 3½% on £965·80) ..		33·80
				Profit and Loss A/c. (second instalment)		965·80
Year 3	Transfer to Machinery A/c. ..		3,000·00	Balance b/d. ..		1,965·40
				Cash (Interest at 3½% on £1,965·40) ..		68·80
				Profit and Loss A/c. (third instalment)		965·80
			£3,000·00			£3,000·00

DEPRECIATION FUND INVESTMENT ACCOUNT

Dr.   Cr.

		£			£
Year 1	Cash (investment)	965·80	Balance c/d. ..		965·80
Year 2	Balance b/d. ..	965·80	Balance c/d. ..		1,965·40
	Cash (investment)*	999·60			
Year 3	Balance b/d. ..	1,965·40	Cash (realization) ..		1,965·40

*This £999·60 consists of the second year's instalment, £965·80, plus the first year's interest £33·80.

MACHINERY ACCOUNT

Dr.   Cr.

			£		£
Year 1	Cash	.. ..	3,000		
Year 2	Balance b/d.	..	3,000		
Year 3	Balance b/d.	..	3,000	Transfer from Depreciation Fund A/c. ..	3,000

CASH ACCOUNT

Dr.   Cr.

		£		£
Year 1			Investment	965·80
Year 1	Dep. Fund A/c. (Interest at 3½% on £965·80) ..	33·80	Investment A/c. (i.e., annual instalment)	999·60
Year 3	Sale of Investments Dep. Fund A/c. (Interest at 3½% on £1,965·40) ..	1,965·40 68·80		

(It is presumed that the third instalment of £965·80 is available in the cash in hand to make up the £3,000.)

BALANCE SHEET

		£		£
Year 2	Dep. Fund A/c. ..	1,965·40	Machinery	3,000·00
			Dep. Fund Investment A/c. ..	1,965·40

WRITTEN EXERCISES

1. Norton & Co., electrical engineers, purchase a machine on 1st February, 19–1, for £500. Show by means of ledger accounts how the machine would be written down in the books, at 31st January, 19–2 and 31st January, 19–3, using:
  (a) The 'straight line' method of depreciation; and
  (b) The 'diminishing balance' method of depreciation.
Take a rate of 20 per cent per annum in both cases.
(Institute of Book-keepers.)

2. The directors of a company acquire a short lease for the term of five years, at a cost of £1,000. They decide to provide for depreciation on the Depreciation Fund principle investing in gilt-edged securities, yield 3 per cent per annum. The amount to be invested annually at 3 per cent compound interest in order to produce £1 at the end of five years is £0·188354. The investments are realized at the end of the five years without profit or loss.
Show all the ledger accounts concerned for the whole period. All figures can be taken to the nearest £.
(C.I.S.)

3. Set out the ledger accounts in the books of a company so as to record the following transactions:
  A company purchased a large furnace for £5,000; £400 was spent on erecting it. A Depreciation Fund, based on the anticipated life of the furnace, was begun; the investments representing the Depreciation Fund were made in British Government 2½ per cent Savings Bonds.
  The furnace was replaced before the end of its anticipated life; some parts of the old furnace were valued at £300 and were used in setting up a new furnace, which cost a further £4,500. The cost of dismantling the old furnace was £90; the erection of the new furnace cost £390.
  When the old furnace was replaced, the Depreciation Fund stood at £2,800; the Depreciation Fund investment was realized at par, namely, £2,800.
(Institute of Book-keepers.)

4. From the following information, write up the Sinking Fund and Sinking Fund Investments Accounts for the year 19—:

Sinking Fund, balance left 1st January £18,000, represented by £20,000 3 per cent Stock and £300 in cash.

Interest received 30th June £65, and 31st December £165.

Instalment set aside 31st December £1,200, £300 was invested on 2nd January in £250 5 per cent Stock on which no interest was received during the year.

Show how the balances at 31st December would appear in the Balance Sheet. *(C.C.S.)*

5. From the following statement make out Trading Account, Profit and Loss Account, and Balance Sheet for The Manufacturing Co. Ltd. for year ending 31st December, 19—:

	£		£
Nominal Capital 160,000 shares of £1 each ..	160,000	Sales	244,000
Subscribed Capital 120,000		Purchases	124,200
shares of £1 each called	120,000	Bad and doubtful debts pro-	
Calls in arrear	2,000	vision	4,500
Freehold premises at cost	36,000	Preliminary expenses ..	800
Plant and machinery at cost	40,000	*Sinking Fund for redemp-	
Interim Dividend paid ..	4,000	tion of debentures ..	16,000
Debentures, 5 per cent ..	40,000	Manufacturing wages ..	60,000
Stock, 1st January ..	37,500	Repairs and renewals ..	2,600
Office furniture at cost ..	1,250	Coal, gas and water ..	4,800
Patterns at cost	12,500	Rates, taxes, insurance ..	2,500
Patents at cost	7,500	Office salaries	2,000
Goodwill	24,000	General expenses.. ..	950
Sundry debtors	75,000	Travelling expenses ..	2,650
Sundry creditors ..	33,600	Discounts allowed ..	4,240
Cash in hand	300	Discounts received ..	3,560
Cash at bank (Current A/c.)	6,000	Directors' fees	1,050
Cash at bank (Deposit A/c.)	24,000	Royalties paid	900
Profit and Loss A/c. credit,		Bank deposit interest ..	600
1st January	1,780	Bad debts	300
Bills payable	31,000	Debenture interest ..	2,000

*Note. This is represented by investments of equivalent amounts and there is one year's interest on them at $3\frac{1}{2}$ per cent per annum due but unpaid at date of making up these accounts.

Write off the whole of preliminary expenses. Depreciate plant and machinery, office furniture, patterns and patents at $7\frac{1}{2}$ per cent per annum. Leave bad and doubtful debts provision at 5 per cent on sundry debtors. Add £4,000 to the Sinking Fund for redemption of Debentures. Stock on hand at 31st December to be taken as £20,174. *(Institute of Cost and Works Accountants.)*

6. On 1st January, 19–1 a business purchased a motor delivery van for £800.

Show how the account would appear in the books of the business for the four following years (until 31st December, 19–4), assuming that depreciation is written off at the rate of £160 per annum.

If, instead, depreciation were written off each year at the rate of 20 per cent of the book value of the machine at the beginning of that year, show how the account would stand on 31st December, 19–4. *(R.S.A.. modified.)*

7. A manufacturing business has a Lease that has six years still to run. The Lease, at this moment, is valued at £5,000. It is decided to depreciate its value in the books by the creation of a Sinking Fund on a four per centum basis; the last year of the life of the Lease is to be excluded from the calculations in order to provide for liability for dilapidations.

Set out the amounts to be charged to Profit and Loss Account during each of the five years. The annual Sinking Fund instalment to provide £1 on a 4 per cent basis over five years is £0·1846. *(Institute of Book-keepers, modified.)*

34

CONSIGNMENT ACCOUNTS

THE records to be considered in this chapter are those which become necessary when one merchant, known as a consignor, sends a consignment of goods to another merchant, the consignee, usually in another country, to be sold on behalf of the consignor.

Two points must be borne in mind in recording such a transaction in the books:

(a) The goods never become the property of the consignee. Therefore he incurs no liability as a result of the transaction until the goods are sold, when he becomes liable for payment of the proceeds. He is paid by a commission.

(b) The consignor wishes to know the amount of profit made on the consignment. He therefore opens a Consignment Account, which is in the nature of a Trading Account. It is debited with all the costs incurred, including the cost of the goods, and credited with the proceeds of the sale. If the amount realized on the sale exceeds the costs (*i.e.,* if the credit side exceeds the debit side), the difference is a profit. Conversely, if the debit side (costs) exceeds the credit side (proceeds), there is a loss. The profit or loss is transferred to the Trading Account at the end of the accounting period.

Illustration: On 1st February, A.B. & Co., of London, send a consignment consisting of fourteen cases of goods to E. Wells, of Sydney, Australia, to be sold by him on their behalf. The cost of the goods was £20 per case, and in addition they pay freight and insurance £85 and other expenses £13. On receipt of the goods E. Wells incurs charges amounting to £14. It is agreed that he should receive a commission of 5 per cent of the gross proceeds. He sells ten cases at £40 each on 29th March, and the remaining four cases on 2nd May at £30 each. The financial year of A.B. & Co. ends on 31st March.

The Consignor's Books

Stage I. The goods are dispatched to the consignee. The entries are:

(a) A debit entry in the Consignment to E. Wells Account, to record the cost of the goods, £280.

(b) It is presumed that these goods have been purchased at some time previous to their dispatch. They will, therefore, be included in the purchases on the debit side of the general Trading Account and will thus be a deduction from the profit shown in that account. Clearly the cost of these goods should not be deducted from the profit in *both* the Trading Account and the Consignment Account. Consequently, they must be taken from the Trading Account by a credit entry.

319

The Trading Account, however, is taken out only at the end of the accounting period. In the meantime, therefore, the amount is credited to a Goods on Consignment Account. At the end of the accounting period it will be transferred to the Trading Account (debit Goods on Consignment Account, credit Trading Account), along with the cost of all other goods sent out on consignment to other people.

At this stage, then, the accounts would appear as under:

CONSIGNMENT TO E. WELLS ACCOUNT

Dr.					Cr.
		£			
Feb. 1	Goods on Consignment ..	280			

GOODS ON CONSIGNMENT ACCOUNT

Dr.					Cr.
					£
			Feb. 1	Cons. to E. Wells	280

The student should not be confused by the similarity in the titles of these two accounts. The Goods on Consignment Account is not used again in this transaction. It is merely a temporary account, and will be closed when the Trading Account is taken out.

If the goods had been purchased specially for this consignment, they would not have been included in the Purchases Account. There would therefore be no occasion to transfer them from the Trading Account and the entry would be simply:

(a) Debit Consignment to E. Wells Account.

(b) Credit the personal account of the supplier (or Bank Account if they were paid for at once).

Stage II. A.B. & Co. pay freight and insurance £85 and other expenses £13.

(a) These expenses, amounting to £98, are part of the cost incurred in offering the goods for sale in Sydney. As such they are a reduction of the profit it is hoped to make on the sale. They are therefore debited in the Consignment to E. Wells Account.

(b) As they would be paid by cheque (presumably), they would be credited in the bank column of the Cash Book.

The Consignment to E. Wells Account will now appear:

CONSIGNMENT TO E. WELLS ACCOUNT

Dr.					Cr.
		£			
Feb. 1	Goods on Consignment ..	280			
„ 1	Freight and Insurance	85			
„ 1	Sundry Expenses	13			

If, at this stage, the Balance Sheet were taken out, the balance of this account (£378) would appear as an asset consisting of stock on hand. The expenses are added to the original cost because together they represent the cost price of these goods in Sydney. That is the amount that would be lost if, for example, the goods were destroyed by fire. There is as yet no profit to record.

E. Wells has also incurred some expenses—£14. This, however, would probably not be known to A.B. & Co. until the goods were sold. E. Wells would recoup himself by deducting this amount (plus his commission) from the proceeds of the sale.

Stage III. Ten cases of the goods are sold by E. Wells at £40 each.

For the first time since this transaction began, E. Wells has incurred a liability. He must pay A.B. & Co. the £400 he received for the goods, less, of course, his just claims. His position would be set out in a document which he would prepare, known as an 'Account Sales'. The following is an example:

To A.B. & Co.
London.   30th March, 19—

Account Sales. No. 1 of 10 cases goods *ex* S.S. *Olivia*, sold by E. Wells of Sydney, Australia, for account of A.B. & Co., London.

		£
Sale of 10 cases at £40 per case		400
Less charges	£14	
commission	20	
		34
		£366

Sight Bill herewith £366.

E. & O.E.

On receipt of this Account Sales, A.B. & Co. would have three things to enter:

(*a*) The amount realized on the sale (£400).

(*b*) E. Wells' expenses and commission (£14 and £20).

(*c*) The receipt of the B/E (£366).

The method of entering these matters would be:

(*a*) *The amount realized on the sale.*

(i) Wells has become a debtor, personally liable for this amount. His personal account would therefore be debited.

(ii) The amount is credited to the Consignment to E. Wells Account. If any profit has been made up to date, it is contained in this sum.

(b) *E. Wells' expenses and commission.*

   (i) Since he is entitled to be reimbursed by A.B. & Co. these items are a reduction of the profit made. They will therefore be debited in Consignment to E. Wells Account.

   (ii) Such expenses are a reduction of the amount owed by E. Wells. They are therefore credited in his account.

The accounts at this stage would stand as follows:

CONSIGNMENT TO E. WELLS ACCOUNT

Dr.			£				Cr. £
Feb.	1	Goods on Con-signment ..	280	Mar. 30	E. Wells. Sale of Part Consign-ment ..		400
,,	1	Freight and In-surance ..	85				
,,	1	Sundry Exps. ...	13				
Mar.	30	Expenses (E. Wells) ..	14				
,,	30	Commission ..	20				

E. WELLS ACCOUNT

Dr.			£				Cr. £
Mar.	30	Sale of Goods on Consign-ment ..	400	Mar. 30	Expenses ...		14
				,, 30	Commission ...		20

(c) The payment of the £366 due from E. Wells would be entered in the same way as any other payment by a debtor: *debit* bank (if he pays by cheque) or B/R account (if he gives a bill) and *credit* E. Wells' personal account.

Del Credere Commission

If E. Wells had sold the goods on credit and himself guaranteed that the account would be met, he might be entitled to a special commission in return for the guarantee. Such a commission would be called a 'Del Credere Commission' and would be entered exactly as the ordinary commission on the sale is entered.

Profit to Date

On 31st March A.B. & Co. took out their Balance Sheet. It will therefore be necessary to assess the profit made on the sale of part of the consignment. This would be done by valuing the stock on hand (*i.e.,* the four unsold cases) and crediting the Consignment to E. Wells Account, the difference between the two sides then being the profit. In other words, the Consignment to E. Wells Account is treated exactly like a Trading Account.

In valuing the stock, the expenses incurred are treated as part of the cost of the stock and are therefore added to the amount paid for it. The total expenses to date (excluding commission) are:

		£
Freight and insurance	... ...	85
Sundry expenses ..	... ...	13
E. Wells' expenses	... ...	14
Total	...	£112

As only four cases out of the fourteen sent are still in stock, only $\frac{4}{14}$ of these expenses relate to the stock on hand. This amounts to £32. The value of the stock on hand would therefore be:

		£
Four cases at £20 each ..	... ...	80
Share of expenses	... ...	32
		£112

Commission is excluded because it was an expense incurred only in respect of the goods sold. No commission has yet been paid on the unsold goods.

(*Note:* It is not necessary to calculate the value of the stock on hand after part of the consignment is sold, unless it is required for Balance Sheet purposes.)

At this stage, therefore, the Consignment to E. Wells Account would be balanced as follows:

CONSIGNMENT TO E. WELLS ACCOUNT

Dr.   Cr.

Date		Particulars	£	Date		Particulars	£
Feb.	1	Goods on Con-signment ..	280	Mar. 30		E. Wells (sale of part consign-ment) ..	400
„	1	Freight and In-surance ..	85	„	31	Stock on Hand c/d.	112
„	1	Sundry Exs. ..	13				
Mar.	30	Exs. (E. Wells)	14				
„	30	Commission ..	20				
„	30	Profit (to Profit and Loss A/c.)	100				
			£512				£512
Apr.	1	Goods b/d. ...	£112				

At the same time, the E. Wells Account would appear as under:

E. WELLS ACCOUNT

Dr.   Cr.

Date		Particulars	£	Date		Particulars	£
Mar.	30	Sale of Part Consignment	400	Mar.	30	Expenses ...	14
				„	30	Commission ..	20
				„	30	Bank	366

As stated before, the balance of the Goods on Consignment Account would be transferred to the Trading Account.

Stage IV. The remainder of the consignment is sold. This is treated in precisely the same way as the previous sale of part of the consignment:

- (*a*) Gross proceeds of sale—Debit E. Wells Account. Credit Consignment to E. Wells Account.
- (*b*) Commission—Debit Consignment to E. Wells Account. Credit E. Wells Account.
- (*c*) Payment—Debit Bank (or B/R) Account. Credit E. Wells Account.

The completed Consignment Account is now shown:

CONSIGNMENT TO E. WELLS ACCOUNT

Dr.			£				£	Cr.
Feb.	1	Goods on Con-signment ..	280	Mar. 30	E. Wells (sale of part consign-ment) ..		400	
„	1	Freight and In-surance ..	85	„ 31	Stock on hand c/d.		112	
„	1	Sundry Exps.	13					
Mar.	30	Expenses (E. Wells) ..	14					
„	30	Commission ..	20					
„	31	Profit (to Profit and Loss Ac-count) ..	100					
			£512				£512	
Apr.	1	Stock b/d. ..	112	May 2	E. Wells (sale of bal. of con-signment) ...		120	
May	2	Commission ..	6					
Sept.	30	Profit (to Profit and Loss Ac-count) ..	2					
			£120				£120	

The Consignee's Books

When the consignee receives the goods, he will also receive a *pro forma* invoice. This is a document in the form of an invoice, sent by the consignor, setting out full details of the goods included in the consignment.

On the *pro forma* invoice, the goods will be priced either at cost price, or at the price the consignee is expected to obtain. As, however, the goods never become his property, this invoice does not indicate that he owes the consignor any money and is *not* entered in the Purchases Journal with the invoices for goods actually bought. It will be necessary, of course, to keep a memorandum of the goods in the consignment and to keep the record of those goods separate from that of his own goods in his warehouse.

His records of the transaction are all contained in the consignor's personal account in his ledger. This account will be similar to his own account in the consignor's books, except that the sides will be reversed. It is shown below:

A.B. & CO. ACCOUNT

Dr.			£				Cr. £
Feb. 20	Bank (Exs.)	..	14	Mar. 30	Sale of Part		
Mar. 30	Commission	..	20		Consignment		400
„ 30	Bank ..	...	366				
			£400				£400
May 2	Commission	...	6	May 2	Sale of Balance		
„ 2	Bank ...	..	114		of Consign-		
					ment	...	120
			£120				£120

WRITTEN EXERCISES

1. W. Ireland, of Belfast, consigned goods to his agent, A. Scott, of London, and forwarded a *pro forma* invoice for £600.

The agent remitted a cheque for £300 on receipt of the goods and the arrangement was that he should receive 5 per cent commission on the gross sales.

A. Scott paid various charges on the consignment amounting to £12. He sold the goods for £715, received a cheque for that amount from the purchaser, and remitted the amount due to the consignor.

Show how these transactions would appear (*a*) in the books of the consignor and (*b*) in the books of the agent.   (*R.S.A., modified.*)

2. The Exfield Company, of Sheffield, consigned to their agents, Le Garde & Co. of Johannesburg, fifty cases of cutlery, the cost price being £4,000, to be sold by the latter on account of the Sheffield company. Le Garde & Co. were to receive a commission of 6 per cent and a *del credere* commission of 1 per cent calculated on the gross amount realized. Le Garde & Co. sold all the cases at an average of £105 each.

The Exfield Company were to pay all charges up to the time the consignment was taken over by Le Garde & Co., and these were as follows: carriage, freight and insurance, £62; wharfage, £5; sundry expenses, £6.

The expenses incurred by Le Garde & Co. were: landing charges, £20; warehouse and insurance charges, £60; distribution expenses, £70; and bad debts amounted to £15.

Prepare the Account Sales sent by Le Garde & Co. to the Exfield Company, and set out the Consignment Account in the books of the latter firm.

(*Association of Certified and Corporate Accountants, modified.*)

3. Produce ledger accounts in the books of John Bull, of London, to reflect the following transactions. All questions of exchange may be ignored.

	19—	£
July 1.	John Bull sent to J. Smuts, of South Africa, a consign-ment of 20,000 books on gold mining to be sold on con-signment terms at £1 per copy, subject to a commission of 15 per cent on gross sales proceeds. Invoiced *pro forma*, at cost ... .. —	12,500

			£
July 1.	Bull drew on Smuts' London Bankers at sight	..	8,000
„ 1.	Bull paid insurance and freight	.. .. ..	500

Oct. 1. Smuts, having notified that the books are not in great demand, is requested to ship 10,000 of the books to A. Digger, of Australia, to be sold by Digger for Bull on similar terms. Insurance and freight is paid by Smuts (£200), but is charged against Bull.

Dec. 1. Account Sales received from Smuts showing that all remaining books were sold at £1 per copy, and that landing charges (£0·05 per copy) had been paid on 20,000 books.

„ 2. Bull pays to Smuts' London bankers the amount due.

„ 31. Account Sales received from A. Digger:
5,000 copies sold at £1 per copy.
Landing charges (£0·025 per copy) paid by Digger on 10,000 copies.
Remaining copies expected to be sold shortly.
Cheque on London enclosed, £3,000.

(Institute of Bankers, Part 1., modified.)

4. B. Abel consigned goods value £1,125 to A. Jones, at Durban. He paid freight £81 and insurance £45. He received an advance of £375 from A. Jones. An Account Sales was received from A. Jones showing that part of the goods had realized gross £1,200 and that his expenses and commission amounted to £127·50. The stock unsold was valued at £375. A bill at one month was received from A. Jones for the amount due. Make the necessary Journal and Cash Book entries for the above transactions, and show the Consignment Account in the Ledger.

(U.E.I., modified.)

5. On 1st September, 19—, Arthur, a London trader, sent 100 cases of goods to Andrew of Cape Town, South Africa, on consignment terms. The cost of the goods to Arthur was £50 per case. All expenses are to be borne by the consignor.
Arthur paid freight and insurance on the consignment, £130.
On 31st December, 19—, Arthur received an Account Sales from Andrew, showing that 75 cases had been sold for £4,600. Andrew had paid duty and landing charges on the whole consignment, £170. Andrew's selling expenses were £40, and he was entitled to a commission of 5 per cent on gross sales.
The Account Sales was accompanied by a sight draft for the amount due to Arthur.
You are required to set out the ledger accounts in Arthur's books, for the above transactions, and to show the transfer to Arthur's Profit and Loss Account at 31st December, 19—.
Note: You are not required to show the entries in the books of Andrew.

(Institute of Bankers.)

6. On 1st January, 19—, A. N. Exporter forwarded a consignment of 200 cases of tropical helmets to A. Trader, his agent in West Africa, together with a *pro forma* invoice for £360. On the following day, the consignor paid the freight charges amounting to £55 and insurance charges £9. On 5th March, 19—, an Account Sales was received from the agent showing that 150 cases had been sold for £380, and that landing and storage charges on the consignment amounting to £28 had been paid by the agent. The agent's commission of 5 per cent of the gross sales was deducted and the balance due was remitted by sight draft.
Record these transactions in the books of the consignor showing the profit or loss on the consignment.   *(R.S.A.)*

INDEX

327